D1713892

This book provides the most detailed analysis to date of the economics of the Soviet urban household sector during the 1970s. It contains nine studies covering the size distribution of incomes and wealth, the incidence and causes of poverty, the labor supply of women, division of labor among household members, and saving behavior. All these studies are based on a unique source of information: the returns of retrospective income surveys of Jewish immigrants to Israel and the United States. In each study, Gur Ofer and Aaron Vinokur employ a cross-sectional econometric analysis of data on individual households and in this they are unique among all Western and Soviet authors on the Soviet household sector. Ofer and Vinokur conclude that socialist achievements in the sphere of economic equality were rather modest. They also show that, even under the peculiar conditions imposed on Soviet households by the socialist system, they responded to economic constraints in a way that is predictable by ordinary Western-type models of household behavior.

Although it is essentially an historical study, *The Soviet household under the old regime* makes an important contribution to current evaluations of the conditions necessary for the smooth transition of the Soviet system. It sheds light on probable changes in household patterns and in entrepreneurship as well as on the refinements needed in the welfare and social security systems. This book will be widely read by students and specialists of Soviet studies, comparative economics, income distribution and women's studies. It will also be an invaluable reference source for government officials and journalists.

The Soviet Household
Under the Old Regime

THE SOVIET HOUSEHOLD
UNDER THE OLD REGIME

Economic Conditions and Behavior in the 1970s

Gur Ofer
and
Aaron Vinokur

CAMBRIDGE UNIVERSITY PRESS
Cambridge
New York Port Chester
Melbourne Sydney

Published by the Press Syndicate of the University of Cambridge

The Pitt Building, Trumpington Street, Cambridge CB2 1RP

40 West 20th Street, New York, NY 10011-4211, USA

10 Stanford Road, Oakleigh, Melbourne 3166, Australia

© Cambridge University Press 1992

First published 1992

Printed in Great Britain at the University Press, Cambridge

A cataloguing in publication record for this book is available from the British Library

Library of Congress cataloguing in publication data

Ofer, Gur.

The Soviet household under the old regime: economic conditions
and behavior in the 1970s / by Gur Ofer and Aaron Vinokur.

p.   cm.

Includes bibliographical references and index.

ISBN 0 521 38398 6

1. Soviet Union − Economic conditions − 1965–1975. 2. Soviet Union −
Economic conditions − 1975–1985. 3. Households − Soviet Union.

I. Vinokur, Aaron. II. Title.

HC336.23.O23 1992

330.947'085 − dc20 91-4224 CIP

ISBN 0 521 38398 6 hardback

ME

To Bella, Mania and Dalia with love

Contents

Acknowledgments

We gratefully acknowledge the financial support over the years of The Ford Foundation; the Israeli Academy of Sciences; The National Council for Soviet and East European Research; The Rand Corporation; the Office of Net Assessment of the Department of Defence of the U.S. Government; The Russian Research Center, Harvard University; The Soviet Interview Project; the Research Authority of the Hebrew University; the Jay and Lonny Soviet and East European Center of the Hebrew University; the University of Haifa, and The Kenan Institute for Advanced Russian Studies of the Woodrow Wilson International Center for Scholars at the Smithsonian Institute.

Credits with thanks for permission to reproduce some of the studies in the book are listed below. Joyce Pickersgill co-authored the chapter on Saving (chapter 3) and Yechiel Bar-Haim co-authored the paper that appears here as the Appendix; we thank both of them, too.

Our special thanks for advice and comments on some of the individual studies to Abram Bergson, Abram Becker, Joseph Berliner, Paul Gregory, Gregory Grossman, James Millar, Jacob Mincer, and a number of anonymous journal referees. We would like to extend special thanks to Konstantin Miroshnik, who oversaw the interview effort in Israel, and to Yechiel Bar-Haim who served as research assistant in the project for a number of years. Etka Leibovitch served during the last year both as research assistant and as editor of the revised drafts. The project of turning the individual studies into a manuscript would not have been at all possible without the dedication and energy of Maggie Eisenstaedt of the Maurice Falk Institute for Economic Research in Israel, who edited the text and tables, and compiled the various drafts of the manuscript in a uniform style and form.

After all this, need we remind the reader that all responsibility for the contents of this book is still the authors'?

Sources

Prologue

The classical Soviet-type 'socialist' system as a social, economic, and political option for the future development of any human society is no longer viable. This seems to be generally agreed upon in the East, West, North, and South, although the ways and means of how to descend from some of its highest doctrinal and institutional paradigms are still far from clear. The countries of Eastern Europe and the Soviet Union, as well as China and many 'socialist' countries of the Third World, are struggling with the transition from the old system into an as yet unclear new one, or are trying to shift to a social variant within the range of a mixed market economy and the democratic political system of the Western hemisphere.

The studies assembled in this book, dealing with different aspects of the economic realities and behavior of the household sector under the 'old (socialist) regime', might nowadays be considered a purely historical endeavour, part of an effort to better understand the effect of the system on the life and behavior of its people, and the extent to which the system was able to attain some of its most important economic, social and ideological goals. All the studies assembled here relate to the 1970s, a period that *post facto* became known as the 'period of stagnation'. They may, however, also shed some light on factors and phenomena that may have contributed to the later demise of the socialist system.

At the present time much attention is focused on the process of transition out of the socialist system. While most of the discussion is directed at the shift from central planning and allocation to the market, and on the 'destatization' or privatization of productive assets, there is also a fair amount of interest in the social implications of the transition and its likely effect on the level of welfare of society as a whole, on various social groups, and on individual households. In both cases it is important to assess the likely response of the population to change, the probable adjustment in its behavior, and the needed level of support. Some clues on these questions are provided in the study of patterns of household behavior and of the economic environment around the household sector under the old regime. For example, a study of patterns of household saving under the rather peculiar conditions of a socialist economy can provide some estimates on what to expect when ownership of real assets is legalized, when interest rates rise, and when the level of economic security declines. Likewise, the established level of income inequality can provide a base for studying the probable reaction of the population to wider income differentials, and of the need to overhaul and adapt the present welfare and support system.

The main lesson emerging from most of the individual studies is that household behavior can be explained by ordinary 'Western' behavioral models, i.e., that Soviet households respond to economic (and other) constraints in the same way as household everywhere. Under the particular conditions imposed by the socialist system, these responses may seem peculiar, but when conditions and incentives ever closer to those prevailing in the West, so too will the responses. In this respect, the main conclusion is one of optimistic expectations as regards the transformation of the Soviet economy, as least as far as household behavior is concerned.

Even with these possible benefits, the studies presented in this book are first and foremost an attempt to better understand the working of the socialist economic system in the sphere of the household sector. Most of the studies were originally prepared long before 1985 and did not deal either directly or indirectly with the ultimate fate of the system. The studies took advantage of the windfall of new information on Soviet society provided by the immigration of tens of thousands of families from the Soviet Union, first to Israel and then to the United States, in the 1970s. The shroud of secrecy and the lack of information, especially in the form of cross-section data of individual households on ordinary matters such as work-supply functions, income differentials and poverty, saving habits, not to mention activity in the second economy, did not allow the kind of penetrating behavioral studies common in the West.

With the advent of *glasnost'*, more and more data on previously secret topics are being published, but most of these data relate to very recent years (post-1985), and reflect, at least partly, the effects of recent developments and recent changes.[1] With time, there may be opportunities to gain access to older data sources which could reveal more of the still hidden facets of past economic realities. Even so, the studies presented in this collection, together with other studies based on the Israeli and the American Soviet Interview Projects, ISIP and SIP respectively (some of whose results are reported here), and other similar efforts, may for a long time remain unique opportunities to understand the economic and social processes of the Soviet socialist system.[2]

This book contains nine separate studies, mostly based on ISIP. They reflect the economic situation in the Soviet Union in the early 1970s. Two of the studies also include results based on SIP, which refer to the late 1970s. All the individual studies were prepared over the period 1979 to 1988 and are presented here with minor editorial changes, mostly in order to reduce duplication. Some duplication remains, in order to preserve the natural development of the presentation in each chapter. Some of the studies have been previously published in journals and in various compendia, and others were presented at conferences or issued as research reports. The acknowledgment paragraph gives the exact publication information.

The decision to leave the studies basically in their original form was taken in order to avoid infusion of hindsight from the post-1985 developments into what was originally a contemporary research effort. A case in point is the long debate over the extent of repressed inflation in the Soviet Union under the old regime. The studies presented here on savings (Chapter 3) and on the second economy (Chapter 2), take a minimizing stand on the extent of repressed inflation in the early 1970s, a view that seems to have been strongly vindicated by recent events. The evolving deep disequilibrium and crisis in the consumer markets and elsewhere during the late 1980s can be credited mostly to post-1985 actions (Ofer, 1990).

One of the drawbacks of the presentation of the studies in their original form is that each is based on a somewhat different sample of the original populations of immigrants, and/or on different variants of adjusted or reweighted samples. The need to adjust the original samples stemmed from the fact that due to their composition most Jewish families come from urban locations in the European parts of the Soviet Union; therefore, their structure does not conform to that of the target population of the Soviet Union. The adjustment or re-weighting procedures are described below. Some of the studies are based on non-adjusted samples while others use adjusted ones, some are based only on the active (non-retired) parts of the samples, others use the entire samples. Finally, as mentioned above, most of the studies are based only on ISIP and two studies also on SIP. In each chapter there is a clear definition of the exact nature of the sample or sub-sample used. Let us point out here that under ISIP two sub-samples were created in two distinct stages of the study, a sample of 1,016 'normal and active' households, made up of two-parent families whose head was under retirement age and worked in the public sector. Later, a second sub-sample of 250 households was added, including singles, retired people, one-parent and other 'incomplete' families, both active and not active in the labor force.

The studies collected in this volume cover the economic activities of the Soviet urban household in the sphere of the second economy (Chapter 2) its saving behavior (Chapter 3), and various aspects of the household's labor supply function. Chapter 8 is devoted to the labor supply of women, while issues of the division of labor among household members are also dealt with in Chapter 2 (on the second economy) and in Chapter 7. The size distribution of wages incomes and wealth are discussed in Chapters 4–7. Following a general study on income and wage distribution (Chapter 4), there are more focused discussions on the distributive effects of the Social Consumption Fund, the Soviet welfare system (Chapter 5), and the incidence and causes of poverty (Chapter 6). Chapter 7 addresses both the distributive issues and the general topic of the economic status of women and discusses pay differentials between males and females. In doing so, the chapter also presents earning functions for both sexes and thereby provides an analysis of the causes of wage differentials and the major characteristics of the Soviet labor market in general. For the sake of brevity, a study focusing on earning functions was not included.

Chapter 1 of the volume presents an attempt to integrate the individual studies into a conceptual framework of the economic behavior of the household under Soviet conditions, as distinct from its behavior in a typical market economy. In doing so it also provides a summary of the main findings. Chapter 1 also discusses the main methodological problems of how to use a sample of mostly Jewish immigrants to study the behavior of the Soviet population and the remaining biases. Finally the Appendix chapter describes in detail the nature, structure, and characteristics of the sample of active households used as the basic sample for ISIP and compares it with the corresponding attributes of the target Soviet population (the urban European population), and whenever possible with those of the Jewish community in the Soviet Union.

At this point it is far from clear where the Soviet Union is heading, as a state, a society, an economic system. Wherever it goes, we hope the studies presented in this book will be included among those that provide a general benchmark of the point of departure into the new era.

Notes

1. Extensive information on wage and income distribution and on poverty was published recently among others in *Sotsialnoye Razvitiye SSSR* (1990) and in *Sostav Semi* (1990) as part of a multitude of new data on the economic conditions of the household sector and on the economic behavior of households.

2. The basic results of SIP are reported in Millar, 1987. Other major studies based on interviews of migrants are the Berkeley–Duke project on the second economy (for an updated bibliography see Grossman, 1990), and the German interview project based on interviews with German immigrants (see Dietz, 1986, 1987).

Chapter 1
Introduction: economics of the Soviet urban household in the 1970s

1. Introduction

Much of our knowledge of the operation of any economic system is gained through the study of the records of individual economic units. Economists interested in household behavior (i.e., work, consumption, fertility), in the market behavior of wages and prices, and in distribution (i.e., wages, incomes, welfare) will turn to one of many available data bodies for records of household or firm behavior. This is so in many countries, including the Soviet Union, where household and firm surveys are conducted by both the central statistical authorities and individual social scientists. The government of a centrally planned system resorts more often to such surveys and records than do market economies. Nevertheless, in order to assure the secrecy of most results, there are severe limitations in the Soviet Union on the use of centrally collected records and on conducting independent surveys, and even more severe restrictions on the publication of detailed results (to say nothing of restrictions on access to the underlying data).

Secrecy and ideological inhibitions have also impeded the full development of theoretical models and statistical methods needed in the analysis of such records. Theoretical and statistical methods lag behind Western developments, as far as can be ascertained from published work. In most cases the analysis is confined, when information is released at all, to cross-tabulations of two or three variables. Secrecy also demands that in many cases no information is provided on the nature of the underlying data. It follows that in only very few cases do Western scholars gain access to the data sources, permission to conduct their own surveys, or an opportunity to reproduce the analysis done in the Soviet Union. Western scholars are thus almost completely deprived of one of the most important types of data needed to understand the Soviet system and the behavior of its main economic units. This is in sharp contrast to the increased volume of macro-economic information that was available to students of the Soviet economy between the mid-1950s and the early 1970s, when renewed restrictions were introduced.

The present study on the economics of the Soviet urban household sector is based on one of the few systematic micro data bodies that have become available to Western students in recent years (another is SIP, Millar, 1987): a full-fledged family budget survey conducted on a sample of 1,250 families who had emigrated from the Soviet Union during the 1970s. This survey deals with these families' economic situation in the Soviet Union prior to their having decided to leave, and covers such areas as work and wages, income from all sources, education, family structure, expenditures, housing, and wealth. The survey was designed to accommodate analysis through the application of Western economic theory and statistical methodology.

Such analysis can improve the knowledge and understanding of the Soviet economy in four ways: first, it provides additional basic information on the Soviet economy in areas where official data have been especially limited, e.g., on the extent of private economic activity, wage differentials across socio-economic vectors, and measures of income inequality. On the basis of the survey's returns, many figures already available from official Soviet statistics are independently estimated. These latter estimates are then used both as a check on the quality and accuracy of the sample's data and — vice versa — as a check on official Soviet statistics.

Second, the microeconomic data are used in the context of multivariate analysis to study the behavior of households in key aspects of their economic activity: for example, decisions on work and the amount of work provided, on consumption and savings, on 'second economy' activities, and on fertility. Microeconomic data add not only new information, but another dimension that provides an opportunity to understand better behavior under the particular conditions of the Soviet system. Likewise, the new data allow one to study thoroughly the determinants of key parameters in various Soviet markets. In this study we place special emphasis on the determinants of wages and wage differentials, but prices can also be studied in a similar manner.

Finally, a number of macroeconomic topics are also studied, such as the determinants of income distribution and income differentials, the incidence of the welfare system, the importance and impact of the private economy, and the general issue of repressed inflation.

The main goals of the study are as follows: to study conditions of life and economic behavior in the Soviet Union of Jewish immigrants to Israel in order to better understand their absorption needs and problems; to compare the economic behavior of the Jewish minority in the Soviet Union with that of the general population; and to estimate family incomes and expenditures of Soviet urban families independently from official Soviet data and in greater depth.

Which economic theory should be applied to the study of Soviet household behavior? of the Soviet labor market? of the level of savings? An extreme (though not uncommon) view is expressed by Igor Birman. After presenting his evaluation of the dangerously large cash overhang, threatening to disrupt the consumer market at any moment, he states:

> Why do most American Sovietologists disagree with me on the issue? Because they unreservedly believe in modern Western economic theories which, they think, are universal. Not true, since their *premises* are not universal, since the subject — a Western economy and/or an economy of the Third World — are very different from a Soviet-type economy. That is why scholars who follow the theory make mistakes in judgments on financial matters, standard of living, GNP accounts, etc. That is why a *special theory of the Soviet-type economy is badly needed.* (Birman, 1981, p. 162; italics added)

An opportunity is presented here to address the specific issue in dispute. It is not even clear that Birman really means that a different theory is needed, so that the quotation is used partly as a pretext for an exposition of the question. The absence of microeconomic data on the Soviet economy could have supported the assertion that Western economic models are inappropriate. It at least stood in the way of seriously testing such questions. Western economic theory is used in this analysis of both household behavior and market patterns under the working hypothesis that such a theory is indeed applicable and appropriate. The test of this proposition is another goal of the study.

2. Western theory and Soviet reality

There is wide agreement that of the three major subdivisions of the Soviet system (the macro system, the production sector, and the household consumption sector), the latter is most similar to its counterpart under Western-type market systems. On the macro level, central planning and the market system in their pure forms are miles apart. Even so, several observers find some similarities between the *modus operandi* of Soviet production units and corporate production sectors in the West (see Berliner, 1959). In contrast, the immediate environment of the household in the Soviet Union is made up of market (or quasi-market) structures so that household members face choices and options that are similar in nature to those of households under a market system. They face set wages and have a large degree of choice regarding occupation, place of work, and even the amount of work. They are confronted with given prices and are free to choose how to spend their income — albeit with limitations — on goods and services available in the market or in the private sector. And they can make their own decisions on savings and on the size and development of their families. At least from the household's point of view, both the labor market and the consumer-goods market may be viewed as not too different in essence from those in a market environment (but see below).

One possible approach to the question of the applicability of Western theory to Soviet conditions is to check how every element of the economic optimization decision — the common element in all economic models of household behavior — fares under such conditions. We will limit the discussion to the question of possible differences in behavior under the assumption of *homo economicus* under both systems. We assume that Soviet households have a material utility function similar in its general characteristics to that of households in market systems, and that they seek to maximize it under their budget (and other) constraints. This does not mean that tastes need be identical in both systems — only that major wants have similar signs.

One abstract case where this may not be so is contained in the concept of the 'New Soviet Man'. Under full communism, such a new personality is expected to work out of inner conviction without or with less need for material incentives. If Soviet educational efforts succeed in pulling Soviet society in the direction of a higher level of altruism than is common elsewhere, then the basis for the market optimization model will be eliminated. In such a case, the efficiency in the labor market can be achieved with a somewhat lower level of wage inequality than realized in market systems. But the general formulation of the model remains unaffected.

This brings us to the examination of the nature of the constraints imposed on the decision-making units by different economic systems. In this area there is more room for the claim of a different model for the Soviet case. The absence of real markets, the central planning mechanism, the intensive intervention of the state in the determination of the product mix of prices and of rules of behavior are obvious grounds for such a claim. In weighing the burden of such claims on the nature of ordinary optimizing decisions, it is helpful first to distinguish between two kinds of constraints: (a) parametric constraints, specified mostly in terms of prices and wage rates given to the decision units in their decision-making process, and (b) institutional, administrative, and regulatory constraints that limit the field of choice allowed by the parametric constraints, or that over-ride choice altogether (e.g., rationing).

(a) Parametric constraints vary across countries, over time, and among different economic systems. The differences may reflect economic conditions, government policy, or the ways in which these are determined. Such differences result in different economic behavior, in different levels of the decision parameters — all other things being equal — irrespective of their initial cause. Government intervention in the determination of the level of the parameters cause changes in the economic behavior of families. Such interventions serve as indications that the authorities believe that some kind of optimizing model is working, and the resulting changes serve as proof that they are right. In such cases, government intervention supports the actual operation of the optimizing model and does not, as is sometimes argued, undermine its operation. If government intervenes, the final behavioral variables are expected to take different values than those arrived at in the absence of intervention. This is as true in the West as it is in the East, and governments in centrally planned economies use prices and other choice indicators as policy tools in many spheres to shape and influence economic behavior. In the Soviet Union, prices are set to affect consumption patterns, wage differentials are determined to create work incentives, minimum wages and welfare payments are set to influence work and fertility — all of which acknowledge rather than reject the relevancy of ordinary models.

(b) The second kind of constraint results in most cases from outside intervention or institutional structures that restrict action, thereby either changing the conditions under which individuals optimize, or strictly preventing them from reaching an optimal solution. But even here, the cases where optimizing behavior completely disappears cover only part of the entire range. In many cases, such constraints are merely another parameter that affects behavior according to the regular model: it must be taken into account, but does not alter the optimizing principles involved (see Portes, 1981; Pickersgill, 1980b). The equilibrium reached is said to be 'constrained' and the optimum points to be 'second best'. In other cases, the constraint dominates the decision completely, leaving no room for maneuver for ordinary optimizing forces. An example may clarify the distinctions: a decision to limit the production of household goods that substitute for time needed to perform household chores will affect the decisions of women to seek outside work, household distribution of work, investment in human capital, and fertility — but not the model that must take the availability level as given. Thus, while the study of the supply of household goods does, indeed, require a different theory, the study of decisions on work, fertility, etc. will take that supply as given and go on to analyze these decisions with the regular model. It seems reasonable to assume that while such quantitative interventions also exist in the West, they are more frequent in the Soviet economy and impose more severe limitations on choices.

The case of savings that prompted the reaction of Birman is a case in point. What Birman is actually saying is that because of different conditions the level of voluntary savings by Soviet households should be lower than in a Western economy, when all other things are similar. In the Soviet Union, he claims, one does not have to save for a house, to pay for the children's education, or for retirement, since these are all supplied by the state. In addition, investing in production assets is excluded and the rate of interest offered for savings is a mere 2 percent. From this Birman concludes that savings are accumulated involuntarily — and as such they jeopardize the stability of the system (Birman, 1981, Chapters VI, VII). We cannot go into a discussion of the substantive argument, but if one reads Birman's argument carefully one finds that it is based on an acceptance of the Western theory of saving rather than on its rejection. Birman assumes similar preferences but different conditions with different expected results — low savings — under optimal behavior. Finally, if savings in the Soviet Union are, indeed, mostly involuntary, then again established theories can analyze the potential pressures that they exert.

The same kind of argument applies to the analysis of wage differentials in the labor market. True, wage rates are determined in the first place by state organs. But considering that the supply of labor is largely in the hands of households, and that people can choose jobs and can, rather freely, change jobs, these facts exert pressure on the labor market to adjust wages in order to accommodate the supply and thus to come closer to a market situation. Therefore, the general human capital approach can be used to study wage differentials (as, indeed, suggested by some Soviet economists; see, for example, Rabkina and Rimashevskaia, 1972; McAuley, 1979, pp. 186–88). The results are expected to reflect special Soviet conditions, like the schooling system, as well as the possible impact of government intervention.

In conclusion, it should be emphasized that the application of Western economic theory to the study of Soviet household behavior is used as an hypothesis to distill those elements that fit the models and those that have to be accounted for outside the models.

3. The sample, the data, and biases

The data for this study come from returns of income survey questionnaires of 1,250 Jewish Soviet families who emigrated to Israel in the mid-1970s and reported retrospectively on their lives in the Soviet Union during their last 'normal' year there. This last 'normal' year, before life started to be affected by the decision to emigrate, turned out to be (for most families) 1972, 1973, or 1974 in about equal shares. Therefore, 1973 was chosen as the reference year for most comparisons with Soviet data.

The twenty-six-page questionnaire includes questions on place of residence; family size and structure; educational attainment; work status, experience, and position of all adults (17 years of age or more) in the family. Each family reported in great detail on the income of each working member from wages and on all other sources of family income; on expenditures by type, item, and place of purchase; on savings, possession of durables and other assets; and on housing conditions. All the questions were 'closed' and related solely to the life of the family being interviewed. They all related to facts of life — not to ideas or opinions.

The interviews were conducted by interviewers and all entries were recorded by them. An average interview lasted about 90 minutes. All the interviewers were themselves Soviet immigrants who had arrived in Israel a few years earlier, and most of them had academic degrees. This may explain why there were very few refusals to be interviewed and why, in the great majority of cases, the information was obtained with no difficulty.

With few exceptions, the sample was not preselected nor prestructured. Interviews were held 'randomly' in the lay meaning of the word, with only general guidelines formulated as the interviews were accumulated. One such guideline was to try and locate as many families as possible with blue-collar workers. As the fieldwork proceeded and 'enough' observations from certain occupational groups were accumulated, interviewers were instructed to discontinue interviewing families belonging to these groups.

The decision not to preselect the sample rested partly on budgetary and logistical considerations, and partly on the fact that the final sample was designed to represent more than one target population, each with a quite different structure: the population of migrants, the Jewish population in the Soviet Union, and the Soviet urban population — the sector which is examined herein. The survey compares the demographic, social, and economic composition of the survey population (SP) with the same characteristics of the Jewish population (JP) and urban population of the Soviet Union (UP).

The predominantly urban character of Jews in the Soviet Union precludes the possibility of studying the Soviet rural population in any systematic manner. The sample and study are therefore confined to the urban sector. Hence, two further restrictions were preimposed on the sample.

(a) Only families of European extraction were included — because of the difficulties entailed in establishing reliable communications with Georgian and Bucharian families from the Asian republics. (b) In the first stage of the survey only two-parent families whose heads were of working age (15–60) and working were included (totaling 1,016 families). At a later date an additional 250 household units, singles and one-parent families, were interviewed, using almost identical questionnaires. Most of the present study is confined to the first stage, the exceptions being the discussion of income distribution, the welfare and social security systems, poverty, and women, topics where the exclusion of the latter population segment would seriously bias the results.

Clearly, the direct estimates derived from the samples are not accurate estimates of the Soviet European urban population (UP). Two types of problem arise: (a) to what extent the data collected truly describe the lives of the families interviewed, and (b) how can these data be used for inferences on the Soviet urban population at large.

Errors or biases of the first type could have resulted from imperfect recall, from difficulties in relating fully to a 'normal' year and of avoiding the interjection of various changes connected with the decision to emigrate, as well as from intentional misrepresentation of facts. The nature and structure of the interview, the emphasis on complete anonymity and on the academic (non-government) nature of the project may have reduced the incidence of some (but by no means all) of the most common reasons for misreporting. On the other hand, the fact that the survey was conducted outside the Soviet Union may have raised the level of reliability of answers (on income, for example) as compared with similar surveys conducted in the Soviet Union, either by the government or by academic agencies. Some errors, intentional or not, may be and have been detected through consistency tests in cases where the same data was sought through different and independent sets of questions. Still, possible biases remain, and their significance must be evaluated in relation to each issue under investigation.

Even if the information gathered is accurate, it clearly reflects the sample rather than the target population. The demographic and economic characteristics of the sample are reasonably similar to those of the immigrant population or the European Jewish minority in the Soviet Union; many remain far removed from those of the target population. In very general terms, the sample population (SP) has a much higher level of education, higher occupational structure, and higher earnings and incomes than the urban population (UP); and was concentrated in larger urban centers and in the western parts of the Soviet Union annexed since 1939. Demographically, however, the differences between SP and UP are much narrower, although SP families seem to have fewer children.

The main characteristics of SP and UP are presented in Table 1.1.[1] We will discuss this comparison further in the following sections and explanatory notes. Let us simply note here that the very high proportion of families from the post-1939 Soviet areas reflect the immigration structure to Israel at the time the survey was conducted. We consider this an oversight on our part — we should have obtained a much higher proportion of families from Russia proper. Still, it must be pointed out that so far we have failed to identify one equation in which the subject's residence in the post-1939 areas made any difference to the results.

How can the sample data be used to study UP? A distinction must be drawn between two situations: one in which the composition of SP is biased, but where all the characteristics represented in UP are also represented as non-zero cells in SP. An example is the distorted occupational structure of SP: proportionally, SP has fewer blue-collar families than UP (even though about a quarter of SP are blue-collar workers). In such cases the bias can be overcome in different ways, depending on the questions being studied and on the nature of the statistical analysis used. When the behavior of a certain subsection of the population is investigated, the structural bias becomes irrelevant — for example, when studying blue-collar workers in isolation. When the question being investigated lends itself to most kinds of multivariate regression analysis, the effect of the structural bias is sharply reduced because what mostly counts is the representation of all the relevant characteristics and not so much their relative weights or frequencies. Finally, when true UP averages or distributive statistics are sought, SP can be and has been reweighted so as to conform to UP, the target population. Reweighting can be done as long as the true distribution of UP by the relevant variables is

Table 1.1.
General characteristics of the sample and the Soviet urban population
(7 western republics)

		Sample population circa 1973	Urban population 1970
1.	Residing in the RSFSR	19.3	69.6
2.	Residing in the 'annexed' areas	61.6	8.4
3.	Residing in cities with population of 1 million or more	20.5	15.5
4.	Residing in cities with population of 1/4 million or less	35.0	72.1
5.	Average size of family[a]	3.39	3.57
6.	Average number of children per family	1.14	1.25
7.	Population of working age (%)[d]	70.9	62.8[c]
8.	Population under working age (%)[d]	22.2	24.1[c]
9.	Population over working age (%)[d]	6.9	13.1[c]
10.	Workers per family[b]	2.1	1.8
11.	Education of labor force (no. of years)	13.0	9.3
12.	Working population with higher education (%)	43.1	10.4
13.	Working population with under 7 years' education (%)	5.5	25.1
14.	Blue-collar workers (% of working)	28.7	65.3[c]
15.	Working in manufacturing	30.2	37.7[e]
16.	Working in services	55.5	38.9[e]
17.	Total monthly net income per family (rubles)	389.0	293.0
18.	Monthly net wage per worker	152.3	124.1

[a] 1974.
[b] RSFSR only.
[c] Excluding singles.
[d] Working age for men: 16–60; for women: 16–55.
[e] Percent non-agricultural workers and employees in the USSR.

Sources: Sample population — authors' own data; Soviet data — Official Soviet sources and calculations based on the Appendix tables in this volume.

available from Soviet sources. Such reweighting was done, for example, for the analysis of income distribution of UP.

When the structural bias of SP involves empty cells, the problem of representativeness becomes much more serious. The absence of rural families restricts the discussion to the urban sector and such is the case with respect to the Asian republics. Extension of the analysis to the entire Soviet population requires inferences based on outside information, and the findings of this research are used as guidelines. The same is true when a shift is sought from the two-parent labor-active population to the entire active population or to the entire urban population. Here, however, data of the second stage of the study is very helpful.

Two key cells in SP are completely empty. Since all families are Jewish and all are migrants, there are no control groups for non-Jews or non-migrants. None of the above-mentioned methods can be used to take into account the migration or the Jewish biases of the sample's returns, nor is it intended to limit the analysis to the Soviet Jewish community or to immigrants. The way to account for these (potential) biases is to evaluate their direction and importance on the basis of outside information on the relevant characteristics of these two groups.

Until recently, migration theory held that voluntary economic migrants are positively (self-) selected from among their peers. If so, the economic performance of would-be emigrants from the Soviet Union may present an overly positive picture of Soviet economic conditions. However, lately the possibility of negative selection of migrants is working its way into the migration literature, so that even the direction of a possible bias is not quite clear. In the case of emigrants from the Soviet Union to Israel, a number of factors may contribute to the muting of a possible positive bias or even to creating a negative one. (a) One should consider the possibility that some migrants chose to leave because they failed to make it in the Soviet Union. (b) Applying for migration involves the risk of refusal and punitive action — the risk being higher the higher the status and position of the applicant. (c) The significance of economic self-selection in any direction may be smaller in the case of migration to Israel (as distinct from migration to the United States) because some of the motivating forces underlying such migration have to do with national aspirations and traditions and with dissatisfaction with the Soviet system on other than economic grounds. (d) The migration bias may have special effects on particular activities; for example, would-be emigrants may be both more industrious and more disenchanted with the Soviet system, in which case they would engage more avidly than average in private, second economy type activities. The bottom line of this discussion, while inconclusive, leads us to speculate that the migration bias is probably not very distorting.

The most serious question raised concerning the use of the sample data to study Soviet conditions is the fact that it consists exclusively of Jewish families. Jews are not only a tiny fraction of the Soviet population — less than 1 percent in 1970 — they are very atypical of the Soviet population in many respects. The differences in economic, demographic, and residential attributes need not, in themselves, cause skepticism or concern. The critical distinction is the one between specific Jewish patterns of behavior that can be accounted for by reweighting the sample, and those than cannot thus be amended. If Jews tend to concentrate in certain occupations and to shy away from others, reweighting can correct the bias as long as there are no empty cells. But if, for example, Jewish physicians differ in their behavior from non-Jewish physicians through unobserved variables, the difference cannot be discovered for lack of appropriate control groups. Since in practice reweighting cannot be based on the ultimate, most detailed, disaggregation, some degree of difference in structure — occupational structure, for example — is left in the unmeasured specific 'Jewish' bias (e.g., if Jews tend to concentrate in specific medical fields). In addition to the above, there might be specific Jewish patterns of behavior that are completely unobserved. One method that may help in estimating the bias is to control for 'degree of Jewishness' assuming that the level of identity with Jewish lifestyle, traditions, etc., is positively correlated with Jewish economic and social behavior patterns. Our sample does not include the data needed to perform such an analysis. Only external information on particular modes and tendencies of Jewish behavior may help to guesstimate possible directions and extent of biases.

The problem may best be illustrated by a key example of potential Jewish bias in estimating earnings. A number of studies on American Jews show that Jews tend to have more education and a higher occupation structure than other groups, and that they tend to concentrate in urban areas, particularly in major cities. (Note, however, that American Jews are mainly migrants or descendants of migrants.) All these attributes contribute to higher earnings than in other groups (see Chizwick, 1982, 1983). The same is true for Soviet Jews, but (at least in principle) differences in earnings attributed to education, occupation, and residence can be estimated and eliminated through reweighting, or can be weeded out in a regression analysis. But Chizwick also demonstrates that some earning advantage remains even after the above-mentioned attributes are controlled. This additional advantage is shown to be strongly correlated with the level of education. It thus supports the hypothesis that rates of return to education among Jews are higher than in other groups (Chizwick, 1983). This constitutes a Jewish bias that, if not correlated with other observable expressions of Jewish behavior, cannot be corrected by statistical methods. As put clearly by Chizwick, higher rates of return to education can result from a more intensive or more efficient production of human capital per year of education and/or from better application of on-the-job acquired human capital. Chizwick's tentative explanation of these phenomena is that the better use of schooling is achieved through more intensive upbringing of children in Jewish families. Jewish families tended to have fewer children *and* a lower labor-force participation rate of mothers (Chizwick, 1983). Whether or not further study substantiates this explanation, the hypothesis provides another example where a behavioral bias can be corrected if the model or reweighting can include labor-force participation and fertility rates. Chizwick claims that his findings rule out the dominance of direct discrimination in education or at work, because discrimination must result in lower rates of return to education. If anticipated discrimination causes Jews to study more years, then this is controlled for by the analysis.

One possible effect of discrimination that Chizwick does not fully consider is that Jews may make special efforts to excel in school and on the job in order to reduce the risk of discrimination by raising its 'cost' to the potential discriminator. Fear of discrimination may also explain the higher investment of parents in their children. This seems to us a very important consideration. If true, the positive effect of expected discrimination may offset the negative effect of actual discrimination. In countries where discrimination is declining over time, such as the United States, fear of discrimination may be more important that actual discrimination, thus contributing to a higher rate of return to education. This is less likely to occur in countries like the Soviet Union, where discrimination is constant and long-standing or rising. There, the Jewish earning premium may be lower or non-existent.

Chizwick estimates the 'pure' Jewish earning advantage at about 8 percent of earnings, which we consider to be an upper limit, unlikely to be realized by the Jewish community in the Soviet Union. We can illustrate these hypothetical considerations with actual figures on wages. On the basis of the Soviet data, the net monthly wage of a Soviet non-agricultural earner in the European USSR in 1973 is estimated at R124.1 (see Appendix). The corresponding SP unweighted return is R149.0. When reweighted by the composition of sex, work status (blue- vs. white-collar workers) and level of education — 18 cells in all — the wage figure drops to R135.8. Reweighting thus explains almost two-thirds of the gap. This reweighting does not account for place of residence or for a more detailed occupation structure. Even so, the upper limit for a 'Jewish advantage' is only about 9 percent.

Other particular 'Jewish' modes of behavior are stronger family attachment (of which higher investment in children may be only one aspect), lower alcohol consumption and, possibly, higher inclination to engage in private economic activities. The case of alcohol consumption is probably the best example of a topic that cannot be studied for the Soviet population on the basis of our Jewish sample. According to the SP returns, families spend about 2 percent of their income on wine and spirits, compared with 13 percent in the Soviet population (Treml, 1982, p. 81). As we shall see below, even the direction (let alone the size) of a possible Jewish bias with respect to private activity is open to question. We are convinced that the Jewish bias — following reweighting when necessary — is much smaller than some popular views have it. Nevertheless, its consideration will come up in relation to every question discussed below (see also Bahry in Millar, 1987).

4.   A framework of analysis in the Soviet environment

Analysis of household behavior calls for a general equilibrium approach
where all the constraints are considered together and all the decisions are
interdependent. Such an approach can ensure, for example, that no family
decides to overwork while at the same time accumulating *unwanted* cash
balances. The present study does not go that far. Every aspect of behavior
is analyzed separately or in conjunction with only one or two others; but the
analysis makes an effort to remain consistent when drawing conclusions about
the following household decisions.

a   Work outside the household. Who works, how much to work, how to
    distribute the work effort among family members, how to allocate
    working time between the public and the private sectors. The underlying
    rule is to equate on the margin and in all directions the utility value of
    units of labor time used.

b   Saving vs. consumption.

c   Consumption patterns by categories of goods and services and by
    different markets (public/private).

d   Family formation (fertility).

The 'price' constraints studied are:

a   The formation and determination of wages in the public and private
    sectors.

b   Prices of goods and services in the two sectors.

Some of the rationing and institutional constraints imposed by the Soviet
system and authorities are:

a   'Pressure' to work and the availability of part-time jobs; price constraints,
    e.g., in the form of very low wages to husbands that induce wives to go
    to work.

b   Rationing of goods and services. On a general level, such rationing may
    take the form of repressed inflation, with people accumulating unwanted
    savings balances in the short run. It may also take the more illusive form
    of dissatisfaction with the assortment of goods or their general availabi-
    lity even after all adjustments to eliminate unwanted balances are made.
    In a particular form, rationing may exert specific pressure in specific

areas of household life. One example is the short supply of goods and services that help relieve the time pressure of household chores, such as decent appliances, better housing, more retail services, domestic help, and child day-care facilities. Rationing in these areas, with relatively limited opportunity for substitution, seriously affect the environment in which women function.

c   Rationing, or, in some cases, the complete absence of investment opportunities in productive (and 'non-productive') capital. This must influence decisions on savings, but also the determination of wage differentials in the public sector and the level of activity in the private sector.

Decisions on the allocation of time under such constraints help shape the size and structure of family earnings and income, and when combined with the emerging demographic structure and patterns of taxation and with the distribution of the Social Consumption Fund, they help form an income distribution pattern for the entire Soviet society.

The final picture that emerges from analyzing the individual household and the broader features of Soviet society is the outcome of the interaction between the Soviet family and the Soviet system. Three major interrelated and interdependent elements of the system help shape the particular outcome. These are the nature, structure, and rules of operation of the centrally planned system, the particular strategy chosen for economic development and growth, and the underlying body of ideological doctrine. It is interesting to trace their individual impacts on the outcome and, if possible, to draw up a balance sheet for them.

5.   The main findings

The following sections summarize the findings reached in the areas of work, the 'second' economy, savings, wage determination, wage differentials, and income distribution, welfare, social services, and poverty.

a   The family work effort

The most singular phenomenon of Soviet household life is the very high rate of labor-force participation (LFP) of women. Most women of working age (16–55) in the European parts of the Soviet Union are at work for most of their post-school lives. This produces a LFP for women of working age that exceeds 80 percent, which translates into a major contribution by women to the family's work effort and earnings. In our sample, women contribute about 45 percent of the family's labor input *outside* the home, and bring in almost a third of all earnings — about 28 percent of total income. The lower share of women (than of men) in total family earnings is due to the different occupational and industrial structure of the two sexes, and, in part to the lower LFP of women, in part to their shorter working hours (women work an average of 40 hours a week compared with 44 hours worked by men), but more than anything else to sex discrimination resulting in lower pay. On average, women earn about 60 percent of men's earnings per month (about 70 percent of men's earnings per hour). Put differently, had women earned the same hourly wage as men, their share in family earnings would rise from 32 to 42 percent. Despite women's lower earnings, the Soviet family distributes outside labor more evenly between husband and wife and consequently its earnings are less concentrated in the husband's paycheck than in most market economies.

What determines the decision of women to join the labor force? Can an economic explanation be offered for their very high LFP rate? The answer to the first question is that the same economic parameters that are relevant in the West go into the decision to participate in the labor force, and in the same manner as in the West. But that alone cannot account for the high participation level.

Women's LFP was estimated twice: once as a short-run phenomenon (participation during the last 'normal' year of life in the Soviet Union, before emigration) and once as a long-run phenomenon (the proportion of years in the labor force after finishing school. Both estimates produce expected, Western-type results: the participation decision in a given year in the Soviet Union, as everywhere else, is affected positively by higher wage rates offered and negatively by other family income sources and by the number of very small children present. These relationships are very robust.[2]

As in most western studies, the response to the wage offer is the strongest, and usually dominates the equation, as well as part (and to some extent future) trends. That is to say, a trend of equiproportional growth in the wages of both husband and wife, with fertility (and all other variables) held constant, will project a continuation of the increase in the LFP rate of women. The negative effect of non-wife family income on participation is relatively weak (see below).

The long-range commitment to the labor force (COMMIT) was estimated with longer-term variables — the level of education and the level of overall fertility. Since fertility and LFP are co-determined, a simultaneous estimation procedure was followed. The results indicate that the proportion of years spent in the labor force following formal study is strongly and positively affected by the level of education, and negatively affected by the number of children born.[3] According to the equation, each child born reduces the labor-force commitment 5.4 percentage points, and a lower level of schooling — between 2.5 and 7.5 points.

Part of the higher LFP rate of Soviet women can be explained by different levels of the determining parameters: Soviet women are better educated and Soviet families have lower levels of fertility and of non-wife income than in other countries with a similar level of economic development. It is also possible that Soviet women enjoy a higher relative (to men) wage. It is highly doubtful, however, that these differences can explain the entire difference in participation. A direct approach to explain this difference requires a comparative international study, which is unavailable at present. Indirectly, we reach the conclusion that since it takes much too much, in terms of changes in parameters, to bring down the Soviet LFP rate to a 'normal' level, something else must be keeping it up. One such factor, we believe, is 'persuasion', a term that extends over a wide range of means, from sincerely motivated ideological education in school to more abrasive propaganda and social pressure. The reason why the latter end of the possibility range is brought up is because relatively little is done to make it easier for women to join the labor force in the sphere of housing and in providing household services. The poor state of the household economy is, indeed, a missing variable that would have had a negative participation coefficient had it been included.

Another piece of indirect evidence that other factors are involved is that the participation equation over-predicts changes in the participation rates over time since the late 1930s. To us, this is an indication that some other factors — probably 'persuasion' — were much more important in the past in enlisting women to work than more recently; that over time, as a result of 'persuasion', women have adjusted their behavior to accommodate a working life, both by going to school more (among other reasons in order to avoid hard physical work on a job) and by planning smaller families. Both phenomena are observed in the historical records and in the results of the COMMIT equations. It is possible to hypothesize that over time 'persuasion' was increasingly internalized into the long-range behavioral parameters conducive to work. This process was compressed into a shorter period of time than is observed in the West, so that today much of what once had to be achieved by pressure is achieved through internal conviction.

An alternative explanation for the over-prediction of the rise in LFP rates over time is that the coefficient of the income effect in the cross-section analysis does not correctly represent the income effect over time. It is widely accepted that the best means of 'persuasion' used by the Soviet authorities to lead women to work has been to keep their husbands' rate of pay low, thereby making it necessary to have two salaries to survive. This does not show up in the statistical analysis, and the only explanation we can offer, other than statistical-technical problems, is that the income effect was, indeed, much stronger in the past, but now — with higher incomes — it is no longer as important.

Whatever the explanation, this issue of female LFP presents a classic example of the methodological argument advanced above, namely, that personal behavior in the Soviet Union can be explained through the use of established Western models, that different behavior is partly caused by differences in the levels of the parameters and that there may be other specific Soviet factors outside the model that share responsibility in determining behavior.

In our survey there are no data on time budgets of the participants. But data published in Soviet sources indicate that the extra burden on women in the workplace is not compensated for by a higher degree of sharing by husbands in household chores. That is to say, husbands of working women take a more active part in household work than husbands of non-working women, but not to a larger extent than American husbands. And working wives in the United States work fewer hours outside the home by taking advantage of part-time work opportunities not available to Soviet women. Also, the household burden on American families with working wives is on average lighter than in a corresponding Soviet home (more Soviet women with young children go to work). It follows that Soviet husbands are, at most, as cooperative as American husbands of working wives, and very likely less so.[4] The implementation of socialism for women in the labor market (in terms of work, not wages) without its implementation in the household, creates the extra pressure that shows up in low relative wages for women and in reduced fertility.

In addition to deciding on work at home vs. work in the market, Soviet families also must decide on the distribution of work between the public and private sectors and on the amount of extra work. Three facts are worth mentioning here. (a) Most outside work beyond the demand of a regular job in the public sector is performed by men. Men average 4.2 hours a week on top of regular hours, while women work only 1.8 extra hours (on average). This provides evidence of the extra non-wage-earning burden on women (extra hours were accounted for when the distribution of work was calculated). (b) Extra hours invariably come at the expense of regular hours. (c) Ten percent of all men and 5 percent of all women devoted some time to private work. The total reported time devoted to private work is just 2 percent of total family work time. We shall return to this point below.

b. Explaining lower pay for women

Remuneration for women is kept at only 60 percent of the comparable market wage for men. This is the exception among wage differentials in the Soviet Union today — the Soviet wage distribution is more equal than in the West — and, according to McAuley (1981), it is also the only wage differential that has not narrowed over the past thirty years while all other gaps have narrowed substantially.

The particular reason, in addition to the possible existence of discrimination as elsewhere, is precisely the heavy burden on women. To some extent, women earn less because they have fewer opportunities to invest in human capital on the job (not, as in the West, because they do not have long working careers, but because during their careers they do not have sufficient time to invest either on the job or after work at home). Being aware of this situation, they opt for the kind of jobs that can accommodate limited effort. In the West, it is claimed, the prospect of a shorter career for women causes less investment in human capital in formal schooling and on the job — leading to lower wages. For Soviet women the effect is the same — except that a short working career, measured in the West in years of work, is substituted by a short working career measured in limited ability to invest in human capital while on the job. In addition to the circumstantial evidence provided in the previous section, the most important piece of direct evidence that this is so is derived from the much lower premium per year of experience estimated in the earning function for women in comparison with that of men (2.5 and 6 percent respectively). This finding implies that in the Soviet Union, as in the West, women's lifetime profile of earnings is much flatter than that of men.

A second factor that may affect women's wages is the structure of the Soviet economy, where relatively few jobs are available in the service sector and in the middle (and lower) white-collar occupations. On the other hand, there is vast demand for women as blue-collar workers. The compensating factor is that a number of traditionally 'male' occupations, such as medical doctors, engineers, economists and the like, are open to women. The case of medicine is interesting: it is dominated by women — over 70 percent of all medical doctors are women, and wages are set at very moderate levels. The same is true with respect to rank-and-file engineers, among whom women are also a majority.

The formal analysis of male–female wage differentials is conducted through the estimation of earning functions for both sexes, a calculation of the hypothetical wage of each sex had it been paid according to the coefficients established for the other, and the assignment of the differences between actual and hypothetical wages to the various explanatory factors. The earning functions include variables for hours worked, schooling, work experience, age and marital status, occupational class, and industry.

Of an average wage advantage for men of about 40 percent, approximately half can be explained by inferior labor-force attributes of women and the other half is left to be explained by discrimination, occupational segregation, and the qualitative factors discussed above. The inferior labor-force attributes of women do not include their level of education, as the educational level of working women is equal to that of men. Historical data show that women have been catching up with men on this score very rapidly. The slight wage advantage of men originating in the educational factor (less than 1 point out of 20) results from a higher concentration of men in work that requires advanced university education, and of women in semi-academic vocations. About one-third of the explained earnings gap (7 out of 20 points) is attributed to the shorter work tenure of women, but about half of it is due to the younger age of wives in our sample.

Over half the explained earnings gap results from choice of occupational role and industry. The main items causing this gap are the absence of women from managerial roles and their concentration in low-paying, semi-academic professions, especially in health services. One interesting and telling finding is that both the wage differential and its breakdown into individual factors are very similar to findings about the same phenomenon in the United States (Malkiel and Malkiel, 1973; Oaxaca, 1973), despite sharp differences in rates of participation and in the size of the service economy. It seems that the gains made by Soviet women in the labor force are offset by low-level services provided by the government to households, by the additional pressure on their time and energies created by household burdens, and (to some degree) by labor-market and household discrimination and prejudices.

c. Private incomes

In addition to income earned from the public sector, we estimate that on average a Soviet urban family earned about 42 extra rubles per month in private income from a variety of sources in 1973. This amount is an addition of 15–20 percent to public income and is a very important supplementary source of income. About 28 percent of all families reported having private sources of income. For these families, total private income averages about R120 — a much higher percentage of total income.

Private income comes from a variety of sources, only some of which are revealed in our survey. Nor do we know the level of legality in obtaining most of this income. In the case of private incomes there is almost no possibility of checking the estimates with official Soviet statistics, and over the years, since the first draft of our paper on private incomes was written, we have accumulated a long list of claims of possible biases in both directions — that is, reasons why estimates based on a sample like ours are too low or too high. Clearly, the anecdotal evidence available (see, for example, Grossman, 1977; Smith, 1976; Simis, 1982) makes our estimate appear too low. What should be remembered, however, is that the anecdotal evidence provides information on those who have private incomes, but does not mention those who do not. If our finding that about 30 percent of households have private income sources is reasonable, then our results look much more consistent with such evidence.

Our estimates of private income distinguish only four different sources: from private work, from private agricultural plots, from rent, and from 'all other sources', with an obvious (implicit) emphasis on illegal sources of all kinds. The estimate of this last category comes partly (40 percent) from direct reporting by the respondents and mostly from our independent estimates based on reported gaps between expenditures and incomes. Of the total, private plot and rent add up to R2.7, private wages are R18.7, and 'other income' to R20.6 — all per family per month.

One of the most striking findings with respect to private incomes is the strong correlation between incomes from a particular source and the occupation of branch in which the recipient is engaged. In Table 1.2 we present a breakdown of private income by the occupation of the head of family (for 1,016 two-parent working families). Despite the fact that the effects of the wives' occupation is ignored, the patterns are very clear: private wages concentrate heavily among workers in the medical professions, in housing and communal services, and in production workers in consumer-goods industries. These people can provide services that are in short supply or of low quality in the public sector, along with the materials and tools needed. Private work is much less common among engineers, technicians, management workers and heavy-industry workers. Other evidence (not shown in the table) reveals that

Table 1.2. Private income by source and occupation of family head

Occupation	Number of families	Public earnings	Private incomes	Private wages	Other private income	$\frac{(3)^a}{(1)}$	$\frac{(2)^a}{(1)}$
		(1)	(2)	(3)	(4)	(5)	(6)
All families	1,011	335.3	42.4	18.7	20.6	7.5	16.9
Engineers	283	365.1	29.0	7.5	18.2	2.8	8.7
Technicians	72	319.9	24.5	9.0	14.8	3.0	10.9
Medical workers	57	350.4	87.1	57.4	29.7	24.9	35.8
Education, culture, and science	140	381.4	39.1	18.9	−18.3	6.7	15.3
Management and administration	45	339.3	20.6	3.2	12.7	0.7	6.5
Trade workers and employees	76	311.2	58.0	3.6	51.5	0.8	24.8
Communal workers and employees	44	302.7	88.8	56.8	30.4	14.5	26.4
Production workers (a)[b]	127	295.5	65.0	44.1	16.6	20.0	14.3
Production workers (b)[b]	167	296.2	28.6	10.0	13.9	5.9	31.0

[a] Calculated as average of individual responses, not as quotient of col. (3) [or col. (2)] entries *divided by* col. (1) entries.

[b] (a) Includes consumer good industries, construction, and transportation; (b) includes heavy industry.

Source: Sample data.

male physicians earn on average R220 in private income compared with R150 in public wages; communal service male workers make R152 in private income compared with R162 in public wages; and consumer-industry male workers make R158 in private income compared with R172 in public wages.

'Other income', which is much more integrated into one's working place — selling under the counter, accepting 'favors', rendering preferential services (in hospitals, for example) — is, indeed, concentrated among workers in trade and again in communal and medical services. The occupational breakdown fails to focus on the role of public administration, but when this is done we find that heads of families in public administration bring home about R30 extra (on average) of this type of income.

In addition to the occupational patterns of private income we find that private *work* comes at the expense of regular hours worked in the public sector, that people with lower public wages tend to engage in it more, and that it is more prevalent in Moscow than elsewhere. Finally, women tend to engage much less in private work than do men. This does not seem to reflect a less favorable occupational structure, quite the opposite: it seems to reflect the recognition of the heavier time and responsibility burdens borne by women due to household labor (as noted above).

The hourly wage rate in private work averages 3–4 times the rate in the public sector. It tends to be higher, the higher the regular hourly wage and level of education of the performer and (communal services excluded) the higher the perceived demand for the service. The very high differential between public and private wage rates is probably explained by the greater effort and better quality of private work; by its irregular nature; by the lack of the equivalent amount of social benefits that come with public employment; and by the risk element associated with private work. All these factors are elements in optimizing the division of labor between public and private work, so that overall the net marginal benefit of both is equal. It is possible, however, that part of the premium for private work manifests dis-equilibrium — the inability to reduce hours of public employment as much as is necessary to reach equilibrium. (If, instead, effort in public employment is reduced, it shows up on the optimal pay differential.) Private work thus becomes the marginal unit of work and demands higher compensation.

Why do people bother to engage in private work or to take the risk and exert the greater effort entailed in providing 'special services' for special fees, especially in view of the heavy time burden on families without such work? The immediate standard answer is that there is great demand for these extra services because people have excess cash balances that they cannot spend in public stores for lack of goods (the repressed inflation explanation). To some extent, the demand for private services is directly motivated by the time pressure on families in that they are ready to pay more in order to substitute money for time spent waiting in line or in searching for goods.

This is clearly one possible explanation of the development of private activities. As Pickersgill (1980b) has shown, the availability of privately supplied goods and services may even cause people to increase their work effort in the public sector, as this new supply is treated as an increase in real wages. But this argument is based on the assumption that total supplies are increased (or more efficiently distributed) and not, as is frequently the case, that a preferential service is to some extent offset by less service to others. In any case, as we have seen above and as is stipulated in Pickersgill's model, people who possess a comparative advantage in supplying such services reduce their hours of work in the public sector. The net benefit to the public sector is unknown. Finally, on this score, repressed inflation may result from the inability of families to reduce their work load in the public sector. There seems to be some evidence to support this argument in our study of obligatory full-time work for women (Chapter 8); a backward-bending supply curve for hours worked for women may indicate some preference for part-time work, which is usually unavailable.

The development of a private sector does not necessarily depend on a repressed inflation situation in the public sector and thus is no proof of its existence. Assume a situation in which the wage fund in the Soviet Union exactly matches the supply of consumer goods at official prices, all markets are cleared, and people hold the optimal amount of cash balances. When an opportunity presents itself to work more and get better services in an alternative sector, the situation changes and people become interested in exchanging more leisure for those better goods. One sure way to finance additional purchases in the private market is to engage in private activities (it is difficult to finance such purchases out of regular wages). We have not estimated the connection between the degree of household dependency on the private market for consumption and the level of its activity in private work in order to finance those extra purchases, but two observations support this notion: (a) expenditures in private markets are estimates (for the unweighted sample) at 16–18 percent of total expenditures, which is a few points higher than the proportion of private income (12 percent for the unweighted sample). The difference is taken up by purchases of food in collective farm markets. (b) Private purchases have uniformly higher income or expenditure elasticities than purchases in the public sector, so that clearly people with higher incomes buy more of them. And, as we shall see below, people with high incomes derive a high proportion of it from private sources. The only element missing in such a story is an increased money supply to facilitate the additional transactions.

A private sector can thus exist without repressed inflation in the public sector, in the conventional sense of the term, and the size of the private sector is not a measure of the extent of repressed inflation. The development of a private sector is a clear manifestation of the fact that people are not happy with what the public sector has to offer, but not necessarily that they have unwanted cash balances to spend elsewhere.

d. Savings

The issue of repressed inflation arises once again in the debate on what explains the secular rise in savings by the Soviet population. To what extent does this increasing volume of savings represent forced savings? To what extent does it represent the accumulation of voluntary savings, expressing household choice?

Our contribution here involves the evaluation of the savings issue on the basis of a cross-section savings function, its properties and parameters. We take into account the special environment affecting voluntary savings in the Soviet Union and conclude that the 1973 rate of savings (about 7 percent of income), the volume of liquid savings including cash (see Table 1.3), and the predictable well-behaved estimates of the savings function do not point to a serious problem of forced savings, at least in 1973 (for details, see

Chapter 3). In addition, we believe that voluntary savings should be lower in the Soviet Union than in comparable countries with market systems, for three reasons:

Table 1.3. Savings and wealth (1,014 families of survey population)

	All families	Families with no private income	Families with private income
Number of families	1,014	765	249
	(Rubles)		
Monthly income			
Net	392.6	367.9	488.6
Private	42.3	4.3	158.9
Savings	32.6	24.0	59.1
Total wealth			
Monetary assets	3,116	2,454	5,150
Real assets[a]	1,082	930	1,542

[a] Including private apartment, car, dacha, garden.

Source: Sample data.

First, in the Soviet Union life-cycle profiles of incomes are flatter than in the West and are more stable, creating less need to shift incomes over the life cycle through savings. The universal, though modest, pension plan extends a significant income stream beyond retirement. In addition, annual incomes — derived mostly from wages — contain fewer transitory elements and are much closer to permanent income. Again, there is less need to shift incomes from year to year. This reduces the expected level of the marginal savings rate in a cross-section analysis. The only exception on the income side is the existence of private incomes, which resemble entrepreneurial incomes in a market economy. Such incomes tend to be unstable, unpredictable, and risk-intensive, and thus call for much higher saving rates.

Second, on the consumption side, Soviet citizens are faced with less need to save money for large expenses that are concentrated in a short period of time. Most of them will never purchase a house, do not have to finance their children through college, receive free medical services, and are insured against accidents or illness that could prevent them from earning a living. All these make their consumption patterns more uniform over the life cycle and reduce the need for savings.

Third, there are very limited investment opportunities in the Soviet Union — almost no investments are permitted in productive assets — and the rate of interest on government bonds and savings accounts is very low (2–3 percent). The relatively vast opportunities to invest in human capital further limit the attraction of money or asset savings.

On the other hand, in addition to private incomes that stimulate savings, savings must be encouraged by the irregular and unpredictable supply of consumer goods and by the almost total lack of public credit institutions available to families. Money has to be held ready in anticipation that desired goods may appear in the market and, in general, money must be presaved for any significant planned expenditure. Availability of credit, in the United States for example, is an important factor that discourages savings. In the Soviet Union the opposite is true.

Finally, people may increase their rate of saving if they are not satisfied with the present assortment or quality of goods, and they have reason to believe that supplies will improve in the future. This motive, it can be argued, borders on forced, rather than voluntary savings. In some sense this is true, but not in what really matters: such savings are voluntary in the sense of choice, and they are not likely to change as long as underlying conditions and beliefs remain unchanged.

Even with these offsetting factors, we expect the rate of savings in the Soviet Union to be low by international standards.

The savings equations estimated are very stable and have relatively high coefficients of determination. They do, indeed, generate lower marginal rates of saving by international comparison, and even lower ones out of public income. Only marginal rates of saving out of private income are high and comparable to those found elsewhere.[5] On the basis of the above arguments it is difficult to judge whether the 7 percent average rate of savings is low enough to exclude the possibility of substantial amounts of forced savings; the rate is low by most international comparisons, and the entire picture, together with the data on accumulated savings, does not support the forced savings notion.

The repressed inflation hypothesis is further weakened when a more general equilibrium approach is adopted. It is especially difficult to support in light of the very high pressure on time of household members and the exceptionally high participation rate of women. A prolonged situation of repressed inflation should reduce unwanted cash or savings balances by reducing the time spent in work or work effort. Factors such as the many women who work in undesirable physical jobs, the quite large proportion of people engaged in extra work, the fact that premiums and bonuses still constitute some 15 percent of wages in the main place of work, all seem to support the claim that most families are engaged in earning more money and are interested in higher incomes. Add to this the argument advanced with respect to the private sector and one must reach a final minimal conclusion that repressed inflation is a much weaker phenomenon — at least it was in 1973 — than is generally assumed.

What remains to be explained is the secular trend of increasing savings rates. We cannot offer a full explanation for this trend, and the survey cannot provide the answer. It may be explained by the rise in incomes; by the increased share of purchases of durable goods such as cars, private apartments, and travel; by an increased effort to improve on government retirement pensions, which decline relative to income and wages over time; by the expansion of private activity in the urban sector; and by raised expectations resulting from a clear trend of improvement in standards of living between the mid-1950s and the early 1970s (see also Pickersgill, 1976, 1980a). Generally, it may be explained by an increasing demand for future economic security, improvement in pensions for retirees, and better provision for children, beyond what the state already provides.

e. The determination of wages

The doctrine of pay according to work performed governs (at least in principle) the formal determination of basic wage rates in the Soviet Union. In practice, a method of skill evaluation for each job, with emphasis on the nature of the task to be performed and work conditions, predominates — as opposed to the amount or kind of training required (Kirsh, 1972, Chapters 4, 5; Chapman, 1977a). Even if one formally rejects the human capital approach as a theory to explain wage differentials under socialism, a number of Soviet labor economists use it nonetheless, or at least a disguised version of it. A few even advocate the formal inclusion of schooling and training as a criterion in the determination of wage scales by the authorities (Kapustin, 1974; Kunelskii, 1968; Maier, 1968; Rabkina and Rimashevskaia, 1972).

In our work we use the human capital approach to explain actual wage determination in the Soviet Union. Even if actual wages directly correspond to prescribed wage rates, the analysis according to a partially different set of criteria than those used to determine these rates may discover to what extent human-capital theory factors are (unintentionally and indirectly) adhered to. In reality, however, actual wages differ from prescribed wage rates, partly because of formal rules on payments of bonuses, premiums and other flexible items; and because of responses of the labor market to pressures of demand and supply for particular kinds of labor. With relatively free choice of profession, location and place of work, the predetermined rate can never directly conform to labor market needs. As in other parts of our work, here too the human capital approach helps to distinguish between common and particular features of the Soviet labor market.

Formally, the analysis is based on estimating earning functions of the general form

$$W = f(SCL, EXP, Xi)$$

where W stands for different concepts of 'wages'; SCL stands for schooling variables; EXP — for work experience; and Xi is a vector of other variables such as place of residence, occupation or economic branch. The actual specification of the function varies, but wages are always presented in natural-logarithmic form as specified by Mincer and others (Mincer, 1974) so that the coefficients of schooling represent rates of return to years invested in school. The discussion here concentrates on earning functions for men.

The most significant result emerging from this work is that earning functions for Soviet workers behave in the same way as do similar functions in market economies. The usual independent variables explain anywhere from 20 to 40 percent of all wage differentials, the variables have the expected signs, and in most cases they are statistically significant. In the Soviet Union, as in other countries, there is a positive premium on both formal education and on-the-job training.

There are, however, important differences in the size and patterns of the coefficients of the major variables that reflect specific Soviet conditions. The most significant departure of the Soviet estimates made in comparison to American earning functions is that in the Soviet Union the premium for one additional year of schooling is much lower: 3–4 percent of the annual salary, compared with over 10 percent in the United States. Put differently, in the Soviet Union the maximum spread among wages between a worker with only four years of schooling and one with an advanced university degree — all other things being equal — amounts to no more than 50 percent. In the United States, the same schooling gap can produce a wage differential of over 350 percent (Mincer, 1974, pp. 92–93).[6]

The lower premium for schooling in the Soviet Union reflects lower rates of return to investment in schooling and lower private (and perhaps social) investment in a year of schooling. Lower rates of return to schooling are possible in the Soviet Union for a number of reasons. (a) There is no material capital market with high rates of return to compete with investment in human capital. The rate of interest paid on savings accounts is at most 3 percent, so that people should be ready to invest in education for approximately the same rate. (b) The rapid expansion of the education system over the post-war period produced an ample supply of professionals and semi-professionals and eliminated the need to pay high quasi-rents as may have been the case in other countries at a similar level of development. The Soviet authorities can definitely eliminate any attempt to block entry into certain professions and to establish monopoly wages. (c) The absence of the alternative of becoming an independent entrepreneur (yet another limitation imposed by the abolition of private productive property) also reduces the competitive pressure to pay high salaries to highly trained professionals who, in a different system, enjoy such alternatives.

It is interesting to note that so far the explanations of lower rates of return for investment in schooling should not affect efficiency considerations as they are all consistent with free market forces under the system's constraints. In this respect we agree with Wiles that top bureaucratic salaries can be cut without affecting efficiency (see Wiles, 1974, Chapter 4). In a broader sense, however, the efficiency problem is how to make public employees in the Soviet Union perform like entrepreneurs, or at least like managers of big corporations in market economies, rather than like public employees. Here, an argument may be made in favor of increasing the premium for schooling in the Soviet Union in order to encourage non-bureaucratic responses. Finally, lower rates of return may be achieved by administrative success in the artificial suppression of schooling premiums below what they should be. This can be partly checked by comparing the schooling premiums for basic wage *rates* with those for actual total wages, which is what we intend to do.

Private investment in schooling is lower in the Soviet Union for two reasons. First, a comparatively high proportion of students attend night school or take correspondence courses while working full time. The amount of forgone earnings for both student and society is thus lower.[7] Secondly, all schooling is free and regular day students in vocational schools and universities get a stipend of R40 per month (compared to a minimum wage of R60–70) along with other subsidies that cover a substantial part of their living expenses.

A second deviation of Soviet earning functions from those estimated in the West is that rates of return to higher levels of education are higher — not lower — than for general schooling. While a year of general school adds 2.3 percent and of technical school 2.7 percent, a year of university education adds 5 or 6 percent to wages. The accepted explanation in the West for a decline in the rates is the general tendency of rates of return to decline with the volume of investment. We do not have a clear explanation why the reverse is true in the Soviet Union. It may reflect the relative abundance of graduates of general schools and the relative scarcity of university graduates. This, in turn, may be caused by the small service sector in the Soviet economy, a sector that usually employs many high-school graduates. Most such graduates take blue-collar jobs in the Soviet Union, where the differences created by a few years of schooling are possibly not very central.

Work experience is introduced into the earning function in the form of the number of years actually worked and the square of this number to allow for the effect of declining investment in human capital over the life cycle. A typical pattern of premiums for investment on the job is a starting increment of 5.1 percent, declining to 4.8 percent per year at an average experience level of about 20 years, and declining further to 4.5 percent after 30 years of work. This pattern is very similar to the one found in similar studies in market economies, but both the basic premiums and the rate of decline are lower in the Soviet Union, and the compensation for years of schooling is lower still. The lower coefficients may be partly explained by the above-mentioned factors that reduce the rate of return to formal schooling. The fact that they are not lower may be explained by the more formal role played by seniority in Soviet wage determination.

Several other conclusions emerge from the estimates of the earning functions. (a) Wages in large cities tend to be higher than wages in small cities. (b) Compared with workers in academic professions, workers in managerial roles get a premium of 12 percent and highly skilled blue-collar workers get a premium of 16 percent, while semi-professionals (graduates of *tekhnikums*) are paid about 9 percent less. (c) Among branches of the economy, using manufacturing as a reference, we find all other branches with negative branch coefficients; the largest deviations are in services (-23 percent), trade (-15 percent), and science (-11 percent). These findings may represent to some degree the preferences of wage-setters in addition to market forces.

f. Inequality of wages and incomes

Having discussed the known determinants of wages, we now turn to examine their overall level of equality. Of the many measures of inequality we use two groups: one consists of percentile ratios (P_x/P_y), ratios between the wage rate of a worker with x percent of all workers above his wage and the wage rate of a worker with y percent below his wage. The most commonly used percentile ratio, especially in the Soviet Union, is the decile ratio — P_{90}/P_{10}. The second group consists of Lorenz measures — the percent of wages accruing to a given top or bottom proportion of the population. Both measures emphasize differentials between people at the extreme ends of the wage (or income) range and ignore what happens in the middle. We agree with Wiles (1974, p. 2) that this is the major aspect of inequality.

The decile ratio of net wages from the public sector for the weighted population of all workers is estimated at 3.31 and as we move further to the edges of the distribution it widens for P_{95}/P_5 to 4.52 and for P_{98}/P_2 to 5.83. That is, excluding at each end 2 percent of the lowest and highest earners, 96 percent of all employed workers belong to a group in which no one earns more than six times anyone else's wage.[8] Turning to the Lorenz measure, the top decile of earners collects 21.4 percent of all public wages and the bottom decile gets only 4.4 percent. Finally, it is worth mentioning that due to the minimum wage the average wage at the lower end of the wage distribution (P_2) is almost half the median wage, which is very high. All disparity measures for earnings from the main public job are only slightly narrower. However, when private wages are added, inequality widens significantly: the decile ratio rises to 3.77 and the total wage share of the top decile rises to 23.9 percent compared with only 1.9 percent for the lowest decile. The main point here is that people who have private wages tend to move up to the top decile and stretch the distribution.

According to Soviet sources, the decile ratio for gross wages from the main place of work dropped from a high of 7.24 in 1946 and 4.44 in 1956 to a low of 2.83 in 1968, when it started to climb again, reaching 3.1 in 1972 and 3.46 in 1976 (Rabkina and Rimashevskaia, 1978, p. 20). One can assume that the figure for 1973 may have been 3.3, compared with our figure for gross wages from the main job of about 3.4. This ratio is typically somewhat above corresponding ratios in other East European countries, lower than American ratios, and certainly not lower (but perhaps higher) than ratios in the developed countries of Western Europe (they are certainly higher than the ratios reported for the UK and Sweden; see Wiles, 1975b, p. 33; Bergson,

1984, pp. 1062–66, and Table 3). Finally, as Bergson has argued, the Soviet rates may be somewhat lower than those for market economies at similar levels of economic development (Bergson, 1984, pp. 1091–96). Considering the discussion in the previous section, it seems clear that the main forces that have brought down wage differentials are the rapid expansion of the educational system and the establishment of higher levels of minimum wages. The main force preventing wages from becoming more equal is the failure to narrow the gap between male and female pay scales.

How does the distribution of wages translate into income distribution per capita? It is easy to see that this transformation involves a long list of factors, only some of which are directly policy- or system-determined. The most important of the latter are how other sources of income are treated, such as entrepreneurial and property incomes (including capital gains) on the one hand, and, on the other, government transfers in the form of taxes, welfare and social-security type payments and the supply of free services (education, health, etc.). Among the other factors that determine income inequality are the composition and distribution of households by size, by number of children, and by the work status of household members (for example, the number of workers employed, their composition, and the number of retired family members).

Taking all these diverse factors into account, the following are our main findings about per capita income distribution in the Soviet urban population.

a. The decile ratio of net disposable income from all sources for the entire urban European population is 3.15; P_{95}/P_5 equals 5.10 and P_{98}/P_2 equals 8.33. The top decile of the population receives 22 percent of all incomes and the bottom decile 3.6 percent.

b. Without private income the decile ratio is slightly *higher,* as are the income shares of both the lowest and topmost deciles: 3.3 and 20.8 percent, respectively. Private incomes are thus more concentrated in relative terms at the extreme ends of the range, rather than in the middle. At least some people at the lower end of the income range supplement their income with privately earned incomes.

c. Monetary government transfers are a major source of income equalization for the entire population. These transfers help reduce the decile ratio based on earnings only from 4.66 to 3.26, and raise the share of the lowest decile from 0.6 percent of income to 3.3 percent. The main factors here are pension payments to the retired. In the Soviet Union all these payments come under the heading of the so-called Social Consumption Fund (SCF) and are not borne by employers.

d. The level of equality achieved with the help of the SCF for the entire population is only slightly lower than that obtained through wages alone for the active part of the population, i.e., for households with working heads. This should be considered a significant achievement.

e. Finally, the level of inequality is further reduced for the active population with the help of SCF payments so that the decile ratio for this group drops to 2.84 when SCF payments are included, but climbs back to 3.05 when private income is included as well. Among the working population, private income gravitates upward.

The most appropriate figures based on our sample for comparison with estimates based on official Soviet data are those for public incomes earned by the active population. Soviet surveys include only a small portion of private incomes, and their sampling procedures have, until recently, excluded households with no workers. In addition, their target population is essentially that of workers' and employees' families in the public sector for the entire country (see McAuley, 1979, pp. 50–55; Migranova and Rabkina, 1979). The 1970–1972 decile ratio for pre-tax incomes based on these official Soviet surveys are put at 3.2–3.3 (Migranova and Rabkina, 1979, p. 106; Nemchinova, 1975, p. 38) compared with our post-tax ratio of 2.84. With tax, our decile ratio would probably go up about 0.2–0.3 to around 3.1. In addition, our figure does not include the Asian urban population, nor any representation of public-sector employees in agriculture. There are other reasons why we believe our estimate is on the low side, but in either case (our figure or the official Soviet one), one has to add the influences on equality of incorporating the non-active segment of the urban population — about 0.4 points — to reach a pre-tax decile ratio of about 3.5–3.6. As stated above, the inclusion of private income on top of this figure may reduce it by about 0.1 point.

One Soviet source gives a decile ratio that purports to include the collective farm population, presumably also excluding non-active units of 3.59 for 1972 (Migranova and Rabkina, 1976, p. 62). If we add to this 0.4 points on account of the non-active population we arrive at a decile ratio of 4.0.[9]

Two income elements are still missing. The first is the value of free or subsidized services provided by the government to households. Our efforts to estimate the value of such services and their distributive impact lead us to the conclusion that they are distributed nearly evenly per capita to everybody, regardless of income, though in practice, high income brackets may get up to 20 percent more (see Chapter 5). We value them at about 20 percent of net public income when money SCF payments are included in income, and they may thus have a significant additional equalizing effect on the distributive measures. A very crude calculation shows a possible decline of the decile ratio by about 0.6 points. This affects the definition of poverty since free services allow persons the use of income that would otherwise go to pay for these services.

The second missing element that we could not estimate is the value of the special consumption privileges of the Soviet elite. While such privileges gravitate down the hierarchy to many 'ordinary' people, most are concentrated at the very top which, according to Matthews (1978), accounts for a mere 0.2 of the labor force. Clearly, their incomes do not belong to the decile ratio, but they do belong to the overall measure of equality. On the basis of data compiled by Matthews, Bergson (1984) estimates that privileges add about 1.5 percent to the total income accruing to the top decile of the labor force, and presumably a similar increment to the top decile of per capita income. While the overall effect on equality is slight, we fully concur with Matthews' final judgment that this phenomenon in itself "removes much of the social justification of the Bolshevik Revolution" (Matthews, 1978, p. 185). If specific elements of inequality could be weighted, we would assign a very high weight to this hypocritical source of inequality under 'socialism'.

It must be clear from the above that international comparisons of equality present many definitional and methodological problems, especially when data for other countries are not much better than those for the Soviet Union. We conclude that there is no question that the level of Soviet income equality is higher than in the United States, Canada, France, and several less developed European countries such as Spain and Italy. We believe that this may also prove true with respect to Sweden and the UK, but the available data preclude a definite conclusion (see Bergson, 1984, pp. 27–31 and Table 6; Sawyer, 1976). In contrast, the level of income *in*equality in the Soviet Union is higher — or at least it was in the early 1970s — than in most, if not all, East European countries (Wiles, 1975b).

The major factor that seems to give the Soviet Union an edge over market economies in terms of equality is the existence of entrepreneurial and property income and the extremely unequal distribution in the latter. Differences across systems of the distribution of wage incomes are narrower, although with respect to the United States, for example, it is still very significant.

6. Conclusion

We hope this introductory chapter outlines the contribution of micro-economic data on Soviet households to a better understanding of this sector. Although important aspects of the economic environment are different under the Soviet system, a meaningful and revealing discussion can be carried out by applying the theories used in the West for similar kinds of analysis. This kind of approach can help to isolate and define the areas where the differences in economic systems really matter. We further hope that the inter-action between the available Soviet statistical information and data generated from the income survey has reinforced the credibility of both. Although we have not discussed a number of potential sources of bias, the general corres-pondence of our estimates with Soviet data supports the proposition that these biases cannot be very great.

The main overall substantive conclusion that can be reached is that, while the three major systemic elements of the Soviet system contribute to the patterns of behavior of Soviet households and to the economic environ-ment surrounding them, whenever there is a conflict among the goals of the Soviet leaders, the goal of rapid growth prevails over all others. This is observed mostly in the interaction between the goals of growth and equality. As long as increased equality is consistent with growth, as when it is facilitated by expanding the education system or eliminating non-competitive wage differentials, equality is advanced. In contrast, wide wage differentials between men and women have been allowed to persist because removing them could involve directing substantial resources of the public sector to the household services required for women to direct more attention and effort to the labor market. Likewise, most welfare payments are work-related and, at least until recently, very little has been distributed as 'pure' welfare, lest it negatively affect labor-force participation.[10] The goal of growth maximization at minimum acceptable rates of consumption also contributes to the degree of tolerance of private economic activity. We do not claim that the size of the private sector is preplanned and optimal, or fully controlled by the center; nonetheless, a case can be made that such activity improves the well-being of the population at a lower net cost to the system in terms of 'growth' than if public production had provided the service currently provided by the private sector. Of course, private activity is tolerated at a high cost to socialist ideology.

The Soviet growth strategy has followed the extensive pattern in that it has achieved growth through the maximization of the non-consumed surplus for investment purposes and the enlisting of the maximum possible supply of labor. In addition to an attempt to bring everybody who can work into the labor force, this strategy imposed a heavy additional time burden on households in the spheres of household services, retail services and, indirectly, in the private sector.

One household response that has exacted a heavy toll on further growth potential is reduced fertility. It is difficult to judge to what extent private activity may have increased and public work effort may have been reduced as additional responses. At the present time, when growth rates are very low, the Soviet authorities will have to pay much closer attention to possible household responses to future policies.

Notes

1. A more detailed exposition of the main characteristics of SP, UP, and the Soviet Jewish community appears in the Appendix.

2. An example of one LOGIT equation with 978 observations would be:

$$\text{WFPART} = 5.672 + 4.54 \text{ LNWFWG} - 1.17 \text{ WFAGE2} - 0.086$$
$$(10.7) \quad (6.6) \qquad\qquad (-4.5) \qquad\qquad (-2.5)$$

$$\text{NWFINC} = 0.011 \text{ PRINC} - 0.66 \text{ CH03}$$
$$(-4.2) \qquad\qquad (-2.7)$$

where: LNWFWG = wives' estimated hourly wage; WFAGE2 = the wife is between 45–54 years of age; NWINC = per capita non-wife family income, derived from the public sector — consists mainly of husband's earnings; PRINC = per capita family income from private sources; CH03 = number of children age 0–3. Figures in parentheses are t values.

3. The COMMIT equations were estimated for a subsample of 'complete' families — with younger child over 3 years of age or wife above the age of 30. The following is a typical equation:

$$\text{COMMIT} = 1.01 - 0.45 \text{ WFTS} - 0.17 \text{ WFGS2} - 0.22 \text{ WFGS1}$$
$$(24.4) \quad (2.5) \qquad\quad (-8.1) \qquad\qquad (-7.4)$$

$$- 0.10 \text{ WFAGE2} + 0.03 \text{ WFRLD1} - 0.054 \text{ BIRTH}$$
$$(-5.6) \qquad\qquad (1.1) \qquad\qquad (1.8)$$

where: WFTS, WFGS2, and WFGS1 = dummy variables for completed technical school, general school (at least 9 years) and lower schooling, respectively, all compared with having university degrees; WFAGE2 = being between 45 and 54 years of age; WFRLD1 = having a managerial job; BIRTH = number of children born. Figures in parentheses are t values.

4. These statements are based on calculations from data in Szalai, 1972, Table III.3, p. 601.

5. The equations are:

For the entire sample: $S = -36.8 + 0.174Y$

For families with no private income: $S = -18.5 + 0.115Y$

For families with private income: $S = -66.5 + 0.25Y$

where: S = savings in rubles; Y = net family income.

In an equation for all families the coefficient for regular income is 0.13 and the coefficients for privately earned income range between 0.14 and 0.40.

6. A typical 'short' earning function for men in the Soviet Union is:

$$\ln W = 2.8 + 0.44(\text{hours}) + 0.023(\text{regular school})$$
$$+ 0.027(\textit{tekhnikum}) + 0.050(\text{university})$$
$$+ 0.063(\text{advanced studies}) + 0.051(\text{experience})$$
$$- 0.0007(\text{experience}^2) - 0.0077(\text{age}).$$
$$R^2 = 0.32$$

Hours are weekly and all other variables are measured in years. W is wage from main job; all coefficients are significant at 1 percent except *age*, which is significant at 5 percent.

7. In the regression shown above we already accounted for lower investment in night schools and correspondence courses.

8. Higher ratios, of up to 15:1, also exist, but these are truly exceptional cases.

9. McAuley (1979, p. 65) estimates a comparable figure for 1967–68 (3.1–3.2), which may not be entirely off the mark if the differentials in income per capita started rising again after 1968 as did wage differentials. We suspect that private incomes in agriculture may have the same equalizing effect on the entire population's income as urban private incomes. We do not know how they are treated in the Soviet surveys.

10. This conclusion is borne out in Chapter 5.

Chapter 2
Private sources of income of the Soviet urban household

1. Introduction

In its pure form, the Soviet economic system is supposed to be based exclusively on public production; all means of production are to be owned by the state and all production conducted through its authority. Nonetheless, since the institution of this public economy in the late 1920s, there have always been certain "private production" activities. Some have received full government sanction (notably private agricultural plots and the collective farm market); some are tolerated but lack explicit approval; and some are conducted illegally. Even so, private production activity has always been ideologically unacceptable and is therefore viewed as a necessary but temporary compromise. With the growth of the public sector's economic potential, on the one hand, and the socialist education of the population on the other, it was hoped that both the need for and the temptation to engage in such activities would decline. Although the relative importance of private farming, the most important legal private production activity, has been declining over time, the final goal still seems to be beyond reach. This is fully recognized by the now famous Article 17 of the new Soviet Constitution, which openly authorizes private labor activity in certain fields.

In such a situation, the loci of private economic activity, whether legal, semi-legal, or illegal, can serve to identify weak areas of performance in the public production sector and on the reeducation front. The study of private economic activity can thus provide another dimension to the understanding of the workings of the centrally planned economic system.

The inclusion of legal activity in the definition of the private sector makes our concept extend beyond what is usually called an "underground" or "second" economy — in the Soviet Union or elsewhere. But given our concern with extralegal activity here, why singly out the Soviet Union when every nation has its "second" economy, which may even be larger than in the Soviet Union? Studying the underground economy helps to clarify the prevalent economic and social system for any country. For the Soviet Union, special interest in this topic derives from the interaction, noted above, between the public and private subsystems within a system that is designed and geared to become completely public. It is for this reason that legal as well as extralegal private activity is included here, as it would not be in a study of the "underground" economy *per se*.

Determining the size of the Soviet private economy is also important for the study of excess demand or repressed inflation in the consumer-goods sector. Pressures created by imbalances between the wage bill and the "consumption bill" (all consumer goods and services produced in the public sector, valued at official prices) may be directed into the private sector. Moreover, as in many other countries, the exclusion of certain private activities may distort estimates of national aggregates such as GNP and private consumption, as well as the structural patterns of the economy such as the ratio of consumption to investment (or defense) and the industrial structure. To cite one example, the cross-section saving function in the Soviet Union is considerably influenced by the existence of private income (see Chapter 3).

By its very nature, private economic activity defies accurate recording in official statistics. Much of what is illegal under Soviet law is not included in the relevant statistical categories. Furthermore, to avoid taxation or exposure, a large share of private legal activities is probably not reported to the authorities. In some cases (such as the column of sales and prices in collective farm markets) the information is gathered by a sampling method (not direct reporting), which leaves room for doubt. As a result, no published official Soviet estimate of the size of the private sector exists, nor is there a full reckoning of this sector in the system of national accounts. While not easy in any country, estimating the size of the underground economy has been much more difficult for students of the Soviet Union living in the West. The double curtain of secrecy which has shrouded information on the private sector within the Soviet Union is responsible for the wide variation of current estimates, ranging from a few percentage points to some 40 percent of GNP, or at least of consumption. The implications of accepting either the minimum or the maximum estimates are very significant for our understanding of the Soviet economy.

Many studies on the private sector of the Soviet economy have appeared in the West in the past few years, ranging from personal experience with private activities in the Soviet Union to methodological and theoretical papers on the definition, scope, and legal aspects of private activity, attempting to estimate the level of these activities and their effect on economic aggregates.[1]

In this chapter we shall provide a comprehensive quantitative estimate of the extent, level, and pattern of private economic activity in the Soviet urban sector and of its effect on the size of major economic aggregates.

The private sector is defined here to include all production activity on private account, including transactions performed outside the accounts of a public enterprise or institution, whether legal or illegal. It includes pure private production or provision of services and also the use of public property, materials, equipment, and labor to provide goods or services to private people for private gain.

Western convention omits all illegal activities from the national accounts. Had we done so with respect to the private sector in the Soviet Union, a significant proportion of the above activities would have to be excluded, some of which, while strictly illegal, appear to be quite common. On both theoretical and practical grounds, therefore, we decided to include in our estimate all activities classified in the Soviet context as economic crimes against the state or the public sector, as distinct from other criminal acts. In principle, we should include, say, pilfering by employees from government stores, but not burglary. The distinction may not be as clear-cut as we would want it to be, but the intention is clear enough. In practice, we include any income reported as earned privately, keeping in mind the limitations of our data.

The analysis is divided into two major parts. The first deals with sources of private earnings and incomes, the second with purchases from private sources. In both parts we first present the data for the sample population as it is and then adjust the estimate and project the findings to fit the target population and the macroeconomic national aggregates.

2. Private sector earnings and incomes

a. The survey evidence

The survey estimates income derived from four different private sources: private work, subsidiary farm, rents, and "other" sources (the latter deliberately remain unspecified in order to bring in, with minimum embarrassment, all legally questionable non-work incomes.[2] The unspecified source of income may thus include "tips" to public officials, the value of goods taken without permission from the public domain for private use or resale, and possibly wages or quasi-wages nor reported as private work.[3] Nevertheless, and for obvious reasons, income from private sources is likely to be under-reported. An attempt to estimate unreported private income is made at the end of this section.

Although income from private work, private agricultural plots, and rented apartments or rooms can be legal, it actually becomes so only if reported or registered and when the appropriate special tax on it is paid. However, these regulations are commonly disregarded, so as to evade taxes, avoid public exposure, or conceal the use of illegally acquired tools or materials. The questionnaire did not distinguish between legal and illegal activities.

1. Private wages

Table 2.1 presents a breakdown of the working habits of the sample population (SP) by the extent of work and sector and by sex. Of the entire adult population of 2,520, 2,146 were working; of those who were working, 173 (8.1 percent) were engaged in some kind of private work or other. Several observations on the incidence of private work can be made from the data in this table.

First, private work appears largely as a supplement to, rather than as a substitute for, a full-time job in the public sector. Only four women worked exclusively privately and only five people (four of them women) who worked privately held only a part-time job in the public sector. All but one of the men and 84.3 percent of the women who work privately were also fully employed in the public sector. The presumption that women might have resorted to private employment as the only way to get a part-time job is not

Table 2.1. Adult population by working status and extra work

		Men	Women	Total
1.	All adults	1,209	1,311	2,520
	a. Nonworking	82[a]	292[b]	374
2.	Working	1,127	1,019	2,146
	a. Part-time	11[c]	26[d]	37
3.	Working full-time	1,116	989	2,105
4.	Working privately	122	51	173
	a. Only privately	0	4	4
	b. Part-time in public sector	1	4	5
	c. Full-time in public sector	121	43	164
	i. Additional work only in private sector	79	32	111
	ii. Additional work in private *and* public sectors	30	3	33
	iii. Additional private work and overtime[e]	9	5	14
	iv. Additional private and public work *plus* overtime	3	3	6
5.	Those working full-time with additional public jobs	140	36	176
	a. In addition to only overtime	11	1	12
	b. In addition to overtime and private work	3	3	6
6.	All those with full-time jobs working overtime	65	50	115
7.	All those with full-time jobs engaged in extra work	270	114	384

[a] Of whom 5 are family heads.
[b] Of whom 118 are wives of family heads.
[c] Of whom 6 are family heads.
[d] Of whom 23 are wives (4 of them work only privately).
[e] Overtime accounts for all cases of more than a full-time job in the main place of public employment.

supported by the data. Indeed, twenty-two out of twenty-six women who work part-time found such jobs in the public sector.

Secondly, while there are opportunities to work more than full-time in the public sector, even here private work serves, at least for some people, as a supplement rather than as a substitute: 115 people work overtime[4] in their main place of work (line 6) and 176 people engage in additional public jobs (line 5); 33 people (19 percent) of those who hold extra public jobs and 20 (17 percent) of those working overtime are also privately employed, both proportions being higher than the incidence of any kind of extra work in the entire population. This indicates a *positive* gross association between additional public and private jobs rather than a negative one, which would have been called for if these two types of employment were real substitutes for one another.[5] This gross association may result either from demand or from supply conditions conducive to extra work for specific groups in both the public and private sectors. However, most people who seek or have the opportunity to engage in extra work choose only one of the three forms available.

Finally, men are much more active than women in private work: 122 men (10.8 percent of those working) but only 51 women (5.0 percent) had such jobs. Correspondingly, more women who work privately do so part-time, and fewer of them (only 11, as against 42 men; lines 4.c.ii to 4.c.iv) are engaged in other forms of extra work. This reflects the overall lower involvement of women in extra work (line 7). The main explanation for these differences between the sexes seems to lie in the very high rate of participation of women in the active labor force. At 78 percent (lines 1, 2), the rate is lower than for men (93 percent), but far higher than the rates for women in any market economy. Faced with both need and social pressure to work, and with a heavy load of household chores to perform, it is surprising that even 5 percent of the working women do engage in extra private work.

In what follows we trace the extent and significance of private work in various sectors of the Soviet economy. The variables used to measure the size and importance of private work are:

W3D   The proportion of all workers in a certain group engaged in private work.

W3	Monthly wage per worker in a defined group, from private work.
H3	Average weekly hours spent in private work.
W1, W2	Monthly net wages from the main place of work and from all jobs in the public sector, respectively.
H1, H2	Weekly hours in the main place of work and in the public sector, respectively.
W3/W1, W3/W2	Private wages as a percentage of total wages from the main place of work and of total wages received from the public sector, respectively.
H3/H1, H2/H1	Private work time as a percentage of time spent on the main job and on work in the public sector, respectively.
WPH1, WPH3	Wages per hour on the main job and in the private sector, respectively.
WPH3/WPH1	Ratio of hourly wages in the private sector to those in the main place of work.

The analysis is carried out for two groups: the privately employed and the entire working population. In the first we focus on the effect of private activities on the families involved; in the second we emphasize the differential impact of private work on various segments of the economy.

The average private work characteristics of these two groups appear in Table 2.2 for men and women. People who are privately employed average R109.8 per month (net) from private work, adding about 78 percent to their wages and salaries from public jobs or some 44 percent of their total wage earnings (Panel A). They devote 10 hours a week to private work, an extra one third or more to the time they spend on their main job. Private work is thus of major economic significance to those engaged in it, and any conclusion drawn on their economic position or behavior based solely on their public work and earnings would be completely misleading.

The hourly rate in the private sector is R3.10 — almost four times higher than the average rate in the public sector. This wide difference reflects the inadequate supply of needed goods and services in the public sector, a risk premium, and a rental charge for the use of facilities and tools.[6] Even when proceeds from private work are averaged out across the entire labor force

Table 2.2. Private work: incidence, wages, and hours, by sex

	A. Working privately[a]			B. Entire working population		
	All	Men	Women	All	Men	Women
1. Number of workers	173 (159)	122 (112)	51 (47)	2,146	1,127	1,019
2. W3D (percent)	100.0	100.0	100.0	8.1	10.8	5.0
3. W3 (R per month)	109.8	127.6	67.4	8.9	13.8	3.4
4. H3 (hours per week)	10.1	10.7	8.6	0.8	1.1	0.5
5. W3/W1 (percent)	80.8	87.5	64.8	6.4	9.6	3.0
6. W3/W2 (percent)	77.8	83.7	63.7	6.2	9.1	2.9
7. H3/H1 (percent)	34.8	34.2	36.3	2.6	3.5	1.7
8. WPH3 (R per hour)	3.1	3.3	2.4	..	..	..
9. WPH3/WPH1 (ratio)	3.7	3.9	3.2	..	..	..
10. W1 (R per month)	150.9	165.6	115.8	152.1	184.0	117.0
11. H1 (hours per week)	38.8	40.3	35.3	40.3	41.6	38.9
12. WPH1 (R per hour)	1.0	1.0	0.9	0.9	1.1	0.7

[a] The figures for those employed privately are based on only 159 workers (112 and 47 women). Excluded from this analysis are individuals who do not hold full-time jobs in the public sector (1 man and 4 women), who did not report on hours worked in the private sector (6 men), and 3 men whose reported wage per hour either exceeded R20 or fell below R0.40.

they remain quite substantial (Panel B): private earnings add R8.9 (5 percent) to the average (net) public wage of *every* worker. Every worker spends an average of 0.8 hours (2.6 percent above regular weekly hours worked) on private activities.

Table 2.2 reveals additional findings on the lower level of involvement of women in private work. As may be seen from comparing the first three with the last three columns of the table, this lesser involvement of women shows up primarily in the lower participation of women in private work and, to a lesser extent, in lower levels of activity for those who do engage in such work. Thus, although only 5 percent of working women take on private jobs (as against 11 percent of the men), women who work privately spend 8.9 hours a week (only 2.1 hours less than men) on such jobs.[7]

Women's earnings from private work are significantly lower than those of men: R67.4 as compared with R127.6 per month. This is a combined result of somewhat lower private-work premiums for women over public wage rates, and of significantly lower public wage rates for women as compared with those for men.[8]

All these factors contribute to the much lower significance of private work for all women workers as compared with men (Panel B): private work adds, on average, only R3.4 to women's net monthly earnings, a mere 3 percent increment, as compared to R13.8 per month (9.1 percent) for men. Women spend only half an hour a week on private jobs, 1.7 percent above regular working hours, as compared to a full hour (3.5 percent) in the work effort of the entire male labor force (Panel B). Men who are engaged in private work add R127.6 (83.7 percent) to their public earnings. Clearly, private work becomes at least as important for these men as their official jobs.

Although private work is spread among all types of workers classified by any relevant criterion, it is obvious that some groups are more deeply involved than others. In what follows we sketch the pattern of differential participation in private work of various groups of workers to determine the reasons behind these patterns. The analysis is carried out first for the entire labor force.

Highly significant differences in private work levels (besides those between men and women) are observed between blue- and white-collar workers, between workers in different branches of the economy, between different professional groups, and to some extent between residents of cities of different sizes. No significant differences are observed on the basis of age, family size, education, and geographical location (republic). A description of the differences by branch and sex is presented in Table 2.3, and by occupation in Table 2.4. The main results are discussed below.

High levels of private work participation (W3D) are observed among workers in housing and communal services, where 19.0 percent of all workers (23.1 percent of all men) engaged in private work; in education and culture (11.0 and 12.3 percent, respectively); and in health services (mainly among men) (9.4 and 19.5 percent).[9] More or less average rates are observed in science, construction and transportation; low rates of private participation are found in manufacturing (4.3 percent overall and 6.2 percent for men); and very low rates are found in trade and public catering (2.0 and 4.3 percent) and in public administration (1.2 percent overall and none among men).

The levels of the other variables, private earnings (W3) and relative private earnings (W3/W2), are highly influenced by the private participation rates and thus follow the same *general* pattern. The following figures are especially interesting: men working in communal services *average* (i.e., including those who do not engage in private work) close to R32.5 a month in private work, adding almost 22 percent to their earnings from public-sector jobs; the corresponding figure for men in health services are R40.5 and 31.3 percent. The high degree of variance among branches is underlined by comparing these figures with the corresponding R2.9 per month (2.5 percent of public earnings on average) for an employee in the trade industry and even less than that for public administration workers. These findings make it clear that the data on wage differentials by economic branch published in official Soviet sources need to be adjusted.

A more detailed picture is presented in Table 2.4, where differences in the level of private work variables are presented by occupation. In many cases it is the occupation rather than the branch of employment that determines the propensity to engage in private work. The table is made up of three parts: one for blue-collar workers, one for white-collar employees, and one for a finer breakdown of employees in the medical professions.[10]

Concentrating first on W3D, we observe that workers are more inclined than employees to engage in private work, and that this average finding results entirely from higher rates for male workers (14.3 percent) than for male employees (8.8 percent). The W3D rates for women belonging to these two groups are very similar, around 5 percent. The private wage differential between workers and employees, again for men, is even wider: workers make R19.7 per month in private work, adding 12.9 percent to their public job income (W2), while employees add only R10.3 (6.9 percent). Correspondingly, blue-collar workers spend more time doing private work than do white-collar employees. The differences between the two groups are narrower when hourly wages in private work and ratios of private to public wage rates are considered. Private hourly rates for all those engaging in private work are quite similar, only those of women are much lower. Relative private hourly rates, however, are similar throughout, at close to four times the public rate.[11]

Among blue-collar workers we find a dichotomous situation in which, on the one hand, all workers in the non-manufacturing occupations, together with industrial workers producing textiles, clothing, footwear and leather, construction materials and furniture have high rates of participation in private work, while on the other hand, workers in heavy industry (mostly in machinery in our sample) and in the food and other sub-branches engage far less in private work. The highest rates are found among construction workers (52 percent of all men, R74 per month). The typical rates for the high private-work occupations (mostly for men) are 15–25 percent for W3D (in transportation, though, it is only 14 percent) and R20–35 per worker per month — some 20 percent above the public wage. In the low-participation occupations, the W3D rates range from 2 to 8 percent, monthly wages from R3 to R8, and the relative increment to public wages — 2–6 percent. We shall return to the discussion of private work rates further on.

Two main observations on employees emerge from Table 2.4 (parts b and c): first, we see a repetition of the patterns observed for the service branches of the economy, except that some specific private work rates, for more restricted occupational groups, are much higher. This is the case with respect to medical employees, employees in communal services, and education and culture groups. This is also the case within the medical profession, especially dentists — the only identified professional group that reported higher earnings from private work than from the main public-sector job (127 percent). Secondly, we observe that major professional groups (engineers,

Table 2.3. Private work by economic branch: all workers (sample returns)

		Number of workers	W3D %	W3D R	$\frac{W3^a}{W1}$ %	$\frac{W3^a}{W2}$ %	$\frac{W1}{R}$
Manufacturing	Total	649	4.3	3.6	2.6	2.5	165.5
	Men	390	6.2	5.3	3.9	3.7	190.0
	Women	259	1.5	0.9	0.7	0.7	128.7
Agriculture[b]	Total	43	7.0	5.7	3.4	3.1	149.9
	Men	28	10.7	8.8	5.2	4.7	268.6
	Women	15	0.0	0.0	0.0	0.0	115.1
Transportation	Total	87	9.2	14.3	7.6	7.5	163.6
	Men	71	11.3	17.5	9.3	9.2	177.7
	Women	16	0.0	0.0	0.0	0.0	101.4
Construction	Total	153	7.8	8.5	4.3	3.8	186.4
	Men	118	10.2	11.1	5.5	5.0	199.4
	Women	35	0.0	0.0	0.0	0.0	142.3
Trade and public catering	Total	200	2.0	1.4	1.2	1.0	130.6
	Men	94	4.3	2.9	2.5	2.1	160.6
	Women	106	0.0	0.0	0.0	0.0	104.1
Communal services[c]	Total	232	19.0	24.4	17.2	17.0	140.7
	Men	139	23.1	32.4	21.9	21.7	161.8
	Women	93	11.8	12.4	10.2	9.9	109.2
Health services	Total	266	9.4	14.2	12.0	11.7	128.9
	Men	77	19.5	40.5	31.3	30.3	171.5
	Women	189	5.3	3.5	4.1	4.1	111.5
Education, science and culture[d]	Total	435	11.0	9.6	7.6	6.9	153.4
	Men	187	12.3	14.7	11.6	10.1	202.4
	Women	248	10.1	5.7	4.6	4.5	116.4
Public administration[e]	Total	81	1.2	0.4	0.3	0.3	124.7
	Men	23	0.0	0.0	0.0	0.0	162.1
	Women	58	1.7	0.5	0.5	0.5	109.8

[a] Computed as averages of individual responses, not as the quotient of table entries for W3 divided by W1 (or by W2).
[b] Only 43 of SP worked in agriculture. Living in cities, they do not represent in any way the Soviet agricultural population.
[c] Including services to housing, repairs, and personal services.
[d] Including art.
[e] Including banking and communications.

Table 2.4. Private work by occupation[a] (all employed, sample returns)

		Number of workers	W3D (%)	W3 (R)	W3/W1[b] (%)	W3/W2[b] (%)	H3 (hours per week)	WPH3[c] (R per hour)	WPH3[b,c]/WPH1 (ratio)	W1 (R)
a. Workers (blue-collar)										
All workers	Total	615	11.2	14.8	10.2	10.0	1.4	3.1	3.8	142.9
	Men	419	14.3	19.7	13.2	12.9	1.7	3.2	4.5	162.5
	Women	196	4.6	4.4	3.9	3.8	0.7	2.8	3.8	101.0
Manufacturing (mach. and other heavy industry)	Total	187	7.5	7.0	5.9	5.6	0.5	3.2	4.0	161.9
	Men	172	8.1	7.7	6.4	6.1	0.6	3.2	4.0	166.5
	Women	15	..	..	..	..	..	..	..	109.1
Manufacturing (wood, textiles, clothing, shoes)	Total	122	15.6	25.3	18.1	18.1	2.6	2.8	3.7	139.1
	Men	70	21.4	36.1	26.8	26.8	1.2	2.3	3.0	159.2
	Women	52	7.7	10.7	6.4	6.4	3.7	5.4	6.6	112.1
Manufacturing (other)	Total	51	2.0	3.1	2.2	2.2	..	..	..	129.2
	Men	31	3.2	5.2	3.7	3.7	..	..	..	142.0
	Women	20	..	..	..	..	..	..	..	109.3
Construction and construction materials	Total	28	50.0	71.1	38.8	36.9	6.6	2.9	3.1	186.9
	Men	27	51.9	73.7	40.3	38.3	6.9	2.9	3.1	188.4
	Women	1	..	..	..	..	..	..	..	145.0
Transportation	Total	46	13.0	21.3	12.0	11.7	1.1	6.5	7.6	185.0
	Men	43	14.0	22.8	12.8	12.6	1.1	6.5	7.6	192.2
	Women	3	..	..	..	..	..	..	..	82.3
Trade and business services	Total	110	0.9	0.9	0.6	0.6	0.2	0.9	1.1	104.1
	Men	37	2.7	2.7	1.9	1.9	0.7	0.9	1.1	124.0
	Women	73	..	..	..	..	..	..	..	94.0

b. Employees (white-collar)

All employees	Total	1,531	6.8	6.5	5.0	4.7	0.56	3.1	3.7	155.8
	Men	708	8.8	10.3	7.5	6.9	0.72	3.6	4.1	196.7
	Women	823	5.1	3.2	2.8	2.7	0.42	2.3	3.0	120.7
Engineers	Total	434	6.5	4.2	3.0	2.8	0.44	2.5	2.7	188.4
	Men	299	7.7	5.3	3.8	3.6	0.51	2.7	2.9	208.5
	Women	135	3.7	1.6	1.1	1.1	0.30	1.6	2.0	143.9
Technicians	Total	158	1.9	2.9	1.4	1.4	0.21	3.4	2.9	142.6
	Men	82	2.4	3.7	1.5	1.5	0.28	3.3	2.5	173.3
	Women	76	1.3	2.0	1.2	1.2	0.13	3.5	3.6	109.6
Medical employees	Total	228	11.4	16.9	14.2	13.8	1.05	4.1	6.0	128.4
	Men	61	21.3	47.1	36.4	35.4	2.49	5.3	7.1	164.5
	Women	167	7.8	5.9	6.0	6.0	0.53	2.8	4.8	115.2
Education employees	Total	373	10.7	8.0	6.5	5.7	0.88	2.6	2.6	161.0
	Men	157	12.1	11.3	9.1	7.4	0.94	2.2	3.1	217.4
	Women	216	9.7	5.6	4.6	4.5	0.84	3.1	2.0	120.0
Planners or administrators	Total	236	1.3	0.7	0.5	0.3	0.09	0.8	1.1	129.5
	Men	49	2.0	2.0	1.1	0.6	..	..	..	180.2
	Women	187	1.1	0.4	0.3	0.2	0.12	0.8	1.1	116.2
Trade employees	Total	83	2.4	1.5	1.0	0.7	0.14	0.5	0.7	144.1
	Men	48	4.2	2.5	1.8	1.2	0.25	0.5	0.7	167.5
	Women	35	..	..	..	..	..	..	..	112.1

c. Medical profession

Doctors	Total	102	5.9	8.6	4.8	4.3	0.49	4.6	5.4	169.4
	Men	37	10.8	21.6	11.6	10.7	1.03	5.8	7.1	196.9
	Women	65	3.1	1.2	0.9	0.7	0.18	2.3	2.0	153.8

(cont.)

Table 2.4. (cont.)

		Number of workers	W3D (%)	W3 (R)	$\frac{W3^b}{W1}$ (%)	$\frac{W3^b}{W2}$ (%)	H3 (hours per week)	WPH3[c] (R per hour)	$\frac{WPH3^{b,c}}{WPH1}$ (ratio)	W1 (R)
Dentists	Total	23	39.1	96.5	88.1	88.1	4.96	5.7	8.6	111.7
	Men	13	53.9	147.7	127.3	127.3	7.77	5.6	7.6	123.5
	Women	10	20.0	30.0	37.2	37.2	1.30	6.3	11.8	96.2
Nurses	Total	65	13.9	6.5	7.3	7.3	0.86	2.1	4.0	87.6
	Men	4	25.0	17.5	13.5	13.5	0.75	5.4	7.4	86.2
	Women	61	13.1	5.8	6.9	6.9	0.87	1.7	3.6	109.5
Others	Total	38	5.3	8.7	6.3	5.6	0.53	3.8	4.9	98.2
	Men	7	14.3	11.4	11.8	8.1	1.43	1.9	3.4	100.4
	Women	31	3.2	8.1	5.0	5.0	0.32	5.8	6.4	97.7

[a] For the sake of brevity, some of the occupations sound like branches; they nevertheless mean occupations. Thus, 'manufacturing' means 'industrial workers' in any branch, etc.

[b] See note a in Table 2.3.

[c] Calculation based on returns of only those who are privately employed. For the number of observations see Table 2.5. See also notes in Table 2.3.

technicians, and administrators) have very low private work participation rates and earnings. The rather high proportion of workers in these groups employed in manufacturing is a major factor driving down the private work rate in this branch. Similar situations exist in other high private work branches, where isolating public administrators (as well as engineers and technicians) helped to focus attention on the higher participation rates of the professional groups that provide the specialized services of these branches.

To complete the picture on private work, Table 2.5 presents data *only* on the group of privately employed persons by (aggregated) occupation. Earnings per month are higher for private work in medical services, communal services, for production workers of type (a) (where private work is high) and in education, than for private workers who are engineers, technicians, administrators, or production workers of type (b), i.e., in low private work branches.[12] In most cases, differences in monthly earnings results from corresponding differences in hours worked and in rates of hourly pay. Workers in all high private work occupations average more than 10 hours weekly in private work (less in education), and all those in low private work occupations, except for the 5 people in administration and trade, spend less than 10 hours a week in private work. Similarly, earnings per hour are highest for medical workers (R5.3) and communal service workers (R3.8), and lower (with administrators and trade workers again an exception) for engineers and technicians, educational workers, and the two kinds of production workers (R2.8–3.1).

A more complete explanation of the propensity to engage in private work must consider, in addition to occupation and sex, such factors as wages, incomes, family size, wage ratios between the public and private sectors, and alternative extra work in the public sector. Such analysis is performed using the following equations:

$$EW_i = a + bRW + cRH + dYR_i + eFS + fED + gMOS \quad (1)$$
$$+ \Sigma_i h_i OCCP_i + kSEX + U_j$$

$$\ln WPH3 = \alpha_1 + \beta_2 \ln WPH1 + \tau_1 ED + \Sigma_j \delta_{1j} OCCP_j + U_k \quad (2a)$$

$$\ln WPH3/WPH1 = \alpha_2 + ... + \tau_2 ED + \Sigma_j \delta_{2j} OCCP_j + U_k \quad (2b)$$

Table 2.5. Hours and wages of persons engaged in private work, by occupation and sex

	No. of workers	W3 (R)	H3 (hours)	W3/W1 (%)[a]	W3/W2 (%)[a]	H3/H1 (%)[a]	WPH3 (R per hour)[b]	WPH3/WPH1[a,b]	W1 (R)	H1 (hours)	WPH1 (R per hour)
Engineers and technicians											
Total	29	75.3	7.3	49.8	48.3	17.8	2.6	2.7	180.0	41.6	1.0
Men	23	79.1	7.0	52.4	50.5	17.1	2.8	2.8	186.1	47.7	1.0
Women	6	60.8	8.3	39.9	39.9	20.3	1.9	2.3	156.7	41.0	0.9
Medical workers											
Total	26	148.3	9.2	124.1	121.4	23.8	4.1	6.0	127.6	41.1	0.7
Men	13	220.8	11.7	170.9	166.2	29.7	5.3	7.1	150.2	41.7	0.8
Women	13	75.8	6.8	77.3	76.6	17.8	2.8	4.8	105.1	40.5	0.6
Education and culture											
Total	35	71.1	8.0	62.1	56.0	65.3	2.6	2.6	135.2	29.9	1.3
Men	17	88.2	7.9	70.0	58.1	72.0	3.1	3.1	156.8	33.5	1.4
Women	18	54.8	8.1	54.6	53.9	59.1	2.2	2.0	114.8	26.5	1.3
Planning and trade[c]											
Total	4	48.0	14.3	35.8	31.5	34.6	0.7	1.0	128.5	41.3	0.7
Men	2	60.0	17.5	42.4	41.5	42.7	0.7	0.9	134.5	41.0	0.8
Women	2	36.0	11.0	29.2	21.4	26.4	0.8	1.1	122.5	41.5	0.7

Communal services[c]										
Total	16	124.1	12.0	87.9	87.2	29.5	3.0	3.8	142.1	40.4	0.8
Men	11	152.7	11.6	89.0	89.0	28.5	3.8	4.0	161.8	40.1	0.9
Women	5	61.0	13.0	85.4	83.3	31.7	1.3	3.2	98.6	41.0	0.6
Production workers (a)[d]										
Total	36	157.1	14.6	101.2	99.4	35.3	3.4	4.0	166.7	41.5	0.9
Men	33	157.6	15.0	100.4	98.5	36.1	3.2	3.7	171.7	41.5	1.0
Women	3	151.7	10.7	110.1	110.5	26.0	5.4	6.6	111.3	41.0	0.6
Production workers (b)[d]										
Total (men only)	13	84.4	7.4	62.5	57.8	17.8	3.1	4.0	149.0	42.2	0.8

[a] See Table 2.3, note a.

[b] Figures based on returns of 159 private workers and employees (see Table 2.2, note).

[c] Workers and employees.

[d] (a) Employed in wood, textiles, clothing, construction and construction materials, and transportation.
   (b) Employed in other branches of manufacturing.

where:

EW$_i$ Dummy variables for extra work, with value 1 when the worker is engaged in some form of extra work, and subscript 1 stands for private work, 2 for extra public jobs, and 3 for overtime work in the main place of work.

RW   Regular wages: net monthly earnings at the main place of work *without* overtime.

RH   Regular hours: number of weekly hours worked at the main place of work *without* overtime.

YR$_i$ Monthly family disposable income *less* RW and earnings from the respective type of extra work (see EW$_i$).

FS   Family size.

ED   Level of education, measured in years of schooling.

SEX   A dummy variable for being male.

WPH1, WPH3, WPH3/WPH1 — as above (p. 50).

OCCP$_i$ Detailed occupations (as in Table 2.4).

OCCP$_j$ Aggregated occupational groups (as in Table 2.5).

MOS   A dummy variable for Moscow.

The estimates include only workers with full-time jobs in the public sector, so that the analysis concentrates on extra work as a supplemental (not competitive) source of income. Since, however, regular working hours vary, those working fewer hours have more time to engage in extra work; in this respect main work and extra work may be gross substitutes — across jobs. We therefore expect a negative RH coefficient with respect to EW$_i$.

For a given number of hours worked (RH), regular earnings (RW) become a measure of wages per hour; the lower it is, the higher should the tendency be to engage in alternative work that may pay more. The coefficients of both RH and RW may also reflect the negative effect of higher income on extra work. The income effect, which is expected to be negatively related to extra work, is estimated by YR$_i$ and family size (FS) which, together, reflect the levels of YR$_i$ per family member.[13] We do not have an *a priori* prediction for the effect or the level of education on extra work, and the expectations on the effect of OCCP$_i$ and SEX are in line with the corresponding gross effects found in Tables 2.2–2.4 above.

Finally, the propensity to engage in private work (EW_i) also depends on the availability and pay rates of the other alternatives for extra work — in the main place of work (EW_3) and elsewhere within the public sector (EW_2). The earnings derived from such alternatives are included, in each case, in YR_i. The competition between these alternatives with respect to other variables (especially occupation) is observed at this point by comparing corresponding coefficients across equation (1).

Equations of type (1) are estimated only for full-time workers. Separate estimates for men and women and for slightly different specifications were also made, and will be referred to when relevant. Since the dependent variables are dichotomous, a discriminant function was estimated, rather than ordinary least squares.

Since there are no data on private wages for most workers — those who do not engage in private work (equations of type [1]) — we cannot estimate the effect of higher private wages on the decision to engage in private work. Equations (2), estimated only for those who do work privately, provide a second-best approach to this problem. In equation (2a) the hourly private wage rate is "explained" by its public counterpart as well as by the level of education and occupation. In equation (2b) the relative private-to-public wage rate is explained by the same variables. Since there are only 160 observations, occupations were aggregated into seven groups with engineers and technicians serving as the reference group.

A full presentation of the estimates appears in the appendix to this chapter. The coefficients of the variables other than $OCCP_i$ in equation (1) are presented in Table 2.6. The main findings, resulting also from equations (2) appear in Table 2.7 and are merged with the following factors to shape the scope and patterns of private work:

1. We again observe the wide difference between men and women in all forms of extra-work activity, including private work. Results of corresponding equations with no $OCCP_i$ variables, or for men only (not shown), reveal that the low participation of women in extra work is only marginally explained by their specific occupational structure.

2. Jobs with fewer regular hours encourage higher private work as well as other forms of extra work. Because there is a strong correlation between

Table 2.6. Engagement in extra work: regression results[a]

	Private work (EW$_1$)	Public jobs (EW$_2$)	Overtime (EW$_3$)	Extra work (EW)
Constant	−1.3785	−4.8753	−3.3269	−2.2372
	−1.4288	−5.6026	−2.8206	−3.3206
Sex	1.3287	1.5952	1.3742	1.6654
	5.6910	7.0167	4.0939	9.7897
Regular wage (RW)	−0.0048	−0.0016	−0.0017	−0.0021
	−3.0241	−1.4068	−0.9872	−2.2503
Regular hours (RH)	−0.0581	−0.0102	−0.0621	−0.0416
	−3.3404	−0.6596	−3.4387	−3.4080
YR$_i$	0.0007	0.0001	−0.0008	0.0038
	1.1933	0.1848	0.9708	9.1669
Education (yrs) (ED)	0.0465	0.0803	−0.0250	0.0380
	1.3059	2.3649	−0.5052	1.4756
Family size (FS)	−0.0160	0.2299	0.4317	−0.0515
	−0.1595	2.5541	3.3698	−0.7431
Moscow	0.6975	0.1898	0.0912	0.1359
	2.4556	0.7206	0.2084	0.6331
$\bar{R}^2$	0.1107	0.1233	−1.2982	0.1892

Small numerals are *t* values.

[a] All the equations include variables for occupations. Full results are presented in the appendix to this chapter.

the occupational structure and the number of regular hours, the RH coefficients are higher (in absolute value) and more significant when $OCCP_i$ variables are excluded from the equations.

3. While all forms of extra-work activity are negatively correlated with public wage rates (RW), only the coefficients for private work and for all extra work are significant. This indicates that people do not turn to overtime work in the same place of work — for the same low wage.

4. Of all kinds of additional work, only private work fails to respond to the income effect; although YR_i is not significant throughout, family size (FS) has significant positive coefficients for extra public jobs and for overtime. This may be an indication that private work is more constrained by non-economic factors. A negative income effect on private work may, however, be merged with the effects on hours and wages.[14]

5. The occupational patterns of private work are very similar in some respects to those shown in Table 2.4 but different in other respects from the occupational patterns of official overtime work. In two or three cases the alternatives compete successfully with private work: medical doctors and educational workers do a lot of extra work in public jobs, within and outside their main place of work, but engage relatively little in private work. The third group where such competition exists (and the only one among blue-collar workers) is transportation workers, where overtime is somewhat more pronounced than private work. On the other hand, private work dominates the field in those blue-collar occupations where private work (or any type of extra work) takes place.

The competition is more balanced — with high levels of extra work of all or most kinds — for dentists, nurses, and transportation workers. Finally, a very low level of all kinds of extra work (private or public) is found among technicians, administrators, trade workers, and employees, as well as among blue-collar workers in the food and heavy industries. Engineers also belong to this last group.

6. Higher relative private-to-public earnings per hour clearly encourage private work. This conclusion is drawn from comparing the coefficients of the various occupations in equation (1) for private work (see appendix to this chapter, column 1) with corresponding coefficients in equations (2) (Table

2.7). According to the equation results, higher relative private wages are found for the medical profession, for workers in communal services (equation 2b) and industries, production workers of both types (a) and (b) (equation 2c). All these occupations (except for production type b) also show high levels of participation in private work. Low levels of relative private wages are found among workers in trade and administration — lower even than the low level of engineers and technicians, the standard of comparison. Again, low private earnings correspond to little private participation and work. Relative private hourly earnings are also low for workers in education, and this may be one reason for the rather moderate level of private participation (the coefficient in equation 1 is not significant) in this branch.

7.   The relative level of hourly earnings is only one of the factors determining participation in private work. In essence, it is a signal, an outcome of the market forces of supply and demand. High rates of private pay reflect shortages of specific goods and services that lure private participation. Indeed, most of the available anecdotal evidence points to a strong correlation between private activity and shortages in the Soviet Union.[15]

8.   In addition to this overriding factor, there seem to be few other supporting explanations for the specific occupational patterns of private work.

Private work in services (including repair services and transportation) is less conspicuous than the production of goods and can be more easily concealed from the public eye. The conduct of many of these services (again, unlike production) is, at least in principle, legal, and thus involves less risk. But a high incidence of private work is also found in areas where workers have access (in their main jobs) to scarce materials and possibly also to equipment that are essential to the performance of the private task. This is clearly the case in the fields of construction, communal services (which include apartment maintenance), type (a) production, and dentistry. In most cases it is impossible to distinguish between the demand for the service and that for the source materials need to provide it, but from what we know of the scarcity of construction materials, household fixtures, wood (for furniture), and the like, it is quite clear that the workers' access in the relevant industries to sources of supply of such materials must be very important in determining the demand for their services.

Table 2.7. Absolute and relative private wage rates: regression results

Independent variables	Dependent variables		
	*ln*WPH3	$\frac{ln\text{WPH3}}{\text{WPH1}}$	$\frac{\text{WPH3}}{\text{WPH1}}$
Constant	2.6148	4.6111	1.4840
	3.8122	12.3107	1.2993
*ln*WPH1	0.4045		
	3.0748		
ED	0.0577	0.0512	0.0779
	0.6927	2.2941	1.1393
$OCCP_j$			
Medical workers	0.5835	0.8418	1.7813
	3.0209	4.3466	3.0414
Education and culture	−0.1474	−0.1311	−0.5684
	−0.8516	−0.7249	−1.0858
Planning and trade	−0.8258	−0.6687	−1.4588
	−2.2225	−1.7591	−1.2955
Communal services	0.2248	0.4364	1.0815
	0.8650	1.6453	1.3466
Production workers (a)[a]	0.5017	0.5119	0.9799
	2.1610	2.1184	1.3305
Production workers (b)[a]	0.5050	0.5797	1.6633
	1.9994	2.2121	2.1347
$\bar{R}^2$	0.1724	0.1824	0.1044

Small numerals are *t* values.

[a] Production (a) includes workers in wood, textiles, clothing, leather and footwear, construction and construction materials, and transportation. Production (b) includes all other workers in manufacturing.

Finally, just as the opportunities for extra jobs in the public sector compete with private work, there are opportunities to earn extra money not only in the course of performing the main job, but at the job site as well. Two groups of workers are likely to enjoy such opportunities: those working in trade (retail, wholesale, public catering), and those holding administrative positions. So far, we have only observed that workers in these branches engage least in private work; we shall have to resort to other sources of private income (other than wages) to reveal the other side of the picture.

2. Other private sources of income

Three other private sources of income are reported in the survey: income from leasing apartments or rooms, income derived from private agricultural plots, and "other" income.

Only 14 families reported income from rent, averaging R51.4 per month, with an average contribution to average family income for the entire sample amounting to only R0.7. Sixty families in our sample had private agricultural plots from which they derived between R3 and R158 per month (the average is R39.2). Averaged over 1,016 families this source adds R2.3 per family per month.[16] About 87 percent of this income is earned by families residing in small cities (of less than half a million inhabitants). Private plot activity is more than proportionally concentrated among families whose heads are blue-collar workers, employed in agriculture, and older people. It should be emphasized that our survey covers urban residents only, and thus only a small portion of the private-plot sector is represented here.

"Other" income was reported in response to the following question: "Did your family receive any other income, no matter from whom or from where?" Since by this stage all possible sources of income had been exhausted by previous questions, "other" income (OI) must be understood to refer to sources of private income of questionable legality. Such incomes most likely include the following. (a) "Tips" received at the main place of work for providing services to clients, either part of one's regular duty or indicating some sort of preferential treatment. We know from the Soviet press and other sources that such "tips" are paid to acquire or expedite the handling of various documents from public officials; to obtain ordinary (or extraordinary) treatment from nurses in hospitals; to get ahead in queuing for scarce goods, and so forth. (b) Payments for preferential treatment in the supply of goods and services, mainly in the retail and services industries. Such payments clearly contain a "tip" element, entailing higher than official prices for goods of higher quality or that are in short supply. (c) "Other" income may include private work either because in some cases the distinction between a "tip" and the provision of a new service is blurred (i.e., a plumber may install a new faucet during regular working hours for an extra fee), or because some of the respondents simply preferred to report on private work under this heading. (d) "Other" income could simply be the value of goods taken from the public sector either for one's own use or for resale. Judging by available evidence, this must be a major source of "other" income. (e) OI could include the proceeds from the sale of used items and interest on savings accounts and government bonds, sources about which we did not ask specifically.

All told, 102 families reported having some source of OI, the amounts ranging from as little as R3 to as much as R400 per family per month. The average intake for a family with OI is R78.9 per month, a significant sum by any count. For all 1,016 families, OI adds almost R8 per family per month, or about 2 percent of total family income.[17]

Being in a position to obtain "tips" or have access to goods belonging to the public sector is closely connected with branch of employment and occupation. The breakdown of OI by economic branch is presented in Table 2.8, and supplementary findings for occupation are given in the text below. Since we have no information on which member of the family provided this income, the data are presented in cells of branch of employment of both husband and wife. The table presents data on three variables: the proportion of families with OI for a given branch; the average monthly level of OI per family in the group; and the average monthly level of OI per family with OI in each group. Since there are only 102 families with OI, the results presented here necessarily depend on a small number of observations for each branch or occupation.

In general, the findings support the expectation that OI is concentrated in branches such as trade, public administration, transport, construction, and other services where such incomes are most likely to be created, and that it

Table 2.8. Reported "other" income by economic branch of family heads
and their wives

	Family heads				Wives			
	No. of fami-lies	% with OI	OI per family (R)	OI per family with OI (R)	No. of fami-lies	% with OI	OI per family (R)	OI per family with OI (R)
All families	1,011[a]	10.1	8.0	78.9	891	10.2	7.5	73.5
Manufacturing	351	8.8	5.1	57.2	224	8.9	5.0	55.6
Agriculture	24	12.5	11.6	92.7	13	15.4	6.5	42.0
Transport	64	15.6	8.7	55.7	12	25.0	15.8	63.3
Communications	5	0.0	0.0	0.0	12	16.7	3.4	20.5
Construction	108	10.2	12.9	126.9	33	6.1	2.4	40.0
Trade and public catering	88	9.1	14.2	156.4	88	4.6	5.4	117.8
Communal services	119	11.8	7.4	62.9	77	18.2	10.4	57.3
Health	69	11.6	8.1	69.6	169	9.5	10.5	110.8
Education and art	91	11.0	10.1	91.9	174	11.5	8.5	73.5
Science	78	6.4	2.9	45.6	52	5.8	3.9	67.7
Banking and insurance	..	..	..	..	12	8.3	6.9	83.0
Public administration	14	14.3	14.5	101.5	25	16.0	15.2	95.3
Wife not working[b]	..	..	..	..	120	9.2	11.3	123.1

[a] Excluding five non-working family heads.

[b] Not included in the average for 891 families.

is greatest where on-the-job opportunities reduce the incentive to seek private work.

Public administration stands out as the branch with almost the highest incidence of OI as well as the highest level of average OI per family: 14–16 percent of all families in public administration had OI (compared with about 10 percent on average), the average increment created for *all* families in this branch being about R15 per month, almost double the OJ average for the entire population. Finally, the level of OI per family with such income in public administration is also among the highest: R101.5 for families whose heads are in this branch, R95.3 when the wives are in this branch. Unfortunately, these results are based on too few cases (2 out of 14 for men; 4 out of 25 for women) to make them conclusive.

The proportion of families in which one of the main earners is employed in trade and had OI is not exceptionally high; in fact, it is below the average for both heads and wives and, in this respect, the results differ from expectations. On the other hand, the OI of such families is the highest of all. In fact, it is so high that despite the relatively low proportion of such families average OI per family of the entire trade group is the second highest among all branches when families are sorted by the branch to which the family head belongs (the top five families with OI in the entire sample have one worker in trade). A similar picture about trade emerges when families are sorted by occupation.

High incidence and levels of OI are also found in agriculture, transport (with lower average income level) and construction. Above average incidence of OI is found among families in which wives are employed in trade, health, or educational services. The occupational breakdown (not presented here) shows high OI levels among families in which wives are doctors, nurses, or work in communal services.

An interesting observation is that families in which wives do not work at all earn more OI: R11.3 as compared with R7.5 for all families and R123.1 as against R73.5 per family with OI. This may be due to an income effect — lacking the wife's income, the family is forced to reach for alternative sources or, vice versa, the existence of additional sources allows wives not to work. But it may also result from the wife helping her husband, in one way or another, to derive this extra income and thus being unable to "afford" an official job.

Finally, we do find some differences in levels and incidence of OI when families are sorted by city size (higher levels in small towns) and by republic (more OI in the RSFSR and in Moldavia). There are also differences according to the level of family income, to which we shall return later.

3. Unreported private income

How accurate are the reports about other income and private work? Despite the precautions taken in formulating the questions and the fact that the interviews were conducted outside the Soviet Union, we believe that such incomes are likely to be underreported. *Overreporting* is also possible — there may be a tendency by some to boast about how they beat the system — but the degree of illegality, or even immorality associated with private earnings certainly overrides such tendencies.

Support for underreporting is provided by the comparison of two other sources of data on income obtained from the questionnaire. One is total expenditures (EX), which, by definition, should equal total income; the other is a declaration made by the family head on total income (Y') before answering detailed questions on each and every income component. Family expenditures are greater than income by R14.3 per month on the average. This difference (YD1) is the net result of all possible errors in reporting both income and expenditures, and as such cannot be attributed exclusively to unreported private income; but some of it may, as we shall see below. One should expect Y' to be lower than Y (aggregated income). Giving a one-shot estimate, people tend to neglect certain sources of income mentioned only at a later stage, and indeed, $Y - Y' = YD2$ averages R30.1. When Y' was found to exceed Y there is reason to suspect that some income elements were not reported and not included in Y.

That YD1 and YD2 contain unreported income is first observed by finding higher levels of YD1 and lower (or even negative) levels of YD2 for families that did not report having private income as compared with families that did report having such income. Thus, for families with private income (from any source), YD1 averages *minus* R5.0 as against R20.3 for families that reported no private income (the average figure is R4.3). The corresponding figures for YD2 are R54.4 for families with private income and only R27.4 for families without such income (YD2 averages R30.1). Similar results are obtained for individual elements of private income and all differences are statistically significant.

Were it not for the fact that YD1 is positive, it could be claimed that differences between families with and without private income result from overstating income by the former rather than non-reporting by the latter. That is not generally the case, as demonstrated by following the patterns of YD1 and YD2 for families classified by branch or occupation. The hypothesis is that if the distributions of YD1 and YD2 are uneven among branches, especially if YD1 tends to be higher and YD2 lower in branches and occupations where we expected private incomes to be created, then much of YD1 and YD2 represents unreported income. We cannot think of another explanation for errors in the reporting of expenditures, income, or the difference between them to establish a systematic relation with economic branch or occupation.

On the basis of YD1 and YD2 we define a new family income variable (YFR): in all cases where Y' is greater than Y and conforms better than Y to total expenditures, we substituted Y' for Y. There are 149 such cases. In addition, EX replaced Y in 29 cases on the basis of the investigation of the saving variable.[18] YFR stands at R398.06, only R1.76 less than EX. Based on YCR we define YD3 = YFR − Y and show its average level by branch alongside those for YD1 and YD2 in Table 2.9.[19]

All income differentials vary substantially among branches (many of the differences are statistically significant) and support the hypothesis that branch of employment affects their size. Specifically, when classified by branch of the family head, we find high income differences (and low YD2) in trade, public administration, and health services (YD2 excepted for the latter).[20] YD1 is also exceptionally high for science. High levels of supposedly unreported incomes are found according to branch of employment in public administration and health services, but to a somewhat lesser degree in trade and in education (YD3 excepted). Naturally, since men presumably bring home most of the private money, the distinctions by branch of wife are less sharp.

Table 2.9. Unreported income by economic branch (R per month per family)

	Family heads			Wives		
	YD1 (1)	YD2 (2)	YD3 (3)	YD1 (4)	YD2 (5)	YD3 (6)
All working	14.3	30.2	12.6	13.2	31.7	11.4
Manufacturing	15.5	32.8	7.9	6.4	39.4	6.9
Agriculture	−7.9	39.3	7.8	−6.2	34.2	6.9
Transport	2.9	27.3	5.4	37.8	40.2	7.8
Communications	55.6	36.8	1.0	2.3	47.8	4.7
Construction	17.4	32.4	5.5	6.1	39.2	5.8
Trade	27.9	10.7	33.1	2.2	13.7	15.9
Communal services	−2.3	21.5	15.9	9.4	17.9	11.1
Health	25.5	41.5	24.3	22.4	26.9	20.7
Education and art	−3.9	42.9	10.0	23.9	33.9	10.6
Science	38.6	26.2	13.6	3.0	47.3	4.8
Banks and insurance	..	..	..	5.2	33.3	0.4
Public administration	20.5	21.9	25.2	62.2	27.8	11.9
Wife not working	..	..	..	22.7	19.1	21.6

As for "other" income, here, too, families with non-working wives are found to "underestimate" their own incomes to a much higher degree than families with working wives: TD1 for the first group is R22.7 as compared with only R13.2 for the second; the corresponding figures for YD2 are 19.1 and 31.7, and for YD3: 21.6 and 11.4, respectively.

One may wonder to what extent the respondents, intentionally or otherwise adopted this method to report on such private incomes whose source they preferred to conceal when the specific question came up. A summary of all sources of private income and their relative importance in total income, by families classified according to branch or occupation of family head is presented in Tables 2.10 and 2.11. Some concluding observations on these data appear below.

Table 2.10. Family public and private earnings by industry of family head

	No. of families	Rubles per month				OI	YD3	%		Index	
		Y2 +YP (1)	Y2 (2)	YP (3)	Y3 (4)	(5)	(6)	$\frac{Y3^a}{Y2}$ (7)	$\frac{YP^a}{Y2}$ (8)	Y2 (9)	Y2 +YP (10)
All families	1,011	377.5	335.3	42.2	18.6	8.0	12.6	7.5	16.9	100.0	100.0
Manufacturing	351	365.4	341.8	23.6	7.5	5.1	7.9	3.8	8.5	101.9	97.8
Agriculture	24	333.6	287.8	45.8	13.6	11.6	7.8	4.5	22.9	85.8	88.4
Transportation	64	355.2	314.4	40.8	21.0	8.7	5.4	6.7	14.7	93.8	94.1
Communications	5	310.8	309.8	1.0	0.0	0.0	1.0	0.0	0.4	92.4	82.3
Construction	108	381.9	346.3	35.6	15.9	12.9	5.5	5.3	13.4	103.3	101.2
Trade	88	368.7	310.9	57.8	4.3	14.2	33.1	1.5	26.3	92.7	97.7
Communal services	119	365.6	297.5	68.1	43.1	7.4	15.9	18.5	30.5	88.7	96.8
Health	69	429.1	348.0	81.1	48.1	8.1	24.3	21.3	32.6	103.8	113.7
Education and art	91	423.2	371.6	51.6	29.7	10.1	10.0	9.8	20.4	110.8	112.1
Science	78	395.5	360.3	35.2	16.7	2.9	13.6	6.0	10.9	107.5	104.8
Public administration	14	351.8	308.0	43.8	0.0	14.5	25.2	0.0	19.3	91.9	93.2

[a] Calculated as averages of individual responses, not as the quotient of column (4) (or column 3) entries *divided by* column (2) entries.

Table 2.11. Family public and private earnings by occupation of family head

	No. of fami- lies	Y2	YP	Y3	OI	YD3	$\dfrac{Y3^a}{Y2}$	$\dfrac{YP^a}{Y2}$
		(1)	(2)	(3)	(4)	(5)	(6)	(7)
All families	1,011	335.3	42.2	18.7	8.0	12.6	7.5	16.9
Engineers	283	365.1	29.0	7.5	5.7	12.5	2.8	8.7
Technicians	72	319.9	24.5	9.0	12.7	2.1	3.0	10.9
Medical workers	57	350.4	87.1	57.4	6.1	23.6	24.9	35.8
Education, culture, and science	140	381.4	39.1	18.9	8.6	9.7	6.7	15.3
Management and adminis- tration	45	339.3	20.6	3.2	1.0	11.7	0.7	6.5
Trade workers and employees	76	311.2	58.0	3.6	21.5	30.0	0.8	24.8
Communal workers and employees	44	302.7	88.8	56.8	6.6	23.8	14.5	26.4
Production workers:								
(a)[b]	127	295.5	65.0	44.1	4.5	12.1	20.0	14.3
(b)[b]	167	296.2	28.6	10.0	8.5	5.4	5.9	31.0

[a] Calculated as averages of individual responses, not as the quotient of column (3) (or 2) entries *divided by* column (1) entries.

[b] See Table 2.5, note d.

1. Private earnings of all types, YP, including YD3, are estimated at R42.2 per family, an increment of 16.9 percent above all earnings from the public sector. This is no doubt a significant figure. It remains so even if only part of YD3 is included in YP.

2. Although private earnings of all kinds exist in all branches of the economy and in most occupations, they are concentrated in certain areas. The observed patterns of distribution of YP and its elements correspond quite closely to deductions made on the basis of the analysis of the economic situation and of qualitative and anecdotal evidence about the realities of life in the Soviet Union.

3. The uneven distribution of YP among the various branches of the economy changes the relative incomes of families by branch of the family head. As can be observed by comparing columns (9) and (10) in Table 2.10, YP raises the relative incomes of families whose heads are employed in health further away from the average; it raises relative incomes of families in trade and communal services, in this case toward the average from below; and it somewhat reduces relative incomes for families in manufacturing.

b. Private income of the Soviet urban population and in Soviet national aggregates

As stated in the Introduction, two distinct sets of steps must be taken to extract data from the sample population (SP) estimates on the scope and patterns of private incomes and earnings for the entire Soviet population. The first set of steps involves reweighting the raw data by structural variables of the target (Soviet) population. The most that such reweighting can hope to accomplish is to produce estimates for the investigated variables for the Soviet urban population (UP) of the non-Asiatic republics, and even this — only if it is assumed that no pure "Jewish" or "emigrant" biases exist. The second set of steps is intended to move the estimates to the level of Soviet national economic aggregates. By the nature of the problem, it is clear than this second set of steps involves rather heroic assumptions based on much less concrete information.

The choice of the structural variables for the first set of adjustments is made on the basis of two criteria and one constraint. The variables should be the most important in determining the levels and patterns of the investigated phenomenon, and those in which the SP–UP differences are wide. The constraint is, of course, the availability of information about the variables to be reweighted. The structural variables that qualify, in our case, are the occupational (or branch) structure by sex or family status. The grouping by occupation and sex explained most of the variation of private work and that by branch of family head most of the variations of other sources of income. Although we can further reduce the unexplained variation of some of the private work variables by adding some more variable, an excessively fine breakdown of the raw data for reweighting purposes results in too small cells reducing the quality of the estimates.[21] The results of a selected number of reweighting schemes are reported in Table 2.12; results for private earnings for individual workers are shown in Part A, and those for all kinds of private earnings per family, classified by family head, in Part B.[22]

In Part A we find, first, that when fully reweighted the proportion of the urban population (UP) engaged in private work is estimated at between 6.2 (column 3) and 8.8 percent (column 5) of all workers, compared with 8.1 percent in SP. The corresponding figures for monthly earnings from private work per worker are between R6.3 and R10.3 for all workers and R8.9 for those in SP; the implied private earnings for those engaged in private work average R101.6, R117.0, and R109.9, respectively. All reweighted figures are not very far from those for SP. Nonetheless, the differences do warrant some explanation.

The sample population is made up of 52.5 percent men and 47.5 percent women, as compared with 52.1 percent women in UP. Since women participate much less in private work, the true UP proportions alone "explain" a decline of about half a ruble in W3. Furthermore, the deficit of women in SP is concentrated relatively more in the branches and occupations in which the overall private work levels are high. A "correction" for this asymmetric deficit further dampens the W3D and W3 estimates for UP. This can be seen by comparing the figures for the above variable in columns 2 and 4 with those in columns 3 and 5. The pure branch effect of reweighting further reduces the figures of private work while the pure occupation effect increases it quite substantially. This results from the fact that, although the industrial

Table 2.12. Private earnings of the urban population (UP) and sample population (SP)

	SP	UP weighted by			
		Branch	Branch and sex	Occupa-tion	Occupa-tion and sex
	(1)	(2)	(3)	(4)	(5)
A. Employed persons					
1. Percent working privately (W3D)	8.1	6.7	6.2	10.5	8.8
2. Monthly private earnings (W3)	8.9	7.3	6.3	13.0	10.3
3. W3/W1 (percent)	6.5	5.0	4.4	8.5	7.0
4. Monthly public wages (W1) (rubles)	152.1	157.3	150.7	150.1	143.9
5. W3/W1 [(2)/1,368]			4.6		7.5
6. W3/W1 [(2)/124.1]			5.1		8.3
B. Families					
7. Private income (YP) (rubles)	42.2	35.4		41.1	
8. Private wages (Y3) (R)	18.7	14.8		22.1	
9. Other income (OI) (R)	8.0	7.9		7.8	
10. Unreported income (YD3) (rubles)	12.6	9.6		7.6	
11. YP/Y1 (%)	17.5	14.0		17.0	
12. Y3/Y1 (%)	7.9	6.1		9.0	
13. OI/Y1 (%)	3.6	3.5		3.6	
14. YD3/Y1 (%)	4.9	3.6		2.9	
15. Earnings from main job (Y1) (rubles)	321.9	322.9		304.0	
16. Earnings from public sector (Y2) (rubles)	335.3	336.1		315.2	

distribution of SP is more concentrated than UP in high private work industries, its occupational structure is further removed than that of UP from high private work occupations. In both cases this results from average or overall tendencies, not necessarily true for each branch or occupation separately.

The figures obtained from the classification by branch result from a high concentration of the SP employed in education, health, communal and related services, and a low concentration in construction and transportation. The relatively high concentration in SP of engineers and technicians (with low private work levels) and the low representation among transportation and construction workers by occupation are enough to more than offset the high concentration in health and some other high private work services and to produce higher levels of W3D and W3 for UP. Judging by the level of statistical significance of the two alternative classifications, the occupational classification turns out to be more dependable.[23]

In calculating the weighted relative increments of private wages (W3) to official wages we used three alternative estimates of public wages: SP wage from main job (W1) reweighted according to the same branch or occupation weights as W3 (line 3); SP wage from main job (W1) reweighted through an alternative weighting scheme which we found more appropriate to W1 (line 5);[24] and finally, as W1 we used the official Soviet (net) wage of R124.1 in 1973 (line 6).[25]

The resulting estimates for W3/W1 range from 4.4 to 5.1 percent based on branch, and 7.0 to 8.3 percent based on occupation.[26] The main difference is still caused by the weighting system, and of all estimates we tend to support the range between 7 and 8 percent. It should be remembered that W3 was found to be negatively related to W1. Since public wages of SP, even when reweighted, remain higher than the corresponding official figures, W3 for the lower official wage may be higher than R9.94 and correspondingly W3/W1 may be above 8 percent. As we have seen, all these figures are very likely underestimates, since they do not include any additional private wages that may be included among other sources of income, either OI or unreported sources.

In Part B of Table 2.12 a similar analysis is carried out for private sources of income of families: total family income from all such sources (YP) is made up of private earnings of all family members (Y3 = ΣW3), OI, YD3, and income derived from subsidiary plots and rentals. The weights are according to the activity of family heads.

Income from private work per urban family is estimated at between R14.8 and 22.1, compared with R18.7 for SP. The estimates for OI are almost identical by all weights (close to R8), and those for "unreported" income (YD3) range between R9.6 (by branch) and R7.6 by occupation (R12.6 for SP). Total private income adds up to R42.2 for SP and almost the same for UP (R41.1 when weighted by occupation), but somewhat less (R35.4) when weighted by branch. Since the main difference stems from the figure for Y3, we are inclined to accept a figure of around R40 per family.

Private earnings add 14–17 percent to earnings from the main job (line 11) and up to a percentage point less if all public earnings (Y2) are considered. More than half of this increment comes from private work (occupational weights), a fifth from other income, a sixth from unreported income, and a tenth from agricultural plots and rents.

The reweighted estimates for Y1 (and Y2) for UP are still about R50 higher than our independent estimate based on official Soviet data.[27] This remaining difference is explained by the presence of more workers per family in SP, by a small difference in the sex composition, by differences in the educational levels not accounted for by the occupational reweighting, and by some other factors. Since YP (and its elements) is slightly negatively related to public earnings, and YP/Y1 more strongly so, it follows that YP for families with an average income of R248 (as in UP) will not be lower than our reweighted figure of about R40. This implies a YP increment of at least 17 percent, possibly up to 20 percent, over public earnings. Even if YD3 is completely eliminated, YP/Y1 would not be less than 15 percent.

We now proceed to move these estimates to the level of national aggregates. Of the various possible ways we elected to convert the absolute figures to a per-worker basis and then multiply them by the number of workers and employees in the urban sector, or by the total number of workers and employees outside agriculture. The latter calculation rests on the assumption that non-agricultural families of rural residents behave similarly to urban families when it comes to the "second" economy.

Based on reweighting by occupation (Table 2.12), we derive the following estimates for 1973 (in billions of rubles):[28]

	Urban population	Non-agricultural population
Total private income (YP)	18.0	21.0
Private earnings (Y3	9.7	11.6
"Other" income (OI)	3.4	4.1
Unreported income (YD3)	3.3	4.0
Agricultural plot	± 1.2	± 1.5
Rent	± 0.3	± 0.4

The figures of R18.0 billion or R21.0 billion are based on urban behavior in the 7 western republics, so that if the levels of privately earned incomes are higher among rural-non-agricultural families or (as is definitely the case) in the Asian republics, then these figures are underestimates. In the following calculation we use the figure for the entire non-agricultural sector; the corresponding figures for the urban sector alone are 0.933 of the former.

How does the figure of R21.6 billion relate to existing estimates of Soviet GNP and its components? How much of it should be added to the various accounts? To GNP (or to any other aggregate) one should add only that part of private income which reflects new value added and not accounted for in existing estimates. This implies subtracting from R21.6 billion (a) private incomes included in existing estimates, and (b) those parts of these sums that are not value added.

Let us consider point (b) first. When GNP is measured in *prevailing* prices, or when its *welfare* equivalent is sought, then the entire value of sales in the private sector should be added simply because these are actual sales. However, when GNP at factor cost is considered, various elements of the private volume of sales should (or at least may) be excluded. Included even in GNP at factor cost is, first, the value of factors and inputs created solely by private activities outside the public sector. The differences between the total volume of private activity and this "genuine" new value added is made up of:

1. Costs necessary to make illegal private production possible. These include bribes and tips as well as risk premiums to cover possible prosecution. Under the existing situation these are genuine production costs and may be included as a special input or factor cost. It is doubtful, however, whether one should include in GNP both the costs of eluding the law and the costs of law enforcement designed to combat these activities.

2. Costs or value of materials, goods, and labor services (working privately on company time) pilfered from the public sector. Since their factor cost to private producers is zero, these inputs are not included in GNP in factor cost. We maintain, however, that even when GNP is measured in prevailing prices there is room to consider their exclusion. Most (if not all) of the value of stolen inputs is already included in GNP as part of the *price* paid by consumers for goods and services purchased from the public sector. This is so because stolen goods, materials, or time figure as a cost element toward the production of goods and services. Since such phenomena are fairly widespread and entrenched, it is very likely that the losses incurred are included in the calculation of normative costs of production that serve as the basis for price information. Stolen time may simply show up as lower labor productivity. When these high prices are charged for consumer goods or for intermediate products for consumer goods, the costs of theft are charged directly to the consumer and are included in the official figures on household expenditures. When theft is from enterprises producing for investment or for public-sector uses (construction, defense, etc.), the charge to the private consumer may show up through taxation (including turnover tax) or wage determination. The data presented in this report and the anecdotal evidence point to the fact that most thefts (with the important exception of construction materials) are in the consumer-goods industries and in the trade system.

3. Finally, an element of scarcity rents, over and above all costs, which constitutes a legitimate element of value added but not a "factor cost."[29]

As stated at the outset, if we follow the formal definition of "prevailing prices" and include all illegal activities against the state — all or almost all of YP should be added to GNP. If, however, we allow for the double-counting caused by theft and legal costs, or think in terms of GNP at factor cost, then part of OI and YD3, including such elements, should be excluded. If half of the income from these sources is excluded, a minimum amount to be added to GNP is about R17.5 billion for the entire nonagricultural population.

Next we have to deduct that part of private income which is already included in Western estimates of Soviet GNP. We use here only one such estimate, that of the CIA for 1970, since this is the only recent estimate that is detailed enough for our purposes (see CIA, 1975). When needed, we move the estimates to 1973 using growth rates from Greenslade (1976, p. 276). This is an estimate at established prices, i.e., official prices for public goods and services and market prices for private transactions. This GNP estimate follows the methodology developed by Bergson, Becker, Greenslade, and others, and is based on four basic accounts: household incomes, household outlays, and public-sector incomes and outlays.

Since in the 1970 estimates, as in others, total Soviet incomes fall short of household outlays, the latter is used as the household sector input to GNP. Included in household outlays are R4.4 billion (4.8 billion in 1973) of private incomes that are also included in our figure of R21.6 billion. The CIA estimate includes, for obvious reasons, a much higher estimate than ours for income from agricultural plots — so that we have to deduct our figure of R1.5 billion. In addition it includes estimates similar to ours for rents, but lower figures than ours for income derived from construction, house repairs and other repairs, personal services, and private educational and health services.[30] Even if we assume that the entire sum of R4.8 billion is new value added, we still obtain a figure of R13–17 billion to add to the Western estimate of Soviet GNP in 1973 (of about R450 billion), which adds another 3.4 percentage points to the nearly 1 percent of urban private income already included. This is definitely not an insignificant figure, considering that it represents only about two-thirds of the population and only the consumer sector.

Similar calculations with respect to total household income in the Soviet

Union show that on the basis of our calculations (for the non-agricultural sector) one should add to the CIA estimate of R230 billion — which includes about R14.4 billion (6.3 percent) of private earnings — R13–17 billion or some 6–7 percent. This brings the share of private income of the average Soviet household to about 11.5 percent.

Going one step back, the most significant figure for us is the estimated share of private income from all private sources in total incomes of the urban sector. In 1973, total net income of the urban population from all public sources, including government transfers, was around R136–140 billion.[31] The figure of R21.6 billion adds between 15 and 16 percent to this amount. This is not as high a proportion as the corresponding one for collective farm members (about 20 percent),[32] but it certainly makes a significant difference in the level of material well-being as well as in the way of life of the Soviet urban population. Such a figure would also justify the large amount of public attention devoted to private activity in newspaper articles and bulletins, in widely disseminated anecdotes, and generally in the urban folklore of Soviet society. There is no point in repeating the evidence that has already been well summarized in several books and articles by Western authors — Smith (1976), Kaiser (1976), and Grossman (1977, 1979), to mention only a few. Let us only note that the stories included in this anecdotal body of evidence tie in with the statistical and quantitative evidence provided by the sample. Not only do the kinds of activities mentioned in the stories find their statistical counterpart here, but there is also a strong correlation between the relative importance of various activities as learned from quantitative sources and other quantitative elements in our study. This correspondence can best be summarized by a curse, cited by Smith (1976, p. 117) as originating in Odessa: "Let him live on his [public] salary alone."

3. Buying in private markets and from private people

a. Introduction

As seen in the last section, some private incomes come directly, in an authorized way, from the public sector. In most other cases the rubles earned by private activity are those spent by other people on purchases from private persons.[33] For this reason, the study of these purchases can be used to corroborate the estimates of private income and to provide a clearer picture of the exact nature of goods and services supplied privately. Beyond that, however, information on such private expenditures (PEX)[34] is important in a full study of the true level and structure of expenditures of the Soviet urban household.

As in the case of earnings, official Soviet information on consumption that draws on retail trade turnover data or on production statistics does not include private purchases other than in collective farm markets and some bazaars where second-hand items are exchanged. Soviet data derived from the family budget survey may include such expenditures, but very little of this survey is published.

Unfortunately, our data on expenditures also suffer from a number of deficiencies, only part of which could be removed by future work. The most important of these is that for several important expenditure categories no questions were presented on the shares or amounts of PEX. This applies to transportation services, culture and entertainment, the purchase of non-durable household goods, and a few others.[35] In addition, there is only partial coverage of purchase through the use of "connections" with a public outlet, which we classify as PEX and which by all accounts is very significant. In these respects the PEX data are not complete and will provide an underestimate of the total.

A second problem is that for our sample, which represents only one segment of the population, there is no full correspondence between private earnings and private expenditures. The leading examples are purchases of fresh food in collective farm markets: all urban families belong almost exclusively to the client side of this market. It may well be that the urban sector is a net exporter of some other private services or goods (construction?) to rural areas, but since the sample is also non-representative of the urban population, such imbalances may also occur as a result of "trade" among various segments of the urban population. Reweighting may rectify some of the intra-urban imbalances, but not resolve them.

Finally, at the present stage the entire body of data on the expenditure side is still in raw form and was not checked for internal consistency and reliability. For this reason, very little work on the general patterns of expenditure was performed. These two (temporary) factors presently restrict the scope of analysis of PEX to the more fundamental results.

This section concentrates on a description of PEX as reported for SP and draws only first estimates of the implied magnitudes for UP as well as a few earnings-expenditure comparisons.

b. Sample results and comparisons with official data

The major source of supply of goods and services for the Soviet urban household is the government and its cooperative retail and service networks. About 85 percent of all private urban consumption needs are acquired in outlets of these two systems. Private purchases can be made through four channels: collective farm markets; private sellers in organized or unorganized "flea-markets"; theft of public property in various forms for own use; and the acquisition of goods and services from public outlets, using some form of preferential treatment or "connections" and paid for by "tips" or bribes. With the exception of the first channel, all transactions are illegal in varying degrees and may involve transactions in goods pilfered from the public sector.

The questionnaire makes only a few distinctions in dealing with these purchases. All four categories appear separately in questions relating to expenditures on food, but they are lumped together in almost all other cases. In some of the latter cases, the nature of the good or service purchased may, however, reveal the type of transaction involved. As mentioned above, in some cases questions on PEX are totally missing.

The basic data on family consumption expenditure by type of expenditure and source of purchase in the sample population are presented in Tables 2.13 and 2.14; the latter gives a detailed breakdown of food purchases.

According to Table 2.13, SP family expenditure on all types of PEX are at least R66.0 or 18.1 percent of total monthly *consumption* expenditure of R364.5.[36] For a family without "connections" for purchasing food, the PEX figures are R57.4 (15.7 percent). The collective farm market (CFM) sales of R37.7 takes the lion's share of all PEX and dominate private food purchases. Of the 1,016 families in the sample, only 79 did not report any PEX. A total of 723 families purchased some food in CFM and more than half the families

Table 2.13. Monthly consumption expenditure by type and source

	Total (rubles per family)[a]	Number of families[b]	Private purchases (rubles per family)[a]	Number of families[b] (3)/(1)	Percent private purchases
	(1)	(2)	(3)	(4)	(5)
1. Total consumption[c]	364.5	1,016	57.4[a]	926	15.7
2. Total consumption			66.0[b]	937	18.1
3. Food	182.8	1,015	51.0	841	27.9
3.a. Food at home	169.8	1,015	51.0	841	30.0
3.a.i. CFM			37.7	723	22.2
3.a.ii. Private people			4.7	109	2.8
3.a.iii. "Connections"			8.6	160	5.1
3.b. Restaurants	13.0	467	*	*	*
4. Non-food consumption	182.1 (109.9)[d]	1,016	14.9	612	9.2 (13.6)[d]
5. Tobacco	5.3	555	*	*	*
6. Clothing, shoes, apparel	43.0	1,007	4.9	232	11.4
7. Household goods: durables	22.0	626	0.8	31	3.6
8. Household goods: non-durables, and jewelry	9.5	1,000	*	*	*
9. Rent	7.8	850	0.3	33	3.8
10. Mortgage and utilities	14.0	985	*	*	*
11. Household repair	2.8	220	1.6	132	57.1
12. Domestic services[e]	1.3	56	1.3	56	100.0
13. Transportation	9.9	969	*	*	*
14. Entertainment and culture	21.8	1,015	*	*	*
15. Vacation	20.8	705	3.7	361	17.8
16. Education	4.8	306	1.3	54	27.1
17. Medical services	2.4	479	0.8	128	33.3
18. Personal services	4.9	691	0.3	50	6.1
19. Dues and other services	11.4	1,000	*	*	*

Please see notes on following page.

Notes to Table 2.13

* Question on private expenditures not asked.
ᵃ Average per family over all families.
ᵇ With positive expenditure in category.
ᶜ In variant (b) (= line 2) private purchases include food purchased from public stores where special "connections" were used to acquire the goods.
ᵈ Figures in parentheses are total expenditures and private purchases on nonfood consumption only in items for which questions on private purchases were asked.
ᵉ Assumed to be entirely private. Also includes R0.2 for work services (typing, driving, secretarial jobs).

reported some PEX other than CFM (food or other purchases). Owing to the special position of CFM in PEX — being legal and best reported in food purchases — the following discussion will consider food first, and other consumption later.

1. Private food purchases

The information on food purchases presented in Table 2.13 was obtained from questions on total consumption of food by source of purchase.[37] In Table 2.14 the total amount is obtained by summing up detailed information on the consumption of many food items as listed there. As can be seen, the figures for total expenditure on food from the two sources are not too dissimilar: R184 in Table 2.14 and R169.8 (excluding restaurants) in Table 2.13. The difference may result from the detailed nature of questioning in the data underlying Table 2.14, for this method improves the memory but creates opportunities for double-counting as well. Correspondingly, the estimates for CFM purchases are R40.3 and R37.7, respectively, in both cases about 22 percent of total food purchases. According to the detailed results of Table 2.14, CFM purchases concentrate mainly in fresh food items: fruit, vegetables and potatoes (about two-thirds of total spending) and in meat and dairy products (12–46 percent of the total). Fruit and melons, meat and poultry, and vegetables (including potatoes) account for the bulk of PEX.

Table 2.14. Monthly consumption of food at home, by category and source

	Total (rubles)[a]	No. of families[b]	Private purchases (rubles)[a]	No. of families[a]	% private
	(1)	(2)	(3)	(4)	(5)
Total food	184.4	1,016	45.3	817	24.6
Collective farm market			40.3	738	21.9
Private individuals			5.0	121	2.7
Bread and bread products	11.0	1,015	0.03	11	0.3
Potatoes	4.7	994	3.4	612	71.8
Vegetables	12.1	993	8.0	655	65.5
Fruit and melons	27.1	984	15.6	681	57.6
Sugar and sweets	12.6	1,003	0	1	0
Milk and milk products (excluding butter)	26.9	988	3.2	213	11.9
Butter	0.7	219	0.4	98	56.8
Fats and oils	15.0	1,003	0.4	35	2.7
Meat and poultry	35.7	1,001	12.0	355	33.7
Sausages and meat preserves	13.0	951	0.1	10	1.0
Fresh fish	3.8	854	0.5	96	14.1
Herring and fish preserves	4.1	896	0.1	19	2.9
Eggs	8.5	992	1.6	184	19.4
Alcoholic beverages	9.2	660	0.01	1	0.1

[a] Average expenditure for all 1,016 families.
[b] Number of families reporting positive expenditures in category.

One still unsatisfactory result affecting most of the findings and conclusions of this section is our estimate of consumption of fruit and melons. Expenditures on these items are R27.1 per family per month for 41.6 kgs. of produce, about three and a half times the Soviet average according to official data and thus rather unreasonable. We tend to believe that people reported on their consumption in periods when fruit was in season (i.e., summer), but we find it very difficult to correct such data on an individual basis. Our *ad hoc* measure is to assume that fruit consumption is half that reported in our sample, which reduces total fruit consumption from R27.1 to R13.5 and private fruit purchases from R15.6 to R7.8.[38]

In addition to CFM purchases, we find that both tables put private purchases of food at around R5 per month, 2.7–2.8 percent of the total, and "connections" help buy about R8.6 worth of food from public stores (Table 2.13). Altogether, about a quarter of all home food purchased by the sample population was provided outside the public sector, some 30 percent of it when "connections" are taken into account. Purchasing food from private sellers is widespread: 841 families reported such purchases, 723 in CFM and 109 from private persons; 160 families reported acquiring food in public stores through special connections.

In order to move from the sample's figures to the Soviet population some adjustments must be made to account for those differences between the two populations that are most important in determining the level of private food purchases. The two main variables considered are income and location.

Income makes its impact on two levels: first, as a determinant of the level of food consumption (including food sub-categories). When the consumption of total food is considered, the proportion of private purchases will change with income if such purchases are distributed unevenly among sub-categories of food with different income elasticities. Specifically, since PEX is concentrated in the high-income-elasticity items of food (meat, fruit, and fresh vegetables; see Table 2.14), the PEX level should be expected to be positively correlated with income simply because the proportion of these items in total food consumption is so tightly correlated with income. Secondly, the proportion of PEX *within* each food category is likely to increase as income rises. Privately bought food is considered to be of higher quality, and its acquisition less time consuming and more predictable than food sold through public outlets. It also costs more. All these attributes should be high-expenditure elastic. Hence the hypothesis.

On the supply side, the availability of food in collective farm markets varies considerably between locations according to city size and distance from major crop areas.

Expenditures on food from the major marketing channels were estimated using the following equation:

$$EI_i = a_i + b_iYFR \ [\textbf{or: } B_iEX] \ + c_iFS + \Sigma_j d_{ij}X_j + U_j$$

where EI_i are food purchases from the different marketing channels, YFR is corrected income (see above), and EX is total expenditure; FS is family size and X_j are dummy variables for different locations. After a number of experiments we settled on separating Moscow, Leningrad and Kiev as individual locations, leaving all other observations to be divided by republic.[39] Owing to existing errors, the use of YFR as income tends to bias the true income response downward, and EX to bias it upward. The true coefficient is somewhere in between.

At the present time we are unable to isolate individual prices for goods by source of purchase, and our estimates are thus not of physical quantities purchased but of total expenditure. The estimated *expenditure* coefficients and elasticities for PEX will under- or overestimate the true *income* coefficients and elasticities, depending on whether the corresponding price elasticities are higher or lower than unity. If, however, we assume that higher PEX prices fully reflect higher quality and better accessibility, it follows that prices no not vary considerably, and expenditure and income are similar. Thus, in our discussion we use income and expenditure elasticities interchangeably. Whenever possible, separate equations were estimated on the basis of data on total food (TF, Table 2.13) and on aggregated food consumption (AF, Table 2.14). A selected sample of results of income and FS coefficients and some other estimated statistics are presented in Table 2.15.[40] In presenting the findings, references are made to other equations. The results can be summarized as follows:

(a) Expenditure on food (total, and from separate sources) rises with income. An income increase of R1 brings with it between 16 and 21 kopecks of additional food purchases (line 1), of which 4–6 kopecks received CFMs (lines 3–4). The implied expenditure elasticities are estimated at 0.35–0.46 for all goods and 0.39–0.62 for purchases in CFMs. CFM elasticities are higher than for food purchased in public outlets in each pair of equations using the

Table 2.15. Expenditures of Food (at Home) by Type of Purchase: Regression Results[a]

| | | Coefficients | | Income elas-ticity[b] | Average propen-sity to spend (APS) | $\bar{R}^2$ |
| | | "Income" | Family size | | | |
		(1)	(2)	(3)	(4)	(5)
1. Total food	EXP	0.2135	22.3981	0.46	0.46	0.95
		17.0311	10.6128			
	YCR	0.1628	23.6044	0.35	0.46	0.89
		12.4262	10.4145			
2. Public food	EXP	0.1342	18.7430	0.29	0.35	0.87
		11.9289	9.8934			
	YCR	0.1027	19.4802	0.29	0.35	0.86
		8.9785	9.8438			
3. CFM (a)[a]	EXP	0.0626	1.8779	0.62	0.10	0.10
		7.1198	1.2687			
	YCR	0.0498	2.1077	0.49	0.10	0.48
		5.6736	1.3890			
4. CFM (b)[a]	EXP	0.0507	−0.4778	0.54	0.09	0.58
		7.4832	−0.4187			
	YCR	0.0368	−0.0777	0.39	0.09	0.57
		5.4238	−0.0662			
5. Private food	EXP	0.0151	1.7964	1.21	0.01	0.10
		3.9230	2.7677			
	YCR	0.0095	2.0063	0.76	0.10	0.09
		2.4795	3.0283			
6. Food through "connections"	EXP	0.0428	0.5098	1.98	0.02	0.07
		8.5960	0.5877			
	YCR	0.0351	0.5726	1.62	0.02	0.05
		6.9984	0.6429			

[a] All the equations except for 4 and 6 are based on data for aggregated food (Table 2.14). Equations 4 and 6 are based on data for total food (Table 13). All the equations except for 6 include locational variables (coefficients not shown here), as explained in the text. Figures in small numerals are *t* values.

[b] At the average point.

same type of data and income variable (column 3). Results similar to those obtained for CFM are found for other private purchases (line 5) and for purchases through special connections: in both cases the expenditure elasticities are typically *above* unity.

(b) Although larger families spend more on food (income held constant), they do not tend to increase purchases through private channels (except "private" that includes one's own agricultural plot). The coefficients for CFM or "connections" purchases are always very small, and statistically not different from zero. Here there seem to be two offsetting effects: the per capita income effect pushing private purchases down, while family size pushes total food consumption up.

(c) There are marked locational differences in the amount of CFM purchases: the lowest levels are found in large cities, notably Moscow and Leningrad (but also in Kiev). The highest levels are found, in descending order, in Central Asia, the Ukraine (excluding Kiev), and — in some equations — in Moldavia and Latvia.[41] In general, the larger the city, and the farther you go from agricultural areas, the sharper the decline in CFM purchases. In many cases, high levels of CFM purchases are correlated with low levels of purchases from public channels and *vice versa*. Again, the clearest examples are Moscow and Leningrad, where the levels of public purchases are far higher than the average; this is the sample's support for the well-known fact that Moscow and Leningrad are exceptionally well supplied with food in the public networks compared with the rest of the country.

We now turn to adjust our SP figures on private food purchases to figures for the entire Soviet population. Since average family size is almost the same in the two groups (3.39; see Appendix, Table A.26), only two adjustments are made: for difference in income level and in residence. As always, the adjustments apply only to the urban population of the 7 western republics and are then extrapolated to the entire Soviet Union population of 147.9 million in mid-1973 (*Narkhoz*, 1973, p. 7). The level of monthly family income of UP is estimated here at R298, including private income as estimated in this report.[42] The adjustments are performed by plugging the UP income level and locational distribution into the relevant equations described above.

According to these adjustments, we estimate CFM expenditures of a

Soviet family at R31.7–36.5 per month. When half the expenditure on fruit is deducted (see discussion above, p. 94), the figures drop to R26.5–31.3. In either case the range is caused by estimates based on different equations. These UP figures are R2–6 lower than those for SP (R37.7–40.3 and R30.5–33.1, respectively) and almost the entire adjustment is due to the income difference. The small net effect of the wide differences between SP and UP in residence is surprising, since (as we have seen) CFM sales vary widely with location. An examination of individual locational adjustments shows that the small net effect results from two large offsetting factors: (a) SP is much more heavily concentrated than UP in regions with high CFM sales, e.g., the Ukraine and Moldavia, and (b) within RSFSR, SP is much more highly concentrated than UP in Moscow and Leningrad, where CFM sales are minimal, and much less so in the other republics where such sales are relatively high.[43]

In percentage terms, CFM purchases for UP range around 21 percent of all food consumed at home and all fruit to 20 percent when only half the fruit are taken into account, compared with 21–22 and 18–19 percent, respectively, for SP.

Aggregating over the entire urban population, the adjusted CFM figures is between R16.6 billion and R19.1 billion (13.9–16.4 billion when only half the fruit is included).[44] These figures are far higher than those published by the Soviet Union — R4.6 billion for 1973 (*Narkhoz*, 1973, p. 647) — which, according to official explanations, is arrived at by sampling *kolkhoz* markets in 256 cities *all over* the Soviet Union (Sarkisian, 1973, p. 43). Such a wide gap immediately raises questions as to the credibility of both figures. A thorough analysis of the gap and its source must await further investigation (see Treml, 1985) but we can suggest some observations about both figures that may either narrow the gap or explain it.

(1) In addition to sales in CFMs, collective farms and individual persons also sell some of their produce to special cooperative stores that resell them to the public, for a commission, at higher than official prices. The high prices and quality, and the fact that most of these stores are located in the collective farm markets, might have induced our respondents to include purchases in such stores under CFM rather than under cooperative stores. The official

figure for commission sales of produce is R1.4 billion, so that together with *kolkhoz* farm market sales the figures that should be compared to our estimates should go up to R6.0 billion. On the other hand, some CFM sales (about 8.7 percent) go to institutions, and should therefore be deducted (CIA, 1975, p. 40).

(2) Official figures on CFM sales in Moscow indicate that the official national figure is downward biased. According to these figures (for 1973), CFM sales in Moscow totalled at least R215 million, probably R238 million.[45] Extrapolating these figures for the entire urban population yields estimates of R4.3–4.8 billion, probably higher than the official national figure. This is very unlikely, given the well-established fact (firmly reestablished by our findings) that CFM sales in Moscow are far below the urban average.

(3) A comparison of CFM purchases according to SP with the official figures shows that *for Moscow* the SP estimates are not nearly so much higher (if at all) than the official figures; but when total SP figures are compared with the official figures for all UP, the gap becomes quite wide. Following are some comparative estimates for a comparable list of produces (in millions of rubles, for 1973):

	Including all fruit	Including half the fruit	Excluding fruit
Official data	215	..	130
Official data *plus* commission sales[a]	280	..	170
SP unadjusted	490	366	241
SP adjusted for income[b]			
(i)	361	259	161
(ii)	420	311	205

[a] Assuming that the ratio between CFM and commission sales in Moscow is the same as the national average.

[b] (i) Is estimated from a regression on total CFM sales. (ii) Is estimated from individual regressions for the main items sold in CFM. In both cases it is assumed that the income *differences* between SP and UP Moscow families are the same as in the entire sample.

(As mentioned above, these figures include only about 90 percent of the turn-over of CFM, so that total CFM purchases are that much larger.) As we can see, SP adjusted figures range from just about the official figure (with commission sales) and 50 percent higher than that figure only if all SP fruit are included. The corresponding differences on the national level are, as we have seen, twice as large. Our interim conclusion is either that official Soviet national figures are very heavily weighted by Moscow (and Leningrad, etc.), thus understating the true figures, and/or that there is some flaw in our reweighting scheme.

(4) Such a flaw might, indeed, be caused by the fact that about 60 percent of UP (in the 7 western republics) are represented by only 45 families in SP, so that even a small error in our estimate of CFM sales can have a serious effect on our results. CFM sales in RSFSR outside Moscow and Leningrad are quite high, thus compounding the error. It should, however, be noted that even when we take RSFSR as a single unit (thereby imposing the low CFM figures of Moscow and Leningrad on the entire republic) our estimated figure for CFM goes down only to R9.6–13.6 billion, still at least 50 percent higher than the official figure. We believe this weighting system biases the estimate downward. An interim conclusion is that the official Soviet CFM figures are very likely understated by at least one-third, and possibly one-half of their true value.

The adjusted UP figures for private food purchases (other than CFM) are estimated by the various equations at between R1.5 and R4.7 per family per month, or R0.8–2.5 billion annually for the entire population (the corresponding SP figures are R4.7–5.0 and R2.5–2.6 billion, respectively). Purchases from public stores using special "connections" add another R4.4–5.2 per family per month, or R2.3–2.7 billion annually for the entire urban population (SP figures are R8.6 and R4.5 billion, respectively).

In relative terms, CFM purchases account for at least 12–14 percent of total home food purchases of the urban population, but the proportion may be as high as 20 percent. Together with private purchases (1.1–2.8 percent of total food) and "connections" (2.6–2.8 percent), the total proportion of food bought outside official channels ranges from a minimum of 16 percent to possibly 25 percent of the total, compared with 30 percent in SP.

2. Non-food private purchases and "connections"

Of total non-food purchases by SP families (R182.1 per month, see Table 2.13), R14.9 worth of goods and services (8.2 percent) were purchased privately. But when items about which no questions on PEX were asked are excluded, the relative share of PEX rises to 13.6 percent (Table 2.13, line 4). Examining the items for which the PEX data are missing, namely private transportation (gasoline, car repairs, etc.) and nondurable household goods (and consumer items including books and jewelry), it seems that the actual share for SP is somewhere between 8 and 14 percent — probably closer to the higher figure.

In Table 2.16 (columns 1–2) we first present the expenditure elasticities derived from the equations for the non-food categories, equations that are structurally similar to the food equations but exclude location variables. Next, the table shows our estimate of private purchases of non-food items by a family of UP (column 3) and by the entire Soviet urban population (column 4), adjusted for SP–UP differences in income levels (they have the same average family size). For comparison and consideration, the unadjusted SP figures are also shown (columns 5–6). Given the relatively weak explanatory power of some of the equations (not shown), as well as the other weaknesses of the data, the figures should be treated as rough estimates.

Owing to the high income elasticities estimated by the equations, the adjusted figures for total non-food private consumption for UP are much lower than the original SP figures (shown in Table 2.13). In some equations the SP figure is reduced by two-thirds or more. For all non-food items, the adjusted estimate is R6.9–9.2 per family per month (depending on the income concept used), or R3.6–4.8 billion annually for the entire UP. This should be compared with an unadjusted figure of R7.8 billion. If, however, we take into account the missing information on private purchases, and assume that it behaves like those purchases for which information is available, the adjusted UP figure may increase to R6–8 billion as a maximum, and the unadjusted figure to R13 billion.[46] When adjusted, total non-food private purchases range between 5.5 and 6.5 percent of total non-food purchases. When adjusting for unreported private purchases, the figures can rise to around 8.0 and 10.5 percent, respectively.[47]

Table 2.16. Expenditure elasticities of nonfood consumption categories, by source of purchase

		Expenditure and income elasticities[a]		Private expenditure of the urban population			
				Adjusted[b]		Unadjusted	
		All expenditures in category	Private expenditures in category	Family per month (rubles)	UP annual[c] (million rubles)	Family per month (rubles)	UP annual[c] (million rubles)
		(1)	(2)	(3)	(4)	(5)	(6)
1. Non-food (all)	EXP	1.20	2.11	6.95	3,639	14.94	7,801
	YCR	0.86	1.49	9.20	4,817		
2. Clothing	EXP	1.21	2.30	2.04	1,068	4.90	2,565
	YCR	0.95	1.47	3.05	1,596		
3. House repair	EXP	2.67	2.58	0.55	288	1.59	838
	YCR	1.32	1.15	1.12	586		
4. Domestic services	EXP	..	3.27	0.22	115	1.28	681
	YCR	..	2.32	0.53	277		
5. Vacation	EXP	1.30	1.22	2.54	1,330	3.60	1,937
	YCR	1.05	1.24	2.51	1,314		
6. Education	EXP	0.74	2.13	0.59	309	1.28	681
	YCR	0.33	1.54	0.77	403		
7. Medical services	EXP	1.04	1.29	0.54	283	0.80	418
	YCR	0.63	0.63	0.67	351		
8. Personal services	EXP	0.71	2.09	0.12	63	0.26	157
	YCR	0.47	2.02	0.12	63		
9. Others		..	..	..	..	1.15	576

[a] Based on linear regressions. Elasticities are at average points. Columns do not add exactly due to rounding.

[b] For income differences (for SP, EXP = R399.1 and YCR = R397.7 as compared with R298 for UP). Family size is 3.39 for both SP and UP.

[c] To move from 'per family per month' to 'UP annual' we divide the former by 3.39, then multiply by 12 months and by 147.9 million (the size of the Soviet urban population).

There is some additional information on purchases of durable goods and appliances using "connections." According to this information, which probably gives an underestimate, connections are exploited for 3.5–4.0 percent of all purchases of washing machines and TV sets, up to 10 percent in the case of pianos and furniture, and 14 percent for refrigerators. It would seem that this particular form of private effort accounts for about 5 percent of the volume of goods purchased in public stores. By inference, the proportion of services should be higher.

4. Conclusion

What are the implications of this chapter for our understanding of the workings and economic potential of the Soviet Union? We found that while the volume of private activity in the urban consumer sector is quite sizable, its impact on our assessment of Soviet GNP is fairly moderate — at most it adds 3–4 percent to existing estimates.[48]

The urban private sector is a significant element in the household economy on both the income and the expenditure sides. About 10 percent, perhaps 12 percent of total income is derived privately, and about 18 percent of all consumption expenditure are conducted between private individuals. On this basis it should first be stated that despite this considerable volume of private transactions, the Soviet urban citizen depends first and foremost on the public sector for his income and consumption needs.[49] However, consideration of opportunities for private gain or private purchase is an essential element in the economy of almost every urban household with respect to decisions on work, income, and standard of living. As an incremental and more flexible source of income, private earnings play an even more important role in family decision-making processes than their relative share in total income would indicate. By the same token, private purchases often bridge part of the gap between the provision of basic needs (as determined by the planners in accordance with their rather austere and unfulfilled standards) and the higher standards and quality of life for which these households strive.

Such a significant private sector clearly testifies to the dissatisfaction of the population with the level, quality, and variety of consumer goods and services supplied by the public sector and with their logistics. Many students of the Soviet economy see the large volume of private activity as one manifestation of a repressed inflation that, they claim, exists in the Soviet Union. If repressed inflation means that people seek and find ways to improve their standard of living beyond what is publicly provided, by earning and buying privately, then these students are right. If it means that there are shortages of *specific* goods and services, or that their supply is so disorganized that people are willing to pay more to acquire them privately, then they are right again. But the existence of a private sector need not necessarily mean that people receive more money from the public sector than they can either spend on public-sector goods or save voluntarily. The last statement represents a narrower, but in our view the correct definition of repressed inflation.

Assume for a moment that this is not the case, and that people are able and willing to spend their entire income on publicly supplied goods and services. This should not prevent them from creating a private sector of any size in which the amount of income generated equals the amount of income spent. All it takes is an increase in the circulation of money or the development of substitutes for official money. The demand for private goods and services could result not from surplus income, but from dissatisfaction with the standard of living and the availability of opportunities to raise it by exerting extra effort (including extra work for higher pay). We do not deny that there may be repressed inflation in the Soviet Union, we only state that the existence of a private sector *per se* is no proof that repressed inflation does exits.

It is very likely, given revealed preference, that private activity raises the average household's level of welfare. However, this rise is probably less than implied by the relative share of the private sector. As we have seen, at least part of the transactions in the private sector deal in goods produced in the public sector or in labor paid by it, and, as we assumed, paid for by the purchaser of public goods and services. This segment of the volume of private activity has a redistribution effect whose welfare impact is unknown, but it certainly does not create a large volume of goods and services.

The existence of private earnings and their uneven distribution among the various occupations and branches of the economy clearly disrupts the functioning of the allocation and incentive schemes built into the official wage structure and bonus payments. Activities or jobs that provide ampler opportunities for private gain may attract more people than the official wage intended, and *vice versa* — if such an activity has low priority and thus intentionally pays a low official wage, the urge for private gain will grow. There is quite a large body of evidence suggesting that people prefer jobs with private-earnings potential in trade, construction, and services. At least one writer points out that this situation makes it more difficult for the authorities to recruit qualified scientists and skilled workers for military R&D and production enterprises, as such people prefer analogous civilian positions. The nature of production and the secrecy and security measures in military production lessen the opportunities for private gain (Agurski and Adomeit, 1977, pp. 31, 39–40).

Opportunities for private gain also compete, of course, with bonus payments and premiums, either directly (in the case of a choice between the two) or indirectly (when more money can be made by exerting extra effort in private rather than bonus-earning activities). Our survey does not contain information on how the authorities react to these problems. Obviously, they can internalize whatever information they have on private gain into the official wage and bonus structure. They may deliberately offer low wages to trade workers, taking the expected private income into account, just as any restaurant operator in the West takes into account the tips his waiters get. Or they can compensate military employees with other privileges unavailable to most civilian workers. The problem can thus be mitigated, but not solved. Private earnings cannot be planned and the action–reaction game of private vs. public incomes may be an unstable (or even an explosive) one.

This brings up the issue of the attitude of the authorities toward the entire private sector phenomenon. There are no new answers in our survey: the extent, spread, and variety of activities that characterize the private sector seem to imply an ambivalent approach by the authorities, similar to the one taken toward private agricultural plots. The private sector makes a positive contribution as long as it invites the population to exert greater efforts, because it satisfies needs that the planning system is very inefficient in supplying, and raises the general morale of the population. It must be checked, however, so that it encroaches as little as possible on the production capacity of the public sector. The translation of this attitude into a set of policy measures is complex, and the result is the same zigzag of restrictive periods followed by more permissive ones, as observed in the context of private agricultural plots. In the long run, the patterns of private activity could be used by the authorities to improve the planning and production of consumer goods and services.

Appendix Table 2.A1. Participation in private work: regression results

Equation:	Private work (EW1) (1)	Public jobs (EW2) (2)	Over-time (EW3) (3)	Extra work (EW) (4)
Constant	−1.3785	−4.8753	−3.3269	−2.2372
	−1.4288	−5.6026	−2.8206	−3.3206
Sex	1.3287	1.5952	1.3762	1.6654
	5.6910	7.0167	4.0939	9.7897
Regular wage (RW)	−0.0048	−0.0016	−0.0017	−0.0021
	−3.0241	−1.4068	−0.9572	−2.2503
Regular hours (RH)	−0.0581	−0.1020	−0.0621	−0.0416
	−3.3404	−0.6596	−3.4387	−3.4080
YR_i	0.0007	0.0001	−0.0008	0.0038
	1.1933	0.1848	−0.9708	9.1669
Education (years) (ED)	0.0465	0.0803	−0.0250	0.0380
	1.3059	2.3649	−0.5052	1.4756
Family size (FS)	−0.0160	0.2299	0.4317	−0.0515
	−0.1595	2.5541	3.3695	−0.7431
Moscow	0.6975	0.1898	0.0912	0.1359
	2.4556	0.7206	0.2084	0.6331
$\bar{R}^2$	0.1107	0.1233	−1.2982	0.1892

$OCCP_i$: White collar

Technicians	−1.0866	−0.4877	−2.4132	−0.8308
	−1.7377	−1.1311	−1.0591	−2.2569
Doctors	−0.2653	0.3510	811.65	1.4406
	−0.5420	0.9104	25.792	5.2316
Dentists	1.9950	−0.1451	2.0768	1.4609
	3.9523	−0.1846	2.7233	2.9328
Nurses	1.3665	−0.8632	3.4869	1.5905
	2.9370	−0.8264	6.1498	4.5378
Other medical	−0.0522	1.0898	0.7224	0.5353
	−0.0664	1.9801	0.6368	1.0827
Education	0.0302	0.7850	1.7996	0.6673
	0.0917	3.1586	3.8647	3.1439
Public administration	−1.1773	0.2379	−0.1163	−0.4663
	−1.8782	0.6960	−0.1453	−1.4663

(cont.)

Appendix Table 2.A1 (cont.)

Equation:	Private work (EW1) (1)	Public jobs (EW2) (2)	Over-time (EW3) (3)	Extra work (EW) (4)
Trade	−0.9231	−0.7970	−0.4016	−1.4916
	−1.2170	−1.2729	−0.3710	−2.6934
Communal services	0.5896	−9.7641	−2.6978	−0.9173
	0.7213	−0.1461	−0.4177	−1.0398
OCCP$_i$: Blue Collar				
Heavy industry (machine building)	0.1688	0.0565	0.0696	−0.1045
	0.4212	0.1572	0.1060	−0.3538
Wood, textiles, leather & shoes	1.3311	−1.2071	−0.7511	0.3493
	3.0568	−1.5526	−0.6714	0.9820
Food and other light industry	−1.0618	−0.5522	0.5746	−0.3944
	−1.0038	−0.7127	0.6392	−0.7452
Construction and const. materials	−0.4498	0.6227	−3.0502	1.7611
	−0.4338	1.0233	−0.5629	3.8955
Transportation	0.9199	−0.6759	1.5758	0.6192
	1.7168	−0.8763	2.2880	1.4810
Trade	−1.5823	−1.6220	−0.4224	−1.4726
	−1.5070	−1.5522	−0.3839	−2.4101
Communal services	1.4210	−0.2689	−0.1975	0.6842
	3.0741	−0.4078	−0.1758	1.7326

Note: Small numerals are *t* values; all equations include variables for occupations.

Notes

1. Some of the more recent works are: Chalidze (1977), Grossman (1977, 1979), Kaiser (1976), Katsenelinboigen (1977), Katz (1973), Schroeder (1977), Severin and Carey (1970), Simes (1975), Smith (1976), Treml (1975), Schroeder and Greenslade (1979), and Ofer (1979).
2. Money received from relatives as gifts or loans was treated separately in the questionnaire.
3. A plumber performing a repair for private remuneration during regular working hours may decide to include such income here.
4. Including overtime as well as extra part-time jobs in the main place of work (e.g., by medical staff, teachers, etc.).
5. The simple correlation between private work and extra public jobs is 0.156, and with overtime, 0.088. There may, of course, be a negative association on the margin, or within specific groups of workers.
6. More data on hours and earnings of those privately employed in various occupations appear in Table 2.5 below, and are discussed later.
7. Thus working women devote proportionally as much additional time on private jobs as men do.
8. Average net monthly wages from the main job are R183.95 for men and R116.95 for women. When corrected for hours worked, the female/male wage ratio goes up from 0.64 to 0.67. See discussion in Chapter 7.
9. The overall proportion in this branch is low, owing to the high proportion of women employed in it.
10. The occupational breakdown differs from that by branch in that the latter classifies according to place of work; thus a construction worker employed in "health services" is classified in different groups by occupation and by branch. However, the available classification by occupation is much more detailed than that by branch, and at least for blue-collar workers within manufacturing, could be considered as a proxy for an industrial classification.
11. Private wages and relative private-to-public wages are calculated on the basis of wages of those actually engaged in both public jobs and private work.
12. See exact description of groups (a) and (b) in notes to Table 2.5.

13. Since YR_i includes the husband's earnings as well as those of other family members, this high income effect includes elements of cross-substitution effects and is not pure. At this level of analysis, and for lack of good data on non-earned incomes, we let it stand as is.

14. The level of education has a positive effect only on extra public jobs. This may reflect multiple job holdings by academics in the form of extra jobs in research and consultation. Residence in Moscow enhances private work, although separate equations for men and women show that this is true only for women.

15. See, for example, Smith (1976, Chapter 3), Grossman (1977), and Simes (1975).

16. Only about a quarter of this income is derived from the sale of agricultural produce; 75 percent is self-consumed.

17. For an illuminating discussion of these sources of income see Grossman (1979, pp. 3–15).

18. See Chapter 3.

19. YFR is used henceforth in the book as the variable for family income in the ISIP sample.

20. Disregarding communications due to the small number of families.

21. Disaggregation into smaller cells simultaneously increases the within-cell uniformity and thus improves the predictive power of the reweighting process, but reduces the number of observations per cell and the dependability of the estimate. There is an optimum degree of disaggregation at reasonable levels.

22. The industrial and occupational structures used as weights are for the entire non-agricultural employed population of the Soviet Union. Only very small and insignificant differences are expected to result from substituting the corresponding structures for those of the 7 western republics only.

23. This observation is based on regression results that are not shown here.

24. See Appendix, Table A.26.

25. *Ibid.*, Appendix, Table A.26.

26. When total earnings from the public sector (W2) are used as denominator instead of W1, the percentages are about 0.3 points smaller.

27. That is, R288–303.3 compared with R248.2 per family with workers. See Appendix, Table A.26.

28. Based on 2.00 workers per family with workers in UP (see Appendix, Table A.1). The number of non-agricultural workers and employees in 1973 is 87.1 million and those in UP about 72.6 million. When Y3 is estimated directly from our estimate of R9.94 per worker, the figure is R10.4 billion. Estimates based on reweighting by branch are slightly higher (by about R0.5 billion for YP), but the share of YD1 is higher and that of Y3 is about R6 billion lower. If YD1 is cut in half, YP as well as YD1 are reduced by about R2.2 billion. Finally, all the figures increase 11.3 percent (YP rises by R23.3 billion) if the estimates are made for all workers or employees (including those working in agriculture).

29. A detailed discussion on the problems of including illegal activities in GNP appears in Ofer (1979). For a debate on the problem of double counting see Schroeder and Greenslade (1979).

30. A detailed account of the two sets of figures may be obtained from the authors.

31. Based on CIA (1975); Schroeder and Severin (1976, p. 653); and our reweighted estimates.

32. The CIA estimates total incomes of collective farmers (for 1970) at BR41.2, of which BR8.3 comes from collective farm market sales. The figure of 20 percent does not include income in kind (CIA, 1975, Table 1, p. 3).

33. Exceptions occur when people provide services to public enterprises on private account (*shabshniki* [private construction groups] working for *kolkhozy*, for example).

34. Although all personal consumption is "private" in the ordinary sense, throughout this report we use the term "private" to mean the *source of purchase* rather than the buyer.

35. As explained in the Introduction, many questions on the private sector were added to the questionnaire at the last moment, and the above omissions are one of the results.

36. Non-consumption expenditures are savings and transfers to other families.

37. Only the questions on alcohol consumption and on expenditures in restaurants were presented separately.

38. It also reduces total food consumption (Table 2.14) from R184.4 to R170.9, very close to the figure in Table 2.13, where no specific questions

were asked about fruit. Correspondingly, total private food purchases in
Table 2.14 go down from R45.3 to R37.5 — below the matching figure in
Table 2.13.
39. Estonia and Latvia are merged, as are all the Central Asian republics,
from which there are twenty-three observations.
40. Full results can be obtained from the authors.
41. The following are deviations from the average CFM purchases in some
locations (in rubles): Moscow — −24.8; Leningrad — −22.0; Kiev — −3.6;
other RSFSR — +1.9; Moldavia — +3.0; Ukraine (excluding Kiev) — +10.9;
Central Asia — +14.5. The figures are from equation 3 in Table 2.15.
42. This estimate is derived as follows: total income from public sources is
estimated at R138 billion (arrived at independently from our calculations in
the Appendix, Table A.26); as well as Schroeder and Severin (1976, p. 652)
and CIA (1975, pp. 3, 4). To this we add R18.0 billion, which is our estimate
of urban private incomes from all sources. Total net urban income is estimated at R156 billion or R298 per family per month (R97.9 per capita).
43. The geographical distribution of SP and UP is as follows (in percentages):

	SP	UP		SP	UP
RSFSR	[18.7]	[69.6]	Byelorussia	4.7	3.6
Moscow	8.6	5.8	Lithuania	4.6	1.4
Leningrad	5.8	0.3	Latvia (Estonia)	3.9	2.1
Other RSFSR	4.3	60.8	Moldavia	28.1	1.0
Kiev	6.4	1.5	Central Asia	2.3	0.0*
Other Ukraine	31.1	20.8			

* No families from Central Asia in the sample.
44. The extrapolation to the entire urban population (beyond the 7 western
republics) is made on the assumption of similar behavior. It is clearly an
underestimate for the central Asian republics.
45. The first figure is based on data from Soviet Union, *Moscow v Tsifrakh,
1971–1977*, pp. 100, 102. Figures for 1973 are based on quantities for that
year and ruble volumes for 1970 and 1975. The figure of R238 million is 10.7
percent higher, and this, according to SP, is the volume of CFM in Moscow

not covered by the items included in the official figures.

46. In both cases the maximum figure assumes that PEX consists of 13.6 percent of all non-food purchases of R24.8.

47. Adjusted non-food purchases per family of UP is estimated at R125.7–142.6 per month.

48. The present study cannot assess the effect of private incomes on the rate of growth of GNP.

49. Even more so if we add to both income and consumption those services that are provided free (e.g., most health and education services).

Chapter 3
Soviet household saving

1. Introduction

According to the conventional theory of Soviet planning, the level of investment is unrelated to the level of household saving. The amount of resources designated for investment purposes is acquired, as are all other public funds, from the household sector, in the form of taxes and profits. With a few minor exceptions, households are not permitted to invest in productive assets directly. For these reasons, private savings have not been considered to be an important element influencing the level and composition of Soviet output. In fact, when private saving started to grow during the latter part of the 1950s and the 1960s, many students of the Soviet economy explained the phenomenon mainly as "forced saving," a manifestation of repressed inflation, since there seemed to be no reason for Soviet households to save (Bronson and Severin, JEC, 1973; Keizer, 1971; and Bush, 1973).

Recent work by Pickersgill (1976, 1977) and Millar and Pickersgill (1977), employing both a time-series analysis of Soviet household saving and an aggregate model of the Soviet economy, cast doubt on the forced saving hypothesis and the consequent separation of the planners' decisions on the level of investment from the households' decisions on the level of their saving. The purpose of this chapter is to extend the analysis of Soviet household saving by developing a saving function based on cross-section data derived from a family budget survey of Soviet emigrants.

We propose to use Western theories of household saving behavior to explain similar behavior in the Soviet Union. Although the Soviet economy is characterized as a planned economy, not all resources are centrally allocated. Despite the planned allocation of natural resources and intermediate goods by the central planners, the supply of labor, the demand for consumer goods, and the allocation of household income between consumption and saving is not directly determined by the planners. To influence household choices in these three areas, the planners must alter the costs and benefits of household decisions, and thus, indirectly, their choices.

Soviet households, like their Western counterparts, make choices with respect to the education, occupation, and employment of the various family members, all of which affect their lifetime income. Soviet workers allocate their time between leisure activities, public employment and, within certain constraints, private employment.[1] Despite the labor controls used by the central planners, workers can supplement income from their official place of employment through moonlighting in the public sector or engaging in legal, quasi-legal, or illegal activity in the private sector. In addition, each Soviet household may allocate the income it earns to the purchase of a variety of consumer goods from the public and private sectors and may save a portion of its income for future consumption.

Given that there is wide room for choice, we proceed by assuming that Soviet households, like Western ones, behave in ways consistent with utility maximization and that neoclassical theories of consumer behavior such as those of Becker and Lancaster are applicable also in the Soviet Union. In particular, we expect to observe behavior similar to that in the West with respect to saving; for example, positive saving when current income is high relative to lifetime income, and zero or negative saving when current income is relatively low.[2] We would expect Soviet household saving patterns to differ from Western patterns to the extent that differences in the respective economic systems influence income patterns and the opportunities for and the constraints on the use of this income.

2. Variables influencing Soviet household saving

In this section we outline Soviet income and expenditure patterns and investment opportunities. Differences between Soviet and Western institutions and practices that may affect saving behavior are discussed, using the approach of the permanent income and life cycle theories of saving and consumption.

a. Income patterns

The pattern of income derived from the public sector in the Soviet Union differs in two major respects from income earned in a market economy. First, Soviet income shows less variation over the life cycle than commonly observed in market economies, and short-run income variations around the long-run trend are narrower. Since one of the major motives for saving is to transfer income from high- to low-income periods, the rate of saving out of public income in the Soviet Union should be lower than that found in market economies. These statements do not relate to income from private sources, which may vary as much or even more than incomes in market economies in both the long and the short run. For this reason, we treat public and private sources of income separately.

1. The Soviet life-cycle income. The reduced income variation is in part due to the fact that the overwhelming proportion of Soviet personal income is derived from wages and salaries, the most stable element in total income. In addition, wage differentials among occupations and according to skill levels and seniority within occupations are narrower than in most Western economies (Chapman, 1977a,b; and McAuley, 1977a). Moreover, these wage differentials have been declining in the Soviet Union since the 1950s. Further, the income of the Soviet household at retirement is cushioned by a mandatory pension system, which, despite a rising trend, is still substantially below the worker's preretirement income. Finally, both preretirement income and, more importantly, retirement income, are supplemented by substantial transfers-in-kind in the form of free education and medical care, low-cost housing and transportation, and the subsidization of some other basic items, all of which contribute to a smoother income trend over the life cycle.

2. Variations in current income around the life-cycle trend. Many of the major sources of short-run income instability in the West are absent or sharply reduced in the Soviet Union. First, labor income is, in the short run, more stable than entrepreneurial income, and its dominance in Soviet personal income thus dampens short-run income variation. Second, short-run wage variations are narrower mainly because of the much lower incidence of open (and unpaid) unemployment in the Soviet Union. This is due to smaller cyclical variations in the level of economic activity and to the fact that Soviet enterprises are not motivated to lay off workers but rather find it in their interest to retain extra workers as a buffer. To the extent that cyclical variations do exist, they affect mainly the quantity and quality of consumer goods, and since prices remain constant, also the level of *real* income.[3] The effect on saving of this last phenomenon is discussed below.

A possible source of income variation over the short run is the supplementary wage or bonus. In 1974 various bonus payments amounted to 11 percent of the wage bill. Bonuses and premiums that are paid as rewards for fulfillment and overfulfillment of targets for sales, profits, labor productivity, etc. are paid on a monthly basis to managerial and technical personnel and at year end to all workers. For the first group, bonuses amount to 30 or even 75 percent of their annual salaries, and this may cause significant income variations. However, in many cases the bonus is used as a more or less permanent addition to a wage rate that is out of equilibrium in periods between wage reforms and in such cases forms a part of anticipated income.

The most important source of household entrepreneurial income in the Soviet Union is the proceeds from the sale of produce grown by farmers and others on legal, private agricultural plots. The probable high variation in these incomes as well as the investment opportunity that the private plot provides (see below) probably causes the Soviet farmer to save more than he would have on the basis of the much more stable income stream he gets from the collective farm. But since our sample is entirely urban, there is no way to test hypotheses on rural saving habits.

3. Private urban incomes. There is a good deal of evidence that many urban families in the Soviet Union supplement their incomes from the public sector with private income; in addition to a small number of private plots and some renting of rooms or dachas, people earn money by a whole range of activities from the provision of medical services on private account to the pilferage of goods from the main place of work (see Chapter 2). In our sample more than 40 percent of all families reported having some private income. For all families private income averages around 12–15 percent of official income. One would certainly expect much greater variation in this unofficial income than in income earned at the main place of work. Also, such incomes are in many cases less than fully legal and thus highly risky. High variance and high risk are the two major characteristics of entre-preneurial earnings in market economies, and the two major reasons that high proportions of such earnings are saved. We should thus expect high rates of saving from private income also in the Soviet Union.

b. Expenditure patterns

In addition to the level and pattern of variation of Soviet household incomes, the propensity to save may be affected by the unique characteristics of Soviet capital and consumer-goods markets. These characteristics include a restricted set of portfolio choices facing the typical Soviet household, the lack of consumer credit, the state provision of a variety of "free" goods and services, the stochastic nature of the availability of consumer goods, the absence of inheritance taxes, and the taste for inconspicuous behavior. In the section below we shall outline these characteristics and their implications for Soviet saving.

1. Portfolio choices. In a market economy households may select a wide variety of real and financial assets, varying with respect to risk, yield, and liquidity. By contrast, Soviet households are not allowed to acquire or hold productive assets (or claims to them), and as mentioned above, investment, financed from the budget of the public sector, is divorced from household savings. They may hold currency, savings deposits, 3 percent lottery bonds, consumer durables, and jewelry. The interest paid on savings deposits ranges from 2 to 3 percent. Although this rate is comparable to or even higher than the real rate paid on savings deposits in the United States today, the lack of higher-yield, higher-risk assets, such as common stocks or direct investment in productive capital, must result in a significant reduction of the proportion of permanent income saved in the Soviet Union.[4]

Perhaps one of the most important assets held by Soviet households is human capital. Given the relative ease with which people may add to their stock of human capital and the relatively high yield in the form of higher status and lifetime income, one would expect to observe Soviet households holding a large part of their wealth in this form. Milton Friedman has suggested that the rate of saving is positively affected by the ratio of human to non-human wealth. Given the extent of education in the Soviet Union and the difficulty of accumulating wealth in non-human form, one would expect to observe the Soviets saving a higher proportion of their permanent income in order to increase the liquidity of their portfolio (Friedman, 1957).

2. Consumer credit. The use of consumer credit to purchase goods on the installment plan is extremely limited in the Soviet economy. Consumers must be prepared to pay in cash for nearly all purchases, including automobiles. One expects that the limited supply of consumer credit will increase the proportion of income saved. The limited availability of credit also makes it more difficult for young Soviet households to transfer income from high to low earning years through the use of installment credit. Thus, households can only dissave if they have previously accumulated positive savings or if they can receive financial assistance or borrow privately (from their parents). One would expect to observe a low incidence of dissaving and a higher average propensity to save throughout the life cycle.

3. State provision of consumer goods and services. The supply of "free" education and medical care and low-rent housing in the Soviet Union reduces the demand for savings compared to market economies. Purchasing a home, sending children to college, and creating reserves as security in case of health hardships are among the main motives for household saving in many market economies. While a small proportion of Soviet households do plan on buying a cooperative apartment or a dacha, and while better medical treatment or even better education may be obtained through side or private payments, the overall burden of these purchases on Soviet households is much lighter, and the demand for savings on their account much smaller.

4. The availability of consumer goods. Many writers have argued that shortages of consumer goods have been the primary cause of Soviet saving, and thus that most Soviet saving is "forced" simply because there is excess demand for goods at the current set of prices.[5] In addition, if official prices are rigid and consistently below the equilibrium level, households can reduce their cash holdings by reducing their labor supply. There have been substantial year-to-year variations in the marginal propensity to save, and recent time-series evidence does indicate higher saving rates in the post-1965 period.[6] If forced saving does occur, the level of saving will, of course, be higher.

Whether or not saving may be increased by repressed inflation, it is certainly affected by the perennial uncertainty and irregularity of the availability of consumer goods, including food items, clothing, and consumer durables. Not only does this uncertainty of supply affect Soviet real income as discussed in the previous section, it also provides a motive for increased liquidity. One would expect the average propensity to save to be higher, since the Soviet household must have liquid assets to take advantage of unexpected opportunities. As the level of income goes up, so must the incremental additions to this precautionary stock of cash.

5. Inheritance. Since 1943 there has been no inheritance or gift tax in the Soviet Union (Diachenko *et al.*, 1964). This fact should increase the proportion of life-time income saved. On the other hand, the absence of the opportunity to invest productively must reduce the incentive to accumulate for future generations as well as the average size of inheritances.

6. Political and social environment. Finally, we should mention the rather unique political and social environment of Soviet households, which may affect their saving behavior. It is difficult to assess the impact of the currency reform of 1947 on saving behavior today. In 1947 the Soviet authorities traded old rubles for new rubles at a rate of exchange that was particularly disadvantageous for holders of cash and large saving deposits. The fear of future confiscations still lingers. In addition, the political authorities look upon the accumulation of private wealth with suspicion, and Soviet citizens have learned to avoid conspicuous consumption.

c. Soviet saving patterns: a summary

The variations in current income around expected lifetime income in the Soviet Union are narrower than in the market economies of the West. Tests of both the life-cycle and the permanent-income hypothesis support the view that the high proportion of transitory income in the West is responsible for the gap between the long-run saving rate and the much higher marginal propensity to save (MPS) observed in Western cross-section studies (Mayer, 1972, p. 350). If our arguments about the nature of Soviet public income patterns are correct, the MPS estimated from Soviet cross-section data will not be much higher than the average saving rate, and the corresponding average rate of saving (APS) will not rise as much, if at all. Rather, the estimated APS will approach the MPS and both will closely correspond to the long-run or permanent saving rate. Figure 3.1 illustrates the classical saving function estimated using cross-section and long-run time series data for a market economy. For a given *permanent* saving function, we expect the Soviet *current* saving function to rotate clockwise toward the permanent function. The impact of income earned from private sources will partially offset this tendency. The rotating effect should thus be best observed when 'private' income is excluded from the analysis.

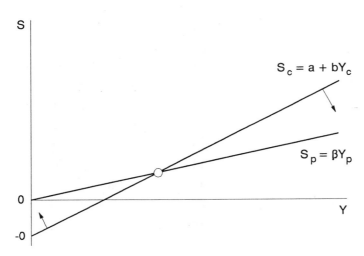

Figure 3.1. Saving out of current and permanent income

The influences on the proportion of permanent income saved are more difficult to summarize, since they point in different directions. On the one hand, the lack of investment opportunities, the access to free education, medical services, and low rent housing, and the avoidance of conspicuous behavior would tend to reduce the proportion of permanent income saved. On the other hand, the uncertainty of supplies, the lack of credit, the absence of inheritance taxes, the ratio of human to nonhuman wealth, and the possibility of repressed inflation would have the opposite effect. A judgment of the net impact will have to depend upon actual results, but it is our strong feeling that the factors that reduce saving tip the balance to bring the saving rate below normal market economy rates.

3. The data and variables

The study of Soviet household saving behavior on the basis of ISIP data suffers from a number of general and specific limitations and biases. First, all we can study directly are saving habits of the urban working Soviet population (of European descent) and even this, only for complete families. All the excluded groups may have somewhat lower tendencies to save, so that our findings may be biased upward. Since we were not able to discover statistically significant differences in saving habits between groups classified by geographic location, level of education, occupation, or even age, for a given income, structural differences between the sample and the target population with respect to these criteria should not affect the results of our analysis. There are, of course, differences in the saving behavior of families with different levels and structures of earnings, income, and wealth, as well as demographic variables. We hope that the use of regression analysis helps to minimize the effect of the rather wide sample to population differences that do exist with respect to many of these variables. For reasons that are explained below, we believe that the variances of savings among people at the lower and upper ends of the income range are not much higher than those with incomes in between, so that biases resulting from a combination of non-representiveness of the sample and heteroskedasticity of savings along the income range should not be serious.

The specific data on saving as well as those on income are, however, subject to a number of more significant limitations and shortcomings. Let us discuss these together with a general description of the variables used in the analysis.

Saving. The data on saving (S) are made up of two elements: (i) direct saving in the form of additions during the normal year to various saving accounts or to bond and cash holdings, as reported by the respondents; (ii) saving includes mortgage payments on apartments. While in principle the respondents could have reported negative saving, no one did so. We conclude that negative saving was not reported because the respondents did not understand that they could report it, not because it did not exist. A broader definition of saving includes credit payments net of purchases on credit. Since credit purchases are rather limited in the Soviet Union, the results using the more inclusive definition were very close to our reported results. The quality of the data on credit activity was not good enough to justify its inclusion. An alternative definition of saving — the difference between total income and total expenditure on consumption — had to be ruled out at this point, since such a residual contains many errors and inconsistencies and is not sufficiently reliable.

The most serious deficiency of our definition of saving is that it overstates saving because of the absence of negative savers. This is in addition to the bias in the same direction created by the total exclusion from the sample of groups like pensioners, student families, and one-parent families, among whom negative savings should be more common. In addition to over-stating the level of saving, this shortcoming may also affect the slope of the saving function with respect to income and wealth variables. However, under Soviet conditions, discussed in the last section, these biases may be less serious than in a market economy. Due to the absence of credit and the resulting necessity to accumulate prior to dissaving, the unknown dissavers may be more evenly distributed along the entire income range, and not overconcentrated among low-income families, as is usually the case. In addition, since savings are used more often to bridge over uneven *expenditure* streams than to bridge over variations in lifetime income, fewer low-income families (compared to a typical Western sample) are temporarily in such a situation, and thus able to afford dissaving on the basis of their long-range, permanent income.[7]

Of the 1,014 families included, 526 reported positive direct saving and an additional 80 families with no direct saving were paying mortgages. Among the non-savers, only 86 had at the end of the normal year a stock of savings of R300 or more. Non-reporting dissavers most likely belong to this group.

In addition to the absence of dissavers, there is also a possibility that some non-savers did, indeed, save but failed to report it. While the interviewers were instructed to insist on getting a definite answer, they may have failed to do so in some cases. The bias created is opposite to that discussed above, but should be considered of smaller significance, since we do find a rather wide and highly significant income difference between the group of savers and nonsavers.

Income. Total income (Y) is defined as disposable family monthly income (in cash and in kind) and is divided into the following:

YO	net earnings from all places of public employment
YWP	net earnings from private employment
YPO	net incomes from unspecified private economic activities (including proceeds from renting rooms or apartments)
YF	net incomes from private agricultural plots
YT	government transfer payments (pensions, educational stipends, social security-type payments)
YG	cash gifts (or loans) from private people
YDIF	the difference between our estimate of Y and the sum of all income elements as reported by the families. This sum was revised on the basis of answers to other questions that were inconsistent with the sum. We have strong support for the supposition that much of YDIF are incomes from private sources that the respondents did not care to report on.[8]

We also define YP (= YWP + YPO + YF + YDIF) as the sum of all income earned from private sources.

Finally, in order to test the hypothesis that saving behavior may vary according to the proportion of private income (YP) in total income, the empirical analysis is also carried out using dummy variables for two subgroups: (i) families for which YP is 10 percent of their income or less —

DYP = 0; and (ii) families for which YP is in excess of 10 percent — DYP = 1.[9]

a. Average saving rates and the permanent income hypothesis

As reported in Table 3.1, the average saving rate for the entire sample is estimated at 7 percent. This rate of household saving falls within the range found in other studies of this type, although it is closer to the average for less developed countries. In his work on international comparisons of saving rates, Houthakker (1965) found that the weighted average ratio of personal saving to personal income for developed countries was 9 percent, while for under-developed countries it was 5 percent. In his study of personal saving in Asian countries, Williamson (1968) estimated the long-run MPS at 16 percent. Both studies found a significantly higher saving rate from nonlabor income, and the saving rate from labor income varied between 0 and 10 percent.[10] The mean household saving rate was calculated for a number of developed and less developed countries for the period 1955–68 and varied from a rate of 1.6 percent for Korea to 14.6 percent for Italy (Lluch *et al.*, 1977). The Soviet rate is below all the developed countries except the United Kingdom, which averaged 6.5 percent, but not significantly below saving rates out of labor income. It seems that some of the 'less developed' characteristics of the consumer sector in the Soviet Union as well as the other dampening factors discussed in the previous sections manage to keep the saving rate low. It should, however, be remembered that this is a net result and thus no judgments on the importance of individual factors, especially those that could have raised the rate, can be made. The APS estimated from our sample is almost identical to the long-run MPS derived from macro time series data by Pickersgill (1980a) for the period 1955–71, although below the rate found for the more recent period, 1965–77.

The average rate of saving for families with a high proportion of private income (there are 249 such families) is 13.36 percent, much higher than the 5.86 percent rate for those with little or no YP (765 families). This finding is clearly in line with our hypothesis, and we shall discuss it in greater detail below.

Following a method commonly used in Western studies, we classify

Table 3.1. Saving rates by educational and occupational groups

	Monthly income (rubles)	Saving rate of (percent)	Number of obser- vations
A. Education of household head			
Entire population	397.5	7.00	1,014
University degree	438.8	7.11	426
Professional secondary	388.7	6.89	187
University uncompleted	375.6	6.29	36
General secondary	370.3	6.67	174
7–9 years of school	354.8	7.68	115
Less than 7 years	325.2	6.88	76
B. Occupation of head of household			
Entire population[a]	397.9	7.02	1,009
Managers	463.9	8.18	258
Professionals	396.4	6.22	324
Technicians	384.3	7.85	56
White-collar employees	352.0	4.19	14
Service workers	377.7	10.12	80
Skilled production workers	378.4	5.87	123
Semi-skilled production workers	327.5	6.14	122
Low-skilled production workers	318.6	5.56	32

[a] Excluding five families whose heads did not work.

households by two variables correlated with permanent income: education and occupation.[11] Households are grouped into seven educational and eight occupational sub-groups, and the mean income and mean saving rate for households in each group are calculated. These are reported in Table 3.1.

If the mean income of each group contains no transitory elements, then the differences in mean income between groups represent the differences in permanent income. If the permanent income hypothesis is correct, one would

expect to observe no significant difference between the saving patterns of the
various groups. Turning to the calculations reported in Table 3.1, we see that
with only a few exceptions the saving rate for each group is clustered around
the mean ratio of 7.0 percent, and does vary positively with income.[12]

Our results provide stronger support for the permanent income hypothesis that do many Western studies using similar classifications (Mayer,
1972). As was mentioned in a previous section, this may be due to the
relatively limited amount of variation in the income of Soviet households.
Support for the permanent income hypothesis is also provided by the failure
to obtain significant coefficients for the ratio of saving to income with respect
to income in a number of regression estimates.

b. Estimating the saving function

In line 1 of Panel A in Table 3.2, we display estimates of a simple saving
function of the form

$$S = a + bY + E \tag{1}$$

where S and Y are the monthly saving and disposable income of the i-th
household and E is the error term. In line 2 we reestimate the equation
adding the dummy term (DYP) discussed above and a product term (YDYP).
The new equation to be estimated is

$$S = a + bY + a'(DPY) + b'(YDYP) + E . \tag{2}$$

The data for the entire population for the two sub-groups are presented in
Table 3.2. When the entire population is undifferentiated (line 1), we obtain
a very high (and significant) negative intercept and an estimated MPS of
0.1744. This last rate is lower than the range of rates of 0.20–0.40, which are
estimated from United States cross-section data, but higher than those
derived from time series; the MPS estimated in time series for the United
States ranges between 0.11 and 0.13. The estimated Soviet MPS is also significantly higher than the average rate of saving (estimated *from the equation*
at 8.2 percent for the average income of R391.5 per month) and from the
long-run MPSs of 7 and 10 percent estimated from time series (Pickersgill,
1980a). Thus, even if the cross-section MPS reflects the stability elements
discussed in Section 2 above, it does so only to a limited extent.

Table 3.2. Regression coefficients of estimated saving functions[a]

A.	Intercept	Y	DYP	YDYP	FS	FS·DYP	R̄²
1. S	-36.7850	0.1744					0.3246
	-10.7944	22.0892					
2. S	-18.5053	0.1154	-47.9865	0.1413			0.3814
	-4.7921	11.8825	-5.8625	8.3703			
3. S	-4.5208	0.1282	-20.3723	0.1453	-5.5480	-8.8972	0.4056
	-0.7959	12.4738	-1.7463	8.4228	-3.3025	-2.9164	

B.	Intercept	YO	YPW	YPO	YF	YDIF	YT	YG	FS	R̄²
4. S	-23.8380	0.1295	0.2903	0.1355	0.1132	0.3960	0.0819	0.0199		0.4289
	-7.1135	14.5055	14.5670	4.2441	1.1527	18.0921	2.0921	0.3827		
5. S	-4.5547	0.1439	0.2921	0.1414	0.1668	0.3912	0.1416	-0.0184	-7.3205	0.4426
	-0.9047	15.5346	14.8339	4.4818	1.7089	18.0575	3.5021	-0.3554	-0.3554	
DPY = 0 (765 observations)										
6. S	-19.4885	0.1256	-0.2731	-0.1919	0.3810	0.1791	0.0111	0.0131		0.2592
	-6.5248	15.5042	-1.2599	-0.9608	1.8736	1.0142	0.3130	0.2750		
7. S	-3.5763	0.1369	-0.3091	-0.1126	0.4788	0.1628	0.0612	-0.0185	-6.0433	0.2777
	-0.7774	16.3296	-1.4430	-0.5686	2.3704	0.9332	1.6698	-0.3877	-4.5071	
DPY = 1 (249 observations)										
8. S	-41.2773	0.1497	0.3259	0.1833	0.1174	0.4255	0.2835	0.0698		0.4607
	-3.7428	5.0644	8.8344	3.4079	0.7199	11.8607	2.4665	0.4670		
9. S	-12.7810	0.1705	0.3216	0.1816	0.1626	0.4144	0.3629	0.0138	-10.3405	0.4733
	-0.8274	5.6568	8.8116	3.4175	1.0030	11.6048	3.0861	0.0925	2.6031	

[a] Figures in small numerals are t values.

The stability hypothesis is, however, upheld when we separate families with regular public incomes from those with significant proportions of private incomes. As can be seen from line 2 of Table 3.2, when only families with little or no private income are included, the MPS falls to 0.1154, much closer to its time-series counterpart or that of the United States, and the intercept — while still significantly different from zero — is much closer to it.[13] Similarly, while in equation (1) the APS varies from 1.4 percent for income one standard deviation below average to 11 for income one standard deviation above it, in equation (2), when only families with little private income are included, the APS varies over the same income range from 3 to 8 percent. The other side of the same picture is observed in equation (2) for families with private incomes: the estimated intercept (a + DYP) is equal to −66.49 and the MPS (Y + DYP) is equal to 0.2667. Both coefficients are highly significant. This is indeed a very steep function, not different from regular cross-section equations in the market economies. The estimated intercepts and slopes for all three groups are presented in Figure 3.2, where the differences are clearly demonstrated.

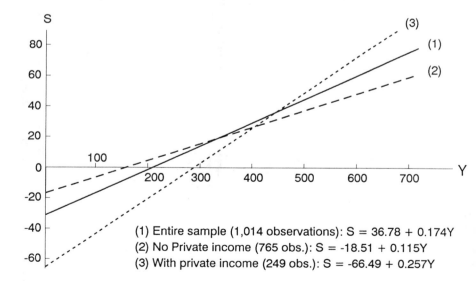

(1) Entire sample (1,014 observations): S = 36.78 + 0.174Y
(2) No Private income (765 obs.): S = -18.51 + 0.115Y
(3) With private income (249 obs.): S = -66.49 + 0.257Y

Figure 3.2. Saving functions

That saving rates vary with different types of income can also be observed from the equations estimated in Panel B of Table 3.2. Total income is broken into its components, which differ by the size of the transitory element as well as by other characteristics. The equation to be estimated is

$$S = a+B(YO)+cY(PW)+d(YF)+e(YDIF)+f(YT)+g(YG)+E . \quad (3)$$

The results for the entire population are shown in line 4 of Table 3.2, and those for the two separate groups of families in lines 6 (DYP = 0) and 8 (DYP = 1).

The most interesting result is that the MPS from components of private income are in most cases significantly higher than for earnings derived from public jobs. The MPSs for YPW and YDIF are between 30 and 40 percent as compared with 13–15 percent for YO.[14] The MPS for YPO, while only 13.5 percent in equation (4), (line 4) goes up to 18.3 percent in equation (8) (line 8). Only the MPS out of private plot incomes remains relatively low and insignificant in both equations (4) and (8). One thus observes very clearly not only the expected results due to the large transitory element in YP and its components but also an element of insurance against the risk involved in acquiring these incomes as well as a tendency to avoid conspicuous consumption.

These results support the view that the higher saving rates found for high private income families do not result merely from their higher incomes. Although, as shown in Table 3.3, such families have an average income of R488.6 per month as compared with only R367.9 for low private income families, the MPSs out of public earnings (YO) for the two groups of families are not significantly different: 0.1256 for the low YP and 0.1497 for high YP families.

We find very low and insignificant MPSs out of private transfers (YG), as should be expected, and low or average MPS out of government transfers (YT). While the first result is stable for all groups, high YP families save a lot from YT, while low YP families save very little out of that source. This dichotomy may be due to the fact that on the one hand YT is temporary (thus transitory), and on the other hand is made up of welfare payments for poor families.

Finally, it should be pointed out that equation 4 has a coefficient of

Table 3.3. Average levels of variables used in the regressions[a]

	All families	DYP = 0	DYP = 1
No. of observations	1,014	765	249
S	32.6	24.0	59.1
Y	397.6	367.9	488.6
YO	334.3	342.8	308.2
YPW	18.6	0.8	73.3
YPO	8.8	1.0	32.5
YF	2.4	0.7	7.5
YDIF	12.5	1.8	45.6
YT	13.8	13.6	14.2
YG	7.2	7.2	7.3
YP	42.3	4.3	158.9
FS	3.39	3.37	3.45
W	3,115.9	2,514.8	5,149.7
SS	2,034.2	1,524.2	3,607.5
APV	828.9	730.9	1,131.5
CAR	208.5	163.5	347.0
GARDEN	36.9	31.6	53.3
DACHA	7.4	6.5	10.1

[a]   All variables measured in current rubles. Flow variables measured in current rubles per month.

determination (R^2) of 0.43, which is higher than those of equations 1 or 2 in Panel A of Table 3.2, and is rather high for cross-section saving functions.

Theory and empirical studies have established relationships between demographic variables and the proportion of income saved. According to the life-cycle hypothesis, saving and age are related because the young and the old should dissave from income saved during mid-life years. Family size should affect saving through its effect on real per capita income. The absence of credit and the exclusion from our data of households headed by pensioners may explain our failure to establish the expected negative relation between age and saving. However, we did establish the negative relation between family size (FS) and saving as can be observed from lines 3, 5, 7, and 9 in Table 3.2.[15] In all the equations the coefficients of FS are negative and significant. In all cases adding FS into the equations significantly raises the MPS of private plot incomes and out of government transfers. In both cases there is a positive correlation between FS and the income component, and the somewhat surprising low MPSs from these sources can now be attributed to the biases created by omitting FS from the equations.

We also examined the effect of the reporting year (1972, 1973, or 1974) and of the location of the family, but found no relationship with saving.

The results presented above support our hypotheses discussed in the summary of Section 2. However, a word of caution on the direction of possible biases and errors is warranted. Two groups of observations have been included in the analysis that may bias the results. For thirty-four families, the estimated level of saving was substantially below the actual level of saving. Eighteen additional families reported saving 50 percent or more of their income. In all these cases total expenditures (including saving) were significantly higher than income, and in most of them we had good reason to suspect (on the basis of occupation) that they could have additional private sources of income. With one exception, these families also had large accumulations of savings to justify their high saving rates. In these cases we decided to include the observations but to use total expenditures as the measure of income. Both groups, 52 cases altogether, are characterized by high accumulation of saving, high saving rates, high incomes, and high proportions of private income. To the extent that the error is not in the reported level of income (as we assume) but in the level of saving, the inclusion of these observations biases the results by raising the average saving rate raising the slope (MPS) and the (negative) intercept of the saving functions. These results are indeed manifested in equations that exclude the 52 observations. For example, the average saving rate falls from 7 to 6 percent; the MPS estimated in line 1 of Table 3.2 falls from 0.1744 to 0.1090; the coefficient for YDYP (line 3) falls from 0.1453 to 0.0369, and the coefficient for YDIF (line 4) from 0.3960 to 0.2057. In all cases the coefficient of determination for equations including all observations are much higher than those without the 52 observations.

c. Saving and wealth

According to the permanent income hypothesis, consumption and wealth should be positively related. An increase in wealth, holding current income constant, will result in an increase in consumption and thus an increase in the proportion of income consumed. The empirical evidence on this proposition, derived from Western budget studies, has been mixed, many studies showing no or negative relationships between consumption and wealth (Mayer, 1972; Evans, 1969). These mixed results may be explained by the confounding of the consumption–wealth relationship by a taste variable. Some of the households with larger amounts of wealth are those who have saved in the past, and thus have a 'taste' for saving. For them, wealth is a result of high saving rates (and lower consumption rates) and wealth and saving are positively related. A negative relationship may exist when wealth comes in as a windfall (inheritance, capital gains, and the like).

In the Soviet Union at the present time, the primary source of household wealth is still past saving. As mentioned earlier, present households received little or nothing by way of inheritance, and the nature of Soviet real and financial assets precludes significant capital gains. One would then expect to observe, at least up to a certain wealth level, a negative relationship between consumption and wealth, or a positive wealth coefficient when wealth is substituted for or added to income in the savings function.

However, as wealth increases and some of the assets for which liquid wealth is accumulated are purchased, the positive relationship between saving and wealth may weaken or even turn negative. This hypothesized non-linear relationship is tested in Part A of Table 3.4 by estimating a savings function of the following form:

$$S = a + bW + cW^2 + dY + eFS$$
$$+ DYP(a' + b'W + c'W^2 + e'FS) + E . \qquad (4)$$

Wealth (W) is defined as

$$W = APV + SS + CAR + GAR + DACHA$$

where:

W	total wealth
APV	value of the equity in an apartment
SS	saving deposits + currency + 3 percent bonds at end of year
CAR	value of car (depreciated)
GARDEN	value of garden
DACHA	value of dacha.

W^2 is introduced to test for the nonlinearity in the relationship between S and W. We also add the dummy variable to test for differences between families with high and low proportions of private income.

We find a positive relationship between saving and wealth that is declining slightly as wealth grows (see lines 1–4 in Table 3.4). When wealth is included, the MPS out of income drops slightly.

Separating the population into high and low   YP   families does not produce different coefficients with respect to wealth — the coefficients of both W.DYP and W^2.DYP are very small. The results of including family size are similar to those reported in Table 3.2.

In Part B of Table 3.4 we substitute the components of wealth — as listed above — for the total, and estimate the equation for the entire population as well as its two sub-groups. Of all the wealth components, only liquid saving retains a positive (and highly significant) coefficient in the three equations. The coefficients for the material components of wealth are in some cases negative, in others positive, and in most cases not statistically significant. This result is consistent with the non-linearity hypothesis presented above: first, part of the accumulation of liquid assets is earmarked for the future purchase of a material asset — like an apartment or a car. When the goal is reached, the saving stream declines. Second, the owners of material assets are also those with larger holdings of wealth, and the positive effects of wealth on consumption may be stronger.

It is interesting to note that despite the fact that mortgage payments are included in saving and that only apartment owners pay them, the coefficient of the apartment value for the entire population is not significantly different from zero. It is positive and significant only for those with low private incomes (line 6), where mortgage payments are an important element in total savings.[16]

Table 3.4. Regression coefficients of estimated saving functions including wealth[a]

	Intercept	W	W²	Y	FS	DYP	WDYP	W²·DYP	Y·DYP	FS·DYP	R²
Dependent variable A											
1. S	13.6787	0.0066	-0.0052×10^{-6}								0.2355
	7.2482	12.6471	-3.4668								
2. S	-32.3427	0.0037	-0.0020×10^{-6}	0.1358							0.3948
	-9.8615	7.4228	-1.4339	16.3355							
3. S	-10.4177	0.0036	-0.0021×10^{-6}	0.1527	-8.3207						0.4150
	-2.1343	7.2907	-1.5897	17.6576	-5.9832						
4. S	-7.9096	0.0065	-0.0022×10^{-5}	0.0951	-4.5016	-18.2487	-0.0040	0.0021×10^{-5}	0.1433	-8.1652	0.4662
	-1.4557	8.4009	-5.2302	8.9788	-2.8183	-1.6313	-3.7051	4.6948	8.0211	-2.7992	

	Intercept	SS	APV	CAR	GARDEN	DACHA	Y	FS	R̄²
Dependent variable B									
5. S(All)	-10.0700	0.0041	0.0006	-0.0011	0.0007	-0.0160	0.1509	-7.6633	0.4354
	-2.0926	12.1875	1.0514	-0.7643	0.1888	-1.6375	17.8055	-5.5902	
6. S(DPY=0)	-3.7907	0.0043	0.0022	0.0003	0.0030	-0.0196	0.0967	4.7492	0.3508
	-0.9255	9.5759	3.7233	0.2518	0.9088	-2.1550	11.9874	-3.9317	
7. S(DPY=1)	-26.6843	0.0033	-0.0016	-0.0024	0.0001	-0.0099	0.2307	-10.5005	0.4616
	-1.7844	5.3460	-0.0663	-0.6948	0.0110	-0.3944	10.5178	-2.7930	

[a] Figures in small numerals are t values.

Finally, the exclusion of the 52 observations discussed above reduces the wealth coefficients, but otherwise the results are unchanged.

5. Conclusion

The empirical evidence does support our hypothesis that Soviet saving behavior can be explained using the same variables found to be significant in Western studies based on the permanent income and life-cycle theories of saving. Saving is a positive function of current income, and the APS is positively related to income — the situation found in nearly all Western cross-section studies. The proportion of transitory income saved is significantly higher than the proportion of permanent income saved. Finally, as in Western studies, family size and saving are negatively related.

The nature of Soviet conditions, however, affected the shape and pattern of the saving function in particular ways: the average saving rate seems to be lower than normal by international comparisons judged by the Soviet level of economic development. If only public sources of income, or families with mostly public income are considered, then the Soviet cross-section saving function is found to be much flatter than ordinary Western ones; that is, the short-run MPS is low by international comparison and much closer to the short-run APS and the long-run saving rate. But the Soviet Union has its own group of high savers in the form of earners of income from private sources, whose saving behavior is very similar to that of the self-employed or entrepreneurs elsewhere. Furthermore, if their weight in the Soviet urban sector is similar to that found in our sample, then the saving behavior of the entire urban sector is closer to the Western pattern than the observed behavior of those families earning only public incomes. We also find a positive relation between wealth and saving, which is not surprising given that wealth mostly represents the accumulation of past saving by the families in the sample.

In conclusion, the proportion of income saved found in this budget study is consistent with that found in time series studies and does not support the proposition that Soviet households save inordinately large amounts of their income for lack of consumer goods and services to purchase. The analysis is not complete enough, however, to exclude the possibility that some saving does represent a response to repressed inflation.

Notes

1. Although the vast majority of the adult Soviet population is in the labor force and has jobs in the public sector, an individual still has some choice with respect to overtime, date of entry into the labor force, and retirement. See Appendix, Table A.26, for details.
2. For a survey of Western studies on saving and consumption see Mayer (1972) and Mikesell and Zinser (1973).
3. From recent econometric work, we know that cyclical variations in Soviet output are largely connected with the fate of the harvest; see Green and Higgins (1977).
4. Less opportunity for direct investment may also be the reason one commonly observes lower saving rates out of labor income (see Houthakker, 1965).
5. See Bronson and Severin (1973), Bush (1973), and Schroeder (1975).
6. See Pickersgill (1976, 1980a).
7. Pensioners may constitute an exceptional group with respect to this proposition.
8. For more details on the derivation of the revised Y, see Chapter 2.
9. The choice of '10' percent as the dividing line was made on the basis of experimentation with other rates. The sensitivity of the results to the rate chosen is small.
10. Lower saving rates out of labor income than out of non-labor income were also found by Johnson and Chiu (1968), Friend and Taubman (1968), and Mikesell and Zinser (1973).
11. For a summary of the results of these tests using Western data see Mayer (1972).
12. The somewhat more bumpy rates among the occupational groups — especially the high rate of saving of service workers — is due to different concentrations of private income families in the various occupations.
13. In this way a and b are the intercept and MPS for families with little private income, and (a + a') and (b + b') are the corresponding coefficients for families with more private income.
14. We did not find differences between the MPS of components of YO, i.e., between earnings from the main job and from extra public jobs.

15. FS may also have captured part of the age effect, since small families concentrate in low and high aged families.

16. When savings are defined to exclude mortgage payments, the coefficient for apartment ownership becomes negative throughout.

Chapter 4
Inequality of earnings, household income and
wealth in the Soviet Union in the 1970s

1. Introduction

At least in the popular mind, socialism is about economic equality. The issue of whether or not incomes in the Soviet Union and the other members of the "socialist" bloc are distributed in a more equal fashion than in the mixed economies of the West has, therefore, been addressed by students in both the East and the West.

The scarcity of relevant data published in the Soviet Union adds to the many natural and methodological problems that any attempt at international comparison of equality must face. Raw data are completely unavailable to Western scholars, and whatever is published in Soviet scientific work is usually restricted to a very few measures of dispersion, mostly the decile ratio, and both the methodology and information about the nature of the samples that were studied are at best obscure. As it is quite clear that Soviet authorities possess that necessary information, withholding it from the public eye must be attributed to the embarrassment that publication would cause. The source of such embarrassment is not entirely clear. Wiles (1974, pp. 1–2) suggests that the main problem is that income in the Soviet Union is distributed less equally than in other East European countries, but one cannot exclude internal considerations or embarrassment on the basis of international East–West comparisons.

Soviet scholars almost unanimously claim that both wage and income distributions in the Soviet Union are much more equal than in the "capitalist" world and that historical wage and income gaps in the Soviet Union are diminishing as Soviet society becomes more homogeneous in all aspects of social life. Soviet studies demonstrating a rather marked decline in the inequality of wages since 1947 are better documented and more convincing than those related to household incomes. As wages constitute the lion's share of incomes in the Soviet Union, however, it is reasonable to assume that incomes followed the same trend. As regards inequality trends for the 1970s, and even the 1960s, there seems to be some dispute even among Soviet scholars. According to one Soviet economist, Maier, for example:

> Analysis of data that relate to the last 15–20 years shows that differentiation of incomes has not changed. And this condition is relevant not only for the total population, but also for the two main social groups, especially for kolkhozniks. (Maier, 1977, p. 51)

In 1979, however, two other Soviet scholars, Migranova and Rabkina (1979) published a different conclusion. They claimed that income inequality measured by decile ratios and relating to per capita income for the entire Soviet population had declined over the "last 15–20 years, from 4.4 to 3.3" (p. 106).

With respect to the more central question of comparison with the West, there are some Western scholars who support the Soviet claim of higher equality. Cromwell (1977, p. 305) concluded that in comparative perspective "socialism as carried out in Eastern Europe has resulted in a true 'income revolution'." If we accept the estimates presented in McAuley's (1979) very careful study, which was based on Soviet data, we must reach a similar conclusion, although somewhat less enthusiastically phrased. An extreme formulation of the opposite conclusion is Morrison's:

> Czechoslovakia excepted, Eastern European countries do not have a more egalitarian income distribution. Admittedly, Czechoslovakia is the most egalitarian of all the countries, but all the other East European countries belong in the same range of income distribution as the most advanced of the Western countries. (Morrison, 1984, pp. 126–27)

Bergson came to the same conclusion regarding the size distribution of wages:

> What emerges is a rather striking similarity in inequality between... the USSR and Western countries. Inequality in the USSR fluctuates in the course of time, but only rarely does any particular percentile ratio fall outside the range delineated by corresponding measures for Western countries. (Bergson, 1984, p. 1065)

On the comparison of income distribution, however, Bergson is a little more cautious in asserting similarities (pp. 1072–73). The careful studies by Wiles and Markowski (1971, 1972), Wiles (1974), Pryor (1973), and Chapman (1977a, 1979b, 1983), all based on Soviet data, reach conclusions not far from Bergson's.

In addition to ISIP, this chapter (as well as chapters 6 and 8) is based also on data of the Soviet Interview Project (SIP), conducted in the United States during the early 1980s. Under SIP 2,793 individuals who emigrated from the Soviet Union to the United States during the late 1970s and early 1980s were interviewed. In this survey respondents also reported retrospectively on their lives in the Soviet Union during the last normal period. In the framework of SIP, 1979 was considered the "average" last normal year and the reference year for most comparisons with Soviet data.[1]

The main goals of this chapter are: first, to analyze the degree of inequality of personal wages, household income, and wealth in the Soviet Union in 1979, as revealed by both ISIP and SIP; and to compare their main results. The second goal is to compare the results of the two surveys with patterns of wage, income, and wealth inequality that are typical for Western countries. With the help of this comparison, a third Soviet claim may be tested, namely, that wages, household income, and wealth in the Soviet "socialist" society are more equally distributed than in Western "capitalist" countries and that the gap between the two socio-economic systems is so wide that it is possible, in comparative perspective, to define what has happened in the Soviet Union as an "income revolution."

The methodology developed by ISIP has been used systematically in calculations and comparative analysis of the "raw" data of both surveys, with only a few changes that were introduced specifically to deal with the SIP sample.

The reweighting of both ISIP and SIP samples so that they will match as closely as possible the target population of the Soviet European urban population was done according to two criteria: (a) the demographic-economic character of households and (b) the educational level of their heads.[2] According to the first criterion, all households were first classified by their working status into "active" and "non-active." If any member of the family was

Table 4.1. Socio-demographic structure of households: USSR and samples

Type of household	USSR 1970[a] %	ISIP sample 1973 Number	ISIP sample 1973 %	ISIP sample 1979 Number	ISIP sample 1979 %
Total	100.0	1,688	100.0	1,980	100.0
Active	89.9	1,508	89.3	1,762	89.0
Complete	61.3	1,022	60.5	1,213	61.2
Husband and wife employed	60.1	815	48.3	892	45.0
Only husband employed		173	10.2	276	13.9
Only wife employed	1.2	34	2.0	45	2.3
Incomplete	10.7	101	6.0	225	11.4
Singles	16.3	350	20.7	324	16.4
Other	0.7	35	2.1	..	..
Non-active	11.0	180	10.7	218	11.0
Households with only husband and wife	3.6	61	3.6	70	3.5
Singles	5.5	25	1.5	110	5.6
Other	1.9	94	5.6	38	1.9

[a] Calculated structure of the urban households in the 7 European republics of the Soviet Union.

employed in the public sector, the household was considered active. Second, households were classified according to type – complete families, incomplete families, and singles – and by sex of head. Complete, active families were also classified by work status of the husband and wife. Weighting according to this criterion was done according to data provided by the 1970 census with a few marginal changes for SIP in order to take account of whatever data are available from the 1979 census.

The adjusted sample of households was subsequently reconstructed for each sex according to the distribution between workers and employees of the active population of the Soviet Union, and within each of the two work categories, by major level of education, of the same population. The reconstruction was done on the basis of the 1970 census (for ISIP) and the 1979 census (for SIP). The resulting reconstructed (weighted) original subsamples are not ideal, but are quite close to the target household and working (active) populations. Table 4.1 compares the demographic structure of both ISIP and SIP after reweighting with that of the Soviet urban population. As can be seen the fit is quite close. Both ISIP and SIP, after reweighting, are very close to that of the target Soviet population. ISIP however, has less active incomplete families and more active singles.

One way to check the improvement brought about by the reconstruction of the SIP sample is to compare the average monthly wage after reweighting with the official Soviet figures for average wages.[3] The official Soviet figure is R163 for 1979, whereas SIP reweighted figures range between R150.7 (average wage in the main place of work) and R154.5 (in the entire public sector). The relatively small remaining difference may be due to a host of reasons, including the fact that at present the weighting does not consider all possible criteria, such as age or size of city. Even so, the estimates are close enough to raise our confidence that wage differentials in the weighted sample also approximate the true differentials in the Soviet Union.

2. Inequality of wages

a. SIP results

For most adult Soviet citizens, work in the public sector is the main source of personal wages and family income. For this reason, the employment status of respondents and their spouses at the end of the last normal period of their lives in the Soviet Union must be determined, and labor-force participation by sex, age, and marital status must be calculated.

Respondents who worked at the end of the last normal period reported their gross and net wages at the main place of work in the public sector and at any additional place of work in the public sector. In addition, respondents were asked to report their net income (or wage) from any private work. The responses to these three questions were used to define the following concepts

of wages (including salaries):
1. Gross wage at the main place of work in the public sector.
2. Gross wage at the second place of work in the public sector.
3. Income from private jobs.
4. Gross public wage (1 + 2 above).
5. Total wage (1 + 2 + 3 above).

Several measures of inequality of wages are used, the coefficient of variation and the Gini coefficient, ratios between earnings at specific percentiles of the distribution (percentile ratios), and distributions of respondents by wage categories and wage deciles. Dispersion measures were chosen to facilitate comparisons with studies on the Soviet Union and on other countries.

Table 4.2 presents findings on wage dispersion in the Soviet Union in 1979 for three wage concepts: categories 1, 4 and 5 above. Only 5.3 percent of all employed respondents reported an additional job in the public sector, and, on the average, such jobs added less than R4 to the average gross wage. For these reasons the impact of extra public work on the distribution of wages is marginal. The discussion will therefore concentrate on wages at the main place of employment only.

The impact of private wages on both wage levels and distribution is more substantial, however. Of all workers, 263 (12.9 percent) reported private wages and when averaged for all workers, private wages are estimated at R21.2 per month.

When only public wages are considered (Table 4.2) it is found that the wage gap between the top and bottom two percentiles (P_{98}/P_2) is 5.75 (6.0 for all public wages); it narrows to 4.29 between the corresponding five percentile points (P_{95}/P_5) and becomes 3.33 for the decile ratio (P_{90}/P_{10}). The overall level of inequality as measured by the Gini coefficient stands at 0.244 for wages at the main place of work. Only 6.2 percent of all earners make less than R70 per month, and a similar segment of the employed make more than R275.

Who, in the Soviet Union, belongs to the group of lowest-paid workers, and who belongs to the highest-paid group? According to the SIP results, women comprise more than 80 percent of the lowest decile of wage earners,

Table 4.2. Distribution of gross wages per earner, 1979

	Wages at main work- place (1)	All wages in public sector (2)	Total wages (public and private) (3)
Mean (rubles per month)	150.7	154.5	175.7
Coefficient of variation	0.51	0.54	0.89
Gini coefficient	0.244	0.249	0.304
Ratio between wages of individual percentiles of distribution			
P_{98}/P_2	5.75	6.00	7.74
P_{95}/P_5	4.29	4.29	5.29
P_{90}/P_{10}	3.33	3.33	3.75
P_{75}/P_{25}	1.80	1.80	1.90
P_{95}/P_{50}	1.87	1.87	2.47
Mean monthly wages in given decile (rubles)			
1.	67.7	68.0	69.0
2.	83.8	84.4	86.2
3.	101.1	102.1	104.9
4.	117.1	117.8	120.4
5.	128.7	130.2	140.3
6.	147.2	147.9	150.7
7.	155.1	156.8	169.1
8.	179.1	182.8	199.9
9.	210.1	217.8	261.7
10.	312.7	324.0	442.8
10./1.	4.62	4.76	6.42

and men 80 percent of the highest decile. In the lowest decile, more than 30 percent are blue-collar workers in the service sectors, 25 percent are employees in positions that require special secondary education (technicians, nurses, and midwives, accountants, etc.), and over 10 percent are non-professional white-collar workers. This lowest decile includes a relatively small number of workers with higher education.

By contrast, over 60 percent of the highest-paid decile occupy positions that require higher education. It is interesting and important to point out that in the highest-paid decile more than 20 percent are blue-collar workers in the production sectors. This reflects the target treatment of certain highly skilled blue-collar workers in the Soviet Union, who may be called a "labor aristocracy."[4]

When we move to total wages (Table 4.2, column 3), we find much wider differentials. The Gini coefficient moves from 0.249 to 0.304, and the decile ratio from 3.33 to 3.75. In general, the impact of an additional element on the overall distribution of total wages depends on the relative importance of the segment, on the level of inequality of the distribution of the specific elements among all employed, and on the correlation between the two distributions (of the particular element and the rest). With respect to the impact of private wages, private wages are distributed in an extremely unequal fashion. Only 13 percent engage in any private work, and in some cases hourly private wages are very high. The evidence is mixed as to the correlation between wages from public and private sources. There are rather high rates of participation in private work by groups with relatively low public wages. It may well be that there is even a negative correlation between the two, and private wages may reduce inequality by compensating individuals or groups with low public wages or low participation rates (see also Chapter 2).

b. Comparison with ISIP and other studies

Thanks to the contribution of Soviet researchers Rabkina and Rimashevskaia (1972, 1978), the careful analysis and compilations by Chapman (1977a) and McAuley (1979), and the pioneering Western work on Soviet wages by Bergson (1944), we have a reasonably detailed picture of the trends in the distribution of wages in the Soviet Union from 1924 to 1970.

For the years 1968, 1972, and 1976, Rabkina and Rimashevskaia compiled and published decile ratios only (1978, p. 20). Two other Soviet researchers, Aleksandrova and Federovskaia (1984, p. 21) published decile ratios for 1981. As for Western studies, we have at our disposal only estimates based on ISIP for circa 1973 and SIP for around 1979.

Table 4.3 compares measures of dispersion of wages in 1968, based on Chapman (1977a), and in 1973 and 1979 based on ISIP and SIP. The SIP and ISIP numbers refer to wages received from main place of work in the public sector. We assume this is also so for Chapman's estimates for 1968, which are based on her interpretation of official Soviet data that were presented in the bizarre and obscure fashion of non-calibrated histograms. Given the span of 11 years, when average wages rose by more than half (see above), and the fact that the three estimates are entirely independent of each other, the similarity of results must be considered amazing. Although other possibilities exist, our inclination is to conclude: (a) that the individual SIP and ISIP estimates are quite reliable, and (b) that there were relatively small changes in the distribution of wages in the Soviet Union over the decade of the 1970s. This conclusion seems to be borne out also by Soviet decile ratio estimates (see Table 4.4). According to these data, published by different scholars, the decile ratio rose from 2.83 in 1968 to 3.4 during the mid-1970s and returned to 3.0 by 1981. Such a cycle seems to be consistent with the various wage reforms that took place during the period. With the raising of the minimum wage to R60 in 1968, Soviet wage distribution attained the highest level of equality thus far. A natural widening of gaps following the reform, and the gradual introduction of the next reform, including another increase in the minimum wage to R70, could have created the cycle of the 1970s (McAuley, 1979).

The last two columns of Table 4.3 present information on the distribution of total wages as estimated by ISIP and SIP. Both show higher levels of inequality than that of public wages, but again the results are remarkably similar.

Table 4.3. Size distribution of soviet gross monthly wages, 1968, 1973, 1979

	Wage at main work place (public sector)			Total wages (public and private)[a]	
	1968	1973	1979	1973	1979
Mean (rubles per month)	105.2	139.6	150.7	152.5	175.7
Mode (rubles per month)	77.6		150.0		150.0
Coefficient of variation		0.50	0.51	0.58	0.89
Gini coefficient		0.275	0.244	0.291	0.304
Ratios between earnings at indicated percentiles of distribution					
P_{98}/P_2		5.46	5.75	6.85	7.74
P_{95}/P_5		4.28	4.29	5.29	5.29
P_{90}/P_{10}	2.83–3.17	3.11	3.33	3.63	3.75
P_{75}/P_{25}	1.83	1.80	1.80	1.86	1.90
P_{95}/P_{50}	2.10	2.01	1.87	2.48	2.47
P_{90}/P_{50}	1.78	1.70	1.67	1.92	2.00
P_{25}/P_{50}	0.74	0.73	0.67	0.74	0.65
P_{10}/P_{50}	0.56	0.55	0.50	0.53	0.53
Ratio between averages of highest-paid and lowest-paid 10 percent	5.0	4.69	4.62	6.05	6.42

[a] Gross wages from public sector and net income from private work.

Sources: Decile ratio for 1968 (2.83) from Rabkina and Rimashevskaia (1978). All other figures for 1968 from Chapman (1977a, p. 261). Data for 1973 based on weighted ISIP sample, and data for 1979 based on weighted SIP sample.

Table 4.4. Selected percentile ratios, distribution of wage earners and salaried workers by gross earnings, USSR and Western countries

	P_{10}/P_{50}	P_{90}/P_{50}	P_{95}/P_{50}	P_{90}/P_{10}
USSR official release, "public" earnings				
1970	0.58	1.7	2.0	
1972				3.2
1976				3.4
1981				3.0
ISIP sample, 1973				
"Public" earnings	0.55	1.7	2.0	3.1
Total earnings	0.53	1.9	2.5	3.6
SIP				
"Public" earnings	0.50	1.7	2.0	3.3
Total earnings	0.53	2.0	2.5	3.8
United States				
1972	0.47	2.1	2.6	4.5
1975	0.45	1.8		4.0
Japan, 1968	0.52	1.9	2.3	3.7
United Kingdom, 1976	0.60	1.7	2.0	2.8
France				
1972				3.8
1977				3.2
Netherlands,[a] 1977				2.8

[a] Data are for full-time employment in all *private* sectors of the economy (Netherlands) and also semi-public sectors such as education (France).

Sources: USSR – P_{90}/P_{10}, 1972 and 1976 – Rabkina and Rimashevskaia (1978); 1981 – Aleksandrova and Federovskaia (1984); for 1976 – calculations based on official Soviet data made by Chapman (1979b). U.S. – Chapman (1977a, 1979b). Japan and UK – Bergson (1984). France and the Netherlands – Saunders and Marsden (1981, pp. 52, 55).

c. Comparisons with other countries

As pointed out by Bergson (1984, p. 1066), "measures of inequality of wages for different countries are apt to be less than fully comparable statistically." Nevertheless, many Western scholars still attempt to do this kind of comparison. The data in Table 4.4 present some measures of the inequality of wages for five Western countries and the Soviet Union.[5] Inequality of *public* earnings in the Soviet Union, measured by decile ratio, is much lower than in Japan (in 1968), the United States (in 1975), or France (in 1972). These results indicate that perhaps the gap between the highest and lowest wage groups, measured by P_{95}/P_5 and P_{98}/P_2 ratios, is also wider in the United States, Japan, and France than in the Soviet Union. Currently, however, we have these ratios only for the Soviet Union.

On the other hand, the Soviet ratios are similar to or even higher than those for the United Kingdom and the observations for France in 1977. When the distributions of total Soviet wages, including private wages, are considered, Soviet decile ratios clearly fall well within those for the market economies presented. It may, however, be claimed that such a comparison is unfair because there may also be side earnings in market economies that are not captured by the data presented. Finally, it must be pointed out that the comparisons presented in the table are for pretax wages. Given the very low income tax rates in the Soviet Union and its relative proportionality, as compared with higher and more progressive rates in most other countries, it is reasonable to assume that a post-income tax comparison would turn out even less impressive for the Soviet Union.[6]

Finally the cross-country comparison must take into account the level of economic development of the countries that are being compared. The degree of equality of wage distribution rises with the level of economic development, due to, among other factors, the spread of modern education into all parts of society and to a secular decline of quasi-rents for scarce skills. If this hypothesis is reasonable, then the Soviet Union must be given credit for achieving a higher degree of wage equality at a lower level of development than the other countries in the comparison. One major explanation for this achievement is no doubt the early and dynamic development of the Soviet education system at all levels and opening access to it to everybody, especially to women. The resulting rapid increase in the supply of skilled workers for the industrialization drive has allowed the Soviet Union to reduce wage differentials drastically since the late 1950s.

3. The level, structure, and size distribution of household income

a. Methodology

Soviet statisticians refer to "family" *(sem'ia)* rather than to household. "Family is understood to be a group of individuals not necessarily related by blood or marriage who share a common budget" (McAuley, 1979, p. 15). This definition of household was used by both ISIP and SIP. In ISIP, the basic unit of analysis is the household. In the framework of this unit any member aged 17 or older was asked to report on any source of personal or family income. In SIP, however, the basic unit of analysis is the individual, not the family or household. The individual respondent could be any member of a household, not necessarily its head. SIP respondents were asked a more limited number of questions concerning income than were ISIP respondents. Defining total family income and its major components has, therefore, posed certain problems of comparability.

Total income may be estimated by the declared total or by summing up the separately reported component elements. In SIP the latter includes only the respondent's gross wages from all sources and the spouse's gross wage in the main place of work. Therefore the declared total family income should by definition be equal to or greater than the sum of reported components. Due to problems of recollection and to some ambiguity as to the relevant period, this is not so in all cases. The decision was to assume that recollection of components, most related to the respondent himself, was more reliable. Thus, whenever the sum of components was higher than the declared family income, the former was used.[7]

The restricted number of questions on income in SIP also limited the investigation on equality to fewer income concepts and components than in ISIP. At one end of the spectrum we can study household income derived only from public sector wages. Here we lack only spouse's wages from a second job in the public sector and any public wages received by a third earner in the household. As both are relatively rare, distortion is minimal. At the other end, we can study the distribution of total money income, including – in addition to all the above elements of private income – wages of others and all money contributions out of the Social Consumption Fund (SCF), mostly pensions, but also other allowances.[8]

According to the results based on the SIP reweighted sub-sample, the average gross monthly money income per household in 1979 was R338.6 for the total population, and R357.7 for the active population. Comparison of these figures with the equivalent Soviet data is problematic for many reasons. First of all, data on average household income of the total population or the total urban population have not been published in the Soviet Union. Data on the average family income of state workers and employees are published by the official Soviet Central Statistical Administration, but in the following form: the total average income per employed person, which includes only two sources – the average gross wage and the total income from the Social Consumption Fund – is multiplied by the average number of employed persons in the family (or household). The Statistical Administration published four figures for 1979: (a) total average income per worker or employee – R224 per month; (b) average gross wage per employed person – R163; (c) average value of total income from social services per employed person – R61; and (d) total income per family – R400 per month (*Narkhoz*, 1980, p. 393). By simple division of the first number into the last, it is possible to arrive at the average number of persons employed per family.

The concept of total household (or family) income used in the Soviet Union includes "free" social services but does not include private income from private work (except income from private garden plots). The concept of gross money income, by definition, does not include "free" social services but does include private income from private work. To compare the results of the SIP survey with Soviet data, the following procedure was followed:

1. The value of "free" social services (R58.4 per month or 14.6 percent of total income) was excluded from the average total income calculated in the Soviet Union for families of workers or employees.[9]

2. Private income from private work was excluded from the average "actual" gross monthly income based on the reweighted SIP sub-sample.

Because SIP respondents were asked to report only their own income from private work and not that of their spouses' as well, the average actual private income of complete active households was doubled. This assumes that the relevant characteristics of the group of respondents and their spouses are approximately the same.

Table 4.5. Level and structure of average gross monthly household income for for active population in USSR and SIP weighted subsample, 1979

| | USSR | SIP sample | |
		Complete families	Complete and incomplete families
Total "actual" gross monthly income	..	390.3	375.7
Total income from private work	..	46.6	37.9
Total comparable gross monthly income	341.6	343.7	337.8
All gross wages from public sector			
Rubles	291.8	286.6	264.9
Percent[a]	85.4	83.4	78.4
Number of persons employed	1.79	1.73	1.62

[a] As percentage of comparable gross monthly income.

Source: For USSR calculations based on *Narkhoz*, 1982, pp. 383, 393.

The final results of all the considerations mentioned above are presented in Table 4.5. It was necessary to include in this table averages for two different populations – complete and incomplete families – because the definition of family (or household) used by the Soviets in their calculation is not clear. Complete families include families where both husband and wife are present. Incomplete families are one-parent families. Unrelated persons were excluded from the calculations presented in Table 4.5. The data presented in this table reveal similarities between the Soviet and SIP data for both types of family. This similarity has to be taken very cautiously due to the relatively "crude" nature of the comparison.

b. SIP findings: income inequality in the Soviet Union

Findings on the size distribution of income are presented for two populations: active households and the entire population (Table 4.6). All the estimates are for the distribution of income per household member over *all households*. We consider this distribution to be more meaningful than that of the distribution of the same income over all people, mainly because the household as a unit earns all incomes (see Kuznets, 1981).

The main link between the distribution of incomes and the distribution of wages is through the distribution of earnings from the public sector to the active population. In both cases it is the same total wage fund that is distributed, once among workers, and – through them – among their families. Starting from inequality of wages, the level of inequality per household member depends on the distribution of workers among the families, on the correlation between wages of workers in the same family, and on the distribution of family size. The two distributions will come close to each other when these additional factors behave in a uniform way or cancel each other out. If, for example, each active household has two workers with correlated wages, and the household size is also uniform, the inequality of income will not be much greater than that of wages.[10]

When inequality is measured by the Gini coefficient, dispersion of public sector rises from 0.249 to 0.324 when we move from workers to their households, which is a significant difference, but not extreme. Corresponding estimates by ISIP are 0.275 and 0.293. Given the problems in estimating income in SIP, mentioned above, there is reason to believe that the Gini coefficient of 0.324 is biased upward and that the effect of moving from workers to households is nearer the ISIP estimate of 0.293. The reason for this is that SIP household income received from the public sector does not

Table 4.6. Distribution of households by income per household member

	All earnings in public sector (1)	Total income (2)
A. Active Population, 1979		
Median (rubles per month)	81.4	100.0
Gini coefficient	0.324	0.374
Ratios between per capita income at indicated percentiles of distribution		
P_{98}/P_2	13.9	12.0
P_{95}/P_5	7.9	5.7
P_{90}/P_{10}	5.2	3.5
P_{90}/P_{50}	2.1	1.9
P_{75}/P_{25}	2.2	2.0
P_{10}/P_{30}	0.41	0.55
Lorenz statistics (income shares of given groups, %)		
Lowest 5%	2.0	1.3
Lowest 10%	2.5	3.1
Lowest 20%	6.8	7.6
Lowest 25%	9.6	10.3
Lowest 50%	32.1	26.4
Highest 5%	14.2	25.1
Highest 10%	23.7	33.0
Highest 20%	39.5	45.8
Highest 25%	46.0	51.5
Decile income groups (average per capita income in given decile; rubles)		
1.	23.5	43.9
2.	40.3	65.7
3.	53.4	78.0
4.	65.7	89.3
5.	76.6	100.5
6.	87.8	112.1
7.	100.7	130.2
8.	116.2	157.4
9.	151.6	183.4
10.	220.0	472.5
10./1.	9.4	10.8

(cont.)

Table 4.6. (cont.)

	All earnings in public sector (1)	Total income (2)
B. Total Population, 1979		
Median (rubles per month)	76.0	100.0
Gini coefficient	0.396	0.382
Ratios between per capita income at indicated percentiles of distribution		
P_{98}/P_2		12.0
P_{95}/P_5		5.8
P_{90}/P_{10}		3.8
P_{90}/P_{50}	2.1	2.0
P_{75}/P_{25}	2.8	1.97
P_{10}/P_{30}		0.53
Lorenz statistics (income shares of given groups, %)		
Lowest 5%		1.2
Lowest 10%		3.0
Lowest 20%	2.6	7.4
Lowest 25%	4.9	10.0
Lowest 50%	22.6	25.3
Highest 5%	15.6	25.3
Highest 10%	25.9	33.4
Highest 20%	42.8	46.4
Highest 25%	49.8	52.1
Decile income groups (average per capita income in given decile; rubles)		
1		41.6
2	21.7	61.4
3	41.4	75.1
4	55.5	86.3
5	69.3	98.0
6	81.0	109.1
7	95.1	125.0
8	110.7	152.1
9	140.8	182.0
10	214.5	467.9
10/1	9.9	11.2

include wages of a third or higher-order worker or second job earnings of anyone other than the respondent. This omission is relevant mostly for large families located in many cases at the lower end of the income (per household member) scale. Further support that this is so is provided by the very high and unreasonable decile ratio for public earnings per household members: 5.2 as compared with the corresponding figure of just 3.33 for public earnings per worker.[11]

Table 4.7. Distribution of households by per capita household income, different estimates

| | Non-farm active households (pretax) 1967[a] | Urban households (pre-tax) | | | |
| | | 1973 (ISIP) | | 1979 (SIP) | |
		Total	Active	Total	Active
Income share (%) of:					
Lowest 10%	4.4	3.7	3.9	3.0	3.1
Lowest 20%	10.4	8.7	9.2	7.4	7.6
Highest 20%	33.8	39.5	38.4	46.4	45.8
Highest 10%	19.9	24.5	24.0	33.4	33.0
Gini coefficient	0.229	0.305	0.293	0.382	0.374
Percentile ratios					
P_{98}/P_2		9.6	9.3	12.0	12.0
P_{95}/P_5		5.4	4.9	5.8	5.7
P_{90}/P_{10}	3.0	3.7	3.7	3.4	3.5
P_{10}/P_{50}		0.55	0.58	0.53	0.55

[a] McAuley, 1979, USSR

Sources: Incomes shares and Gini coefficient for 1967 calculated by Bergson from frequency distributions compiled by McAuley (Bergson, 1984, p. 1,070; McAuley, 1979, p. 57). Decile ratio for 1967 from McAuley, 1979, p. 57.

As we move from public earnings to total money income (still for the active population), we add, in addition to the omitted element of public earnings just mentioned, all private incomes and all money payments from SCF. We expect the first element to raise the level of inequality and the second to reduce it. As the latter is not very large for the active population, however, the combined impact is to raise the Gini coefficient from 0.324 to 0.374.

When we turn from the active population to the entire population (Table 4.6) we see first that the overall distribution of public earnings becomes less equal. The Gini coefficient rises from 0.324 to 0.396. This is the obvious result of adding 10 percent of non-earning households to the bottom of the sample. The interesting result is, however, that when private income and a very significant increment of pensions and other SCF payments are added, the distribution of income per household member is almost as equal for the entire population as for the active population alone. The meaning of this finding is that pensions and other SCF payments, and possibly also private incomes, are concentrated in the group of non-earners to a sufficient degree to assure that their addition to the population does not widen income gaps. This is definitely an achievement of the support system and of private activity. A similar finding also emerges from the ISIP estimates (see Table 4.7). What is somewhat surprising is that the Gini coefficient does not decline for the entire population when non-wage income is added. It may be an artifact of the less than full account of wages discussed above.

c. Comparison with ISIP and other studies

Information on the distribution of household income is far more scarce in the Soviet Union than are data related to the size distribution of wages. In the rare instances when some statistics do appear, the types of population, concepts of income, and the structure of the sample are not clear. For these reasons, our comparative analysis is restricted to only three sources of data: Western computations based on Soviet literature as presented by McAuley and the results of ISIP and SIP surveys. These are shown in Table 4.7.

As presented, most measures of dispersion, with the exception of the decile ratios, demonstrate a clear rise in the level of income inequality over

the period 1967–1979. However, a careful analysis of differences in methodology and biases in the data put this conclusion in some doubt. First, McAuley
himself and others pointed out that his estimates understate inequality in
1967–68. This is a conclusion reached by Bergson (1984, pp. 1068–69), among
others, on the basis of an alternative estimate by Wiles (1974) of a decile
ratio of 3.5–3.7 for 1966, which is similar to those estimated by both SIP and
ISIP for later dates. Considering McAuley's sources, mostly official Soviet
sources, it is highly likely that he was not able to take full account of private
sources of income that contribute to a higher level of inequality in the other
two samples.

Second, the rising level of inequality between ISIP (1973) and SIP
(1979) also raises some questions of comparability. There is a much stronger
impact on inequality by the group of unrelated active individuals on SIP
results than in the case of ISIP. This difference alone explains about half of
Gini differences between the two estimates, and it is unlikely that it can be
exclusively linked to time trends. More likely, the difference results from
sampling and reporting differences, one of which may be the different nature
of the two samples. A higher concentration in the SIP sample of individuals
who made a lot of money in the Soviet Union, especially through private
activities, may he explained by a greater entrepreneurial spirit of emigrants
who chose to go to the United States rather than to Israel. A similar
argument may be extended to the entire SIP sample, namely, that it includes
a higher proportion of people with higher (sometimes very high) private
incomes, another contribution to the higher level of inequality. If one adds
to this the fact that the decile ratios of ISIP are somewhat larger than those
of SIP, it becomes doubtful whether any residual is left for a trend toward
increasing inequality over the 1970s.

The last relevant piece of evidence on the issue is a pronouncement by
Soviet scholars that the decile ratio for per capita income in 1973 for the
entire Soviet population (including farm population) was 3.7 (Aleksandrova
and Federovskaia, 1984, p. 21). Since the addition of the rural population
may add about 0.2 to the ratio, the implied urban ratio comes to about 3.5,
almost exactly those for SIP and ISIP. It is hard to believe that the Soviet
estimate fully includes private incomes, which makes the estimate even more

of a surprise. It is also much higher than McAuley's similar estimate for 1968, of 3.1 (McAuley, 1979, p. 65).

Our conclusion is that there is no evidence in the data so far of a trend of declining inequality of incomes in the Soviet Union over the 1970s, as sometimes claimed by Soviet scholars. In fact, our results point to a stable distribution of income and do not rule out the possibility of rising inequality.

d. Comparison with other countries

Are incomes in the Soviet Union distributed more equally than in Western developed countries? A priori reasoning has it that indeed this should be the case, at least for public incomes of the urban European Soviet population. It goes as follows: start with a distribution of wages per worker that is as equal or even slightly more equal than in the West. The exceptionally high level of participation of women in the labor force should make wage distribution per household member even more equal. The small size of the average family and the small variance in family size that goes with it should keep the distribution of wages per household member almost as equal as that of wages per worker. Finally, considering that non-wage sources of public earnings (such as property income and the like) are almost completely absent in the Soviet Union and that the impact of SCF payments is at least similar to that for other countries, it follows that a greater degree of equality ought to be found in the Soviet Union. These considerations exclude, however, a number of factors working in the opposite direction in the Soviet Union, namely, the existence of a substantial Moslem population with demographic characteristics that tend to raise inequality, the relatively large rural sector with a similar effect, and the phenomenon of private incomes.

The SIP and ISIP data in Table 4.8 for the Soviet Union exclude the Moslem and rural populations, and some entries exclude private income. They are compared with data compiled by Sawyer (1976) and with further calculations by Bergson (1984) for Western countries. By and large, it can be stated that the 1973 ISIP estimates, with or without private incomes, are consistent with the above considerations and show a more equal distribution of income in the Soviet Union than in 6 of the 7 countries presented. The differences are significant between the Soviet Union and France, Canada and the United States, and marginal when compared with Australia, Norway, and the United Kingdom. The comparison with Sweden, on a post-tax income basis, shows obvious greater Swedish equality. However, when the Soviet 1979 SIP estimates are considered, they show a higher Gini coefficient than that of all other countries with the sole exception of France.

In both comparisons the Soviet distribution is "stronger" in terms of equality at the lower end: the lowest tenth and fifth of households receive relatively higher shares of total (per capita) income than in most countries. Even according to the 1979 estimates these shares are higher than those in France, Canada, and the United States. Although not shown in the table, McAuley's estimates for 1967 put the Soviet Union at a much more equal point than all other countries along the equality scale.

Due to the considerations given above, inequality as estimated by the SIP sample may be somewhat exaggerated. It is highly unlikely that income in the Soviet Union would be distributed as unequally as in the United States. Even so, the SIP estimate certainly brings the Soviet Union nearer to the other countries for which data are available.

A number of additional considerations qualify the comparisons as presented in Table 4.8 in different directions. First, according to Sawyer, the data related to Western countries tend to underestimate the inequality of income due to possible underreporting or entire omission of capital gains, fringe benefits, and investment and entrepreneurial income (Sawyer, 1976, p. 4). Most of these income elements are distributed rather unevenly. Their omission may justify comparisons with only public incomes in the Soviet Union. On the other hand, although there are good reasons to assume that in both SIP and ISIP there was fuller reporting of incomes, the Soviet samples exclude households that belong to the "elite" group in the Soviet Union, a group that enjoys many extra monetary and non-monetary benefits. On the basis of data assembled by Matthews (1978), Bergson estimates those perks as adding about 1.5 percent of all incomes in the upper tenth or fifth of all households (Bergson, 1984, pp. 1070–71). Such a correction may add a not insignificant degree of inequality to the Soviet estimates.

Second, there is reason to believe that free services and subsidies provided to the Soviet household by the government have a higher impact on

Table 4.8. Income shares of selected percentile groups and Gini coefficients: distribution of households by gross money income per household member (USSR and Western countries)

	Income share (%) of:				Gini coefficient	Ratio between income shares at highest and lowest deciles
	Lowest 10%	Lowest 20%	Highest 10%	Highest 20%		
Urban households (USSR, ISIP, 1973)						
Pre-tax total money income	3.7	8.7	39.5	24.5	0.305	6.6
Post-tax total money income	3.8	9.0	39.5	24.6	0.302	6.5
Post-tax money income from public sector	3.7	9.3	36.7	22.0	0.270	5.9
Urban households (USSR, SIP, 1979)						
Pre-tax total money income	3.0	7.4	46.4	33.4	0.382	11.1
All households, pre-tax						
Australia, 1966–67	3.5	8.3	41.0	25.6	0.317	7.3
Norway, 1970	3.5	8.2	39.0	23.5	0.306	6.7
France, 1970	2.0	5.8	47.2	31.8	0.398	16.3
Canada, 1972	2.2	6.2	43.6	27.8	0.363	12.6
US, 1972	1.8	5.5	44.4	28.6	0.376	15.9
All households, post-tax						
Sweden, 1972	3.5	9.3	35.2	20.5	0.254	5.9

Sources: For all Western countries, income shares form Sawyer (1976, p. 17; all Gini coefficients for Western countries computed by Bergson (1984, p. 1,070) from income shares of decile groups.

equality of total income than in most Western countries. Education and health services in the Soviet Union are almost entirely free, and there is a very substantial rent subsidy. Estimates based on ISIP for 1973 show that the overall impact of non-money SCF allowances on overall inequality, like the Gini, amounts to more than 10 percent (the Gini coefficient for the entire population declines from 0.305 to 0.260; see Chapter 5).

Third, one has to consider the impact of taxes. Unlike those in the West, Soviet income tax is very low and of limited progressivity. Most taxes are turnover taxes with different rates on different consumption goods. There is reason to believe that post-tax data for Western distributions would move them nearer to the Soviet distribution. The comparison with Sweden in Table 4.8 may also point in this direction.

Finally, Bergson brings up the point that in such comparisons some normalization for different levels of economic development must be made. Distributions are typically much less equal for countries at earlier levels of development and tend to become more equal as development progresses. Among the groups of countries represented in Table 4.8, the Soviet Union has the lowest level of gross national product (GNP) per capita, a common approximation of the level of development (see Bergson, 1984, p. 1070). Thus, normalization for this factor gives the Soviet distribution some more credit in the comparison. Part of this credit, however, is taken away because rural and Moslem populations are excluded. This exclusion is important as an offset because one of the reasons for a lower level of income inequality in less-developed countries is the higher share of rural population and the larger variance of rural household size. A small additional measure of "credit" may also be allowed to the Soviet distribution on account of its very large size, which is bound to create higher variance of conditions of life and thus incomes, compared with smaller countries of more uniform character (see Wiles, 1974).

Although the analysis is somewhat inconclusive, it is still reasonable to conclude that with normalization for level of development, income in the Soviet Union is distributed in a more equal fashion than in most Western countries. We also conclude that this holds, in all probability, even without normalization. The fact that these conclusions are not easy to demonstrate, however, testifies that the edge in equality for the Soviet Union is not very significant.

4. A note on the concentration of wealth

Under Soviet socialism the private ownership of the "means of production," that is, productive capital, is almost completely excluded. Exceptions are mostly private agricultural plots. In addition, most residential housing is also publicly owned. Accumulation of wealth is therefore limited to some private houses and cooperative apartments, private plots, household appliances and cars, valuables such as jewelry, and a limited list of financial assets – savings accounts and government bonds and cash. There is also the illegal production of capital of the "second economy." These limitations, plus the relatively short time span over which wealth could have accumulated and the rather low level of private income, must limit the extent of accumulation thus far and in the future as well. Nevertheless, both ISIP and SIP asked about wealth, and they provide one of the first opportunities to look into this aspect of equality in the Soviet Union. At this point our observations are very preliminary.

The conventional definition of wealth relates to the sum of several kinds of assets. In both our surveys, these assets include family possessions (such as houses, cooperative apartments, dachas, and cars) and family financial assets (such as savings in the bank, cash, and government bonds). The SIP survey also asked about furniture and other valuable items like jewelry. Another difference is that ISIP asked about the purchase price, whereas SIP asked about current (resale) value. Questions about liabilities, such as mortgage and money owed, were included only in ISIP. On the basis of ISIP, therefore, it is possible to calculate gross and net wealth; on the basis of SIP, only the former.

The main results concerning the size distribution of total wealth and financial assets in 1973 and 1979 are presented in Table 4.9. The results show that inequality of wealth is much greater than inequality of personal wages or income of households. The top 1 percent of the households own approximately 5–7 percent of the total sum of wealth; the top 5 percent own 23–28 percent, and the top 10 percent own more than 40 percent. At the other end, nearly half of all households under ISIP and a quarter under SIP reported no assets. The Gini coefficients for all households are 0.77 in ISIP and 0.61 in SIP.

Table 4.9. Concentration of wealth and financial assets[a] in the USSR, UK, and US (total population)

Lorenz statistics	Gross wealth (USSR)		Wealth		Financial assets (USSR)	
	ISIP 1973	SIP 1979	UK 1979	US 1972	ISIP 1973	SIP 1979
Share of given group						
Lowest 25%	0.0	0.3	..	..	0.0	0.0
Lowest 50%	0.0	8.9	..	..	0.0	5.9
Highest 1%	4.8	7.0	24.0	26.0	8.3	11.5
Highest 5%	23.4	28.7	45.0	45.0	35.8	28.6
Highest 10%	41.2	42.9	59.0	..	54.9	43.1
Highest 25%	70.7	69.5	..	..	83.0	72.8
Gini coefficient	0.77	0.61	0.74	0.76	0.83	0.64
Percentage of households with no wealth or financial assets[b]	58.0	19.0	..	..	68.0	28.0

[a] "Wealth" and "financial assets" in ISIP and SIP contain the *same* elements.
[b] Differences in the percentage of households without financial assets, 68 and 28, may be explained by "anticipation of emigration."

Source: Atkinson (1983, pp. 164, 173–74). For the UK, shares of adult population; for the US, shares of families. Gini coefficient for the US refers to 1962.

The size distribution of capital assets is more unequal than the distribution of total wealth. The top 1 percent of all households own between 8 and 11 percent of the total sum of these assets, and the top 10 percent own approximately 45–55 percent. The lowest 50 percent of households have 0–6 percent of the total sum of financial assets. The Gini coefficients are 0.83 for ISIP and 0.64 for SIP.

Table 4.9 also presents information on the distribution of wealth in Western countries. Needless to say, comparability with the Soviet data is highly problematic. Even so, there is a much higher concentration of wealth in the West among the very few rich families than in the Soviet Union. The differences between the Gini coefficients seem to be narrower, but the main reason for this is most likely that the proportion of households without wealth in the Soviet samples (at least those reporting no wealth) is much higher than in the West. In principle, current income derived from wealth should have been included as part of income and its offset on inequality already taken into account. We have seen that for both the Soviet Union and the West the inclusion of income from assets was not complete. But even if it were, the distribution of wealth itself contributes to the degree of economic inequality, in the form of economic security, attending to emergencies, and social and political status and influence. The impact of the distribution of wealth on overall economic equality depends (in addition to its own size distribution) also on its quantitative weight, relative to current incomes, and on the correlation between the distributions of income and wealth. It is very likely that, as in the West, the correlation between income and wealth in the Soviet Union is also rather high. The impact of wealth on economic inequality in the Soviet case is also weaker by comparison, for the amount of privately owned wealth relative to income is less than in the West.

5. Conclusion

Without normalization for the level of development, and also due to the large size and the heterogeneity of the Soviet Union, the findings in this chapter support the view that public income per household member is distributed among households more equally than in most advanced Western countries.

Wages per worker are also somewhat more equally distributed, but the Soviet advantage here is narrower. The incorporation of privately earned incomes draws the Soviet distribution even closer to earned incomes in the West. Normalization, however, especially for the level of development, may put the Soviet Union one step above most Western countries on the equality chart. If, indeed, after normalization, even wages are more equally distributed than in the West, then credit should be given to the historically intensive process by which the Soviet Union has raised the educational level of the labor force. It is very likely that the resulting increased supply of highly trained academics, technicians, and skilled workers made possible the significant reduction of the earnings differentials that took place in the 1950s and 1960s. According to Soviet sources, the decile ratio of wages fell between 1946 and 1967 from 7.2 to 2.8 (Rabkina and Rimashevskaia, 1978, p. 20). Further study is needed to substantiate this proposition.

A second probable explanation for the better showing of the Soviet Union is the high level of participation of (especially female) workers in the labor force. The exact effect of this factor on the size distribution of income also deserves further study, but here, too, as in the sphere of education, the Soviet Union started the process earlier than others.

A third contributing factor is the high level of demographic uniformity in household size and structure achieved in the Soviet Union, at least as far as non-Moslem populations are concerned. Variation in household size, especially in the number of children, is an important explanation for differentiation in income per capita. The hardships and economic pressures imposed on the Soviet population by the regime helped to expedite the natural process of declining fertility and household size. It also probably contributed to raising the level of income equality at a relatively early developmental stage. To the extent that these policies in the spheres of education and female participation in the labor force, plus the demographic consequences of Soviet consumption policies, may all be included as an integral component of Soviet "socialism," it deserves credit for the higher degree of equality that has been achieved. The fact is, however, that the elements that are considered the essence of socialism – that is, a higher degree of equality brought about by the elimination of property income, by better welfare programs and by given demographic and human capital conditions – have yielded only a marginal difference and that a portion of even this contribution is offset by inequality in the distribution of income derived from the second economy on the one hand and the special privileges enjoyed by the elite on the other.

Socialism was established for a number of reasons, and this is not the place for its overall evaluation. When we consider its achievement in the sphere of income equality, however, our conclusion is that it is highly doubtful whether this small advantage in equality, assuming it exists, outweighs the heavy cost that the Soviet society has been paying in terms of denial of basic freedoms, not to mention the price in terms of the level of income. When socialism was advocated, or even when it was established, its claim to greater equality was based on comparison with the more or less pure market economies. Since then, the market system has undergone drastic changes in the direction of mixed economies with a substantial degree of government intervention in the supply of public services and in income maintenance and distribution. This alternative has presented a constant challenge to Soviet socialism. It seems that in the sphere of income distribution the Soviet Union may be a slight winner, but even at that, a Pyrrhic winner.

Notes

1. A detailed description of SIP and studies based on it are included in
Millar, 1987. Many similarities and differences exist between ISIP and SIP.
The Israeli project dealt only with the economics of Soviet urban households
and was, therefore, properly termed a family budget survey. The US research
project, on the other hand, is interdisciplinary, and questions related to the
family budget comprise only a small part of the total questionnaire. From the
outset of SIP, however, the intention was to compare the results of the two
surveys. Consequently, basic questions about personal wages and household
income were included in the SIP questionnaire and, where possible, exactly
in the form of the ISIP survey.

     The surveys have similar problems, as respondents in the Israeli sample
and the vast majority in the SIP are Jews who came to the West from various
urban areas of the Soviet Union.

     While 1979 was chosen as the representative last normal year for SIP
only 47 percent of the observations reported it as their last normal year.
Another 40 percent reported the same for 1978 or 1980, but other families
had a more distant year. Since there is some change in the economic variables over time, such as wages and incomes, some of the measured variance,
indeed a small part, is due to these changes and not to cross-sectional
variance. A number of experiments were made to adjust non-1979 wages to
those of 1979, using official Soviet data on wages. The differences found were
too small to justify the arbitrary adjustment of individual wages on the basis
of group averages.

2. Reweighting for SIP was done on the basis of only 1,995 households out
of the total of 2,793, for which full information on the income of both heads
and spouses was available.

3. Similar comparisons for ISIP are discussed in chapter 1.

4. See Nove, 1982.

5. This table is a short version of a table originally prepared by Bergson, but
the part of the data relating to the Soviet Union is new and based on the
Israeli and SIP weighted samples. Also new in this table are data related to
France and the Netherlands.

6. The ISIP estimates for post-tax decile ratio of wages is 2.9 as compared with 3.1 for pre-tax wages.

7. The question on total income was: "On the average, what was the total gross income received per month by you (and all the members of your family) during the last normal year." The marginals for this question show that there are 2,749 valid cases, two cases with income equal to zero, and 44 missing cases.

8. See discussion in Chapter 1 and the Appendix (Table A.26) for the corresponding problems with ISIP.

9. According to the results of family budget surveys done in the Soviet Union, in 1980 the "free" social services were 14.6 percent of total income (*Narkhoz*, 1981, p. 383).

10. In principle, it can be even more equal. See Kuznets, 1981; Gronau, 1984.

11. The fact that the decile ratio declines sharply to 3.5 also supports the claim about the bias in the distribution of public earnings in SIP.

Chapter 5
The distributive effects of the Social Consumption Fund in the Soviet Union

1. Introduction

The Social Consumption Fund (SCF) is a Soviet term that encompasses all additions to household incomes — such as money allowances or direct services — made by the public sector that are not strictly wages. The early foundations of the term can be found in Marx's *Critique of the Gotha Program* in the form of deductions from the total value of production prior to payment of wages for two consumption purposes: (a) "for the common satisfaction of needs, such as schools, health services, etc." and (b) "funds for those unable to work, etc." (Marx, 1966, p. 14). Given the necessity, during the socialist stage, to pay workers wages that are "proportional to the labor they supply" (*ibid.*, p. 16), the SCF stands out as a major contribution to equality and to income maintenance.

In 1980 the total value of SCF payments to families of state employees was more than R130 billion — almost 70 percent of the entire net wage fund of about R188 billion.[1] Put differently, almost 40 kopecks out of every ruble (= 100 kopecks) worth of consumption a Soviet family enjoys comes from this fund. In principle, such a fund can be used as a major instrument of income policy, both as an equalizer of incomes and as a vehicle of income maintenance. One would expect this to happen in a socialist country that is forced to maintain significant wage differentials dictated by efficiency considerations. Soviet and Western analysts have different evaluations of the contribution of SCF to these two goals. These differences result, on the one hand, from the use of alternative definitions of the SCF and a variety of data-bases of different population segments and, on the other hand, from different views on what constitutes a satisfactory contribution to equality and welfare.

The main aim of this chapter is to describe and analyze the impact of the SCF transfers on incomes of the Soviet urban population, based on the ISIP. The main elements of the Soviet SCF system will be discussed, but a detailed description of the system and its regulations will not be provided. The interested reader is referred to Minkoff and Turgeon (1977), McAuley (1979), and Madison (1979). The primary emphasis is on macrodistributive effects rather than on effects of specific programs on specific segments of the population. Because of the sample used, the analysis concentrates on urban families of state employees from the European republics of the Soviet Union.

The role of SCF in Soviet income policy

The sum of the SCF and the (net) wage bill in any given year is equal to the amount of consumption households can claim and receive from the public sector.[2] Unlike in market economies, the Soviet government controls the consumption pie, and can determine how to slice it among different types of payment or service and the distribution of each payment or service to the population. Three major considerations have to be balanced in the program adopted: (a) The system of payments must have enough allocative power and built-in incentive structure so that the allocation of labor among different jobs and the level of effort exerted on the job will approach optimality. (b) The payment structure must encourage the highest possible rate of participation in the labor force. This consideration assumes special significance at the borderline between minimum wages and welfare payments, and has added weight in the Soviet Union, where the maximization of growth rates has always been the goal and where growth depends on maximum mobilization of inputs, including labor. (c) The third consideration is to increase social equality and to prevent poverty. At least in the short run, there is a conflict between efficiency (as defined by the first two considerations) and the third consideration, which clearly requires payments that are independent of wages or amount of work done. Any non-wage payment has a negative income effect on work. In addition, if the total consumption fund is fixed, as in the Soviet case, it will have a negative substitution effect because wage rates will have to go down. Both income and substitution effects are of special significance at the low-wage, poverty level, where almost any welfare payment implies a high rate of taxation imposed on those joining the work force.

Finally, any injection of equality considerations into the wage structure may weaken it as an allocative instrument.

Faced with such conflicts and committed to production and growth, the Soviets came up with a compromise that was significantly tilted toward the production goal. Their overall income policy can be summed up as follows.

a. Everybody who can work should work. In addition to social and ideological pressures, there are economic pressures because wages are set at levels that make it very difficult to support a family with one salary.

b. Involuntary unemployment is ruled out. This is a matter of principle, but also an outcome of overambitious plans and the control mechanism. It enables the state to avoid the problem of fixing the level and structure of unemployment compensation so as not to affect work incentives.

c. Non-wage monetary and other support is conditioned on work and as much as possible attached to wages. In addition to the holiday pay that the Soviets include in some of their SCF statistics, there are pensions of all kinds, sick pay, maternity leave, etc. Wherever possible, these benefits are structured to reduce work interruption. Other services, such as housing, child-care facilities, health, and recreation are generally provided through the work place on a priority basis. When these services are not proportional to wages, they can play an equalizing role — at least among wage earners. To avoid granting non-wage payments, the wage structure has also been used as an income maintenance instrument, mostly through raising the minimum wage. Such a policy has made it possible to support low-income families while at the same time raising participation rates of women. The alternative of welfare payments with low minimum wage rates would have had the opposite effect on participation rates. Furthermore, without raising the minimum wage above the sheer subsistence floor, there is no room for "pure" welfare payments.

d. Pure welfare, like child allowances and income supplements, should be used only as a last resort, and even then — very cautiously and in small amounts. Many of these programs are relatively new.

The overall outcome of these policies is that family units with high dependency rates, or who rely solely on pensions for income, make up the majority of the poor in the Soviet Union. The general response of the population to this income policy has been to work if possible, even if difficult (as in the case of mothers to infants or of pensioners), or to reduce the dependency rate by raising fewer children. The long-term costs of very low birth rates, the "demographic problem" facing the Soviet Union, and the high cost of child-care centers combined with basic welfare considerations to bring about rather late increased allowances under maternity leave and children's programs (see Lapidus-Warshofsky, 1978, Ch. 8).

Compared with money welfare payments, the Soviet Union is much more generous in providing free public services — education and health — and in heavily subsidizing basic needs like housing, public transportation, and (recently) food. In principle, education, health, and rental housing are allocated according to need on a universal basis to all, but as noted some of them accrue in greater measure to workers, especially workers in priority industries. With the exception of the food subsidy, the ability to pay is not a factor in determining the amount received. All fall under the principle of providing basic services to the population on an equal basis at low cost. Education and health also have direct productivity implications as well as long-run income equalization effects.

A full discussion of the equalization potential of SCF payments beyond the degree of equality embodied in the wage structure is presented below. It must be obvious from the above analysis that the SCF system is not intended only to promote equality: a large part of it is linked to wages, and most other parts are distributed on a universal basis and without income tests. It will be shown how well SCF deals with poverty.

2. The SCF in 1973 official data and immigrant samples

According to the official definition, the SCF includes free educational and health services, money payments and allowances for vacation, pensions, educational stipends, sick leave, maternity leave, children's and income supplementary allowances, and a list of subsidized services: rental housing, extracurricular activities for children, vacation homes, etc. (*Narkhoz*, 1980, p. 381). McAuley (1979, p. 262) points out that holiday pay is probably included as a transfer rather than as a part of wages because it is not strictly a

Table 5.1. SCF allowances: official data and sample, 1973

	Soviet official data				Immigrant sample data		
	Rubles (billions)		Rubles per month[c]		Rubles (billions)	Rubles per month	
	Total	State employees[a]	Per employee	Per capita	Total	Per employee	Per capita
	(1)	(2)	(3)	(4)	(5)	(6)	(7)
1. SCF total A[b]	93.0	81.0	69.3	33.0	87.7*–93.5[d]	64.4	40.2
2. SCF total B	78.0	66.0	56.4	27.0	68.5	48.0	30.0
3. Money transfers	40.5	34.6	29.6	14.2	38.1	28.0	17.5
4. Holiday pay	10.8	9.2	7.9	3.8	10.0*	8.5	5.3
5. Pensions	20.8	17.7	15.1	7.2	19.1	12.5	7.8
6. Allowances	7.0	6.0	5.1	2.5	7.9	6.3	3.9
7. Sick leave	4.3	3.7	3.2	1.5	5.4*	4.6	2.9
8. Others[e]	2.7	2.3	2.0	1.0	2.5	1.7	1.0
9. Stipends	1.9	1.7	1.5	0.7	1.1	0.7	0.4
10. Non-money transfers	52.5	46.5	39.8	19.0	49.6*–55.4	36.4	22.7
11. Subsidies[f]	20.1	20.1	17.2	8.2	29.7*–35.5	23.3	14.5
12. Housing	4.4	4.4	3.8	1.8	10.5	6.9	4.3
13. Food	15.0	15.0	12.8	6.1	19.2*–25.0	16.4	10.2
14. Others[g]	0.7	0.7	0.6	0.3	..	..	..
15. Free services	32.4	26.4	22.6	10.8	19.9	13.1	8.1
16. Education	21.0	17.1	14.6	7.0	12.0	7.9	4.9
17. Health	11.4	9.3	8.0	3.8	7.9	5.2	3.2

[a] Column 2 is derived by assuming that state employees receive the following shares of the total: lines 4, 5, 7, 8, 9,10: 85 percent; lines 12, 13, 14: 100 percent; lines 16, 17: 81.5 percent.

[b] A includes all items; B excludes food subsidies.

[c] Calculations of figures in columns 3, 4, and 5 are based on 97,466,000 state employees and 203.6 million people in the families of state employees.

[d] All figures with asterisks are based on per employee figures; all others are based on per capita figures. Aggregate figures are sometimes mixes of both calculations.

[e] Maternity pay, children allowances, and other.

[f] Exclude subsidies to education, which are included under free services.

[g] Probably a mix of free and subsidized items.

payment for work done. Excluded from the Soviet definition are food subsidies, which have been growing very rapidly, and several other transfers and subsidies. Since data on food subsidies are available, they are included in Table 5.1 as part of the official data on SCF (Treml, 1978; Kraeger, 1974).

Table 5.1 compares official Soviet data on SCF for state employees with data derived from our immigrant sample made up of state employees and their families. The first four columns contain the official Soviet information on SCF. Column 1 relates to the entire population, and column 2 to state employees and their families (including retired state employees). The figures in column 2 were derived by guesstimating the probably shares of state employees in each SCF component, taking into account their share in the population and the nature of the program. The share of total SCF going to state employees was made consistent with available Soviet data (see notes to Table 5.1). The figures in column 2 are then calculated per employee and per capita for the population of state employees (columns 3 and 4).

The correspondence between the restructured sample and the target population is in general quite good, but differences remain that will be noted when relevant.

Returning to Table 5.1, let us outline the methods and assumptions used in estimating the sample data on SCF expenditures (columns 5–7).

a. The survey data relate to a range of years around 1973 — mostly 1972–74; therefore they are compared with Soviet data for 1973.

b. All the data on money transfers (lines 3–9) are presented as reported by the families after the adjustment of reweighting.

c. Data on non-money transfers (lines 10–17) are usually calculated on the basis on information given by the families on the extent of use of the services and information from Soviet or Western sources on the cost involved in supplying each service and the extent of the subsidy. In many cases information on the use of a service is available only for the group of 1,016 two-parent families, so that figures for the rest of the sample had to be estimated by indirect methods. For example, estimates of consumption of meat and dairy products for the rest of the sample were derived on the basis of their reported incomes, using consumption patterns of the main sample. The value of education services received were calculated by multiplying costs given in

Soviet sources by the number of children attending various types of schools or institutions. The education figure includes some of the subsidized services which the Soviets include under a different category ("other" in the table). It does not include the value of extracurricular youth activities. The value of the rent subsidy was calculated by multiplying the rent actually paid by two — the average rate of public support grants (*Potrebnosti*, 1979, p. 110). The food subsidy is for dairy products and meat only. It was calculated as the product of purchases in government and cooperative stores and the rate of subsidy as given by Soviet sources. The sample survey does not have good data from which to determine the value of health services received. It was therefore assumed that each family received the per capita level of services as reported by Soviet sources, proportional to the number of days its adult members spent in hospital during the year of the report.

d. The sample survey data are first determined on a per capita and per employee basis, and then a total annual figure is calculated by multiplying each SCF element by the number of state employees *or* the number of members of families of state employees. The total sum of each element is different when calculated by the alternative methods because the number of people per employee in the sample population differs from that in the real Soviet population of state employees. The ratio of population to state employees in the real population is 2.09 and in the adjusted sample population — 1.60. This happened, despite the adjustments, for two reasons: (a) while the two populations have the same proportion of active households, the sample population has more workers per household; (b) there are differences between the European-urban target population and that of families of all state employees (the latter includes rural families and families from the Asian republics, both of which have higher dependency rates). One way to get the Soviet total from the sample data is to use the per-employee figure when the payment is made to employees or when it depends on the family's income, as in the case of food subsidies. In doing this we correct for the higher income of the sample families resulting from more employees per capita. In all other cases per capita figures are used.

Despite these methodological problems, the comparisons of the Soviet and the sample SCF figures produce very reasonable results — that is, the sample estimates are not out of line. Among the cash payments, the sample estimates for pensions, holiday pay, and sick leave are higher than our estimates of the official figures. The first is due to the higher proportion of employees in the sample population, and the other two to the fact that even after reweighting the sample wages are still somewhat higher than in the target population. Other allowances are similar by both estimates, and stipends are lower in the sample, probably because of the absence from the sample of students living alone.

Total monthly cash transfers, including holiday pay, are estimated by the sample at R17.5 per capita and at R28.0 per employee, compared with the official Soviet figures of 14.2 and 29.6, respectively. The 1973 cash part of SCF allocated to state employees is about R34.6 billion according to official sources and R38.1 billion as estimated from the sample data. (Without holiday pay the figures are R25.4 and R28.1 billion, respectively.)

In the categories of free and subsidized services, the official and sample estimates for health services are similar, but the sample estimate for education is significantly lower. We were unable to estimate the value of some activities in education, but that explains only part of the difference. On the other hand, the sample estimates of food and housing subsidies are much higher than those derived from Soviet sources (housing) or Western estimates (food). These differences may be due in part to the higher incomes of the sample families and to their concentration in major cities, where the housing subsidies are higher and more meat products are bought in government stores at prices below those in the collective farm markets. Because the difference in food subsidies is so great when the sample estimate is calculated on the basis of per capita figures we also provide an estimate based on per employee figures as a possible alternative. Thus, depending on which method is used for estimating the food subsidy, the annual non-cash SCF estimated from the sample data is R49.6–55.4 billion compared with the official Soviet figure of R46.5 billion.

Finally, the per capita estimate for the total SCF based on the sample data is R40.2 per month compared with R33 according to the official figures; the corresponding figures per employee are 64.4 and 69.3 rubles, respectively. The total 1973 SCF allowance for state employees is estimated from the sample data at R87.7–93.5 billion compared to the "officially" reported total of R81 billion.

The purpose of this rather tedious exercise was to give credibility to the sample estimates of the SCF. This accomplished, we can move on to examine how the various SCF elements are distributed according to levels of income.

3. Distribution of SCF allowances by work status and income groups

The estimates presented in this section are mostly for two populations: the entire sample population (adjusted to resemble the Soviet European-urban population), and the "active" population, a sub-section of the sample comprising all households with heads working in the public sector. A weighting system was also applied to this sub-sample to make it very similar in its main characteristics to its Soviet counterpart. In this section we examine the distribution of SCF allowances across a range of incomes where the basic ordering criterion used is public-sector earnings per household member. Public earnings (rather than total income) were used as the ordering income criterion to emphasize the impact of SCF on the distribution of income generated by public net earnings. Since this is the distribution that the authorities most likely consider when they plan any intervention, private incomes were also excluded. In all the following tables, *per capita* earnings are used rather than household incomes, despite the fact that the distribution is for *entire households*. Per capita income represents better than total household income the real economic position of the family. When public earnings are the ordering criterion, all non-active families fall by definition to the bottom of the distribution. There are 180 such families in the sample who make up almost exactly the lowest decile of the total population (169). In Table 5.2 we present data on the household characteristics and SCF distribution by work status for the entire sample population and two sub-sections: active and non-active populations. In Table 5.3 we present similar data for the active population only by income deciles.

Table 5.2 provides data on the relative size of the SCF compared with the total public wage bill. Even without holiday pay, SCF comprises about one third of all public-sector transfers to households; with holiday pay, SCF

Table 5.2. Household characteristics, SCF allowances and income by population groups

	Entire population		Active population		Non-active population	
	(1)	(2)	(3)	(4)	(5)	(6)
1. Number of households	1,688		1,508		180	
2. Household members	2.53		2.66		1.42	
3. Earners	1.58		1.77		0.02	
4. Children	0.48		0.54		..	
5. Age of head (years)	45.1		42.6		66.2	
Income categories (per month)	R	%	R	%	R	%
7. Public income	285.1	100.0	303.7	100.0	129.7	100.0
8. Public earnings	196.8	69.0	220.2	72.5	1.5	1.2
9. Holiday pay	13.5	4.7	15.1	5.0	0.4	..
10. SCF (total)	88.3	31.0	83.5	27.5	128.2	98.8
11. Money payments	30.8	10.8	24.7	8.1	82.3	63.4
12. Retirement pension	14.3	5.0	6.4	2.1	80.8	62.3
13. Non-money income	57.5	20.2	58.8	19.4	45.9	35.4
14. Subsidies	40.4	14.2	40.5	13.3	39.6	30.5
15. Education	3.5	1.2	4.0	1.3	..	..
16. Housing	10.9	3.8	10.6	3.5	13.5	10.4
17. Food	25.9	9.1	25.9	8.5	26.1	20.1
18. Free services	17.1	6.0	18.3	6.0	6.3	4.9
19. Education	8.9	3.1	9.9	3.2	..	..
20. Health	8.2	2.9	8.4	2.8	6.3	4.9
Reference (per month)						
21. Public money income (8 + 11)	227.6	79.8	244.9	80.6	93.7	64.5
22. Private income	43.4	15.2	45.1	14.9	27.6	21.3
23. SCF including holiday pay (9 + 10)	101.8	35.7	98.6	32.5	128.6	98.8

reaches 36 percent, compared to 64 percent in the form of wages. SCF clearly has significant potential for affecting the levels of income equality and poverty. The most important aspect of Table 5.2 is the comparison of SCF allowances between active and non-active households. The different characteristics of the two groups of households are readily apparent. Non-active households are smaller, with many singles and couples, virtually all of whom are retired; only the levels of education of the two groups are similar. Correspondingly, the levels and structures of incomes of the two groups, including incomes from SCF, are different. By definition, virtually all the public income of non-active households comes from SCF. Of the total of R128 per household per month, almost two-thirds come from retirement pensions and the remaining third is mostly in the form of food and housing subsidies and free health services.

Active families receive less from SCF overall, but still get R83.5 per month (R98.6 including holiday pay) — about two-thirds the amount received by non-active households. Obviously, most of this support comes in the form of subsidies and free services, including education, and much less in the form of money transfers. Money transfers are concentrated in work-related payments such as holiday and sick pay, and to a lesser extent in children-related transfers — stipends and various child allowances. While it is clear that SCF narrows the income gap between the two groups, it is interesting to note that only 13.4 percent of all SCF transfers go to the non-active population — just slightly above its share of the entire household population. (On a per capita basis, however, the equalization impact is much stronger.) We discuss distributive effects in greater detail below.

Turning to the active population, Table 5.3 shows the two primary sources of differentiation among the income deciles: household characteristics and earning capabilities (see Kuznets, 1982, p. 697). Families in higher deciles are generally smaller, and while the number of earners per household starts to go down past the sixth decile, the number of earners per household *member* rises throughout and the dependency rate declines. The negative association between income per capita and family size causes income inequality to be wider for income per capita as compared with income per household. In addition to the demographic factors, income differentials are also increased by differences in earning capacity as manifested here by the strong association between the level of education of the family head and the rank of the income decile.

The main elements of the distribution of SCF transfers among households at different deciles are the following:

a. Without holiday pay, total SCF per household declines from close to R100 in the lower deciles to about R75 in the top deciles (line 9). With holiday pay, however, the absolute difference narrows to R105–108 at the bottom to almost R100 at the top decile. Under both definitions, however, the relative importance of SCF in total public income declines as the decile rank rises. SCF makes up half the public income of households in the lowest decile, but only 18.5 percent for households in the top decile (with holiday pay the proportions are 54 and 24 percent respectively).

b. Money transfers per household (without holiday pay) are the most progressive elements of SCF. They decline over the income range from R37.8 in the lowest decile to R19.2 in the top decile and from 19.3 to 4.8 percent of public income. This progressivity is made up by an interplay of the various allowances included. While pensions are concentrated in the bottom decile and then rise from very low levels in lower deciles to a high level in the top decile, sick pay allowances increase and then decline, while other transfers are very progressive. In each case the pattern is determined by the number of recipients of a specific allowance and by the size of the allowance. There are relatively more receivers of pensions in the lowest decile, but a few high individual pensions increase their relative importance for the top decile. More sick people are concentrated among the lower deciles, but the rate of sick pay is higher for those with high earnings. Stipends for higher education are available to families with children from the lower deciles, but children from higher income families are more likely to attend universities. Holiday pay, which rises at a faster rate than earnings, is the only SCF element in public income (if included) that is regressive. It contributes 3.4 percent to the income of families in the bottom decile, but 5.8 percent to the highest incomes.

c. Non-monetary subsidies and services as a whole decline only very moderately as income rises. The bottom decile receives R61.5 per month, and

Table 5.3. SCF allowances and services per household in active population, by decile

| | Deciles of households[a] | | | | | | | | | | | |
| | Low 1 | | 2 | | 4 | | 6 | | 9 | | High 10 | |
	R	%	R	%	R	%	R	%	R	%	R	%
1. Household members	3.14		3.28		2.93		2.89		2.28		1.75	
2. Earners	1.31		1.78		1.94		1.95		1.86		1.49	
3. Children	0.89		0.76		0.72		0.66		0.33		0.23	
4. Age of head (years)	50.6		43.7		44.6		41.9		44.9		42.8	
5. Education of head (years)	7.6		8.6		8.1		10.0		11.3		12.6	
Income categories												
6. Public income	195.4	100.0	256.3	100.0	292.6	100.0	332.2	100.0	374.8	100.0	402.2	100.0
7. Public earnings	96.0	49.1	158.6	61.9	200.1	68.4	251.1	74.2	300.7	80.2	327.8	81.5
8. Holiday pay	6.6	3.4	11.2	4.4	12.6	4.3	17.3	5.1	23.7	6.3	23.5	5.8
9. SCF (total)	99.4	50.9	97.7	38.1	92.5	31.6	87.1	25.8	74.1	19.8	74.4	18.5
10. Money payments	37.8	19.3	37.4	14.6	27.8	9.5	25.2	7.5	18.7	4.9	19.2	4.8
11. Retirement pension	20.8	10.6	3.8	1.5	1.6	0.5	9.4	2.8	7.3	1.9	17.3	4.3
12. Non-monetary services[b]	61.5	31.5	60.4	23.6	64.7	22.1	61.9	18.3	55.4	14.8	55.3	13.7
13. Education	17.6	9.0	17.2	6.7	18.1	6.2	17.5	5.2	8.1	2.1	7.6	1.8
14. Health	8.5	4.3	10.5	4.1	9.1	3.1	8.5	2.5	8.2	2.2	6.1	1.5
15. Housing subsidy	13.4	6.9	9.2	3.6	10.1	3.5	9.9	2.9	12.5	3.3	11.6	2.9
16. Food subsidy	22.0	11.3	23.5	9.2	27.4	9.4	26.0	7.7	26.6	7.1	30.0	7.5
Reference (per month)												
17. Public money income (6 + 10)	133.8	68.5	196.0	76.5	227.9	77.9	276.4	81.7	319.4	85.2	347.0	86.3
18. Private income	115.1	58.9	39.6	15.5	56.5	19.3	30.9	9.1	41.9	11.2	29.7	7.4

[a] Deciles are defined by monthly public earnings per household member (see text).
[b] Part in the form of subsidy, part as free services (see Table 5.2). Stipends are included under money transfers.

the next several deciles receive almost that much or more. Only for the top two deciles do the allowances decline — to about R55. The progressiveness of these allowances is maintained, however: they make up almost one-third of the incomes of the lowest decile, but only 13.7 percent of incomes for the highest decile. The outcome is a result of varying tendencies among the different elements. The most progressive element is the support for education (excluding university stipends) and the progressivity is determined mostly by the fact that poorer families tend to have more children. (When stipends are included, the progressivity declines only slightly.) It should be noted that the absolute amount of the allowance for education starts to decline only after the sixth decile, despite a consistent decline in the number of children per household, implying that the allowance per child is rising with income at that point.

Health services and housing subsidies are fairly constant per family at all income levels. Only the top decile receives less than the average in health services, due mostly to the smaller household size. At the lower income end, smaller household size is "compensated" for by higher use of medical services due to older age. Health services are thus distributed progressively.

Subsidies for housing show somewhat higher support at the bottom and top income levels. The distribution of residential apartments for rent is managed by government and municipal agencies and family size is a major formal criterion governing it. The somewhat higher subsidy for non-active families may reflect historical needs — i.e., when their families were larger. The higher subsidy for the lowest decile of families is probably due to their larger families, but the higher subsidy to the top decile families is less easily explained. Not only are they smaller families, but also a higher proportion among them own cooperative apartments, which we assume are not subsidized. If the estimate is correct, it may point to a preference in practice in the wrong direction.[3] Even so, housing subsidies are distributed in a progressive manner.

The general principle that more affluent families with higher consumption levels receive larger amounts of consumption subsidies is true also in the Soviet Union. Among active families, based on their own reports, those in the lowest decile receive R22 per month in food subsidies, while families in the

Table 5.4. SCF allowances and services per household member by decile groups in entire and active populations (Rubles)

| | Deciles of household members[a] | | | | | | | | | | | |
| | Entire population | | | | | | Active population | | | | | |
	1	2	3	5	9	10	1	2	4	6	9	10
1. Public income	97.8	72.1	80.3	116.5	167.1	249.2	72.6	79.5	109.6	120.8	172.0	258.2
2. Public earnings	..	31.6	50.0	71.4	128.5	199.9	31.2	48.4	68.1	87.0	134.1	206.3
3. Holiday pay	..	2.1	3.5	4.8	9.8	13.1	2.1	3.4	4.3	6.0	10.4	13.4
4. SCF (total)	97.8	40.5	30.3	45.1	38.6	49.3	41.4	31.1	41.5	33.8	37.9	52.0
5. Money payments	62.4	17.7	11.6	17.6	8.3	13.2	18.2	12.4	17.3	11.5	8.9	13.1
6. Retirement pensions	57.3	11.0	1.2	1.1	3.2	4.8	11.4	1.3	0.3	5.9	2.4	5.4
7. Non-money payments	35.4	22.8	18.7	27.5	30.4	36.0	23.2	18.6	24.2	22.3	29.0	39.0
8. Education[b]	..	4.6	4.3	4.8	2.5	2.2	4.5	4.6	5.2	5.5	2.5	2.2
9. Health	4.3	2.9	3.4	3.1	4.0	3.7	2.9	3.4	3.3	3.1	4.1	3.7
10. Housing subsidy	10.2	5.3	3.0	4.3	7.5	8.1	5.5	3.0	3.3	3.4	7.2	9.0
11. Food subsidy	20.9	10.0	7.9	13.7	16.4	22.1	10.3	7.6	12.4	10.3	15.2	24.1

[a] Deciles are defined by monthly public earnings per household member.

[b] Part is subsidy and part is free services (cf. Table 5.2).

highest decile get R30. As we shall see, the gap is even wider on a per capita basis (Table 5.4). The inequality would be greater but for the relatively large purchases of meat by affluent families in the unsubsidized, collective farm markets. The only exception to this general pattern is the food subsidy received by the non-active segment of the population (see Table 5.2), which is higher per household (and even more so per capita) than the subsidy for the higher deciles in the active population. This may reflect the better ability of non-active people to purchase subsidized items in government stores by having more time to wait in lines and screen more stores. Even so, the distribution of food subsidies to households is still progressive. These subsidies contribute 20.3 and 11.3 percent respectively to the incomes of the bottom non-active and active deciles, compared with 7.5 percent to the income of the top decile.

So far attention has been focused on SCF allowances per household. But, as noted earlier, because lower income households are typically larger, a higher allowance per household need not mean a higher allowance per household member. (This distinction is important only when *absolute* size allowances are discussed, since the *relative* importance of any transfer to income is the same whether total income or per capita income is considered as long as the ordering of the families is unchanged.) The data for allowances per household member for the entire and the active population are presented in Table 5.4. Note that for a number of categories, with some exceptions in the non-active decile, absolute SCF allowances per household member are larger for the rich than for the poor. Thus, while total SCF transfers (holiday pay excluded) are at least twice as high per non-active member as for any active member, they are higher for members of top income active households than for lower income active households. The top decile members receive R49.3 per month as compared with R40.5 for the second decile members or R30.3 for third decile members. When holiday pay (where transfers per member rise steeply with income) is added to the SCF total, the advantage of the rich increases significantly. In non-money transfers, top income members receive not only as much as the corresponding non-active decile, but much more than members of active households with lower incomes. The only SCF category that gives more to the poor, active or non-active, on a per capita basis is total money transfers. But even here, the rise of sick pay is partly due to increasing support with income, starting from the third decile. The positive association between support per capita and income levels underlines one aspect of the Soviet support system noted above: it is tied very strongly to earnings and levels of consumption and is not attentive enough to family size.

4. The effect of SCF on poverty and income distribution

The two main distributional motivations behind the provision of SCF are (a) to assure a minimum level of income and of specific services to poor families and (b) to intervene in the distribution of income in the direction of greater equality. While the two goals are complementary, the first affects primarily the lower deciles of the population while the second can affect everyone.

The degree to which SCF in the Soviet Union is directed toward the poor is reflected in Tables 5.5 and 5.6, which provide data on overall income and SCF distribution in the Soviet Union. Among other things, Table 5.5 shows how SCF transfers help to reduce the number of poor families, while Table 5.6 shows what proportions of the total SCF and its different elements are devoted to the various income groups. (For a definition of who is poor and what is the poverty line, see Chapter 6.)

It is interesting to note that while more than half the potentially poor by official Soviet standards are pushed out of poverty by SCF money transfers, only about one-fifth of those with earnings below R75 per household member are pushed above that level by such transfers. A major part of the push above the poverty line, especially the R50 line, is provided by retirement pensions, but other money transfers also play a role.

On the basis of the crude calculation that non-money SCF transfers to the poor are about R25 per capita, Table 5.5 provides data for estimating the proportion of poor households remaining after all SCF is accounted for. For the entire population, the proportion is 39 percent (all with *total* public income of up to R100), and for the active population it is 37.5 percent, higher proportions than those calculated before. In the same way it can be observed (by comparing relevant figures in lines 1 and 5 on the one hand and lines 4 and 8 on the other) that the impact of SCF transfers in reducing poverty according to this definition is even smaller than that calculated above.

We have shown elsewhere (Chapter 4) that the proportion of poor estimated from the sample may be somewhat too low for the target population. On the other hand, the above calculations are based on public income only and disregard all private sources of income. Our estimate of private income is much higher than the Soviet government's, but even in official Soviet statistics there is some private income from private agricultural plots and other sources (*Narkhoz*, 1973, p. 632). Since the two biases are in opposing directions, we can ignore this issue here. But even if a small distortion remains, the composition of the poor as estimated from the sample is close to the mark for the Soviet European-urban population. We have previously shown (in Chapters 4 and 6) that almost half of all the poor are retired units, and nearly a quarter of them are working-age, one-parent (woman) families. Put differently, while constituting only 8.4 percent of the households, the poor include 30 percent of all retired people, 20 percent of all one-parent families, but only 3.4 percent of two-parent, active families. A higher than proportional share of children is found only in the next income group of per capita income (R50–75 per month). So while the SCF payment in 1973 did allow about 14 percent of all households to move from the lowest income bracket (up to R50) to the next higher one, there were still 10–15 percent of urban families who lived below this level and who were getting SCF cash payments from the government of no more than R12.4 per capita monthly (not including holiday pay for employees). This reflects both the low level of pensions and an unwillingness to provide enough support to units with high dependency ratios (see Chapter 4; McAuley, 1979, Chapters 4, 11, 12).

Turning to Table 5.6, we can see that of the total SCF received by the entire population (again not including holiday pay), the lowest decile of households received just over 15 percent of the funds and the lowest quintile just over a quarter — i.e., 50 percent and 25 percent more than their respective proportions in the population. On the other hand, the top quintile received 17 percent and the top decile 8.1 percent of all funds — slightly below their respective population shares. When only the active population is

Table 5.5. Distribution of households by income per household member (percent)

	Income bracket (rubles)[a]					
	0–50	51–75	76–100	101–125	126–150	150+
Entire population						
1. Public earnings	26.1	20.9	27.0	10.5	7.9	7.7
2. Public money income	11.0	26.2	27.5	14.4	7.9	12.9
3. Public money income and subsidies	4.3	12.4	27.4	21.1	13.9	21.0
4. Total public income	2.8	9.6	26.6	21.6	15.8	23.6
Active population						
5. Public earnings	17.4	23.3	30.2	11.7	8.8	8.6
6. Public money income	8.4	24.5	28.9	14.9	8.8	14.5
7. Public money income and subsidies	4.0	11.0	27.4	20.5	14.2	22.8
8. Total public income	2.8	8.0	26.7	20.8	16.3	25.5

[a] According to money income categories.

Table 5.6. Percentage distribution of SCF among groups of households

	Households belonging to percentile group[a]									
	Entire population					Active population				
	Lowest			Highest		Lowest			Highest	
	10%	20%	50%	20%	10%	10%	20%	50%	20%	10%
1. All SCF	15.2	25.8	56.8	17.1	8.1	12.0	23.6	54.0	17.6	8.7
2. Money allowances[b]	27.9	39.4	66.7	12.8	6.5	15.4	30.4	59.0	15.2	7.6
3. Subsidies and free services	8.3	18.5	51.4	19.4	8.9	10.5	20.7	51.5	18.8	9.4
4. Subsidies	10.2	19.2	50.7	20.7	9.4	9.7	19.2	49.5	20.5	10.2
5. Education	..	9.2	51.2	8.8	1.4	8.6	17.6	48.3	21.7	11.4
6. Health	12.9	24.3	52.7	21.9	9.4	12.7	21.3	49.6	22.5	10.7
7. Food	10.5	18.5	49.7	21.8	10.5	8.6	17.6	48.3	21.7	11.4
8. Free services	3.8	16.5	53.2	16.2	7.7	12.3	24.0	57.3	14.6	7.0
9. Education	..	15.3	55.1	14.3	7.8	14.2	25.4	60.1	12.6	6.9
10. Health	8.0	17.9	51.4	18.2	7.7	10.1	22.5	54.0	17.0	7.2
11. Holiday pay	..	2.3	28.3	32.4	17.0	4.2	11.5	37.5	29.4	14.9
12. Percent population	5.6	18.0	53.1	16.0	7.2	11.8	24.1	55.9	15.2	6.6

[a] According to public earnings.
[b] Excluding holiday pay.

considered, the preference given to the low-income households is even smaller.

In line 12 of Table 5.6 there are data on the distribution of the population across the household deciles which enable us to evaluate the distribution of SCF on a per capita basis. In only one instance — the two lowest deciles of the entire population — does SCF distribution significantly reflect more attention to the poor on a per capita basis. Here a quarter of the total SCF fund is devoted to only 18 percent of the population and 15.2 percent of the fund to the poorest 5.6 percent. In all other cases the per capita distribution points to a lack of attention to the poor and to equity considerations in general. Thus the poorest 24.1 percent of members of active households receive less than their proportion in the population — only 23.6 percent of all SCF transfers. On the other hand, the affluent segment of the population consistently receives slightly more that its proportional share. All this demonstrates either that the distribution of SCF is influenced to some extent by considerations unrelated to distribution or that the policies for distribution are not very effective.

Table 5.7 also shows how each SCF element is distributed. It can be seen that, from the distributional point of view, the most effective programs are the money allowances (other than holiday pay), where 40 percent of all disbursements are directed to the two lowest deciles. Among the non-money elements only the housing subsidy pays more than the proportional share to the poor of the entire population. For the active population, education and health services also slightly favor the poor households, but not when people are counted. The least helpful to the poor is, of course, holiday pay.

The effects of SCF allowances on the overall distribution of incomes depends on three factors: (a) the weight of the element in total income; (b) the size distribution of the elements itself; and (c) the degree of correlation between the distribution of the individual element and total income.[4] These effects are estimated here for a number of commonly used inequality measures, and the results for the size distribution of income per capita for the population of all households are presented in Table 5.7.

All measures of inequality show significant movement toward equality

Table 5.7. Selected Measures of the Impact of SCF on Income Inequality

	Gini	Measures of dispersion[a]				Income share (%) received by percentile group					
						Households				Household member	
						Lowest					
		$\dfrac{P_{98}}{P_2}$	$\dfrac{P_{95}}{P_5}$	$\dfrac{P_{90}}{P_{10}}$	$\dfrac{P_{50}}{P_{10}}$	10%	20%	50%	Highest 20%	Highest 10%	Lowest 10%
	(1)	(2)	(3)	(4)	(5)	(6)	(7)	(8)	(9)	(10)	(11)
Entire population											
1. Public earnings	0.357	..	..	..	..	..	4.7	31.3	31.6	16.5	..
2. Public money income	0.270	8.3	5.3	3.3	1.7	3.8	9.5	36.4	29.0	15.1	6.6
3. Public money income and subsidies	0.252	7.4	4.3	2.9	1.6	4.8	10.9	38.5	27.8	14.2	8.2
4. Total public income	0.240	6.6	3.9	2.7	1.6	4.7	11.3	39.2	27.1	13.9	8.2
Active population											
5. Public earnings	0.281	7.7	5.5	3.6	2.0	4.4	11.5	38.1	28.3	14.6	3.4
6. Public money income	0.263	7.5	4.5	3.1	1.7	5.5	13.4	40.2	27.0	13.9	4.8
7. Public money income and subsidies	0.281	6.5	4.5	2.9	1.6	6.1	14.2	41.5	26.0	13.4	5.4
8. Total public income	0.240	5.8	4.1	2.7	1.5	6.5	14.8	42.5	25.4	13.0	5.7

[a] P_i/P_j is a ratio of incomes received by household members with incomes higher than i and j percent of the population.

when SCF transfers are added. The Gini coefficient goes down from 0.357 to 0.240 for the entire population and from 0.281 to 0.240 for the active population. The most significant equalizing contribution for the entire population is rendered by money transfers, which reduce the Gini coefficient to 0.270. In the case of the active population, however, the equalization impacts of the money and non-money transfers are about the same. The SCF impact is seen in a similar fashion in the decline of the various dispersion measures (columns 2–5). To illustrate, the decile ratios decline from 3.6 to 2.7 for the active population and from technical infinity to 2.7 for the entire population (column 5). Finally, the same impact is seen through changes in a number of Lorenz measures — the percent of income received by segments of the population. For example, the share of public earnings earned by the bottom 20 percent of the active population is only 4.7 percent, but its share in total public income after SCF transfers rises to 11.3 percent. Correspondingly, the income shares of the richest 20 percent of the population decline in the process from 31.6 to 27.1 percent (column 9). It is interesting that the distribution of all public income for the entire population is more equal than that of public earnings for the active population. Compare the Gini coefficient of 0.240 (line 4) with that of 0.281 (line 5). Similarly, it is interesting to note that the overall inequality of total public income is equal for the entire and the active populations. This means that SCF transfers have incorporated the non-active part of the population without widening the income gaps of the entire population. This is due mostly to the pension system, but also partly to the fact that a full third of all retirement age heads of households keep jobs in the public sector and continue to work.

5. Comparisons and conclusion

In order to make the sample findings comparable to some of the results published by Soviet scholars, it is necessary to make some more reweighting and adjustments in our sample. In many cases even these will not help because the exact structures of the Soviet samples are not specified. In general it can be stated that most of the studies relating to the 1970s obtain results that are in the same ball park as ours. It seems that studies that are based on samples that do not include, or under-represent retired (non-active) units find that total SCF transfers are higher for high income than for low income families (see, e.g., Mamontova, 1975, p. 298). When retired units are included in a sample, poor families get more SCF per capita (*Potrebnosti*, 1979, p. 113), as in our sample.

All the studies we examined show (or claim, without showing) a rise in the money payments of SCF across the income range (Mamontova, 1975, p. 198; *Potrebnosti*, 1979, p. 114). Our findings show that this results from the pattern displayed by holiday and sick pay. Our sample that includes the same proportion of retired units as in the Soviet urban population probably shows higher money payments to households in lower income brackets. One wonders why Soviet studies fail to take notice or advantage of such a "positive" phenomenon.

On free services, especially education, all studies but one (Gerasimov, 1978, p. 82) show or claim that low-income families get larger values of services, mostly because they have more children (see Mamontova, 1975, p. 296; *Potrebnosti*, 1979, p. 114). In this connection Gerasimov (1978, pp. 77–78) points out that the level of health services provided to workers is somewhat higher than that for non-working people. If true, it raises doubts whether low-income families enjoy a higher level of health services per capita.

Turning to findings on the distribution of subsidies, most studies reach the conclusion that high-income families receive more services from this source. This is the case with respect to food and rent subsidies (Mamontova, 1975, p. 297; Gerasimov, 1978, pp. 82, 102). Only one study finds equal absolute amounts of subsidies for all income groups (*Potrebnosti*, 1979, p. 114). Although food subsidies were not included, this is nevertheless somewhat surprising.

One study based on a survey in one industrial city of the Russian Republic comes to the conclusion that, through SCF, inequality (actually "incomes difference") was reduced 40 percent and the share of low-income families declined by a factor of 1.5 (*ibid.*, 115). Direct comparisons with this study are impossible at this point, but while the decline in the share of low-income families seems reasonable, a 40 percent decline in the decile ratio (provided this is what is meant by "incomes difference") seems a little too optimistic.[5]

Three points can be made by way of summary. First, the entire Soviet SCF program has quite a significant effect on the level of income equality — especially when the entire (urban) population is considered. The impact on the active population is less impressive. When the distributive impact of SCF is evaluated, one must take into account that Soviet income policies are geared to achieve very high labor participation rates, that the distribution of earnings is already somewhat more equal that in market economies (due mostly to the elimination of most property incomes; see Bergson, 1984), and that the tax system is not nearly as progressive as in many other countries.

Second, through SCF payments a significant proportion of families with no earnings or with low earnings was pushed above the Soviet poverty line. But relatively low pensions and the reluctance to significantly raise the level of pure income maintenance leave many retired, one-parent and large families below the poverty line. A sizable proportion of retired people manage to stay above the line by continuing to work. Other families try to stay at reasonably low dependency ratios by limiting the number of children.

Finally, if the Soviet Union has a higher level of income equality and a lower incidence of poverty (at least when defined in relative terms) than Western societies, it is only partly the outcome of the distribution of SCF. Partly, or perhaps mainly, it is a result of a much broader range of policies.

Notes

1. Collective farm members receive another R14 billion in SCF payments and services (*Narkhoz*, 1980).

2. We shall disregard savings, the private sector, and the problem of market disequilibrium here. Also put aside is pure public consumption such as administration and defense.

3. The advantage shown here to the affluent may be an indication that many of them have larger apartments that they are entitled to and are paying higher rent that they should (McAuley, 1979, pp. 288–89). Or, it may result from the fact that they received the rented places *before* they became affluent, and figured it was worthwhile keeping them so as not to be considered rich. On the other hand, if a high percentage of high-income families own cooperative apartments, then among those who rent the bias in favor of the affluent is greater than shown by the figures.

4. In the calculation of the Gini coefficient, the total effect is exactly the product of these three elements (see Lerner and Yitzhaki, 1984).

5. Several other comparisons between our findings and those of Soviet studies can be found in the Appendix (Table A.26).

Chapter 6
The size and the structure of population in poverty in the Soviet Union

1. Introduction

The era of Gorbachev brought with it new words and definitions, unexpected acknowledgments, and some innovations in the social welfare policy for the most deprived parts of the Soviet population. In previous periods of time, it was impossible to find the word "poverty" (*bednost'*) in Soviet socio-political vocabulary related to "socialist" society in general, and to Soviet society, in particular. Twenty or more years ago, the only category recognized was *maloobespechennost'* — which implied the underprovision of some segments of the population compared to their needs or to the conditions of the rest of the population. In May 1985, the Central Committee of Communist Party, the USSR Council of Ministers and the All-Union Central Council of Trade Unions adopted a resolution "On Immediate Measures to Improve the Financial Well-Being of Low-Income Pensioners and Families and to Step Up Concern for Single Citizens" (*Pravda*, May 21, 1985). This decision brought with it the first official recognition of the existence in the Soviet Union of persons and families suffering from what was officially defined as "acute need" (*ostraia nuzhda*).[1] In the same resolution several changes were introduced to the Soviet income maintenance policy, to help these persons.

These changes in words, definitions, and lately also in policy measures reflected first of all, the fact that inflation in the Soviet Union significantly reduced the purchasing power of persons and families who had lived on a fixed income for many years (e.g., pensioners). As a result poverty evolved into the absolute and relative deprivation of some groups. Secondly, the gap between "very poor" and "very rich" in the Soviet Union is wider today than it was 15–20 years ago and is widening every year. Thirdly, the new Soviet leadership and the rise of *glasnost'* created new and raised old expectations, perhaps to reach some compromise between *social* justice and so-called *socialist* justice, which are theoretically and ideologically based on the well-known principle "from each according to his ability, to each according to his work."

The poor in the Soviet Union have been ignored by Soviet researchers. We could not find any book or article published in the Soviet Union in the last fifty years that dealt with this problem. But we do not agree with Matthews (1987, p. iii), who contends that "the condition of the poor in the Soviet Union has been sadly neglected by researchers in the West." One of the first steps toward ending this neglect was, in fact, taken by Matthews himself (1972), and also by McAuley (1977b; 1979) and Bernice Madison (1978b, 1981, 1988).

This chapter addresses the following questions: How many poor households and poor persons were there in the Soviet Union in the beginning and at the end of the 1970s? What is the composition of households at the poverty level and the incidence of poverty among different types of households? What are the main patterns of the convergence of poverty-linked characteristics? In addition, we will describe the Soviet government's policies toward the poverty problem and their actual impact. An attempt will be made to evaluate the dynamics of the poor population during the past 10–15 years and the prospects of alleviating poverty. Data from the two independent surveys, ISIP and SIP, offer a unique opportunity to examine private economic activity as a means to escape poverty in the Soviet Union. The data actually used are the two reweighted samples as explained in Chapters 1 and 4 (for ISIP and for SIP).

The reweighted samples are not perfect, but as can be observed in Table 4.1 they are a very close approximation of the target population along the dimensions of family type and economic activity.[2]

Due to the relatively small number of cases in the samples, two additional dimensions — family size and city size, potentially very important for understanding the problems of poverty in the Soviet Union — were neglected. It was found in examining these two variables that the reweighted samples are different from the target populations. The distribution of the ISIP reweighted sample by size of families underestimates the actual proportion of relatively large urban households in the Soviet Union, and the

distribution in SIP overestimates this proportion. Therefore for the final
estimation of the poor in the Soviet Union, and in this case only, further
standardization in order to adjust for family size was carried out. We also
took into account that the original and reweighted samples of SIP represent
only urban families living in the middle-sized and large cities of the Soviet
Union.

Even so it is important to stress at the outset that all our results and
conclusions have to be treated with some caution owing to the peculiar
nature of the two samples.

2. Concepts of income and poverty and definitions of poverty lines

a. A semi-official approach

As pointed out by McAuley, the Soviet government and most (if not all)
Soviet sociologists and economists adhere to an absolute concept of poverty
which they call *maloobespechennost'* (see above, and McAuley, 1977b, p. 5).
On the basis of this concept, Soviet researchers constructed a few "normative"
budgets. Notions such as "normative" budget and in particular "normative
budget for guaranteeing minimum material well-being" crop up repeatedly in
Western and Soviet scientific literature since Sarkisian and Kuznetsova
(henceforth: S&K) published their book *Potrebnosti i dokhod sem'i*, in 1967.
According to these authors, "the budget of minimum material well-being is
characterized in practice by the minimum level of consumption of goods, the
costs of the goods determining the expenses of the family, and by the income
the family needs at that level of consumption" (S&K, 1967, p. 56).

S&K constructed three types of "normative" budgets. The first was
defined as a "budget of minimum material well-being *(obespechennost')* for
the current period." The time span was specified not only by Sarkisian and
Kuznetsova but also by Karpukhin and Kuznetsova as the period from 1965
to 1970 (S&K, 1967, p. 56; Karpukhin and Kuznetsova, 1968, p. 423). The
second type of "normative" budget was defined as the "budget minimum ... for
the nearest perspective," i.e., for the period immediately followed the current
one — 1971–75 or longer. In both cases, a budget that could sustain minimum material well-being was calculated, first of all, for a worker's family of

four (the father, a machine operator, mother working in light industry, two school-age children). For the "current" period, the minimum material satisfaction was calculated as a net income of R51.4 per month per household member and R205.6 per month for a family of four. For the second period the corresponding figures are R66.6 and R265.8 respectively (S&K 1967, pp. 66, 125).

Soviet socio-economic literature widely employs the first figure (R.51.4 rounded to R50) as a cut-off point between poor (*maloobespechennost'*) and non-poor populations. Exactly the same poverty line was used by McAuley in his research on poverty in the Soviet Union in the second half of the 1960s (1977, 1979). The second number (R66.6 sometimes rounded to R70), was seldom used in Soviet literature as a similar cut-off point between poor and non-poor for the 1970s. Only in one case, relating to the active urban households in 1973 living in Estonia, was this cut-off point (R66.2 per month) used as a "minimum budget" (Khansberg, 1977). Rounded to R70, this cut-off point was, however, used by Matthews (1986) as the main poverty line.

The R50 cut-off point was accepted by McAuley without any serious critical examination and was deemed "liberal" (McAuley, 1979, p. 20). Indeed, for the non-agricultural active population in 1967, this minimum per capita income was equivalent to 84.5 percent of the median income (*ibid.*, Table 3.2, p. 57). In his research on poverty in the Soviet Union Matthews (1987) accepted this poverty line with some critical reservations although not as critical as those expressed in, of all places, the Soviet literature.

In a survey of the Soviet economic literature related to the family budget studies Bornycheva (1968) critically examined some of the considerations and calculations that had been made by S&K, and concluded that the minimum expenditures accepted by S&K on some items were patently unrealistic. For example, accepted expenses on housing and communal services were so low that they did not cover outlays on gas, electricity, routine repair, radio, and many other sub-items (*ibid.*, p. 263). Bornycheva also pointed out that in their construction of "minimum budget" S&K assumed that the families lived only in government-owned apartments, ignoring the fact that many Soviet families lived (and live) in their own private houses — with correspondingly higher expenditures. According to one family budget survey, analyzed by Bornycheva, expenses for persons living in private houses increased by about 50 percent (*ibid.*, p. 263). Unrealistically low, too, were expenses allowed for public transportation, postal and telegraph services. In the later years all critical remarks that Bornycheva had made in 1968 were confirmed by some Soviet publications related to the individual family budgets (see e.g., Kalinnick, 1977; Inoveli, 1977).

However, according to our analysis of Soviet socio-economic literature, the critical stance of Bornycheva was not accepted by other Soviet researchers. Some of them, in fact, found the term "poverty" (and even the neutral term "minimum") so distasteful that they redefined the first "normative" budget proposed by S&K in attempt to present it as sufficient for normal life. For example, Gordon and his co-authors (1974, p. 36) presented this budget not as a "minimum" budget, but as the budget of "sufficiency" (*dostatok*). In another major work, Gordon and Klopov (1972, p. 36) declared a per capita monthly income of R50 to be sufficient for satisfaction of "necessary" consumption (1972, p. 36). Their purpose is absolutely clear: by presenting the official poverty line as more generous than the "subsistence minimum" they were denying the existence of poverty in the Soviet Union.

b. The official poverty line

In 1974 the Soviet government introduced a means-tested family income supplement; it set the eligibility threshold at R50 per month per household member, which was not changed in the course of the 1974–84. After 1985 the threshold was raised to R75 a month in northern and eastern regions of the Soviet Union, remaining at its original level in the rest of the country (Kriazhev, 1985). In this study we adopt a per capita income R50 as the official poverty line for the 1970s.

The differences between the first semi-official poverty line developed by S&K and the official one, though not large, are important. All the calculations made by S&K rely on the concept of *net* minimum income (per capita and per household) needed to provide a minimum level of subsistence. The concept of income underlying the official poverty "line" is *gross* household income divided by the number of household members. To be eligible for the special income supplement this income must include not only gross wages of all employed family members and money income from Social Consumption Funds (SCF), and also income from private plots. To calculate the latter, special "norms" have been developed and accepted on the local level (*Sotsialistisheskii trud*, 1977, No. 10).[3]

Accounting for the differences in the *income* concepts, the poverty standard adopted by the Soviet government in 1974 is lower by about 10 percent than the S&K concept developed for the middle and later 1960s.[4]

In principle, the Soviet concept of poverty line is based on a calculation of minimum absolute needs, and in this it is similar to those developed by Rowntree (in England), Orshansky (in the United States) and, indeed, by the U.S. Social Security Administration (McAuley, 1977b, p. 5). But behind some general similarities lie a number of very significant differences. The poverty standard accepted by the U.S. Social Security Administration is linked to the cost of living index and is periodically adjusted for inflation. When, in 1974, the Soviets introduced a means-tested family income supplement, eligibility was set at R50 threshold per month per capita rather than at R58-60, as would have been indicated by one of the more modest Western calculations of the cost of living index and inflation rates in the Soviet Union in the late 1960s and the early 1970s. Since 1974, the official poverty line has never been adjusted for the rising cost of living and inflation. In England, official poverty "lines" are linked not only to the changes in the cost of living index but also to the real changes in the standard of living. In the Soviet Union this adjustment has also been ignored until very recently. Consequently, the gap between poor and non-poor populations and the relative deprivation of the poorer segments of the Soviet society has been growing wider over time.

In view of these considerations, we have expanded our analysis beyond the official (or the first semi-official) poverty lines, developing additional and alternative concepts, definitions, and cut-off levels.

c. Poverty lines for the present study

In the following study we deal with three poverty levels for the period 1973-79 bounded by ISIP and SIP. (a) The very poor (or "in acute need" according to Soviet terminology), are households with per capita income of R50 or less. Accepting a rate of inflation of 1.5 percent per year between

1965 and 1979, the real purchasing power of such an income in 1965 would have been lower by 10–20 percent than the minimum level for that period of R51.4.[5] The very poor during 1973–79 were thus worse off than people who had the same minimal income in 1965.

(b) Poor people or households are defined as those with a per capita income, during 1973–79, equal in real terms to the minimum subsistence level in 1965, that is a net income level of R58–60 in 1973 and R63–65 in 1979.[6] In what follows the two categories of "very poor" and "poor" combined constitute the "total population in poverty" in the Soviet Union in the 1970s.

(c) The third category of poor are those "on the verge of poverty," and include households with real per capita income of between R61–70 per month during the 1970s. This level is consistent with the second "minimum" budget developed by S&K for the "nearest" future (according to Karpukhin and Kuznetsova — for the 1970s), of R66.6 per capita per month.

In his research on poverty in the Soviet Union in the late 1970s Matthews (1987) used only one main cut-off point — per capita income of R70 per month. The rationale for our more differentiated approach is based on the fact that a poverty line of R70 constitutes about 70 percent of the median income during the late 1970s, which is quite high when a relative approach to poverty is used.[7] In different countries and at different times the relative poverty threshold was set at 40–50 percent of the median income (adjusted for differences in the type of household and its size). The two other poverty lines used here are more in line with the above convention, and the sole threshold used by Matthews is much too high.

A note on income concepts is warranted. In the periodic surveys of household income during the period 1967–81 the Soviet statistical administration used the concept of gross (*sovokupnyi*) income, which included all money incomes from the public sector (wages, salaries, pensions, stipends, allowances, and other) and income in kind (mainly from private plots). The 1984 survey introduced a new question related to income from private economic activity other than private plots: income from private handicrafts and provision of services to other people (Dumnov, 1984, p. 30). In the ISIP and SIP surveys this last (and more inclusive) concept of income was used and defined as the relevant gross and net disposable incomes. In addition to the above, mainly for purposes of comparing results between ISIP and SIP on the one side and Soviet data on the other, the following concepts of income were also defined: (a) pre- and post-tax public earnings received by all members of the household; (b) pre- and post-tax public earnings plus public money transfers received by all members of the household. The uses of different income concepts also facilitates the tracing of both the separate and combined effects of income tax, public money transfers, and private income on the extent of poverty in the Soviet Union.

3. The extent of poverty and its characteristics
a. How many poor?

The main results of the ISIP and SIP surveys, using the concept of net disposable income and related to the total urban population are presented in Table 6.1. In 1979 the very poor households constituted about 10 percent of the total number of Soviet urban households, the total poor — 16 percent, and the total poor plus those on the verge of poverty — 22 percent. In each case the proportion of persons in poverty is higher than of households in poverty (more than 12 percent in the first case, around 20 percent in the second, and around 28 percent in the third), and this reflects the higher incidence of poverty among larger families. ISIP figures for 1973 are lower, especially with respect to the very poor. It is our judgment that the ISIP to SIP differences are due mostly to less than full representation in ISIP, even after reweighting, of the group of individuals of retirement age (see Table 4.1).

According to official Soviet statistics, the population with per capita income less than or equal to R50 per month constituted 8 percent of the total population in 1980 (Dostovalov and Titova, 1984, p. 97). For the very poor category, then, this result fall nearer to the ISIP estimates, probably for a similar explanation, i.e., that they are based on a sample that did not fully represent the non-active population.[8]

A much higher estimate of the proportion of poor, this time those below R70 per capita is provided by Matthews (1987, p. iii) who concludes that "a perusal of Soviet data suggests that in the late seventies some two-fifths of the non-peasant labor force earned less than the sum needed to achieve the

Table 6.1. Share of households and persons in poverty: total population (ISIP and SIP samples)[a] (percent)

	Very poor		Total poor		Total poor and on the verge of poverty	
	1	2	1	2	1	2
ISIP, 1973						
Households in poverty	6.8	7.1	14.4	14.9	24.7	27.3
Persons in poverty	7.7	8.2	15.8	16.5	28.2	32.9
SIP, 1979						
Households in poverty	10.1	9.5	16.8	15.9	24.6	21.7
Persons in poverty	13.0	12.4	20.7	19.6	30.7	27.8

[a]   In each poverty category the numbers in column 1 refer to the population in poverty before standardization for differences in the distribution of households by size between referent and sample populations; numbers in column 2 — after standardization.

minimum level of subsistence...." This estimate is higher by between one and two-thirds than both ISIP and SIP estimates for the late 1970s (Table 6.1).

Most of the existing evidence indicate that the proportion of the Soviet population living in poverty, when defined by a constant nominal figure, had declined over the period since 1965. Estimates on the changing proportion of the very poor (with R50 per capita or less) were made by McAuley (1977b, 1979), Nemchinova (1973, p. 134), Sarkisian (1978, p. 11) and Dostovalov and Titova (1984, p. 94), produce the following time trend:

Year	Percent of Soviet population in acute need
1965	50
1970	25
1975	16–17
1980	8

Table 6.2. Relative income deprivation of households in "acute need," selected years: 1967–1985

	Per capita income of R50 per month as percentage of:		
	Average wage of state workers and employees	Average wage of industrial workers	Average per capita income of state workers' and employees'families
1967	48.4	45.9	84.5[a]
1970	41.0	38.3	77.3[b]
1975	34.2	31.1	57.9
1980	29.6	27.0	49.2
1981	29.1	26.3	48.6
1982	28.2	25.4	47.5
1983	27.5	24.9	45.4
1984	27.2	24.3	44.9
1985	26.3	23.6	42.5

[a] Our calculations, based on McAuley (1979, Table 3.2, p. 57).
[b] For the years 1970, 1975, and 1981–85, average per capita income of state workers' and employees' families calculated on the basis of the official Soviet statistical publications.

The above figures do not reveal to what extent the same trend of decline of the proportion of people or households under a nominal poverty line also applied to wider poor groups under higher poverty lines. It may be reasonable to assume that the same trend took place though maybe at a somewhat flatter slope. Some indication that this may be so is provided by recent information that the proportion of people under R75 per capita in 1988 was about 15 percent (*Trud*, January 12, 1988). Assuming comparability this is also a radical decline as compared with the 1975 figures in Table 6.2.[9]

As mentioned above the declining trend poverty defined by a nominal poverty line is misleading because it ignores inflation and the rise in the average real standard of living of the rest of the population. If there was a rate of inflation of at least 20 percent per decade since the mid-1970s, then the proportion of poor people since 1975 may have not gone down at all. Table 6.2 goes one step further and compares the changing relationship of the poverty-level income of R50 to median per capita income, to the average wage of state workers and employees, and to the average wage of industrial blue-collar workers. The widening gap over time between this poverty level and the other incomes is a clear manifestation that the relative deprivation of poor households in the Soviet Union increased significantly during 1965–85.

b. Who are the Soviet poor?

As in most other countries, poverty in the Soviet Union exists in all types of household but with a higher incidence among retired, non-active, incomplete, and large households. This similarity of patterns may be a peculiarity of sorts in relation to expectations from the Soviet welfare services; the only significant diverging aspect is, however, the importance of female labor-force participation in raising a household above the poverty line. Tables 6.3 and 6.4 present a breakdown of the incidence of poverty among households of various types and of the relative distribution of the poor population. The following are the main observations.

Poverty is first of all more widespread in the non-active population; and within this population — among single, older women living alone. The probability of being very poor in the non-active population is three times higher (and for singles living alone, four times higher) than for active households.

The second group with a relatively high proportion of households at or below the first and second poverty levels consists of active, incomplete families, most of whom are mothers with children. The probability of being very poor or poor in this case is more than twice as high as for all active households. These two categories account for over 50 percent of the total number of the very poor, and over 46 percent of the very poor and poor combined (see Table 6.4). It is therefore possible to talk about the "feminization" of poverty not only in the United States but in the Soviet Union as well.[10]

Third, the SIP results also reveal that the incidence of poverty among

Table 6.3. Incidence of poverty by type of household: ISIP and SIP samples[a] (percent)

Type of household	SIP, 1973			SIP, 1979		
	Very poor	Total poor	Total poor and on verge of poverty	Very poor	Total poor	Total poor and on verge of poverty
Total	6.8	14.4	24.7	10.1	16.8	24.6
Active	4.7	11.2	20.9	6.4	13.8	22.0
Complete	6.0	13.0	25.5	8.2	14.7	25.0
Husband and wife employed	3.3	8.5	19.6	6.2	11.9	21.8
Only husband employed				13.9	21.1	32.6
Only wife employed	..	..	..	11.8	28.8	39.2
Incomplete	7.9	7.9	8.9	21.5	28.5	36.1
Singles	..	6.6	10.8	..	..	0.9
Other	..	..	..	..	..	..
Non-active	24.4	41.2	57.2	23.8	41.4	45.5
Households with only husband and wife	37.7	63.9	72.1	10.0	24.3	25.7
Singles	11.7	27.7	72.1	32.7	52.7	60.0
Other	40.0	40.0	40.0	23.7	38.5	39.5

Active population

Household size	Very poor	Total poor	Total poor and on the verge of poverty
ISIP, 1973			
2	2.6	5.5	9.1
3	5.4	8.7	21.4
4	10.1	25.8	38.3
5+	9.0	16.0	44.0
SIP, 1979			
2	2.0	3.1	4.8
3	3.2	7.5	17.1
4	15.0	23.9	38.0
5+	23.3	35.7	47.5

[a] No standardization for differences in distribution of households by size.

Table 6.4. Socio-demographic composition of households in poverty, ISIP and SIP samples[a]

Type of household	ISIP, 1973 — Structure of households in poverty				SIP, 1979 — Structure of households in poverty			
	Structure of total sample	Very poor	Total poor	Total poor and on verge of poverty	Structure of total sample	Very poor	Total poor	Total poor and on verge of poverty
Total	100.0	100.0	100.0	100.0	100.0	100.0	100.0	100.0
Active	89.3	61.7	69.1	75.3	89.0	73.9	72.9	79.4
Complete	60.5	54.8	56.3	64.5	61.2	48.7	53.6	62.3
Husband and wife employed	48.3	..	..	..	45.0	27.6	31.9	40.1
Only husband employed	10.2	..	..	..	13.9	19.6	17.8	18.5
Only wife employed	2.0	..	..	..	2.3	2.5	3.9	3.6
Incomplete	6.0	6.9	3.3	2.2	11.4	24.1	19.3	16.7
Singles	20.7	..	9.5	8.6	16.4	..	..	6.7
Other	2.1					..	..	..
Nonactive	11.0	38.3	30.9	24.8	11.0	26.1	27.1	20.6
Households with only husband and wife	3.6	20.0	16.1	10.6	3.5	3.5	5.1	3.9
Singles	5.5	9.6	10.7	11.8	5.6	18.0	17.5	13.4
Other	1.9	8.7	4.1	2.4	1.9	4.5	4.5	3.1

[a] No standardization for differences in distribution of households by size.

complete active households depends on the employment status of husband and wife, more particularly on whether the wife also works. When only one of the spouses is employed, the probability of being very poor or poor is about twice as high as when both spouses are employed. This observation can be generalized much further by observing that the incidence of poverty in households where both spouses work, would have gone up by factors of between 8 and 3 if the wives did not work. To illustrate: without the income derived from the wife's wages the proportion of total poor would go up from 11.9 to 52.2 percent (SIP).

Both samples also indicate a strong correlation between the probability of being very poor or poor and household size (Table 6.4). Since the data presented are only for active households, it is likely that among the large households there are at least two people employed, and therefore larger households could be those contributing to the incidence of poverty among two-parent two-workers households. However, since there are only very few large families in the urban European parts of the Soviet Union, the main explanation for poverty among normal active families is not demographic but economic. The incidence of poverty among complete active families (both husband and wife employed), according to the widest definition is around 20 percent and such families comprise 40 percent of all poor families (1979).

In his first study on poverty in the Soviet Union, McAuley came to the conclusion that "in 1965–68 poverty was almost exclusively a family affair" (McAuley, 1977, p. 18). In his later (major) work on the standard of living, poverty, and income distribution in the Soviet Union, he formulated what amounts to the same conclusion, in greater detail: "At least among non-agricultural state employees, the minimum wage is high enough for the vast majority of those with jobs to support themselves, if single, at a standard of living above the poverty line. Deprivation now depends upon whom one marries, whether one's spouse works, the number of children or other relatives that reply upon one for support" (McAuley, 1979, p. 88). One of the main goals of the present study is to challenge this conclusion. Our results, as we have just seen, reveal the presence of poverty among all household types, including families in which both husband and wife were employed and had not more than one or two dependents.

Table 6.5. Incidence of poverty by occupation of households: ISIP and SIP
          samples (percent)

	ISIP, 1973			SIP, 1979		
	Very poor	Total poor	Total poor and on verge of poverty	Very poor	Total poor	Total poor and on verge of poverty
Active households with husband and wife employed	3.3	8.5	19.6	6.2	11.9	21.8
a. Occupation of head of household						
White-collar	3.2	4.0	7.7	7.7	11.6	18.2
Academic level	1.9	2.9	5.2	7.3	10.3	16.9
Technical level	4.9	5.2	8.4	6.0	10.8	18.6
Non-professional level	4.6	6.5	16.3	13.3	20.0	24.4
Blue-collar	5.6	15.2	28.4	9.1	15.2	24.6
In production sector	5.1	16.8	27.4	7.8	13.2	21.8
Skilled	2.9	8.8	17.6	5.8	10.8	19.6
Semi-skilled	3.4	11.9	21.3	7.1	14.6	20.7
Unskilled and with lowest skill level	7.6	23.9	36.1	12.3	17.4	27.2
In services sector	6.5	12.2	30.0	13.7	21.7	34.1
b. Occupations of husband and wife						
Husband and wife with academic level of occupation	0.2	1.0	3.9	4.1	5.7	14.5
Husband and/or wife with technical level of occupation	6.9	9.2	24.3	6.0	11.2	34.9
Husband and wife blue-collar workers in production sector	3.5	8.7	20.5	12.3	18.7	29.9
All other combinations including employment of husband or wife in the services sector or as non-professional white-collar worker	1.1	11.8	24.2	16.4	27.8	39.9

Table 6.5 probes into some of the economic sources of poverty among otherwise poverty-proof families: it breaks down all double active normal families into the major occupational groups of either the head of household, which is mostly the male (part a), or of both spouses. The general pattern of the distribution of the incidence of poverty is as expected: it is lower for the academic professions and higher for unskilled and service workers. It is interesting to note that these differences are quite narrow for most occupations among the "very poor." Especially noteworthy is the low incidence of such poverty among the skilled and semi-skilled workers in manufacturing. Also worth noting are the generally narrower differences across occupations in SIP as compared with ISIP.

The relative importance of the income contribution of women to the household income, lends itself to an hypothesis that their occupational status also, and its correlation with that of their husbands may affect the incidence of poverty. The first step is to classify households as homogeneous and heterogeneous in the different occupational groups. As in most other societies also in the urban population of the Soviet Union nearly two-thirds of all families are homogeneous from this point of view (see analysis by Iankova, 1979, pp. 114–15 on the basis of the 1970 population Census, 1970, Vol. VII, Table 29, p. 252). The proportion of homogeneous families in SIP is 57 percent not very significantly different. The high proportion of homogeneous families creates the possibility of more extreme poverty positions when families are classified by the occupational status of both spouses, as indeed we can see at the bottom of Table 6.5: the lowest incidence of poverty is among families where both spouses are in academic professions, while the highest is where both spouses are employed as unskilled workers or in services (SIP only).

Two more variables affecting the distribution of poverty are touched upon in Table 6.6.

The geographical distribution of poverty. Some Soviet socio-economic studies have discovered a positive correlation between size of city and standard of living, measured by per capita income: the larger the city, the higher the per capita income of its residents. For example, a study of urban life in Kazan', Al'metevsk, and Menzelinsk shows that in 1967 per capita

Table 6.6. Incidence of poverty by size of city and by age, ISIP and SIP samples (percent)

	Very poor	Total poor	Total poor and on the verge of poverty
a. City size			
ISIP, 1973			
Large	2.6	6.5	14.0
Middle	5.5	17.3	25.9
Small	10.5	15.5	29.0
SIP, 1979			
Large	8.0	14.8	21.6
Middle	13.6	19.8	33.1
Small	20.7	29.3	43.1
b. Age group of husband (active population only),[a] SIP, 1979			
Up to 29	1.5	11.0	17.1
30–34	4.3	10.8	22.6
35–39	10.3	20.4	30.2
40–44	11.3	20.6	35.9
45–49	7.0	13.7	28.4
50–54	7.6	7.6	12.4
55–59	0.9	0.9	5.5
60–64			6.3
65+			8.0

[a] Only households in which both husband and wife were employed.

monthly income in the relatively large city of Kazan' was R59.9 as against R46.7 in the small city of Menselinsk (our calculations, based on Arutunian *et al.*, 1973). Other studies found that in 1967–68 the proportion of very poor households (according to our definition) in relatively large, industrial cities is lower than in small cities — 32 and 47 percent, respectively (our calculations, based on Gordon and Klopov, 1972). The results of the ISIP and SIP surveys reveal the same pattern: the extent of poverty in middle-sized and (particularly) small cities is significantly higher than in large cities. For example, according to the ISIP survey, the proportion of the very poor in small cities is four times higher than in large cities.

Age and the extent of poverty. How long do people remain poor? Is poverty a permanent condition for some families, or do they move into and out of poverty? The ISIP and SIP surveys where mostly cross-sectional and therefore cannot provide full answers to these questions except by implication to one aspect: what happens to poverty over the life cycle? Here a cross-section of households at different stages in life is used to address this question. Relevant data based on the SIP sample and relating only to families in which both husband and wife were employed, are presented in Table 6.6. The relationship between age and the extent of poverty shows a bell-shaped curve distribution, indicating that families tend to move in and out of poverty. The most significant reduction in the proportion of households in poverty comes after age 50–54, i.e., 5–10 years before the officially designated age of retirement for men. This means that some families live in poverty for prolonged periods before moving out of it. For some households this "full circle" includes three phases: move into poverty, move out of poverty, and (after retirement) move back into poverty. The reason for the last phase is low pensions.

c. The convergence and structure of poverty-linked characteristics

So far we have presented poverty-linked characteristics as separate dimensions. After examining the results derived from the one-dimensional approach, many questions remain unanswered. Two of these are: What are the main patterns of convergence of poverty-linked characteristics? What is the independent "contribution" of each factor in creating a poverty-stricken population? One of the results based on the ISIP and SIP surveys is the non-negligible presence of poverty among Soviet households in which both husband and wife are or were employed in the public sector. This type of household composed roughly 50 percent of the total number of households, over 60 percent of all active families, and over 70 percent of complete families (Table 4.1). It was found that among these households the shares of total poor were 8.5 and 11.9 percent (ISIP and SIP, respectively), and the shares of total poor and those on the verge of poverty were around 20 percent in both surveys (Table 6.3). The list of poverty-linked and converged characteristics related to these households includes:

a. Families with more dependents (usually, but not always, children).
b. Families in which the head-of-household was unskilled or low-skilled.
c. Heterogeneous families in which the husband or wife was a blue-collar worker or a nonprofessional white-collar employee.
d. Households living in relatively small cities.

All these characteristics are clearly and significantly correlated with each other and with all three poverty income levels.

The next question addresses the inner structure of poverty-linked characteristics, or the relative weight of each of them. We employed a log-linear ("logit") model with the following specifications of dependent and independent variables:

Dependent variable. Being or not being poor, where 1 = poor; 2 = non-poor.
Independent variables. The homogeneous/heterogeneous types of household ("Homhet") were: 1 = household in which both spouses held different but non-academic professions; 2 = households in which one or both of the spouses held academic occupations.

Size of household ("Hhsize"): 1 = households consisting of 4 or more members; 2 = households consisting of 2–3 members.

Age of household head ("Hedage"): 1 = head of household age 35–49 (middle age), 2 = head of household age less than 35 or over 49.

Size of city ("Citygr"): 1 = small and relatively small cities; 2 = large and relatively large cities.

For the final evaluation and interpretation of the results based on the logit model we used a regression-like model and an analogous multiplicative

Table 6.7. Independent effect of poverty-linked characteristics (coefficient of regression-like and analogous multiplicative models)

| Coefficients: | Income poverty groups | | | | | |
| | Very poor | | Total poor | | Total poor on the verge of poverty | |
	Log-odds (1)[a]	Odds (2)[b]	Log-odds (1)[a]	Odds (2)[b]	Log-odds (1)[a]	Odds (2)[b]
Independent parameters						
HOMHET[c]	0.324	1.383	0.306	1.358	0.628	1.874
HHSIZE[d]	1.694	5.442	1.160	3.190	1.228	3.414
HEDAGE[e]	0.396	1.486	0.586	1.797	0.474	1.612
CITYGR[f]					0.062	1.064
Goodness of fit test statistics						
Likelihood ratio Chi-square	0.027433		0.77406		7.3076	
DF	3		1		3	
P	0.965		0.77		0.063	

[a] Regression-like coefficients.
[b] Coefficients based on an analogous multiplicative model.
[c] Socio-economic homogeneous/heterogeneous dichotomy of households.
[d] Household size dichotomy.
[e] Age-of-household head dichotomy.
[f] City-size dichotomy.

model of the following form:

$$(Fijkls/Fijkl2) = T \times T(A)i \times T(B)j \times T(C)k \times T(D)l$$

The coefficients of both forms are shown in Table 6.7. The main results with respect to the group of total poor are as follows:

a. The likelihood of being poor as a nonacademic family relative to an academic family, other things being equal, is 1.358:1.

b. The likelihood ratio for being poor as a large family compared with being a small one, other things being equal, is 3.190:1.

c. Other things being equal, the likelihood of being very poor for the "middle age" group vs. the other age groups is 1,797:1.

These results do not change significantly when we move from the "very poor" category to "total poor" or from "total poor" to "total poor" combined with those "on the verge of poverty" (Table 6.7). Accordingly, household size and the age of household head have greater impact on the determination of poverty than the net effect of the spouse's occupation or the family's place of residence.

4. The effect of SCF, taxes and private income on poverty[11]

Our aim in this section is to describe and analyze the impact of the Social Consumption Fund (SCF) money transfers by the government, of taxes levied on the population, and of private incomes derived through activities in the second economy on poverty. The Soviet Social Consumption Fund (SCF) is a concept that encompasses all increments to household incomes, such as money transfers or direct services made by the public sector, that are not strictly wages. According to Soviet convention, these transfers include holiday pay, pensions, allowances (sick pay, maternity pay, child allowances, family income supplements, and some other elements), and students' stipends.

The degree to which money transfers from SCF in the Soviet Union reduce the population of poor households can best be observed with the help of Tables 6.8 and 6.9, which, among other things, compare the incidence of poverty on the basis of alternative sources or definitions of income, and therefore the contribution of various income elements to the elevation of otherwise poor families above the different poverty lines.

Table 6.8. The extent of poverty according to different concepts of per capita household income and different concepts of poverty: ISIP and SIP samples (percent)

	Very poor		Total poor		Total poor / on verge of poverty	
	Total popu-laton	Active popu-lation	Total popu-lation	Active popu-lation	Total popu-lation	Active popu-lation
ISIP, 1973						
1. Public earnings, pre-tax	21.6	12.4	31.3	23.2	40.1	33.1
2. Public earnings, post-tax	26.1	17.4	35.2	27.5	43.9	37.2
3. Public earnings and public money transfers, pre-tax	9.3	6.5	18.3	13.9	26.7	21.6
4. Public earnings and public money transfers, post-tax	10.9	8.3	21.2	17.0	30.9	26.4
5. Total income, pre-tax	5.9	3.7	12.4	8.9	19.9	15.4
6. Total disposable income, post-tax	6.8	4.7	14.4	11.2	24.7	20.9
SIP, 1979						
1. Public earnings, pre-tax	31.5	23.0	38.7	31.1	46.0	39.3
2. Public earnings, post-tax	34.2	26.1	42.2	35.2	50.7	44.6
3. Public earnings and public money transfers, pre-tax	10.2	8.4	15.9	12.7	23.6	20.7
4. Public earnings and public money transfers, post-tax	11.3	9.7	28.3	25.4	26.9	24.4
5. Total income, pre-tax	8.9	7.1	14.8	11.5	21.6	18.6
6. Total disposable income, post-tax	10.1	8.4	16.8	13.8	24.6	22.0

Table 6.9. Separated and combined effect of scf and private economic activity on the transitions in the framework of poverty lines and out of poverty, active population, ISIP sample (percent)

	Total	Very poor	Poor	On verge of poverty	Non-poor
a. Separated effect of SCF Public earnings, post-tax[a]		Public earnings and public money transfers			
Very poor	100.0	47.9	19.0	12.8	20.3
Poor	100.0		53.5	23.6	22.8
On verge of poverty	100.0			48.9	51.1
b. Separated effect of private economic activity Public earnings, and public money transfers, post-tax		Total disposable income, post-tax			
Very poor	100.0	56.0	13.0	8.7	22.3
Poor	100.0		61.5	11.7	26.8
On verge of poverty	100.0			84.8	15.2
c. Combined effect of SCF and private economic activity Public earnings, post-tax		Total disposable income, post-tax			
Very poor	100.0	26.8	13.5	15.9	43.8
Poor	100.0		40.5	28.6	30.9
On verge of poverty	100.0			41.6	58.4

[a] In the framework of each income concept the first group (very poor) includes households with per capita net income of R50 or less per month; the second group (poor) – R51–60; the third group (on verge of poverty) – R61–70.

Figures presented in Table 6.8 show that according to the ISIP survey, and on the basis of public earnings alone, 26.1 percent of the entire population and 17.4 percent of the active population are "very poor" (the corresponding figures according to the SIP survey are 34.2 and 26.1 percent).[12] When SCF transfers are added, the ratio of the very poor declines considerably in both populations, to 11 and 8–10 percent respectively, according to both the ISIP and the SIP surveys. SCF money transfers also reduce the share of total poor households and that of total poor and families on the verge of poverty. Compared to the reduction in the share of the very poor, however, the latter two reductions are less impressive though quite substantial in their own right. For example, according to the ISIP survey, SCF money transfers reduce the ratio of total poor households and households on the verge of poverty in the total population from 44 to 25 percent, and in the active population from 37 to 26 percent. The SIP survey yields similar percentages: from 51 to 27 percent and from 45 to 24 percent, respectively.

Data in Table 6.9, panel a, show the distribution of *active* families who would be poor on the basis of public *earning* alone after the allocation of SCF payments. The main findings can be summed up as follows: out of the total number of very poor families, 48 percent did not receive enough income support from the SCF or none at all, and consequently remained in the very poor group; 19 percent of the very poor moved up into the "poor" category; 13 percent moved up into the group on the verge of poverty. SCF money transfers helped only 20 percent of the very poor to escape poverty entirely. The results are the same for the second group, that of "poor" households. The results for those groups on the verge of poverty, however, are more encouraging: with SCF income support over 50 percent of these households moved out of poverty. Therefore, in examining the first two groups (the very poor and the poor), i.e., the total number of poor families, and restricting the examination to the active urban population, we see that money transfers via SCF fail to bring relief to about 50 percent of these groups, do bring relief to some 30 percent, and enable 20 percent to escape poverty entirely.

We have restricted the analysis here to the active population only since for the vast majority of non-active households, retired individuals, and couples living alone, SCF money transfers (mainly in the form of pensions) are the main source of income. According to ISIP, SCF money payments constitute for this group 98 percent of all public income (the other 2 percent is made up of earnings in the public sector), and 74 percent of total net income (with the remaining 26 percent accounted for by private income; see Chapter 5, Table 5.2). Finding out why "only" 24 percent of non-active households were very poor, "only" 40 percent were poor, and roughly 50 percent were poor and on the verge of poverty is another question entirely. The answer lies in the level of pensions and variations in private economic activity as a means of relieving poverty or moving out of it (see more on these below).

The impact of income tax on poverty. Data in Table 6.8 show that the extent of poverty based on "pre-tax" incomes is lower than its extent based on "post-tax" income. Income taxes increase the proportion of households in poverty by 3–5 percentage points. This result from the fact that income taxes are levied on the basis of earnings of individuals and are not always adjusted back to take account of the per capita income of the family as a whole. Married workers and employees who receive the officially defined minimum wage and have at least one child are exempt from income tax on personal wages, but families earning the officially defined minimum per capita are not exempt. An example may clarify this: if, in a family of four (husband, wife and two children), the wife's gross monthly wage is R70 and the husband's is R150, income tax on the husband's wage (nowadays R14.2) will reduce the net per capita income of household to a level defined as the minimum income in the 1960s (R51.4). In addition, according to the Soviet tax system, only families with three or more dependents are eligible for some tax reduction.

The effect of private incomes on poverty. Private income includes different sources which, in the Soviet Union, can be either legal, semi-legal, or illegal. As we have shown elsewhere (Chapter 3 above), the private economic activity that generates such income takes on various forms and can be found among different occupational and income groups. Here we concentrate only on the findings related to the effect of private income on poverty. The results of both ISIP and SIP demonstrate that private incomes significantly reduce poverty in the Soviet Union. For the total population it reduces the proportion of poor households from 21 to 14 percent according to ISIP and from 28 to 16 percent according to SIP. For the active population, the decline is from 17 to 11 percent and from 15 to 14 percent respectively (see Table 6.8).

The impact of private income on the distribution of the otherwise poor is shown in Table 6.9, panel B: due to private economic activity, 22 percent of the very poor move completely out of poverty, another 20–22 percent move up to the "poor" category, and the same percentage rise to the verge of poverty. The results are approximately the same for poor households, but less significant for those on the verge of poverty. As hypothesized in Chapter 2 above it is possible that opportunities to earn high incomes in the private sector encourage some people to reduce their level of activity in the public sector, thus technically becoming poor on the basis of public income alone.

Table 6.9 (panel C) also reveals that the combined effect of SCF money transfers and private incomes produces a significant reduction in the number of very poor and poor families.

5. The causes of poverty

Despite the existence of different kinds of income maintenance programs and flourishing private economic activity, the size of the Soviet population in poverty at the end of the 1970s was still significant. The identification of the types of households or incomes with high incidence of poverty also points to the explanations of poverty — old age, large family, low paid jobs etc. In this section we try to go one step further and to examine directly the levels of pensions, child support, and minimum wage as the main explanations for the resulting poverty.

The causes of poverty differ from one type of household to the next, and we examine them one by one. First is the group of non-active households where the incidence of poverty is the highest. This group is composed primarily of retired singles and couples living alone, whose principal source of income is pensions. Any analysis of poverty in this group must focus on the level and distribution of pension payments and their development over time.

In 1959, 1966, and 1972 three surveys of pensions received by retired state workers and employees were carried out by the Soviet Statistical Administration (TsSU), and some results from these surveys were published by Pavlova and Rabkina (P&R, 1976). They showed that in 1959, 1966, and 1972 the average monthly pensions equalled R47.8, R49.5, and R58.3 and the median pensions stood at R43.8, R45.9, and R52.3, respectively (P & R, Table 2). This means that in 1972 roughly half of the pensioners received pensions of less than R52 per month, i.e., only sufficient for living "in acute need." In the same year 62 percent of all pensioners received a pension of less than R60 (*ibid.*).[13] Only in 1988 did the Soviet Statistical Administration (TsSU) published the following distribution of pensioners, by size of their pensions (*Narkhoz*, 1988, p. 89):

Size of pension (rubles per month)	Percent of pensioners 1983	1987
Up to 60	49.5	31.4
60–79	17.8	19.0
80–99	11.5	14.9
100–119	8.5	11.3
120+	12.7	23.4

These figures reveal that in 1983 half, and in 1987 more than one-third of all pensioners received pensions below the poverty line. It is clear that the low level of pensions provided by the Soviet state is the main cause of the widespread poverty among the non-active population. Low pensions also contribute to the poverty of the active population. Owing to relatively low pensions, many pensioners living with active or semi-active families not only depend on the state, but also on working members of the family.

As we have seen above, the existence of poverty among active households where both husband and wife are employed cannot be explained only or predominantly by the presence of children or old-age dependents. Low wages also play a role and therefore are also an important poverty issue. In Soviet socio-economic literature the definition of *nizkooplatsivaemye* (low paid) is no less acceptable than *maloobespechennye*. Let us start with those receiving the minimum wage. The introduction of a minimum wage of R70 began in 1971, and it was accomplished in 1975. Since then the minimum wage has not changed. As a result, the ratio between the average wage of state workers and employees and the minimum wage has increased from 1.8 in 1971 to 2.4 in 1980 and to 2.6 in 1985. In that year a minimum wage was equal to or a little higher than a third of the average wage. In addition as we have seen since 1971, inflation significantly reduced the real purchasing power of R70. Perhaps as a result of this it was decided in 1981–85 to introduce a new minimum wage level of R80. But implementation of this decision was postponed until 1986–90 (*Narkhoz*, 1985).

The level of minimum wages and other low wages are strongly connected with the contribution of working women to the family income. According to SIP 80 percent of all workers at the lowest wage earner decile and 74 percent at the second decile are women. Most of them are employees with special secondary level of education, non-professional white-collar workers, and blue-collar workers in the services sector. This "feminization" of the low paid positions, in addition to the fact that the earnings of a second earner plays a significant role in family income, combine to explain an important cause of poverty of active families. Indeed over 50 percent of all very poor families and over 35 percent of all poor families belong to the group where gross wages of women do not exceed R80 per month. Even so, it is important to stress that in about half the poor families the low wage of the husband contributes to the state of poverty as much as the wife's.

The existence of groups of women with relatively low wages also explains the widespread poverty among fatherless active households.[14] The results based on the SIP reweighted sample show that over 40 percent of the very poor, fatherless families belong to the lowest wage group of up to R80 per month, and over 65 percent belong to those with up to R90 per month.

As shown above, there is a strong and significant correlation between household size, the number of dependants in it (elderly persons and children), and the scope of poverty. This is related to the policy of the Soviet government with respect to child allowances. Child allowances were reconsidered by the Soviet government at the end of 1974. Beginning in November 1, 1974 all families with per capita gross income of R50 per month or less were eligible to receive an allowance for each child under the age of

8 years (raised to 12 years in 1985). For most families the sum of allowances remained a constant R12 a month. This is a modest, but important income supplement for households in poverty. In 1974 it was equal to some 9 percent of the average net wage of state workers and employees[15] or to 4 percent of the gross personal per capita income if a family had one child under 8 years of age (around 19 and 8 percent, respectively, in the case of two children). In 1985 this supplement stood at about 7 percent of the average wage and 3 percent of per capita income for families with one child (around 13 and 6 percent in the case of families with two children).

Different calculations show that for families eligible for child allowances the established size of these income supplements can lift them above the first level of poverty, but not out of poverty entirely.

6. Some international comparisons

How does the Soviet record on poverty compare with that of Western market economies? The first attempt to compare the extent and incidence of poverty in the West was made in 1976 by the OECD (1976). For the purpose of comparison a "standardized relative poverty line" has been defined as a per capita income level below two-thirds of the average per capita disposable income for each country. Per capita income was adjusted by an adult equivalence scale as follows:

1 person	66.6 percent
2 persons	100.0 percent
3 persons	125.0 percent
4 persons	145.0 percent
5 persons	160.0 percent

Income distribution data in each country were checked for complete coverage of the household sector and are all in terms of post-social-benefit money income (OECD, 1976, p. 66). The results based on this research relate to the early 1970s.

A second comparative study of poverty was made by the Commission of the European Communities, for a group of European countries. The

poverty line was defined as 50 percent of the net income of an adult equivalent unit, which is calculated by using a weight of 1.0 for the head of
household and 0.7 for additional members (Commission, 1981, p. 83).

A third comparison of poverty levels has been made by Peter Hedstrom
and Stein Ringen in the framework of the Luxembourg Income Study (1987).
These authors used a concept of adjusted disposable income, using the
following equivalence scale:

No. of family members	1	2	3	4	...	7+
Equivalence factor	0.50	0.75	1.00	1.25		3.0

The poverty line is then defined as 50 percent of the median adjusted
per capita income of all families (Hedstrom and Ringen, p. 236).

The main methodological differences between the three comparative
studies relate (a) to the basic unit of analysis: in the first and second studies
the basic unit is the household, in the third — the individual; (b) to the
income concept: in the first and second studies — mean income, in the third
— median income; and (c) to different estimations of "equivalence scales."
The first study relates to the early 1970s; the second — to the period between
1973 and 1979; and the third — to the late 1970s and early 1980s.

For purposes of comparison of the Soviet data with the above three
studies we followed the same definitions in each case and adjusted the Soviet
data accordingly. However, due to our suspicion that the average level of
income for SIP is biased upwards, we have used for the comparison of the
late 1970s poverty lines based on both average and median levels of
income.[16]

The authors of the Western studies often emphasized the problematic
nature of their comparison, as the adopted methodology "does not of course
provide a precise measure" (OECD, 1976, p. 66) and that "the figures for
each state should be interpreted as broad orders of magnitude" (Commission,
1981, p. 81). Needless to say, all these remarks (and others not cited here)
are relevant to the comparison of the Soviet Union with other Western
countries.

In such a framework of "broad orders of magnitude" it is possible to

Table 6.10. The incidence of relative income poverty of households in the 1970s: the Soviet Union and Western countries (percentage of households or persons below the poverty line)

| | Comparative studies | | |
	First	Second	Third
The Soviet Union			
1973	10.2	12.2	8.6
1979	12.5	17.4 (7.8)	7.9
Fed. Rep. of Germany	3.0	6.6 (1973)	7.2 (1981)
Sweden	3.5	..	5.0 (1981)
The Netherlands	..	4.8 (1979)	..
Norway	5.0	..	4.8 (1979)
United Kingdom	7.5	6.3 (1975)	8.8 (1979)
Belgium	..	6.6 (1976)	..
Australia	8.0	..	..
Canada	11.1	..	12.1 (1981)
United States	13.0	..	16.9 (1979)
Denmark	..	13.0 (1977)	..
Luxemburg	..	14.6 (1978)	..
France	16.0	14.8 (1975)	..
Italy	..	21.8 (1978)	..
Ireland	..	23.1 (1973)	..
Israel	..	..	14.5 (1979)

Sources and notes: Numbers in the first column relate to the early 1970s: OECD, 1976, Table 27, p. 67. Numbers related to the second comparative study: Commission, 1981, Table 1, p. 83. Numbers related to the third comparative study: Hedstrom and Ringen, 1987, Table 6, p. 23. All numbers related to the Soviet Union based on ISIP (1973) and SIP (1979) surveys. In the second column the first number (17.4) was derived on the basis of mean income and the second (in parentheses) on the basis of median income.

conclude that the proportion of households or persons in relative poverty in the Soviet Union in the 1970s was higher than in Sweden, Norway, the Netherlands, the United Kingdom, Belgium, and the Federal Republic of Germany, and lower than in the United States, Canada, Italy, and Ireland (Table 6.10). In the OECD study the authors noted that the countries under comparison have different socio-economic population structures that could have explained part of the differences in the results. For example, the high proportion of poverty in France (13 percent) is partly accounted for by the high levels of poverty in the relatively large agricultural sector and by the fact that, until very recently, the minimum pensions received by large numbers of elderly persons was relatively low (OECD, 1976, p. 67). It is not difficult to predict what would happen to the proportion of the population in poverty in the Soviet Union if the representative sample were to include not only the urban but also the rural population.

7. Conclusion

The results of the ISIP and SIP surveys confirm the official Soviet claim that from 1965 to 1980 the proportion of households at or below the absolute official poverty line declined significantly. But poverty in the Soviet Union is still widespread. In 1979 the very poor households accounted for roughly 10 percent of the total number of Soviet urban households, 16 percent of total poor households, and 22 percent of total poor plus those on the verge of poverty. Except for unrelated working individuals, no other type of household totally escapes poverty; it is more prevalent, however, among the retired, non-active population and among incomplete families, most of whom are single mothers.

One of the main findings is the non-negligible presence of poverty among Soviet households in which both spouses were employed in the public sector. In this case the probability of being poor is high (a) for families with two or more dependents (mainly, but not only, children); (b) for families in which household heads are predominantly unskilled or semi-skilled workers; (c) for heterogeneous families in which husband or wife is a blue-collar worker or a non-professional white-collar employee; and (d) for families living in small or relatively small cities. It was also found that poverty is the outcome of the convergence of these poverty-linked characteristics.

Through Soviet income maintenance programs (namely SCF money transfers) a sizable proportion of families with no public earnings at all or with low earnings can rise above the official Soviet poverty line, i.e., move out of "acute need." But money transfers from SCF fail to bring relief to about 50 percent of the active urban households in poverty, afford only some relief to 30 percent, and enable only 20 percent to move out of poverty entirely.

In trying to escape poverty and to raise their standard of living, people in the Soviet Union engage in various types of private work. Private incomes reduce the extent of poverty considerably. ISIP findings show that with the help of private economic activity, more than 20 percent of the very poor families move completely out of poverty, and another 20 percent move upward on the poverty scale into the "poor" or "on the verge of poverty" categories.

Poverty in the Soviet Union cannot be explained only, or even predominantly, as the consequence of "a family affair." Structural factors are also at work. Relatively low pensions, reluctance to significantly raise the level of pure income maintenance, and low pay for women leave many retired and one-parent families and large families below the poverty line.

The first attempt to compare the extent of poverty in the Soviet Union with the situation in Western countries does not show that the first "socialist" society has any advantage. On the contrary, the number of Soviet households living in relative poverty in the 1970s was higher than in Sweden, Norway, the Netherlands, the United Kingdom, Belgium, and the Federal Republic of Germany, and lower than in the United States, Canada, Italy, and Ireland.

Notes

1. In trying to grasp Soviet understanding of these words, we found in the Russian-English dictionary published in Moscow that the expression "to be in need" means "to live in *poverty*."
2. In addition both samples were also reweighted according to the educational structure of the target population. (In the ISIP this reweighting was carried out only for active population.)
3. For example, according to a German-language newspaper published in Kazakhstan, in computing "total gross family income" the income from livestock husbanded on a private plot is reckoned as follows: *kolkhozniks* — R60 per month; workers and employees in rural areas — R50; urban settlements — R35; towns — R5 (Bush, 1973, p. 60).
4. According to our calculations for the standard family of four where both husband and wife are employed and where the wife's wage is around 70 percent of the husband's, the *net* per capita income accepted as the official poverty line is equal to R46.8 as compared with R51.4 as proposed by S&K.
5. The assumed rate of inflation over the above period is based on estimates made by Howard, 1976, Schroeder and Severin, 1976, Gilbertson and Amacher, 1972, and CIA, 1988. A level of per capita income of R51.4 per month in 1965 was equal in 1973 to R45.5 and to R41.6 in 1979.
6. Let us note that the first official acknowledgment of the need for a new poverty threshold of R60 appeared in the mid-1980s. The amount of per capita income below which children are entitled to exemption from maintenance charges in preschool facilities was set at R60 per month (Kriazhev, 1985).
7. According to the results of the SIP reweighted sample in 1979, median net per capita income for total urban population (active and non-active) was R96 per month, and the gross median income was R100. The latter figure is the same as the official one, and was published in the Soviet Union in 1980 as follows: "In 1980 approximately half of the population had a per capita monthly income over R100" (*Narkhoz*, 1980, p. 380). If these figures are correct, then the late 1970s per capita "minimum" income of R70 was equal to 70 percent of the median income.

8. Rabkina and Rimashevskaia (1978, p. 28), report that data related to the total population of the Soviet Union (active and non-active) that pensioners living alone were included in the income distribution survey for the first time in 1978. It is also very likely that most Soviet data on this issue is related only to state workers and employees.

9. The level of R75 per capita is now considered by Soviet students and officials as an acceptable poverty line for the 1980s (Levin, 1988).

10. See Pearce (1978). The title of her article is "The Feminization of Poverty: Women, Work, and Welfare."

11. This discussion repeats some of the material in Chapters 2, 4, and 5, but also includes some new results. Most of the discussion on the effects of SCF are based on ISIP only.

12. These figures overestimate the number of very poor households (according to the income concept defined as post-tax public earnings) because in the case of the SIP survey, public earnings include wages and salaries of spouses only.

13. P & R did not publish the size of the group with pensions less that R45 per month.

14. In a SIP weighted sample this group includes only 216 households, a sub-sample that hardly represents the referent urban population of the Soviet Union. For this reason, the following results have to be treated with caution.

15. The average net wage was calculated as gross wage *less* income tax paid by a person with no more than three dependants.

16. The source of the bias seem to be that the reported income of unrelated active individuals in the SIP sample is unreasonably high. Consequently, the poverty results based on too high average income are also relatively high. We are inclined to believe that the "true" figures lie somewhere between the two estimates.

Chapter 7
Earning differentials by sex in the Soviet Union:
a first look

1. Introduction

At work, women in the Soviet Union earn on average less than two-thirds of a man's wage; at home they spend more than twice as much time on household chores as do their spouses. In these two respects Soviet urban society resembles urban societies in most developed market economies. However, Soviet women are much more active in the labor force. When coupled with unusually high participation in the labor force, undiminished (perhaps even greater) work at home imposes on women in the Soviet Union an exceptionally heavy double burden.

For women to bear such a heavy work load and then to receive low pay — compared to men — would appear to be in direct conflict with the egalitarian principles of socialist ideology.[1] The obvious embarrassment created by this conflict may be one reason for the reluctance of Soviet sources to provide data on male/female wage differentials.[2] On the other hand, the broader questions of the status of women in the family and in society, the double burden of married women, restricted access to various occupations, high participation in the labor force — together with the possible demographic effects of these phenomena — are dealt with in dozens of books and scores of articles by Soviet scholars.[3] Many of these studies emphasize how greater equality for women has been achieved with respect to education, occupational choice, income independence, and social and political activity. They also discuss rather frankly areas in which inequality is still significant. In this respect, reasons for wage inequality are in most cases treated qualitatively, not quantitatively.

The increased interest in the West regarding the status of women has now directed even more attention to the place of women in Soviet society.

Some very good surveys and studies covering the available Soviet data as well as Soviet views on many of these issues have been produced in recent years by Western scholars. New tools of analysis have also been used to further analyze the issues, sometimes in a comparative setting.[4] The main factors contributing to earning differentials by sex have been discussed and their consequences analyzed, within the above-mentioned limitations of the available data. In only one case, however (Swafford, 1977), could the analysis of earning differentials be carried to the level of multivariate analysis based on (semi)micro data on earnings of individuals. The general lack of such micro data has prevented Western students of the Soviet Union from performing the kind of multivariate analysis that is so common in similar studies in the West. Such an opportunity is provided by ISIP.

The main purpose of this chapter, therefore, is to use these data to analyze earning differentials by sex in the urban sector of the Soviet Union and to study and compare the earning functions of men and women. The abundance of recent studies on the status of women, mentioned above, allows us to present only short summaries of the broader issues and to concentrate mostly on the empirical analysis and its implications.[5]

In Section 2 we formulate our hypotheses on expected earning differentials by sex in the Soviet Union, based on theories of earning functions, intra-family distribution of labor and household roles, and discrimination. The data are described in Section 3, where the variables and estimated equations are also defined. Section 4 presents and analyzes the results. This chapter presents only our initial findings and leaves many questions for further research.

2. The theory of earning differentials by sex

a. A summary of Western and Soviet theories

Broadly speaking, there are three bodies of theory to explain observed earning differentials by sex: the human capital approach, the theory of comparative advantage, and the theory of discrimination. These three approaches compete with each other in some aspects, but are complementary — and even overlapping — in others. The human capital approach attributes wage or earning differentials to differences in formal education, experience or on-the-job training, the depreciation of human capital, and (one might add) hours of work, intensity of work, and so on. The lower pay received by women is thus to be explained in part by their lower investment in all forms of human capital, less intensity of work, and shorter hours.[6] An additional manifestation of these features would be the small proportion of women holding managerial jobs and other positions demanding great responsibility, extensive involvement, and a good deal of time.

A major explanation of why women invest less in human capital — both formally and on the job — choose less intensive jobs, work fewer hours, and so on, and get paid less for work, is that they devote much more of their time than do men to family affairs and responsibilities. Some believe that this division of roles is due to the (alleged) comparative advantage of women in performing family-type tasks. Women are said to be more fit, and perhaps more inclined, than men to bring up children and perform various other household chores. If optimal behavior requires women to award first priority to managing their family affairs, they naturally participate less in the labor force, thus investing less on the job. Shorter and more frequently interrupted work careers also make investment in human capital less attractive. Women therefore tend to choose less demanding (and thus lower paying) jobs closer to home, with shorter hours, and so on. Because, in this system, the man becomes the principal earner, his choice of work place takes precedence within the family; his wife must then restrict her job search, which in turn obliges her in many cases to select less suitable jobs for which she tends to be, on the average, relatively over-qualified and underpaid compared to her husband (Frank, 1978).

The theory of comparative advantage by sex also includes jobs in the labor market. Alleged differences between men and women in ability and inclination to perform different tasks are thus said to explain part of the occupational segregation by sex observed to varying degrees in most societies. No doubt some "natural" differences between the sexes do enhance the performance of one or the other at a given job. The comparative advantage of men in performing hard physical labor is perhaps the most natural example. Yet at present there is no general agreement as to how much of the observed occupational segregation can be explained in this way.[7]

Sex discrimination can explain part of the observed earning differentials, either directly or indirectly, by being the underlying and ultimate reason for some of the explanatory factors mentioned above. It may exist openly in the labor market: lower wages may be paid to women performing identical work to men, or less money may be paid to women for what is essentially the same job but which has been disguised as a different (inferior) job, role, or occupation. Discrimination in the labor market can also take the form of blocking the entry of women into certain occupations or roles (management) or denying them equal opportunities to invest in certain forms of human capital. Both means constitute an alternative explanation for occupational segregation as opposed to the theory of comparative advantage.

On a deeper level, it is claimed that the lopsided distribution of family burdens, which is responsible for so much of the wage differential, is a direct result not of comparative advantage, but mostly of social or family norms created by men in a world dominated by men.[8] Even without open discrimination in the labor market or the family, women themselves are said to "freely choose" to behave in such a way as to create wide pay differentials, this "choice" being determined by and conditioned upon a system of "role segregation" deeply entrenched in the values, traditions, and educational systems of most societies to the benefit of men (Fuchs, 1971, pp. 14–15).

The actual mix of factors explaining the earnings gap varies among societies, over time, and even by the approach of the student who studies it. In all cases, however, there is a high degree of complementary interaction between most of the explanations listed: some discrimination in the labor market raises the relative advantage (per hour) of women in family work, which in turn reduces their incentive to invest in human capital, and so on.

It is interesting to note that although the human capital approach is formally rejected by Soviet scholars (Goilo, 1971, 1976) and that discrimination as such is formally preserved to explain only earning differentials in capitalist countries (Ershova, 1979), the study of why women are paid less in the Soviet Union adopts all three approaches described above.[9]

b. Sources of earning differentials by sex in Soviet society: a comparative approach

Even without a definitive explanation of earning differentials by sex, it seems possible to hypothesize on the relative size of this differential under Soviet conditions compared with developed market economies. As the data available are limited to the urban sector, the discussion here does not enter into the additional complexities involved in dealing with rural communities. Three possible sources of the male/female wage differential specific to the Soviet system are treated: ideology, Soviet growth strategy, and the system of wage determination.[10]

1. Ideology

All other things being equal, the ideological principles of Soviet society, if implemented, should considerably narrow the earning differential by sex. The official doctrine on wages is to pay everyone according to his or her contribution — that is, on the basis of productivity. Even if there is little room for preferential treatment for women within the wage system, this principle does guarantee equal pay for equal work; it rejects any form of irrelevant wage discrimination.[11] Women are granted equal access to almost all jobs and occupations, and there is no sex barrier to their entry into educational institutions. The ideological principles call, moreover, for women to enjoy equal status in the home and in society at large; a woman's personal and economic independence is to be on a par with that of men. Although these ideological principles — which called for deep changes in perceptions, values, and cultural traditions — could not be fully implemented even during the sixty years of Soviet rule, efforts to adopt most of them have raised the status of women in many respects and thus should have worked toward more equal pay.

There is, however, one major exception to this tendency: the equalization of the status of women within the family has lagged behind. At the same time as the proportion of women in the labor force and in the educational system increased rapidly, the status of women at home changed slowly, if at all. Working women in the Soviet Union still shoulder more than two-thirds of the household tasks (Kolpakov and Patrushev, 1971, pp. 83, 89), a burden that significantly reduces their relative productivity in the labor market. Apparently, it is much easier to create changes in the social sphere than to alter basic mental and cultural values within the family unit. As demonstrated below, in this state of affairs even the (net) effect of ideology on the relative pay of women is not clear.[12]

2. Soviet growth strategy

The specific growth strategy adopted by the Soviet Union has also contributed to the asymmetrical change in the status of women and, in this respect, has aggravated its consequences with regard to their relative pay. Rapid growth, especially via the "extensive" model, meant, first of all, enlisting most women into the labor force. This pressure gained further momentum during the 1960s and 1970s, during which some 86 percent of all women of working age (15 to 54) were employed (Turchaninova, 1975, p. 254), a figure 15–30 percentage points higher than in most Western societies (based on ILO, 1977, Table 1, and OECD, 1979, p. 28). The actual difference between the Soviet Union and the West is even wider, however, because there is very limited opportunity for part-time work in the Soviet Union.

On the other hand, efforts to maximize the rate of investment call for low consumption levels, especially with respect to consumer goods and services, but also regarding housing, household appliances, and childcare centers[13] Under such conditions, household tasks demand not only more time but also much more mental and physical effort. Were these tasks equally distributed within the family, they would not affect relative pay for women; but since they are not — as is so well documented by Soviet time-budget studies — most of the extra burden is shouldered by women, further reducing their ability to demonstrate equal productivity and thereby obtain equal pay in the labor market.

The coexistence of a heavier household burden with a higher rate of participation in the labor force adds further to the negative effect on women's pay. Among the non-working women in Western societies are those with higher-than-average family obligations. As their counterparts in the Soviet Union do work, the average negative effect of household tasks on women's pay in the Soviet Union is intensified; the almost complete absence of part-time work opportunities makes the situation even worse. Some of this pressure on the Soviet woman is relieved by raising fewer children (Berliner, 1977, pp. 13–22; Lapidus, 1978, pp. 262–63, 292–309) and/or children of "lower quality" (Berliner, 1977, pp. 23–39). Other possible consequences include the breaking up of families or the avoidance of family life altogether (Berliner, 1977, pp. 8–12; Lapidus-Warshafsky, 1978, pp. 236–40). The present study, however, is limited to women in families. As long as there is little change in the intrafamily distribution of household work, Soviet growth strategy will continue to be in direct conflict with the goal of achieving equal productivity and thus equal pay for women.

The planner may be interested in going even further and paying women less than their marginal product. This will be the case when he tries to maximize not total product but the "public surplus" of each worker above and beyond his private consumption. To engage a second family member in public-sector work, the planner must relieve the family of certain household tasks by supplying them through the market. This provision of additional services is considered by the planner as a cost that should be subtracted from the wages he would otherwise be willing to pay a second worker.[14] Given that families consider women members to be secondary earners (whether because of discrimination or on grounds of comparative advantage), the planner will want to pay women even less than their marginal product. If there is a reasonable amount of occupational segregation, such a policy may even be implemented, but we do not have any direct evidence to show that this is indeed attempted.[15]

A rapid rise in the number of women in the labor force in conjunction with a limited and slowly expanding supply of women-oriented jobs — as indeed is the case in the Soviet Union — can also negatively affect relative pay for women. By emphasizing heavy industry and construction and by limiting the extent of mechanization and automation of auxiliary and low-priority production processes, the Soviet growth strategy creates at each stage of economic development many more "male" jobs. It creates fewer "female" jobs by constraining the development of the service industries. Women who join the labor force may simply be obliged to take jobs in which they have a comparative disadvantage, such as work involving hard physical labor.[16]

Even with normal availability of female jobs, the higher-than-normal influx of women into the labor force may affect their relative pay. To the extent that the prevailing occupational segregation of the sexes is based on comparative advantage and on the assumption that the penetration of women into additional occupations and jobs proceeds according to principle, a higher proportion of women in any given profession means lower average productivity. On the other hand, to the extent that the initial occupational segregation results from discrimination, with men monopolizing the best jobs, the penetration of more women into high-paying jobs raises their average productivity. This process of rising productivity may be delayed, however, if the occupational segregation is achieved through well-developed social norms and perceptions. In such cases, women do not train for male jobs and thus appear as if they actually did have a natural disadvantage in performing them. In this way, actual comparative disadvantage may, in fact, be simply conditional upon accepted norms and values.

In reality, it seems to us that both discrimination and comparative advantage, part of which is not really natural but learned, account for occupational segregation. But even if discrimination is important in occupational segregation, the rapid entry of women into the labor force does not necessarily mean higher relative productivity or rate of pay, at least in the short run.

The higher priority given to heavy industry and the lower priority enjoyed by light industry, the service sector, and white-collar jobs in general, may also result in lower pay for women, who concentrate more in the latter group. The preferential pay awarded to important sectors may reflect an allocative goal — a premium above actual productivity — or it may enter into the concept of productivity as seen by the planners. Priority treatment (in investment allocation), coupled with restricted movement across sectors, can also create the same effect of higher marginal productivity in some branches.

A final aspect of Soviet growth strategy, but by no means the least important, is the drive to raise — as rapidly as possible — the level of education, qualifications, and training of the labor force. The fast growth of the Soviet educational system has enabled women to close the vast educational gap with men and to prepare themselves better to enter the labor force on an equal footing. Here, too, ideology and economic growth have converged to bring urban women more or less to equality with men in terms of the average length of their formal schooling. This should clearly reduce earning gaps resulting from different educational levels or from quasi-rents of holders of scarce skills.[17] It should also open up certain traditional male jobs to women. According to human capital theory, increased participation in the labor force, expressed here in the form of longer work careers for women with fewer and shorter interruptions, is complementary with a greater demand for education. In this sense the two reinforce each other to reduce male/female earning gaps.

3. The Soviet wage system

How are all the aforementioned factors translated into actual wages? How does the Soviet system of wage determination affect the relative pay of women? The major difference between the Soviet system and a market economy in this respect is that wage rates in the former are determined from above by the planning organs. Wages are based on such factors as output, working conditions, and the priority awarded to a particular industry or occupation.[18] The system ostensibly precludes, therefore, any direct discrimination, but it does prescribe lower pay for lower productivity, even if the latter results from indirect discrimination. Both Chapman and Lapidus — as well as many Soviet scholars — cite the allowances for conditions of work and the high rates of pay for preferred sectors as at least indirect sources of lower pay for women (see note 15). Even so, one is left with questions concerning the relation between officially prescribed wage rates and actual wages paid or the extent to which actual wages are determined by market forces.

Following the pioneering lead of Bergson (1944), most observers tend to believe that actual relative wages paid have a tendency to move toward labor market equilibrium levels[19] — that the household supply of labor and the demand for labor by managers are strong enough to mold wage rates to wages reflecting market conditions. In periods between wage reforms this is done with the help of various wage supplements — bonuses, premiums, changes in job definition, piece rates, and so on — which are more flexible than basic wage rates. Furthermore, changes in wages that take place between wage reforms due to market forces eventually find expression in various ways in the new wage scales determined by the next wage reform. The adjustment toward equilibrium does not have to take the form of changing wages, however; it can be achieved by the movement of people of different quality and commitment from one job to another to obtain wages suiting their qualifications. If we assume that market forces prevail, the existing overall wage differentials by sex and those within occupations and industries represent (a) measurable differences in labor quality — education, experience, hours, etc.; (b) differences in labor quality that cannot easily be measured, such as the degree of responsibility, intensity of work, and actual amount of on-the-job training required (as distinct from years of working experience); (c) differences in conditions of work or degree of disutility from work; (d) occupational barriers; and (e) elements introduced to promote dynamic adjustments toward equilibrium.

Applying all these factors to the question of wage differentials by sex, we believe that, first, occupational barriers external to women's own tastes do exist, but to a lesser degree than in Western societies. This follows from both the doctrine and growth needs of the system; it was further enhanced by the relative shortage of men during the last generation because of the war. Even with fewer barriers, however, the pay differentials may be just as large as in the West if the labor supply of women is relatively abundant. Second, we expect to find greater equality between the sexes with respect to the measurable quality variables, especially the level of education, length of experience, and hours of work. Third, we expect to find relatively wider wage differentials caused by items (b) and (c) above as women try to lighten the quantitative pressures on their time by reducing the quality and intensity of their work. In this way women develop tastes for less demanding jobs — with less on-the-job training, in low-priority industries, closer to home, with shorter regular hours and lighter physical and mental strain. There is, indeed, plenty of evidence in the Soviet literature on these qualitative adjustments to quantitative pressures (a common phenomenon in many other areas of economic activity).[20] This inclination to take lighter jobs increases the supply pressure on relatively low-level white-collar jobs, which, as we have seen, are in limited demand, and thus acts to reduce even further the wage paid there.

The lopsided development of more equality and opportunity for women in the labor market on the one hand, but heavier household pressures on the other, locked together in a system in which almost every woman is made to work, but with fewer female jobs, creates a situation in which it is not clear whether the relative pay for women should be higher or lower than under a system of possibly greater labor market discrimination but with smaller household burdens, a much lower participation rate for women, and a more ample supply of female jobs. As a minimum we think there are enough good reasons to assume that pay differentials by sex in the Soviet Union should not be significantly narrower than in the West.

3. Equations, variables, and data

a. The model, equations, and variables

The analysis in this chapter is based on unweighted data for 1,016 families. In addition to the general problems or biases discussed in Chapter 1, there are a number of specific problems relevant to the topic of this chapter. First, since all families are two-parent and active[21] it precludes the possibility of comparing the relative earnings of married women with those of single independent women.[22] This is unfortunate, because this last comparison is often used in Western studies to estimate the effect of family responsibilities on the productivity and earnings of women. On the basis of the previous discussion and Western findings, single (career) women should earn more than married women, but it is not clear if this should be the case for single mothers.

Second, specific biases may be created by the Jewish and emigrant character of SP to determine if Jewish husbands share more in household tasks, if Jewish mothers devote more time to family affairs, or if emigrant (or Jewish) families are less conservative and more open to new ideas, as, for example, that of women's liberation. Biases may be due to the many structural or compositional differences between SP and UP (to illustrate, two-thirds of SP are white-collar families, whereas UP is two-thirds blue-collar). Similarly, there are differences in levels of education, industrial and occupational structure, geographical location, and in other characteristics as well.

These differences, or most of them, can be accounted for or corrected simply by reweighting the findings on any given phenomenon by the relevant structure of UP instead of SP. Thus, if the relative earnings of blue-collar women are lower than those of university graduates, with respect to the corresponding groups of men, SP will show a higher overall relative women's earnings figure because blue-collar workers are underrepresented. This bias can be corrected by multiplying the two specific relative earnings by UP weights. The findings presented in this chapter have not yet been so corrected, but work in this direction is in progress.

Third, some bias in data for relative wages of women may be caused due to the fact that the SP data was not reweighted to conform to UP. Such biases seem however to be rather small.[23] It should be noted, however, that the structural ifferences do not affect, under reasonable conditions, the results of estimates based on multivariate (regression) analysis.

The main analytical approach used in this chapter is that of earning functions in which earnings and earning differentials are determined or explained by hours of work, level of education, experience, type of job (industry, role), and a number of other variables. Following Oaxaca (1973), Malkiel and Malkiel (1973), Mincer and Polachek (1974), and others, earning differentials by sex are explained by male/female differences in the aforementioned characteristics and an unexplained residual representing missing variables, errors in variables, and/or direct discrimination. The general form of the earning functions, following Mincer, is:

$$\ln W = a + (b \text{ sex}) + \Sigma c_i X_i + U_i$$

where W is earnings and X_i the explanatory variables. Such equations can be estimated for all workers with a dummy variable representing sex (as in Swafford, 1977), or for males and females separately. We have performed both estimates, but present only results based on separate equations. The gross earning differential can be attributed to the various factors and to the unexplained residual by multiplying the sex differential in any given variable by the coefficient of the same variable estimated by either the corresponding male or female earning function (Oaxaca, 1973, pp. 695–98).

The main earning variables and the variables used to explain earning differentials are as follows:

1. Earning variables

The analysis uses four different concepts of earnings (each with a corresponding male/female ratio), all net of direct taxes, per month:

W0 (W0R)   Basic wages or salary from the main place of work, i.e., excluding bonuses or premiums, overtime, etc.

W1 (W1R)   Total wages and salaries from the main place of work, including bonuses etc.

W2 (W2R)   Total earnings from the public sector, i.e., W1 *plus* all earnings from extra jobs in the public sector.

W4 (W4R)   Total earnings, i.e., W2 *plus* any private earnings reported by the respondents.

Of all these, gross W1 is closest to the wage concept published in official Soviet publications.

2. Explanatory variables

Earning ratios by sex are explained by the following variables:

1. *Hours of work.* The present analysis is carried out for full-time workers only, so that differences in regular hours worked (HO) represent differences in what constitutes "full time" (hours per week) in different jobs. The values of the other variables — H1, H2, and H4 — which correspond to W1–W4, vary, of course, according to the amount of extra work performed.

2. *Education.* Two sets of variables are used: years of formal schooling and level of schooling completed. The regressions include mostly the former, with a small correction for the type of school (regular, night, or correspondence) in the case of university studies:[24] RS, years in regular school (up to 10 years); PS, years in secondary vocational (professional) schools; US, years toward first university degree; and AS, advanced university studies.

3. *Experience (EX).* A proxy for on-the-job training is estimated by using the actual number of years worked (not life following formal schooling, as in many Western studies). Following conventional theory, both EX and $(EX)^2$ are introduced into the equations.

4. *Age (Age).* When both schooling (in years) and experience are present

in the regression, *Age* measures years of neither work nor school, the depreciation of human capital, and the quality (vintage) of formal education. *Experience* and *Age*, however, are closely correlated, as are their respective coefficients.

5. *Branch and role.* The introduction of such characteristics into earning functions as independent variables is controversial, especially when near-perfection in the labor market is assumed. We introduce these variables in the following analysis as proxies for differences in labor quality unaccounted for by other variables and/or as estimates of the effects of occupational segregation under conditions of market imperfection, as explained above. The variables included are for industry (IND1 to IND12) with IND1 for manufacturing as the reference variable, and IND2 — agriculture; IND3 — construction; IND4 — communications; IND5 — transportation; IND6 — communal and housing services; IND7 — trade; IND8 — health services; IND9 — education and culture; IND11 — science; IND12 — administration and social security.

The dummy variables for *Role* are ROLE1 (managerial jobs); ROLE2 (high professional jobs, which require university education) — the reference role; ROLE3 (low professional jobs, requiring secondary vocational education); ROLE4 (nonprofessional white-collar jobs); ROLE5 (skilled blue-collar jobs); ROLE6 (semi-skilled workers); ROLE7 (unskilled workers); and ROLE8 (service blue-collar workers of all skill levels).

A dummy variable for non-married status was added to some of the equations, but as mentioned earlier, the non-married in SP belong to active families and are typically either young or old and thus earn less than their married counterparts, who are normally heads of families or wives of prime working age.

Other variables that were included in the analysis but did not contribute to the explanation of wages or wage differentials include location variables, health information, and the number of children of various ages. The effect of the number of children and their ages on earnings at a certain point in time is not straightforward and needs to be studied further.

4. Results and interpretation

The results are presented in two forms. In Tables 7.1 and 7.4–7.7 and in Figure 7.1 we present results on wages and wage differentials by sex, classified by one or more of the main explanatory variables. These results are gross in the sense that the levels of other variables are not kept constant, and they are presented mainly as a source of data for the interested reader. The regression, multivariate results are presented in Tables 7.2 and 7.3. Table 7.2 contains results of four earning functions, two for men and two for women, with ln W1 as the dependent variable. In each case, one regression ("short") excludes, and a second ("long") includes the variables for role, industry, and non-married status. The levels of the relevant variables are also shown for men (column 1), women (column 2), and the differences between them (column 3). Table 7.3 contains an analysis of the male/female earning difference according to the variables included in the long earning functions.

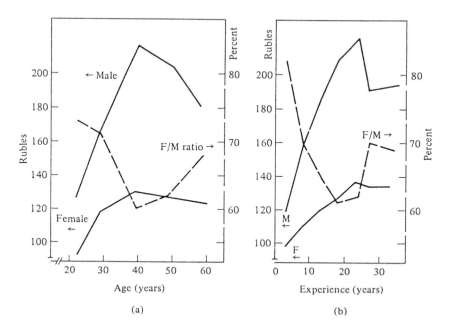

Figure 7.1. Wage profiles by sex and (a) age group; (b) experience group

Table 7.1. Earnings and hours of work by sex

	All (1)	Male (2)	Female (3)	F/M ratio (4)
1. Number	2,106	1,117	989	0.47[a]
2. *Earnings per month* (rubles)				
a. Basic wage (W0)	130.5	153.6	104.6	0.68
b. Main workplace (W1)	153.8	185.1	118.8	0.64
c. Public sector (W2)	160.2	194.8	120.9	0.62
d. All work (W4)	168.8	208.5	123.8	0.59
3. *Hours per week*				
a. Regular hours (H0)	38.1	39.0	36.6	0.94
b. Main workplace (H1)	39.9	41.1	37.6	0.91
c. Public sector (H2)	41.1	42.4	38.2	0.90
d. All work (H4)	41.9	44.1	38.6	0.88
4. *Wage per hour* (rubles)				
a. Basic wage (WPH0)	0.79	0.91	0.66	0.73
b. Main workplace (WPH1)	0.89	1.04	0.73	0.70
c. Public sector (WPH2)	0.90	1.06	0.73	0.69
d. All work (WPH4)	0.93	1.09	0.74	0.68
5. Level of education (years)	13.0	12.9	13.0	0.1[b]
6. Work experience (years)	17.2	19.6	14.4	−5.2[b]
7. Age (years)	37.2	38.7	35.5	−3.2[b]

[a] Proportion of women in labor force.

[b] Female/male difference in years.

The entire earning differential[25] is broken down into "explained" and "unexplained" segments. The explained segment, which appears in Table 7.3, is calculated as the sum of the products of the male/female differences in levels of the variables (Table 7.2, column 3) multiplied by the corresponding (male or female) regression coefficients (Table 7.2, columns 6 and 7). This is equivalent to calculating the hypothetical earnings of women (men) had they been paid according to the men's (women's) earning function and comparing them to actual earnings (see Gronau, 1979; Malkiel and Malkiel, 1973; Oaxaca, 1973). The explained portion of the earning differential is attributed to the several variables in an aggregated form. Table 7.3 contains an analysis of earning differentials for the entire population (as in Table 7.2) and for three sub-groups thereof: those with university degrees or more, those with secondary professional diplomas, and those possessing a lower level of education (the corresponding equations are not shown). Since our main interest is in the earning differentials, the discussion will follow the findings of Table 7.3, referring back to Table 7.2 when necessary. A few remarks will also be added on the results obtained for the other earning variables discussed above, which are not shown here.[26] In comparing the results in the other tables with those in Tables 7.2 and 7.3, the reader is reminded that in the former the earning differential is defined by W_{female}/W_{male}, whereas in the latter we use $\ln W_{male} - \ln W_{female}$.[27]

Data on the overall earning differential by sex are presented in Table 7.1. Net monthly earnings from the main job average R185.1 for men and R118.8 for women, 64 percent that of men (line 2b). Since W1 is the (net) wage category closest to that published in official Soviet data, given the small effect of the structural difference between SP and UP (see Chapter 1, Section 3), this earning differential should not be too different from the one that would have been observed from Soviet data on net wages.[28]

Wage rates (W0) are more equal than monthly main-job earnings (W1), but total earnings, including extra public (W2) and private (W4) jobs, show wider gaps. Thus, in terms of basic wage, women earn 68 percent of what men earn, but the rate falls to 59 percent when all earnings are taken into account (Table 7.1, line 2d). Part of the growing gap is explained by the widening hours gap over the range from H0 (basic hours) to H4 (total

Table 7.2. Earning functions of males (M) and females (F)

| | Level of variables | | | Regression coefficients | | | |
| | Males (1) | Females (2) | M/F difference (3) | Short equation | | Long equation | |
				Male (4)	Female (5)	Male (6)	Female (7)
1. Monthly earnings from main job (lnW1)	5.1297	4.7165	0.4132	..	..	..	..
2. R^2/standard error of estimate	..	..	..	0.32/0.35	0.31/0.29	0.39/0.33	0.43/0.26
3. Regression constant	..	..	..	2.799	3.584	2.830	3.900
Independent variables							
4. Regular hours (ln H1)	3.7193	3.6600	0.0593	0.440	0.139	0.425	0.086[a]
5. Regular school (RS; years)	9.24	9.57	−0.33	0.023	0.024	0.028	0.031
6. Professional school (PS; yrs)	1.09	1.15	−0.06	0.027	0.019	0.031	0.021
7. University (US; years)	1.93	1.88	0.05	0.050	0.065	0.047	0.052
8. Advanced studies (AS; years)	0.26	0.06	0.20	0.063	0.076	0.070	0.090
9. Experience (EX; years)	19.58	14.41	5.17	0.051	0.026	0.036	0.017
10. $(\text{Experience})^2$ $(EX)^2$	507.59	282.96	224.63	−0.0007	−0.0004	−0.0005	−0.0002
11. Age (years)	38.69	35.51	3.18	−0.0077	−0.0006[a]	−0.0030[a]	0.0011[a]
12. Unmarried (years)	0.099	0.117	−0.018	..	..	−0.006[a]	−0.063[b]
Roles							
13. Managerial	0.235	0.068	0.167	..	..	0.119	0.181

14. High-level professional (ref.)	0.321	0.418	−0.096	:	:	‥	‥
15. Semiprofessional	0.057	0.290	−0.233	:	:	−0.092[b]	−0.124
16. Other white-collar	0.014	0.032	−0.018	:	:	−0.018[a]	−0.285
Blue collar							
17. Skilled	0.120	0.004	0.116	:	:	0.162	−0.103[a]
18. Semiskilled	0.121	0.030	0.091	:	:	0.087[b]	0.040[a]
19. Unskilled	0.049	0.036	0.013	:	:	−0.107[b]	−0.017[a]
20. Services	0.082	0.121	−0.039	:	:	−0.085[a]	−0.134
Industry							
21. Manufacturing (ref.)	0.349	0.260	0.089	:	:	‥	‥
22. Agriculture	0.025	0.013	0.012	:	:	−0.070[a]	−0.109[a]
23. Transport	0.063	0.016	0.047	:	:	−0.056[a]	−0.138[b]
24. Communications	0.007	0.013	−0.006	:	:	0.305	−0.124[a]
25. Construction	0.106	0.035	0.072	:	:	0.007[a]	−0.037[a]
26. Trade and catering	0.084	0.107	−0.023	:	:	−0.147	−0.085
27. Communal services	0.123	0.090	0.033	:	:	−0.041[a]	−0.025[a]
28. Health services	0.068	0.189	−0.121	:	:	0.227	−0.216
29. Education and culture	0.091	0.176	−0.085	:	:	−0.027[a]	−0.166
30. Science	0.071	0.056	−0.015	:	:	−0.108	−0.209
31. Administration and banking	0.013	0.045	−0.013	:	:	−0.111[a]	−0.038[a]

Note: Except where otherwise indicated, coefficients are significant at 1 percent.

[a] Not significant at 5 percent.
[b] Significant at 5 percent.

Table 7.3. Sources of earning differentials by sex (M = male; F = female)

		Entire population		University graduates		Secondary professional		General schooling or less	
		M eq. (1)	F eq. (2)	M eq. (3)	F eq. (4)	M eq. (5)	F eq. (6)	M eq. (7)	F eq. (8)
1.	Wage differential[a]	41.32	41.32	35.71	35.71	47.08	47.08	43.98	43.98
2.	Explained[b]	20.35	16.24	17.17	15.39	21.74	19.08	23.84	12.97
	Due to:								
3.	Hours	2.48	0.50	3.61	1.22	2.74	1.22	1.34	−0.27
4.	Education	0.49	0.80	3.20	3.81	0.85	1.63	−0.25	−0.93
5.	Experience	7.73	4.14	2.94	−0.25	5.53	9.03	11.99	3.27
6.	Age	−1.04	0.35	2.29	2.26	−0.30	−1.39	−2.46	−.26
7.	Role	7.03	6.35	4.35	6.42	5.56	−1.10	7.34	8.07
8.	(Managerial)	(1.98)	(3.04)	(3.95)	(6.69)	(−0.08)	(−0.10)	(1.43)	(0.68)
9.	(Semi-professional)	(2.15)	(2.92)	(0.42)	(0.10)	(4.07)	(5.14)	(2.24)	(5.66)
10.	Industry	3.66	4.10	0.82	1.88	7.42	9.68	5.30	2.12
11.	(Health services)	(2.77)	(2.60)	(1.13)	(1.01)	(10.26)	(6.85)	(1.28)	(0.76)
12.	Unexplained	20.97	25.08	18.54	20.32	25.34	28.00	20.14	31.01
Percentages									
13.	Total wage differential	100.0	100.0	100.0	100.0	100.0	100.0	100.0	100.0
14.	Unexplained	50.7	60.7	48.1	43.1	46.2	40.5	54.2	70.5
15.	Explained[c]	49.3	39.3	51.9	56.9	53.8	59.5	45.8	29.5
16.	Explained percent	100.0	100.0	100.0	100.0	100.0	100.0	100.0	100.0
17.	by: Hours	12.2	3.1	21.0	7.9	12.6	6.4	5.6	−2.1
18.	Education	2.4	4.9	18.6	24.8	3.9	8.5	−1.0	−7.2
19.	Experience	38.0	25.5	17.1	−1.6	25.4	47.3	50.3	25.2
20.	Age	−5.1	2.2	13.3	14.7	−1.4	−7.3	10.3	2.0
21.	Role	34.5	39.1	25.3	41.7	25.6	−5.8	30.8	62.2
22.	Industry	18.0	25.2	4.8	12.2	34.1	50.7	22.2	16.3
23.	Number of observations	1,117	989	448	376	244	319	425	294

[a] $\ln W1_m - \ln W1_f$; see note 30 for correspondence with arithmetic ratios of $W1_f / W1_m$.

(Notes continued on following page.)

b The figures in columns (1) and (2) are calculated on the basis of the un-
   rounded figures underlying those shown in columns (3), (6), and (7) in
   Table 7.2.

c Small effect of being unmarried included in total but not shown.

hours). At their main job, women work fewer regular hours than men (36.6
vs. 39.0) because they are highly concentrated in jobs with short work weeks,
especially as teachers and nurses. On top of their regular working week,
women also work fewer additional hours both at their main place of work
(H1) and in extra public (H2) or private (H4) jobs. When all hours of work
are accounted for, women work 38.6 hours per week, only 88 percent of the
44.1 hours a week that men work. The second part of the growing gap is due
to the higher pay per hour received for extra work in general and by men in
particular. For this reason, women's wages per hour go down from 73 percent
of men's for basic hours to 68 percent for all hours. The widening of the gap
between W0 and the other wage concepts may reflect in particular the
influence of market forces on the wage rates determined by the planners.

A side implication of the data in Table 7.1 is that in addition to being
employed for a longer regular working week, men engaged much more than
women in extra work of all kinds (5.1 hours per week for men, 2.0 hours for
women). In this way, part of the observed imbalance in household work in
the other direction is offset.

Additional information on the overall earnings gap, this time for sub-
groups of the population, is included in Table 7.3. The wage gap (based on
W1) is narrowest for academics, the male advantage being only 35.7 percent
compared to the average advantage of 41.3 percent, and widest for semi-
professionals (47.1 percent). It is somewhat narrower (44.0 percent) for those
with general education or less (line 1).[29] The high inequality of the middle
group is somewhat surprising, as one would expect inequality to be negatively
correlated with the level of education. We shall come back to this special
feature later.

Roughly half of these earning differentials are explained by the independent variables included in the analysis according the male equations — only about 40 percent when the female equations are used (Table 7.3). The unexplained part of the pay differentials represents lower pay for women of the same age, education, and experience as men, who work the same number of hours, in the same industry, and at the same job level. This unexplained difference may result in principle from lower quality (rather than quantity) of experience or education, from lower productivity, or from other factors such as the second burden at home, comparative advantage or discrimination. We tried, without success, to estimate directly the possible effects of having small children and sickness-related absenteeism from work.[30] The pure children effect may show up in earning functions for women in those age groups, such as 25–45 (not estimated yet), where their presence should hurt most. We believe that the household burden is very important in the unexplained portion of the gap, but at least until further work is done one cannot exclude the influence of other factors.

The impacts of the main independent variables on the explained part of the earning gaps are as follows.

1. Differences in the *number of hours* worked account for only a small part of the explained segment, at most one-fifth for academics according to one equation, but usually less than 10 percent. Although the difference in hours by sex is itself relatively small, this result is also due to the low coefficients for hours estimated by the equations — 0.425 for men and (non-significant) 0.086 for women (Table 7.2, long equation). Part of the hours' effect is due to the shorter working week prevailing in a number of sectors; as a result, the elasticity of hours in the short equations is slightly higher. The lower elasticities of hours in the female equations probably result from the higher pay per hour received by women in jobs that require fewer hours. The relative importance of hours does increase, however, as we move to more inclusive earning concepts. This results from a widening of the male/female difference in the number of hours worked and from a rise in the elasticity of earnings with respect to hours.[31] But even when we account for the larger contribution of hours in explaining the gap of total wages (W4) there remains a difference in the earning gap between W4 and W1: for the entire

population, based on the men's equation, the differentials are 42 percent for the former and 39 percent for the latter.

2. The contribution of *education* to earning differentials by sex is on the average very small, less than 1 percent (Table 7.3). This is a combined result of the overall equality in the level of education between the sexes (Tables 7.2 and 7.4) and the relatively low rates of return to formal education in the Soviet Union (Table 7.2). The latter average 2–3 percent per year for regular schooling and for secondary professional training, but reach 6–9 percent per year for advanced studies. These should be compared to rates of over 10 percent in the West (see, e.g., Mincer, 1974, pp. 92–93).

For a number of reasons the picture is somewhat different when education is broken down into its various stages. First, women are under-represented in groups of both high and low educational attainment and over-represented in the group possessing secondary vocational education. Whereas they constitute less than one-fifth of those with advanced degrees (less than half their average proportion), women account for almost three fifths of those with secondary vocational training (Table 7.4). An implication of this structural difference is that although women study only slightly more than men, they spend on the average more time in regular and secondary pro-fessional schools and less time in universities, especially in advanced studies (0.26 year for men and 0.06 year for women, and 0.65 and 0.49 year, respectively, for academics; see Table 7.2). For this reason, education reduces the sex earning differentials for the low educational groups but raises them considerably for university graduates.[32] The male advantage created by edu-cation in the semiprofessional group (Table 7.3) results from more professional schooling for men who belong to this group.

Second, for higher levels of education, especially for advanced studies, female rates of return are higher than those for males. This differential might reflect the existence of a comparative advantage for women in jobs that require high education as well as the operation of a selection process in which only the most highly skilled women can overcome the difficulties involved in obtaining jobs demanding such advanced training. The difficulties of penetrating into jobs requiring advanced degrees are demonstrated by both the low proportion of women found in such jobs and their low relative pay

Table 7.4. Female-to-male earning differentials by education, age, and experience

	Female/male ratios				
	Percent women in group (1)	Monthly wages		Hourly wages	
		W1 (2)	W4 (3)	WPH1 (4)	WPH4 (5)
All	47.0	0.64	0.59	0.70	0.68
A. Level of education					
Advanced degree	18.2	0.64	0.59	0.70	0.69
University degree	48.0	0.70	0.67	0.80	0.80
University incomplete	46.0	0.64	0.61	0.71	0.70
Secondary professional	58.6	0.59	0.53	0.62	0.58
Secondary general	43.5	0.62	0.57	0.66	0.63
7–9 years	41.3	0.63	0.57	0.66	0.63
6 years or less	31.6	0.65	0.57	0.71	0.68
B. Age groups (years)					
17–24	55.3	0.72	0.69	0.79	0.76
25–34	50.3	0.71	0.63	0.77	0.73
35–44	48.3	0.60	0.56	0.67	0.66
45–54	44.0	0.63	0.59	0.64	0.63
55+	20.3	0.68	0.68	0.75	0.75
C. Experience groups (years)					
0–5	63.0	0.82	0.78	0.86	0.84
6–10	49.0	0.70	0.64	0.75	0.71
11–15	55.0	0.65	0.57	0.77	0.72
16–20	54.7	0.61	0.57	0.66	0.65
21–25	43.1	0.62	0.59	0.69	0.68
26–30	37.6	0.70	0.63	0.73	0.70
31+	18.2	0.69	0.70	0.67	0.70

(Table 7.4). Comparative advantage seems to play a greater role for university graduates without advanced degrees, because there women are adequately represented and their relative pay is high.

3. The female/male ratios by *age* and *experience* show definite U-shaped forms (Table 7.4 and Figure 1): the relatively high ratios for young age and experience groups decline with rising age and experience but start rising again at older ages and after long experience. The earning ratio patterns correspond to an inverted-U-shaped development of male and female earnings through the age groups and a logistic or parabolic shape of the experience-wage profiles. At least the form of all these patterns are well established by human capital theory and closely resemble findings in the West. At young ages (and low experience) women earn 72 (82) percent of an average man's wage — 79 (86) percent per hour (based on W1 and WPH1). These ratios decline to 0.60 (0.67 per hour) at 35–44 years of age, and to 0.61 (0.66 per hour) after 16–20 years of experience. The climb back to 0.68 (0.75 per hour) at higher ages and to 0.70 (0.73 per hour) for the group with long (26–30 years) experience. The U-shaped patterns of the male/female wage ratios reflect a situation in which the intensive accumulation of human capital by men during work is offset at older ages and long experience by a selection process in which (mostly) women of lower earning capacity leave the labor force. This process can be observed by the declining proportion of women in high-age and long-experience groups. Part of the initial rise in the ratios may also reflect a time trend of declining direct and indirect discrimination against women. Another part of the pattern is explained by a sharper decline in number of hours (relative to men) worked by women of prime working age with relatively long experience.

When translated into the regression analysis, sex differences in work experience are found to be a major source of pay differentials for all groups except academics (Tables 7.2 and 7.3). They explain between 5.5 and 12 points of the total differential for the other groups, but only 2.9 for academics[33] (male equations), or between one quarter and one half of the entire explained portion. As seen in Table 7.2, the EX coefficients are in general not very different from those for education although, unlike education, the decline (as expected) over time flattens out completely after

32–36 years.[34] However, they seem to be higher than those found in most Western studies, but this may result from the direct estimate of experience in our study in contrast to the "years following schooling" used in many Western ones.[35] In all cases the EX coefficients in the female equations are much lower than the corresponding ones for males, not only initially, but — with one major exception — at all relevant experience levels. Since the rates of return to investment in education are not lower for women, this would seem to indicate that the rate of investment in human capital on the job per year of work is lower for women than for men. That such is indeed the case is fully documented in Soviet sources; the main reason given there is that women have less available free time because of family responsibilities (Parkhomenko, 1972, p. 78).

The difference of over 5 years in work experience between the sexes contributes, of course, to the experience part of the earning differential. By Western standards, however, this is a small experience gap. Analytically, it can be divided into one gap resulting from the lower average age of women (3.2 years in SP, Table 7.1) and an experience gap between persons of the same age. Controlling for age, the experience gap narrows by almost half, to 2.6 years.[36] The pure experience effect is thus only about half of what is shown in Table 7.3; the rest should be added to the age effect. It may be, however, that because of the high correlation between age and experience, there is some shifting of effects between them; the results should be viewed in this light.

The age coefficients in earning functions are expected to represent depreciation of human capital and obsolescence of old vintage education, as well as interruptions during schooling or working careers. They are thus expected to be negative, as indeed they are in three of the four equations of Table 7.2. The age coefficient is positive, however, in the equations for academics and in some other female equations. Positive or non-significant values may reflect the collinearity with experience, mentioned above.

As mentioned above, up to one year of the age difference — and a resulting 0.7 year of experience gap — may be due to a bias of SP. This may account for up to one point of the earning gap by sex.

In the short equations the coefficients for hours, experience, and advanced studies are higher that in the long equations, so that despite lower coefficients for the other schooling stages, the variables explain more of the earning gap in the short run than in the long equations. Part of the impact of hours, experience, etc. is absorbed in the long equations by roles and industries correlated with the main variables, such as a positive correlation between managerial roles and experience.

4. That *role* is an important explanatory factor is shown by the gross female/male ratios by role (Table 7.5), the relevant regression coefficients (Table 7.2), and the contribution of role in explaining the earning gap (Table 7.3). To put it concisely, women are underrepresented in high-level roles that pay well and overrepresented in low-level roles that pay less. The product of this negative relationship explains between 6.35 and 7.03 points of the entire earning gap, between 34 and 40 percent of the explained portion (Table 7.3). The most important contributors to this large role effect are:[37]

a. Only 7 percent of all women fill managerial roles that pay a 12 percent (men's equation) to 18 percent (women's equation) premium over wages of high professional workers (which is the reference group; see Table 7.2, line 14). The results on the earning gap, as shown in line 8 of Table 7.3, demonstrate that this factor along absorbs more or less the entire role effect for academic workers.

b. 29 percent of all women are semi-professionals against only 6 percent of all men, and here there is a negative premium of 9–12 percent. This factor alone reduces women's wages for the two schooling groups of workers by 22.–5.6 points, a major part of the total role effect.

c. Skilled workers, and to a lesser degree semi-skilled workers, earn wage premiums of up to 16 percent (over high professionals' wages!), but women are almost totally absent among their ranks (Table 7.2).[38]

d. Women are overrepresented among service workers who earn a premium of 8.5–13.4 percent. The last two factors affect predominantly the lowest schooling group, mostly blue-collar workers

Table 7.5. Earning differentials by sex: job level and role

	Female/male ratios				
	Percent women in group (1)	Monthly wages		Hourly wages	
		W1 (2)	W4 (3)	WPH1 (4)	WPH4 (5)
1. All	47.0	0.64	0.59	0.70	0.68
2. *Employees: All*	51.9	0.62	0.58	0.67	0.66
a. Managers	20.4	0.75	0.70	0.74	0.72
b. High-level professionals	53.5	0.72	0.66	0.82	0.80
c. Semi-professionals	81.8	0.67	0.64	0.67	0.67
d. Other white-collar	66.7	0.55	0.49	0.55	0.52
3. *Workers: All*	31.4	0.61	0.57	0.66	0.63
a. Managers	2.9	0.57	0.49	0.56	0.52
b. Skilled workers	18.2	0.75	0.66	0.76	0.71
c. Low-skilled workers	39.6	0.85	0.75	0.86	0.81
d. Service workers	56.6	0.70	0.65	0.72	0.71

workers, accounting together for 4 points of the earning gap. Again we find that the role coefficients in the female equations are usually positive and higher than those for men for roles in which men predominate; they are negative and larger (in absolute terms) for roles where women predominate.

The importance of role as an explanatory variable is also demonstrated in Table 7.5 in that intrarole earning ratios (with two unimportant exceptions) are much higher than the average ratio. Table 7.5 also demonstrates a rather complicated relationship between the proportion of women in a certain role

Table 7.6. Earning differentials by sex and industry[a]

		Percent women in group (1)	Female/male W1 wage ratio (2)	Monthly wage from main work-place W1 (rubles) (3)
All		47.0	0.64	185.1
1.	Manufacturing: All	39.7	0.68	190.0
	i. Workers	(31.8)	(0.68)	(169.9)
	ii. Employees	(45.2)	(0.65)	(209.7)
2.	Transportation	18.6	0.56	179.7
3.	Construction	22.9	0.71	199.4
4.	Trade and catering: All	53.0	0.65	160.6
	i. Workers	(53.8)	(0.64)	(139.5)
	ii. Employees	(52.5)	(0.66)	(174.3)
5.	Communal services: All	39.4	0.69	162.2
	i. Workers	(25.9)	(0.69)	(156.3)
	ii. Employees	(59.3)	(0.65)	(178.3)
6.	Health services	71.1	0.64	174.6
7.	Education and culture	65.3	0.63	189.4
8.	Art	21.4	0.47	242.1
9.	Science	41.8	0.58	218.8
10.	Administration[b]	71.3	0.68	162.1

[a] According to official Soviet classification.
[b] Includes social insurance, banking, and communications.

and their relative pay: among employees (with one exception) this relation-ship is negative, whereas among workers (again with one exception)[39] it is positive. We shall come back to investigate this relationship for a more detailed breakdown by occupation.

Table 7.7. Relative earnings and the proportion of women: 35 occupations

Occupational group[a]	Percent women in group (1)	Female/ male wage ratio (2)	Average male wage (rubles per month) (3)	Total number in group (4)
Average 35 occupations	46.2	0.82	180.5	2,106
1. Enterprise managers	0.0	..	387.4	5
2. Highly skilled workers, heavy industry	0.0	..	198.1	96
3. Skilled workers, heavy industry	4.3	0.71	167.4	116
4. Senior faculty members	5.9	0.66	350.9	16
5. Highly skilled workers, light industry	9.5	0.59	188.4	42
6. Unit production managers	11.7	0.81	232.7	60
7. Head engineers	13.2	0.72	253.3	53
8. Senior research personnel	18.4	0.62	316.7	38
9. Department managers	18.7	0.84	213.7	75
10. Artists	19.4	0.66	233.0	31
11. Low-skilled workers, light industry	25.0	0.82	127.2	44
12. Senior engineers	32.9	0.76	192.9	79
13. Employees in services	33.3	0.87	137.8	18
14. Senior trade employees	35.9	0.76	166.3	59
15. Engineers	39.8	0.75	174.1	216
16. Senior doctors	40.0	1.01	210.4	25
17. Dentists	43.5	0.78	123.5	23
18. Skilled workers, light industry	51.0	0.85	145.0	49
19. Chief planners, economists	52.6	0.84	188.1	57
20. Low-skilled workers, light industry	53.2	0.90	115.5	47
21. Junior faculty members	56.2	0.97	153.6	16
22. Service workers	56.6	0.70	139.0	212
23. Junior trade employees	58.3	0.52	172.0	24
24. Junior research personnel	60.6	0.90	133.3	33

(cont.)

Table 7.7. (cont.)

Occupational group[a]	Percent women in group (1)	Female/male wage ratio (2)	Average male wage (rubles per month) (3)	Total number in group (4)
25. Chief editors, writers	60.9	0.61	190.7	23
26. Journalists	62.2	0.63	142.4	37
27. Technicians	62.3	0.73	154.5	77
28. Medical doctors	71.3	0.77	188.6	80
29. Teachers	74.8	0.79	162.0	155
30. Planners, economists	85.2	0.91	139.8	27
31. Accountants	86.8	0.61	177.3	136
32. Pharmacists	87.5	1.18	78.3	32
33. Laboratory assistants	91.3	1.29	75.0	23
34. Nurses	92.4	0.81	106.8	66
35. Secretaries	100.0	..	..	16

[a] In increasing order of female representation.

5. The different *industrial structure* of the sexes is less important than role for the entire group as well as for all sub-groups, except for those with secondary professional schooling (Table 7.3). Its effect is very small for the academic group, where none of the industry coefficients in the male equation are significant. Academic salaries apparently vary least between branches. But for those with secondary professional schooling, industrial structure is the most important explanatory factor. As can be observed from line 28 in Table 7.2, the branch that is mostly responsible for the industry effect is "health services." All the equations have large negative coefficients for this branch (as compared with salaries in manufacturing) — and in every group of workers women are represented in this branch to a much higher degree than men.[40] A high concentration of women, plus negative coefficients for education and culture, also contribute a little to the industry effect, especially for the low-

schooling group. On the whole, however, much of the gross industry variation in relative pay for women observed in Table 7.6 seems to be absorbed by the other variables.

6. Table 7.7 includes data on the proportion of women, female/male earning differentials, and men's wages for 35 *occupational groups* of workers. This disaggregation goes far beyond what is included in the regression equations. In deciding not to include the detailed occupational breakdown in the regressions, we shared Fuchs' (1971, p. 14) conviction "that if one pushes occupational classification far enough, one could 'explain' nearly all the (earning) differential." On the other hand, such analysis may shed more light on the question of occupational segregation.

As indeed found by Fuchs and others, intraoccupational wage differentials by sex are much smaller than the overall differences. Within occupational groupings the unweighted, average male/female monthly pay ratio is 0.82; per hour, the ratio rises to 0.85. This implies a significant degree of occupational segregation, with women being concentrated in lower paying occupations. In seventeen occupations, comprising 41.6 percent of all those employed, the proportion accounted for by one sex is at least 75 percent of the total. Included here are three single-sex occupations: enterprise managers and highly skilled workers in industry on the one side, and secretaries on the other. The predominantly male occupations are either characterized by high managerial content and the need for advanced studies, or call for skilled work in (heavy) industry; the predominantly female occupations are nurses, pharmacists, planners, economists, accountants, teachers, and doctors (only the last group differs from the pattern commonly found in the West). Another 38.1 percent of all workers and employees work in occupations with 60–75 percent majorities for one sex or the other, and only 20.3 percent (seven occupations) work in balanced groups.[41]

That women concentrate in low-paying occupations can be seen by comparing the proportion of women (column 1) with the level of wages paid to men (column 3). The simple correlation between the two (for 34 occupations) is −0.66; the regression coefficient of the latter with respect to the former — controlling for education, hours and experience — is −0.346 (t = −4.6071).[42]

A second observation from Table 7.7 is, however, that the relative pay of women is positively correlated with the proportion of women in a given occupation. The simple correlation between the two (for thirty-two occupations) is 0.39 and a regression coefficient of the latter with respect to the former is 0.24 (t = 2.3398). This second finding may be partially dependent on the first (the male wage is the denominator of the pay ratio), but it also has independent significance. The two findings together are consistent with most of the findings on segregation by role and with all the theories explaining occupational segregation.

The concentration of women in low-paying jobs may result from heavy family burdens with all that they imply, whereas the high relative pay may reflect derived or genuine comparative advantage and/or the consequences of the "over-qualification" of women in the jobs they perform. Also, the large demand by women for such jobs may force a decline in average wages for everybody, crowding out the more qualified men. But the same pattern of concentration of women may just as well reflect artificial entrance barriers to the best-paying jobs and all the rest follows. In both cases it is possible to use the existing occupational segregation to artificially reduce wages in women's jobs below marginal productivity. Again we tend to believe that the first set of factors dominate, but more study is needed to substantiate this claim.

The figures in Table 7.7 as well as the findings in Tables 7.2 and 7.3 point to a large cluster of women with inferior pay, which is "responsible" for a major part of the earning differential. These are women with secondary vocational education working in semi-professional roles and occupations in economic branches (such as health and education) with great demand for such workers. These women constitute the majority of the middle educational group in Table 7.3, where the earning differential is the widest. This situation best symbolizes the problems of the Soviet working woman, who tries to avoid physical work on the one hand, and for whom many jobs with high professional training are too demanding under the circumstances. The relative scarcity of such jobs creates the pressure that helps to reduce relative wages in these areas and branches.[43] The most striking example on the border of this group is that of medical doctors: unlike anywhere in the West, women make up about 70 percent of this group in the Soviet Union, but — also unlike anywhere in the West — doctors in the Soviet Union are paid very low salaries. Finally, because medicine is public, the burdens of the job are much lighter than typically in the West. In short, the medical profession was opened to women and adapted to their needs; the rate of pay was reduced accordingly.

5. Conclusion: observations in a comparative context

The main conclusions to be drawn from the foregoing analysis is that by and large both the levels of the pay differential by sex and the main explanatory factors in the Soviet Union are similar to those in the developed Western economies. A full-scale comparative analysis is beyond us at this point, but the following observations on the major similarities and possible differences may be offered.

First, as stated in the introduction, the average differential for the Soviet population is rather similar to what is found in other countries; it may be slightly smaller than in the United States. For 1969, Oaxaca placed the relative hourly pay of women for the urban white population at 0.65, compared to our figure of 0.70 to 0.68 (WPH1 and WPH4, respectively); Malkiel's yearly ratio for university graduates was 0.66, whereas our monthly measure for the same group was 0.65 or 0.64.[44] The Soviet ratio seems, however, to be lower than in other East European countries and in several countries in Northern and Western Europe.[45] The similarity of the Soviet ratio to that of the United States stands out all the more, given the extreme difference between the two countries with respect to overall wage equality.[46] This indicates that some of the factors causing higher inequality by sex operate outside the general labor market, affecting women in particular — especially household responsibilities.

A second observation is that, by and large, and within the limitations imposed by the data, the direct factors explaining the wage gap by sex in the Soviet Union do not differ, either qualitatively or even quantitatively, from those found in the United States:

    a.   In the more recent studies on the United States, the levels of education for the sexes are found to be more or less equal, so that even if the rates of return are lower in the Soviet Union, the contribution of formal schooling to the wage gap is not typically or significantly higher that in those studies.[47] This may not be the case when comparisons are made between the Soviet Union and other countries of the same level of development, in which comparisons we expect to find larger educational gaps and higher schooling coefficients.

b. Although the differences in experience between the sexes, especially for persons of the same age, are much smaller in the Soviet Union, experience still seems to explain at least as much of the wage gap as in the West. In some cases (such as those in Oaxaca, 1973, pp. 705, 706), it results from the much higher experience and age coefficients in the Soviet earning functions. However, where the estimated experience coefficients are high (as in Mincer and Polachek, 1974, p. 423), experience accounts for a higher proportion of the gap than in our study. In all studies the experience coefficient is significantly higher for men than for married women. According to Mincer, the results in the West reflect women's lower attachment to work and greater household responsibilities (*ibid.*, pp. 424–25). With the much greater relative attachment to work of Soviet women (measured in years of work), more explanatory burden is shifted to lower intensity of attachment and lesser ability to devote time and energy to job advancement due to their relatively heavier family responsibilities.

c. The Oaxaca study, which includes industry and role variables in a way similar to our study, gives higher explanatory power to industry and less to role than do our results, but we are not in a position to attribute this difference to underlying factors.

d. Finally, with a list of variables that is more or less similar to that of Oaxaca and the Malkiels, our study also explains up to half of the wage gap. The rest of the gap is due to missing variables and qualitative dimensions of existing ones.

Third, the general similarity in the pattern of the gaps across countries, when viewed through the prism of the explanatory variables, does not lead to the conclusion that the underlying intrinsic factors responsible for the gaps are the same. As we have shown, the difference explained by experience may be caused in one country by the lower labor-force participation of women, and in another by low ability of women to take advantage of training. As in many other areas in the Soviet Union, women find shelter against heavy quantitative pressures under an umbrella of lower-quality response.

In a review article, Barbara Jancar (1976) claims that industrializing societies, both capitalist and communist, have encouraged women to assume "male" roles while losing none of their "female" roles by entering men's industrial world. "But adoption of male roles in many ways is a step backward for sexual equality" (*ibid.*, pp. 71–72), mainly because of the handicap created by the family role, which although now degraded in status still carries its unlightened burden.

One does not have to subscribe fully to these views to see that at some stages "half" or one-sided equality may not bring about more equity. In Jancar's terms, the Soviet system is very intensively industrialized, over-emphasizing industrialization on the one hand and neglecting leisure-augmenting development and changes in family roles on the other. At least temporarily, it thus accelerates the one-sided equality that helps to preserve both a wide pay gap and a heavy double burden on women.

Notes

1. It is our contention that the Soviet record with respect to earning inequality by sex is less favorable, when compared to other countries, than that of overall income inequality. This is definitely true in comparisons with the United States. See, for example, Chapman (1978, pp. 45–47 and Table 11 there); see also Chapter 4, Section 2c. in this volume.

2. Almost exhaustive lists of such situations can be found in Lapidus (1978, pp. 190–94) and McAuley (1979, pp. 10, 13).

3. A partial list includes Danilova (1968), Gordon and Klopov (1972), Kharchev and Golod (1971), Kotliar (1973), Kotliar and Turchaninova (1975), Kotliar *et al.* (1973), Mikhailiuk (1970), Novikova *et al.* (1978), Pimenova (1966), Porokhniuk and Shepeleva (1975), Sakharova (1973), Shishkan (1976), Sonin (1973), Trufanov (1973), and Turchaninova (1975). More complete lists can be found in Atkinson *et al.* (1978) and in Lapidus-Warshofsky (1978).

4. Some of the main and most recent Western studies are Atkinson *et al.* (1978), Berliner (1977), Desfosses-Cohn (1973), Geiger (1968), Lapidus-Warshofsky (1978), McAuley (1981), Mandel (1975), and Sacks (1976).

5. We have therefore economized on citations in all places where the studies cited above have sufficiently covered the specific points discussed. In most cases Soviet references are cited only if they have not been covered by the above-mentioned studies.

6. See Fuchs (1971), Gronau (1979), Malkiel and Malkiel (1973), Mincer (1974), Mincer and Polachek (1974), and Oaxaca (1973), to mention only a few studies of this type.

7. The feminist school tends, of course, to minimize the scope of natural differences between the sexes in this respect. A presentation of the theoretical discussion in the West and in the Soviet Union is found in Lapidus-Warshofsky (1978, pp. 322–34).

8. It is interesting to note that most studies that estimate earning functions take the intrafamily division of labor and roles as given, whereas most studies that analyze intrafamily optimizing behavior assume a wide earning gap between men and women as one determinant of their dependent variable.

See, for example, Mincer and Polachek (1974) vs. Gronau (1973b).

9. See Chapman (1979b), Kotliar and Turchaninova (1975), Lapidus-Warshofsky (1978, Ch. 5), and Parkhomenko (1972, pp. 77–78).

10. The following discussion is based partly on Ofer (1973, pp. 64–67) and on the literature cited in note 4.

11. Women are entitled to maternity leave of 112 days and to some other privileges during pregnancy and while the children are in their infancy. Women are also entitled to a retirement pension 5 years earlier than men are. They also benefit most from the legislation on minimum wage because they are overrepresented in the lowest-paid groups. As pensions and maternity leave benefits are paid by social security, the employer directly bears only the burden of minimum wage payment and the work interruptions in connection with birth. See more in Lapidus (1978, pp. 125–26) and Madison (1978a).

12. Even Mandel (1975, Chs. 10, 11), who has more praise for the achievements of Soviet women than many Soviet students, admits that inequality within the family is a main obstacle to achieving full equality.

13. Although there may indeed be more places for preschool children per 1,000 children in the Soviet Union than elsewhere, it is quite clear that there are not more of them per 1,000 working mothers. See Lapidus-Warshofsky (1978, pp. 128–35).

14. We assume that the planner has recourse to other policy tools (such as the husband's pay level or social pressures) to encourage women to work.

15. Janet Chapman (1979b) claims that there is no evidence of any official policy along such lines. But both she and others indicate that premiums paid for difficult working conditions are lower in women's jobs (*ibid.*, p. 229), that women's jobs offer fewer bonuses (*ibid.*, p. 233), and that production norms for women are more demanding (Sakharova, 1973, p. 25). Other examples may be found in Lapidus (1978, Ch. 6). All these may, however, be responses to market forces, as we claim below.

16. Although this phenomenon is still pronounced in agriculture, which we do not cover, it is also very important in the urban sector (see McAuley, 1979, pp. 20–21).

17. The rapid growth of the educational system is considered to be one of the

major factors contributing to the greater equalization of earnings in the Soviet Union, at least since the 1950s. For women, the educational level has risen faster than for men (Chapman, 1978, p. 238). See also Lapidus-Warshofsky (1978, pp. 134–60).

18. A description of the system can be found in Chapman (1978), and its relation to the wages of women is discussed in Chapman (1979b) and Lapidus-Warshofsky (1978, Chapter 5).

19. The absolute wage is determined at such a level that, with the help of social and legal pressures, every able-bodied person will tend to seek a job.

20. Among others, see Dubovoi (1969), Gordon and Klopov (1972, p. 11), Iuk (1972, pp. 40–44), Kharchev and Golod (1969, pp. 441–43), Kolpakov and Patrushev (1971, pp. 110, 112, 149), Lebin and Leiman (1972, pp. 136–41), Pankratova and Iankova (1978, p. 26), Parkhomenko (1972, p. 78), Riurikov (1977, pp. 118–19), Sakharova (1973, p. 46), Slesarev and Iankova (1969, p. 423), Turchenko (1972, pp. 141–45), Velichkene (1970, p. 96), Zdravomyslov *et al.* (1967, pp. 265), and many, many more.

21. There were five families in which the head of the family did not work.

22. Included in the sample are 116 unmarried working women, but they are typically young and reside within an active family.

23. The wage of all full-time working women relative to that of men in SP is 0.64296; when reweighted by work status (white-collar/blue-collar), it comes to 0.64120, and when reweighted by work status and level of education (three to four groups within each work-status group), it comes to 0.63020 (Ofer *et al.*, 1979, Appendix Table A.16; data on structural differences are given in Chapter 1, Section 5b. of this volume).

A second possible source of structural bias is that the age difference between the sexes in SP may be somewhat wider than that for UP and thus exaggerate the true effect of work experience and age on earning differentials. The 1970 census does not provide any data on the average age of the Soviet urban civilian labor force, but statistics from the 1959 census and the more general data for 1970 lead us to believe that women in UP are younger by at least 2, possibly 3, years than men as compared with the 3.2 year gap in our sample.

For 1959, the average age of working men in the nonagricultural sectors (excluding the army) is estimated at 35.5 years, and that of working women at 33.3 years (based on Soviet Union TsSU, 1959 Census, Tables 33 and 39 and the discussion on armed forces figures in Rapaway, 1976, Table 9, pp 19–25). Demographic development since then, especially the retirement of working cohorts of advanced age, with a high proportion of women, and the introduction of more balanced cohorts of younger age, should have widened this gap by raising the average age of working men. The implication of this possible bias is discussed below.

24. The correction was made only when the coefficients for the different types of schooling differed significantly from each other. The correction for university studies is to assign 0.6 year for every year of night or correspondence studies toward the first university degree.

25. $\ln W1_m - \ln W1_f$ or the percent increase of men's wages over women's estimated by the respective geometrical averages.

26. Results not presented here can be obtained from the authors by request. They also include regression results for the entire working population, with sex as a dummy variable, as in Swafford (1977, Table 5).

27. On the basis of data for W1 the first ratio is 0.64 (Table 7.1, line 2b) and the second is 0.4132 (Table 7.2, line 1).

28. The corresponding male/female ratio of gross wages is roughly calculated to be 0.63, slightly lower because of the progressiveness of income taxes.

29. Based on the geometrical average, the corresponding male/female ratios are 0.71 on the average, 0.74 for academics, 0.68 for semi-professionals, and 0.69 for the low educational group. The corresponding ratios based on arithmetic averages are 0.64, 0.67, 0.60, and 0.63.

30. Women in SP did report higher absenteeism rates for health reasons than men did. Presumably, this is due in part to illness in the family.

31. For $\ln W4$ and the entire population, hours contribute (according to the male equation) 7.4 points to a male earning advantage of 48.3 percent, or more than 30 percent of the total "explained" segment.

32. Which, in Tables 7.2 and 7.3, include all those with advanced degrees. Almost the entire explanation of education comes from the stage of advanced studies.

33. Together with age, the difference in experience explains more than 5 points. Since there is high correlation between age and experience, their respective effects may have shifted from one to the other.

34. The marginal rates of experience per year go down for males from 5.1 percent in the first year (3.6 percent according to the long equation) to 3.7 (2.6) percent after 10 years, 2.3 (1.6) percent after 20 years, and 0.9 (0.6) percent after 30 years. The corresponding figures for women are 2.6, 1.8, 1.0, and 0.2 percent, respectively, according to the short equation, and 1.7, 1.5, 1.3, and 1.1 percent according to the long one.

35. Thus the initial experience coefficients estimated by Oaxaca (1973, pp. 700, 703) are approximately 2 percent for men and 15 percent for women. When experience is estimated directly, the coefficients are much higher, as in Mincer and Polachek (1974, p. S102), where the average rate for males age 30–44 years is estimated at 3.4 percent.

36. The calculation is based on a weighted average of differences in experience in the various age groups. The experience gaps for specific age groups go up from 1.1 years for those younger than 25 to 4.6 years for the 45–54 age group, indicating the cumulative effect of raising children.

37. All the following observations on the effects of specific roles are additional to and relative to the reference differential between the sexes that exists for high-professional workers in manufacturing.

38. There are only four such women who obtain a negative premium of academic workers. This result may be typical, but we cannot judge on this basis; in this case the results based on the female equations should not be relied upon. The same problem creates a negative role effect on the advantage of males with respect to semi-skilled in the semi-professional group of workers.

39. The exceptions are for white-collar employees and service workers, in both cases a rather diverse collection of occupations with women at the lower range in both.

40. Among academics, 207 percent of women but only 10.5 percent of all men are engaged in health services. The corresponding figures for secondary professionals are 27.6 and 7.0 percent; they are 7.1 and 2.8 percent for the low-schooling group.

41. If engineers, with 39.8 percent women, were shifted from the second to the third group, each group would contain approximately 30 percent of the sample labor force.

42. These results are generally very similar to those obtained by McAuley (1978, pp. 18–41), Sacks (1976, pp. 79–92), and others.

43. See also the discussion on these points in McAuley (1978, pp. 33–34).

44. See also Mincer and Polachek (1974, p. S103), where the hours wage gap for the 30–44 year age group is 0.66 (p. S101).

45. See Galenson (1973), Kýn (1979, pp. 280–88), McAuley (1978, pp. 11–12), MEMO (1974, p. 156), Michal (1975, p. 267), OECD (1979, p. 32).

46. See note 1 above. Kýn (1978, pp. 280–81) observes a similar phenomenon in Eastern Europe.

47. Fuchs (1971, p. 10) and Oaxaca (1973, p. 705) find that education explains less than 1 point of the wage gap; see also Mincer and Polachek (1974, p. S102). Malkiel and Malkiel (1973), however, show a wider gap in years of higher education for a group of academics than in our group of academics (1.7 years' difference as compared with 0.4 year in our sample).

Chapter 8
Work and family roles of Soviet women:
historical trends and cross-section analysis

1. Introduction

Changes in the way of life of Soviet women over the past two generations are very similar to those experienced by women in most industrialized and industrializing societies in the West. Millions of married women were drawn into the labor force, most moving from farms to the cities, some switching from family agricultural work to work outside the household. The rate of participation of women in the labor force also increased substantially. This movement was accompanied by a marked rise in the level of women's general and professional education. As a result, women occupy more white-collar positions and fewer manual jobs than in older generations. These developments and the newly enhanced material and social independence of women are reflected in reduced family size and lower fertility rates, later marriages, a higher divorce rate, and more one-parent family units. Even with the compensating adjustments on the family front, women and social scientists complain about the double burden imposed on women by this one-sided emancipation process: increased responsibilities and opportunities outside the home that have not been synchronized with an adequate increase in men's sharing of household and child-rearing responsibilities, nor with technological and institutional changes that could ease those chores.

This double burden is in turn blamed by many for the less than complete integration of women into the labor force on an equal standing with men. In most countries the increased involvement of women in the labor force has not resulted in equal wages for women or in full occupational integration — vertical or horizontal. Women are underrepresented in better-paid "male" occupations and are barred or discouraged from top managerial positions. While some cite the too-slow shift in the division of labor at home as a reason for the discrimination in the labor market, others maintain the opposite. Discrimination in the labor market leads to higher involvement of women in household responsibilities, in accordance with the principle of optimal allocation of time. Still others invoke the argument of comparative advantage to explain these phenomena, but differ on pinpointing its source. The comparative advantage is seen by some as a neutral and "natural" phenomenon, while others emphasize its cultural and social determinants.

In all these trends and interpretations, the Soviet experience is qualitatively similar to that of the rest of the developed world. Differences are found mostly in rates of change of the main variables, in absolute terms and in relation to each other, and in specific aspects of the patterns of integration of women into the labor force. However, the accumulation of quantitative differences add up to a different qualitative outcome.[1] The unique Soviet socialist economic system, ideology, and growth strategy has played a key role, together with specific geographic and historical circumstances, in changing and shaping the role of women at work and in the family. The system, together with historically determined factors, are more closely examined below. The combined impact of most of these systemic and historical factors has, on the one hand, hastened the incorporation of women into the labor force and, on the other hand, delayed developments that could make the transition less burdensome, particularly in regard to housing and household services. As a result, the dissonance between work and the household has become more pronounced in the Soviet Union that in other countries, and women and families look for outlets to alleviate some of the extra pressure.

Thus we find a sharp rise in the rates of women's participation in the labor force — higher levels combined with deeper penetration into occupations previously considered "male." On the household front, a larger lag is observed in the provision of services, appliances, and amenities. Considering the proportion of working mothers of small children, even the number of day-care centers for young children is inadequate. Rapid social and economic changes in the labor market help to widen the gap between those developments and much slower changes in mentality and roles within the family unit. One result is a lower level of fertility. Other possible results are low salaries relative to men's and the persistence of both vertical and horizontal occupational segregation.

The systemic and ideological factors contributing to this somewhat uneven development are discussed in detail in Chapter 7. The goal of growth maximization along an extensive (input-intensive) growth path called for maximum enlisting of women into the labor force and a rapid expansion of the educational system. The accompanying goal of maximizing the (non-consumed) surplus meant slower growth in housing, services, and consumption levels. The ideological doctrine of gender equality encouraged the move toward higher participation and educational levels for women, but paid only lip service to supporting this move on the household front.

Historical events — the revolution and civil war, the collectivization drive and the second world war — amplified some of these trends beyond the changes called for by normal economic development. Women's labor force participation was accelerated especially during and after the war to compensate for the heavy loss of men.

The only factor to play a moderating role in otherwise more extreme *average* trends of the key variables is the presence and growing weight of the Moslem population. With lower levels of social and economic modernization and with strongly rooted traditions, Moslem women still have low labor participation rates, high and non-declining fertility rates, and larger, more stable families.

Different accounts in the literature explain the historical changes in women's role, emphasizing the nature of relationships between participation, wages, incomes, fertility, education, and labor market conditions. In many cases cross-section data and analyses are used to project back to the past with different levels of success.[2] Likewise, the Soviet story is told by many, though in a less rigorous statistical manner.[3] In this chapter we hope to contribute to the understanding of the Soviet story in two ways. First, in Section 2, we survey the evidence about long-term changes of the major variables, where possible, since the 1920s. The section has greatly benefitted from a more comprehensive survey prepared by McAuley (1981). The third part of the chapter (Sections 3, 4) provides an additional layer to the investigation of cross-sectional behavior of women in their multiple roles in the early 1970s. Based on SP, two theoretical and estimating approaches are used and compared. We demonstrate that Soviet married women react much like women elsewhere to economic and demographic variables in shaping their decisions about participation in the labor force and the number of working hours.

Section 3 focuses on the issue of women's short-term labor supply that uses a partial equilibrium approach. It follows Ben Porath (1973b), Gronau (1978) and Nakamura *et al.* (1979) and others in separating the total short-term female labor supply into a participation function and a conditional function of hours worked. As customary in such models, estimated wages of women from earning functions are used in the participation equation. The participation equation is a short-term one in that it uses current participation as the dependent variable rather than a longer-term labor-force commitment, and in that fertility is included in the analysis as an exogenous variable and in that only a short-term fertility effect is addressed — the presence of small children at the time of the survey.

A second theoretical and estimation approach (Section 4) takes a longer time view and a more general equilibrium outlook: first, a long-term participation equation is estimated, the dependent variable being the proportion of working years over the lifetime of women after the termination of formal education (labeled "life-participation"); second, a simultaneous estimation of this life-participation equation and a corresponding long-term fertility equation, is performed. In both long-term equations the decision on the (long-term) level of education also plays a role.

All in all, the model has four equations (each appears in a number of specifications) named after the dependent variables:

(1) The expected hourly wage of wives (in log natural form).

(2) A short-run participation equation — a logit equation with values of one and zero according to whether the wife worked or not at the time of the survey; this equation uses the expected wage estimated by equation (1) as a variable (for justification of this procedure see Schultz, 1977, p. 16). Equations (1) and (2) are estimated for the entire sample of married women.

(3) A life-participation equation.

(4) A fertility equation.

Finally in the concluding section there is a discussion on the ability of the cross-section models to "predict" long-term trends and of the basic applicability of household optimization behavior models under Soviet conditions. It is concluded that, while somewhat more constrained in the degree and nature of choice, Soviet households are confronted with alternatives and are responding to them in a way similar to other households in freer societies. However, this study also finds that the exceptionally high participation rate cannot be explained entirely by these factors, and that some additional system-related or long-term influences must also play a role.

2. A survey of historical trends

Some of the available information about the key variables is presented in a concise form in Tables 8.1–8.4. In a few cases the data presented are not available or relate only to the most relevant aspect in the category. For example, the Soviet Union publishes few statistics on participation rates of women (or men) in the labor force. Most of the gender- and age-specific data are calculated on the basis of separate data sets, one for sex and age distribution of the population and one for the labor force. Data are completely unavailable on wages by sex, or, for that matter, almost every other classification. In these cases we depend fully on the data sample of immigrants.

The Moslem population of the Soviet Union — more than a quarter of the Soviet population in 1980 — has very different demographic and labor force attributes than the majority of the population, mostly of European origin. In particular, fertility rates among the Moslems are much higher and labor participation rates of women much lower than for the rest of the population. While changes over time in these and other characteristics make them more like those of the entire country, the rise in the proportion of the Moslems has the effect of moderating rates of change or even reversing them. In the following survey overall national figures are shown and the likely effects of the Moslem population are discussed qualitatively.

a. Labor-force participation (LFP)

The official working age for women in the Soviet Union is between 15

Table 8.1. Labor force participation rates of women, by age: 1926–1990 (C = Census) (percent)

| | Working population | | | | | | | | | | |
	All	15+	15–54	20–54	15–64	15–19	20–24	25–44	45–54	55–64	65+
1926 (C)	51.3	71.1	75.4[a]	..	95.2	..	..	..	..	..	38.2[b]
1939 (C)	47.3	..	..	..	..	..	..	..	..	..	34.8[b]
1950	48.1	64.3	70.2	69.4	84.4	75.4	74.1	70.0	63.5	47.2	35.0
1955	49.3	65.1	70.9	86.1	..	68.7	75.5	74.9	67.7	44.2	30.9
1959 (C)	49.3	63.2	(71)[c]	..	87.4	60.2	..	..	..	..	32.0[b]
1960	48.2	65.9	75.8	77.4	89.1	62.0	76.9	79.8	72.0	41.3	26.8
1965	46.7	64.2	78.9	..	90.0	49.1	79.7	86.4	78.1	29.9	15.4
1970 (C)	45.3	61.5	(83)[c]	89.4	88.8	37.4	..	..	..	..	..
1970	45.4	61.4	80.9	..	83.3	36.2	82.4	93.0	84.3	18.4	4.1
1975[d]	46.2	60.4	79.6	88.2	86.2	33.9	84.1	93.0	84.1	18.0	3.7
1980[d]	46.2	59.6	79.8	..	82.3	31.5	80.4	92.9	83.9	17.6	3.3
1990[d]	44.4	58.0	80.7	..	86.8	27.6	78.7	92.8	83.6	17.0	2.8

Note: All noncensus data are based on full-year equivalents for labor force.

[a] 16–59.

[b] 60+

[c] Estimate.

[d] Projections.

Sources: 1926, 1939 – Eason (1963, pp. 54, 56); 1939, 1959 – USSR Census Bureau (1959, pp. 50–51, 99); 1959, 1970 (C) – USSR *Census 1970* (Vol. 5, Tables 10, 11, pp. 154, 162–63; Vol. 2, Table 3, pp. 12–35), and McAuley (1981, p. 36). All other years – ILO (1977b, Tables 2, 5).

and 54, the official retirement age is 55 (that for men is 60). Since a significant proportion of women above the retirement age continue to work, various measures of overall participation rates are presented in Table 8.1, some of which include older ages. In order to have consistent series of historical trends we have included participation ratios calculated with "all working" in the numerator but only the population of working age in the denominator.

The main features of the long trends since 1926 are as follows:

(a) Of the crude overall measures of women's LFP, only those in the 15–54 and the 20–54 age ranges show some increase over the 1926–80 period. Together with data on the 20–54 age group, these are the only series showing increased LFP since 1950. All the other measures reflect a decline in participation rates (Table 8.1).

(b) At the other extreme we observe sharp rises in specific LFP rates for the prime working ages, 25–44, and also for ages 45–54 since 1950 (Table 8.1) and for urban women overall, especially the working-age range since 1959 (Table 8.2, lines 4–6). Information on age-specific participation rates of urban women in 1926 and 1931 gives figures of 30–40 percent for the prime working age in the former data and 35–54 percent in the latter, thus further underscoring the very sharp rise in these rates in the long run (*Zhenshchiny v SSSR*, 1937, p. 17). Still, the figures for the early Soviet period are quite high and already reflect the impact of the Soviet system.

(c) The gap between sharp rises in the LFP of urban women at prime working ages and the decline in the overall crude measures is mostly explained by the following factors: first, women's LFP in agriculture are always high, especially if all women who do even part-time work around the farmhouse are included. Hence, urbanization and the decline in the importance of agriculture have the effect of reducing average participation rates. Second, modernization and urbanization, the expansion of the educational system, and the enactment of social and pension legislation all help to reduce the LFP of children and young adults and of persons above the established retirement age. All these trends have been very strong in the Soviet Union, as can be observed in Table 8.1. Finally, roughly since 1950 there has been a secular decline in the proportion of working-age women in the population

Table 8.2. Participation rates of women: urban and rural locations, employees and collective farm members, 1959 and 1970 (percent)

	1959	1970
Total population		
1. All working / total population	49.3	45.3
2. All working / population of working age	87.4	88.8
3. All working / population 15–69	69.6	67.0
Urban population		
4. All working / total population	41.3	48.8
5. All working / population of working age	67.5	86.2
6. All working / population 15–69	56.5	67.4
Rural population		
7. All working / total population	56.6	40.8
8. All working / population of working age	108.5	93.1
9. All working / population 15–69	85.3	66.5
10. Employees (urban and rural)[a]	44.6	48.7
	(38.2)	(46.9)
11. Collective farmers[a]	59.1	35.4
	(48.4)	(32.8)

[a] Figures in parentheses exclude women employed only in their private agricultural plots.

Sources: 1959 – USSR Census Bureau (1959, Tables 12, 13, pp. 49, 50–51; Table 29, pp. 93–94; Table 30, pp. 96–97). 1970 – USSR *Census 1970* (Vol. 2, Table 3; Vol. 5, Table 2, p. 7; Table 4, p. 26; Table 11, p. 162).

of women, which also contributes to the small decline in the overall participation rate. Between 1926 and 1950, however, this proportion increased, affecting participation in the opposite direction.[4]

(d) Our main interest is focused on the working-age-specific participation rates (Table 8.1) and on the rates for urban women (Table 8.2) (we do not have age-specific data for urban or non-agricultural women separately). Already in 1950 the participation rates of women between the ages of 15 and 54 (or 20–54) were around 70 percent (these data include women in agriculture, but on a full-time basis). By 1980 the overall figure climbed to 80 percent — 88 percent for the 20–54 age group, the difference reflecting the sharp decline in the LFP of the 15–19 age group. For prime working ages, 25–44, the rate climbed from 70 to 93 percent, and for ages 45–54 from 63.5 to 84 percent. An even sharper rise, of almost 20 points over 11 years, is observed for working-age urban women (Table 8.2). Considering the very high initial (1950) rates, both the trends and the terminal levels are rally remarkable. However, the rates peaked around 1970. There is no further rise in the rates for prime ages and only a very slight rise in those of the younger and older ages (Table 8.2).

(e) The rise in participation rates and the levels of LFP of non-Moslem women is even more remarkable. Detailed data are presented in McAuley (1981, p. 37), from which the following example comes: the participation rates of women (calculated as all working divided by working-age population) between 1960 and 1970 rose, in the Russian republic, from 66.7 to 85.1 percent; in the Baltic republics from 65 to 88.4 percent; but in the Central Asian republics only from 60 to 66.5 percent.

(f) There are no data on specific participation rates of married women. However, data on marriage rates reveals that in 1970 more than 80 percent of all women between the ages of 25 and 44 were married, and this proportion was equal to or higher than in any year since 1926 (USSR Census, 1931, 1959, 1970). The conclusion to be drawn is that only a small fraction, if any, of the total increase in participation can be attributed to an increase in the proportion of single women. Most or all of this increase came about through a sharp increase in the participation rate of married women.

(g) There is almost no provision for part-time work in public employment in the Soviet Union, so that only a very small fraction of women are thus employed. According to McAuley (1981, p. 27), less than half of 1 percent of the entire public female labor force was employed part time in the early 1970s. Therefore the Soviet participation rate is even higher relative to that in other countries where full-time equivalent ratios are compared.

(h) The increased LFP of women raised their percentage share in the entire labor force. In public (non-collective-farm) employment their share rose from 25 percent in 1922 to 39 percent in 1940, 47 percent in 1950–60, and up to 51 percent since 1970. After the second world war the share of women in the entire Soviet population and in the working-age population rose to 56–57 percent. In 1980, however, although less than half the working-age population, women made up more than half of public employment and almost half of all persons working on collective farms (*Vestnik Statistiki,* 1980–81; USSR Census, 1973).

(i) To complete the section on employment, let us point out that *unemployment* was officially abolished in the Soviet Union long ago, thereby precluding the possibility of reporting it statistically. One may read of pockets of unemployment, especially of women, in small, one-industry towns with no work opportunities in services or in light industry. Nonetheless, unemployment should not be considered a significant macroeconomic problem (see Feshbach and Rapaway, 1973, pp. 536–37).

A second category that will have to go unreported in a systematic manner is data on women's wages. Data on wages do exist, but are not reported by sex. McAuley (1981, pp. 11–26) reviews all the recent, available, fragmentary Soviet data. A more systematic analysis is presented by Swafford (1977) and in Chapter 7 above. All find that women's wages are between 60–65 percent of men's on average, and about 70 percent of men's hourly wage, and that the gap is narrower within occupational groups. There are indications that over time there has been limited narrowing of the wage gap between the sexes, but no hard systematic evidence can support such an assertion. Average annual real money wages of *all* non-agricultural public employees (of both sexes) behaved in the following manner (in index form; see Chapman, 1963, pp. 238–39; Schroeder and Severin, 1976, p. 629; *Narkhoz,* 1978, p. 372):

1928	119	1960	138
1937	99	1965	149
1940	93	1970	179
1950	100	1975	196
1955	128	1978	210

It may be assumed that women's wages went up slightly faster.

b. Education

Since 1939, the proportion of women with a university education increased more than 10 times, and those graduating from technical and professional higher schools — a level similar to that of junior colleges in the United States — by a similar factor. (The data are presented in Table 8.3.) While in 1939 only 10 percent of all women 10 years and older had more than 7 years of schooling, by 1979 this proportion had grown to 80 percent among working women and 60 percent among all women age 10 and older. While this revolution in education affected both sexes simultaneously, women were closing the educational gap with men. Today, the proportion of working women with university degrees is almost equal to that of men (it remains lower for higher degrees, however), and the proportion of working women with technical and general high school diplomas is higher than the corresponding proportion among men. The comparison of the level of education by sex for the entire (age 10+) population is less favorable to women. By 1979, 15.7 percent of all women had less than 4 years of schooling, compared with merely 6.1 percent among men. The main factors responsible for this are demographic: there are many more women than men among the older age groups. In 1980 there were some 18.4 million women and only 7.9 million men in the 65+ age group (Baldwin, 1975, p. 24). This difference is partly due to the longer life-expectancy of women, and partly reflects the heavy loss of life during the second world war. Furthermore, many of the older women are concentrated in the countryside, where education levels are lower.

Secondary technical and higher education is a more important route to the labor force for women than for men because of the nature of jobs that women tend to prefer. The advance of women into white-collar occupations since 1939 is indeed impressive. In that year, only 13.6 percent of all working

Table 8.3. Level of education of the Soviet population (age 10+) and labor force by sex, selected years: 1939–1979 (per 1,000)

	Working population			
	1939	1959	1970	1979
Females				
Completed higher education	9	32	62	98
Completed technical school[a]		84	132	292
Completed general high school	104	68	162	271
Incomplete general high school		247	295	240
Elementary school	887	272	228	160
Less than four years		297	121	39
Males				
Completed higher education	16	34	68	102
Completed technical school[a]		69	103	143
Completed general high school	136	60	156	242
Incomplete general high school		271	327	283
Elementary school	848	368	268	166
Less than four years		198	78	24

Note: Soviet children start school at age 7. They attend a general school where the first four years are considered elementary and first eight years or so "incomplete" general school. General school is completed after 10 or 11 year, at age 17–18. They can leave earlier to join various vocational schools or a technical school. The latter is a professional school for teachers, nurses, technicians, bookkeepers, etc. Graduates of general (and technical) schools can enrol in universities and earn a diploma after 5–6 years of study, depending on the field (see McAuley, 1981, pp. 135–39).

[a] Including incomplete higher education.

Sources: 1939 – *Vestnik Statistiki* (1980, No. 2, p. 22). 1959, 1970 – USSR Census Bureau (1973, Vol. 5, Table 7, p. 66; Vol. 3, Table 3, p. 206); *Vestnik Statistiki* (1981, No. 2, p. 63). 1979 – *Vestnik Statistiki* (1980, No. 2, p. 22; No. 6, p. 43).

women had white-collar jobs and only 2.5 percent had jobs that required technical or higher education. In 1970, almost one-third of all working women were white-collar workers (only 22.5 percent of all working men) and they outnumbered men among professional workers by a ratio of almost 3 to 2. This change took place in an economy where less than one-third of all jobs are white-collar jobs. Two disclaimers are in order at this point. First, the very low proportion of white-collar jobs available in the Soviet economy still forces more than two-thirds of women to do manual work. Second, women are less well represented in occupations that require the highest schooling levels, especially above first university degree. In 1980, women were 13.8 of all doctors of science and 28.1 percent of all Ph.Ds in science (*Vestnik Statistiki*, 1980, No. 11, p. 95; see also McAuley, 1981, p. 91).[5]

c. Fertility rates, marriage, and divorce

Fertility rates in the Soviet Union have dropped steadily from 159 births per 1,000 women aged 15–49 in the late 1920s to 65.7 around 1970. Since then they have climbed very slowly, reaching 70.5 in 1980 (Table 8.4). The decline was indeed steeper and the subsequent rise almost non-existent for the non-Moslem population of the Soviet Union. The typical fertility rate in the Moslem republics today is around 150, and the proportion of Moslems in the Soviet population is also rising. As in most processes of declining fertility, the steepest relative decline occurred among the upper age groups, as fewer children are born. The rising proportion of the Moslem population is responsible for the recent rise in fertility of the 15–19 age group. The decline in fertility took place in both urban and rural areas, and was sharper in the latter. Further decline was affected by population movement from rural to urban areas, where fertility rates are traditionally lower.

Two factors instrumental in the decline in fertility are the rise in the marriage age and the decline in the proportion of married women at childbearing ages over the period 1926–59 (and slightly later). These trends were reversed during the 1960s as the proportion of the Moslem population grew and as the imbalance between the sexes, created during the second world war, was gradually corrected. According to one Soviet source, the marriage age for women declined between 1965 and 1973 from almost 25 to 22.5 years

Table 8.4.   Trends in fertility rates (births per 1,000 women age 15–49), 1939–1979

	Births per 1,000 women age 15–49
1926–27	159.1
1938–39	139.5
1954–55	86.2
1958–59	88.7
1960–61	90.6
1965–66	70.8
1969–70	65.7
1972–73	66.4
1974–75	67.8
1978–79	69.9
1979–80	70.5

Sources: Eason (1976, p. 158), *Naselenie SSSR*, 1973 (1975, p. 136), *Vestnik Statistiki* (1980, No. 11, p. 75), *Vestnik Statistiki* (1981, No. 11, p. 71).

(*Naselenie SSSR*, 1973, p. 172). One factor that offset this trend was the rise in the divorce rate. In the 1950s there were above five divorces for every 100 marriages, but by 1980 the number had risen to 34 per 100. Here, too, the trend is steeper for non-Moslems.[6]

In sum, over the 40 year period from the late 1930s, participation rates of married women of prime working age went up from 50–60 percent to 93 percent, women's level of education rose from about 3 years to 8–9 years of schooling, and real wages more than doubled. During the same period fertility rates dropped from 140 to 70 births per 1,000 women age 15–49.

3. Short-term cross-sectional analysis of participation and hours worked

a. The equations and hypotheses

Like everywhere else, the probability that Soviet women will join the labor force depends on the level of income from other sources (negative relationship), on the offered net wage (positive), and on the marginal value of her time in non-market activities — rearing children, doing household chores — and in leisure (negative). Similar factors determine the number of hours worked, sometimes in different ways. The model itself need not be repeated here (see, for example, Becker, 1981; Gronau, 1978). What may be of value is to discuss in what ways the situation in the Soviet Union is different from that of "similar" countries in the West and how these differences may create (a) higher permanent rates of participation among women, and (b) different responses to changes in the main variables affecting the decision to participate and how many hours to work.

The formulation of the model is as follows:

$$PAR = f(Y, W_a, W_b, W)$$

$$Hrs = f(Y, W_a, W_b, W)$$

where
PAR   rate of participation
Hrs   weekly hours worked
Y   vector of non-wife family incomes
W_a vector of personal characteristics affecting the offered wage
W_b vector of variables of labor-market conditions
W   vector of variables affecting the value of time.

Four main elements of the Soviet system, or a stereotyped version of it, bear on the levels of women's labor participation: (a) under the Soviet system non-wage property income is almost completely eliminated, especially outside of agriculture; (b) the main goal of the Soviet system is to maximize growth, and this is achieved by maximizing the use of inputs — labor and investment; (c) the goal of maximizing women's labor is thus qualified by the requirement that there will be a net gain in the non-consumed social product; (d) but women's work is a goal in itself, emanating from socialist ideology.

In terms of the vectors of variables affecting women's labor participation in the model, the absence of property income should raise participation through the negative effect of income. Encouragement of women to work can also be achieved by raising the wages offered to them relative to their husbands' wages (and even at the expense of those wages), by providing labor-market conditions favorable to women's work, by lowering the price of their own time through better household and child-care services, and finally by "shaping" their tastes in favor of outside work and against staying at home. With the exception of the first and last methods, all the other instruments cannot be pushed too far since the gain in the participation of women may result in a decline of the social surplus. Thus, when compared with conditions in market economies of similar levels of economic development — similar GNP per capita or product per worker — one should expect to find lower non-wife family income and at least higher relative wages for women. However, it is not clear whether there should be a difference in the real cost of one's own time (see below). In addition, one should expect to find a higher "taste" for outside work among Soviet women resulting from ideological education and persuasion.

That nonwife income in the Soviet Union is lower than that in the countries of comparison can be deduced from the fact that even with women's earnings, the share of private consumption in Soviet GNP is considerably lower than in most market economies (Bergson, 1983, Tables 3–4, pp. 8–11). The situation is only slightly affected by a somewhat higher Soviet share of free and subsidized public services.

It is hard to determine whether the offered wages for Soviet women are higher in equally developed Western countries, even if only relative to wages of men. Comparative data on the ratio of actual female to male wages is inconclusive, but may show a slight Soviet lead (McAuley, 1981, pp. 20–26). Since most of the cited comparisons are with advanced market economies, a larger Soviet lead may emerge when compared with countries of similar income levels. Furthermore, comparisons of actual wage ratios may underestimate the Soviet lead in the ratio of *offered* wages since a much higher proportion of Soviet women work outside the home.

The level of education of Soviet women (especially urban women) has been growing very fast during the last generation and is by comparison higher than, for instance, in Italy, Austria, and Finland (see Unesco, 1981, Tables 1-4, pp. 1-37-1-39). They also enjoy somewhat better job opportunities. Both factors contribute to higher offered wages. In addition, some increase in women's absolute and relative wages was the outcome of the rapid rise in minimum wages during the 1950s and 1960s, affecting mostly women at the margin of joining the labor force (McAuley, 1979, pp. 200-1; McAuley, 1981, p. 26).

The effect of conditions of the Soviet household on labor participation is difficult to determine. The poor quality of housing and of household appliances, the unavailability of domestic help, the short supply of most consumer goods and food and their low quality, and the difficulties in the retail supply system all point to high demand for, and low productivity in, household work — and a high value of women's household time. The low priority accorded in the Soviet Union to the provision of consumer goods and services should make the Soviet Union relatively less productive in the household sector for a given level of overall productivity. Offsetting this negative impact on women's work are the low fertility — which is taken here as exogenous, but may be one outcome of the high participation rate — and the availability of child-care centers and nurseries for children of women who do work.

If the average impact of conditions of the household is undetermined, we tend to think that it may have a more positive, or less negative, effect on labor participation of women with a higher level of education and a more negative effect on less educated women. This results from weighing the psychic incomes derived from outside work and household work by women with different levels of education. Job opportunities for educated women seem to be much more rewarding than work in the environment of the typical Soviet household as described above. On the other hand, jobs available to less educated women — many work in construction, heavy industry, and in municipal services — must be less appealing than jobs for women with comparable education in the West. If correct, this should increase the (positive) effect of education on labor participation rates.

Under Soviet conditions the participation variable is the most important one since most of the employed have to work full-time (McAuley, 1981, pp. 27–31). Only through choice of occupation and the decision on overtime work can women affect to some extent the length of their workweek. Possible consequences of the largely noncontinuous choice that must be made are discussed below.

Finally, there is the effect of the severe restriction on the option of part-time work. While it certainly increases the hours of work of those women who decide to participate, we believe that under Soviet conditions it has only limited negative effect, if at all, on the participation rate. A woman with a low level of "other" income, facing the alternative of working full time or not at all, will tend to make the first choice even if optimally a part-time job would be preferred, as is the case for many women in the West.

The above analysis presupposes, with one exception, that the high labor-force participation rates of Soviet (urban) women are the outcome of their optimizing behavior under the constraints imposed by the system. If so, we should observe differences in participation rates between Soviet women corresponding to individual differences in "other" income, wage rates and market conditions, level of education, and family household conditions confronting them as we see in any other society. However, the higher the role of education, persuasion, and social pressure in influencing women to participate, the weaker should be their response to change in the economic variables. The only possible exception is higher response to changes in the level of education, as explained above. The expected responses of hours of work to changes in the level of the economic variables should be weaker than those of the participation rate.

In the following analysis, based on a cross section of Soviet women, we shall concentrate mainly on the response to changes in factors affecting participation and not on international comparisons. The findings will, however, throw some light on the latter question.

b. The variables

Information on the variables used in the analysis as well as categories of the population are given in Table 8.5, which presents the basic sample data and the average values of relevant variables for four groups of married women of working age (17–54): women working full-time, working part-time, non-working students, and non-working women. Detailed definitions and explanations of the variables are in the notes to the table. As can be seen, the two middle groups are too small to give high credence to the figures related to them.

Labor participation is defined in this study as "working during the last normal year of life in the Soviet Union." Therefore the estimated rates of labor participation will be higher than those estimated on the basis of "last week" work as in many Western surveys. They also may relate to a somewhat more permanent situation at the time. The annual labor participation rate may be biased downward if some of the women who worked only part of the year chose to report themselves as not working. Such may be the response of women who stopped working during the year.

The sample has a participation rate of married women of 89.3 percent, perhaps a little higher than the corresponding Soviet average, but no much so (McAuley, 1981, pp. 35–38). Only 2 percent of all women reported having part-time jobs; again, if not accurate, it is certainly indicative (McAuley 1981, pp. 27–28).

The findings that can be drawn from Table 8.5, while "gross" in nature, are highly revealing.

(a) Women who do not work belong to families with a higher level of non-wife income, total and per capita, compared to full-time working women. The extra income comes from higher husband's earnings, higher earnings of other family members, and higher incomes from private sources, including private agricultural plots. However, the income advantage of families where the wife does not work outside the home is less than the total earnings of working wives. In a way, this tells us that there are other factors determining the work decision. At least some of the women who do not participate in work in the public sector are apparently partly substituting activity on private plots or some other non-employed private endeavor. This is one explanation for the higher level of private activity of families with a non-working wife. It should be emphasized, though, that only part of the extra private income is earned by women and that most such private jobs pay more per hour and are performed at home and in convenient hours.

Table 8.5. Economic and demographic characteristics of women (17–54 years), by work status

	All women	Working full-time	Working part-time	Stu-dents	Not working
1. Number of women	990	862	22	10	96

Family income variables (rubles per month)

	All women	Working full-time	Working part-time	Stu-dents	Not working
2. Total family income	399.6	406.3	429.9	358.1	337.3
3. Wife's earnings	112.1	126.8	76.0	..	..
4. Nonwife income	287.5	279.5	353.9	358.1	337.3
5. Husband's earnings	215.4	214.5	214.9	150.3	230.2
6. Other members' earnings	27.3	24.8	35.5	95.2	46.5
7. Nonwage income	44.8	40.2	103.5	112.6	60.6
8. Private plot	2.6	1.8	20.0	..	5.6
9. (Family private income)	42.3	35.7	105.6	57.6	85.8
10. Wife's private work	2.8	2.6	25.5	..	..
11. Per capita family income	116.5	122.8	140.6	99.3	106.4
12. Nonwife family income per capita	83.8	83.5	114.9	99.3	106.4

Labor-force characteristics

	All women	Working full-time	Working part-time	Stu-dents	Not working
13. Average age (years)	36.1	36.0	29.9	20.9	40.4
14. Percent below 25 years	16.8	15.2	50.0	100.0	14.6
15. Percent 45–54	24.8	22.5	13.6	..	51.0
16. Years of schooling	12.8	13.2	13.2	14.4	9.4

17. Expected hourly wage[a] (rubles per hour)	0.65–0.67		0.69		0.42–0.50
17a. Actual hourly wage (rubles per hour)	..	0.69	0.70	..	..

Labor-market conditions

	All women	Working full-time	Working part-time	Stu-dents	Not working
18. Percent in large cities[b]	21.0	22.3	31.8	20.0	7.3
19. Percent in small cities[b]	13.9	12.5	27.3	0.0	25.0

(cont.)

Table 8.5. (cont.)

	All women	Working full-time	Working part-time	Stu-dents	Not working
Family data					
20. Number of children age 0–3	0.26	0.25	0.41	0.60	0.31
21. In nurseries	0.10	0.10	0.09	0.00	0.06
22. At home	0.16	0.15	0.32	0.60	0.25
23. Age 4–16	0.65	0.68	0.59	0.10	0.42
24. Non-working adults	0.30	0.31	0.18	0.00	0.29
25. Non-working women	0.21	0.21	0.05	..	0.17
26. Other working adults	0.23	1.22	1.10	1.80	1.31
27. Total family size	3.43	3.44	3.27	3.50	3.33
28. Husband's education (years)	13.2	13.5	14.2	13.5	10.3

[a] Expected hourly wage is calculated from a regression equation including the level of education, work experience and city size; see text.

[b] Large cities are Moscow, Leningrad and Kiev. Small cities are those with less than 250,000 inhabitants.

(b) The personal labor-force qualifications of the nonworking wives are considerably below the qualifications of those who do work: non-working wives have only 9.4 years of schooling compared with 13.2 years for the workers, and they are 4.4 years older than working wives. Particularly, more than half the nonworking wives are over 45 years of age, contrasted with a quarter among working wives. This combination of less education and higher age most likely points to a labor-market disadvantage for hard physical jobs.

(c) The labor-market conditions are estimated in this study by the size of the city of residence. Under Soviet conditions, large cities offer more jobs for women in both manufacturing and services (public and private). In many small cities there are no light industrial enterprises where women can work and the demand for service jobs is more limited. In small cities there are, on the other hand, more opportunities to cultivate private plots. Indeed, we find that 22.3 percent of all working wives reside in large cities and 12.5 percent in small cities, compared to 7.3 and 25 percent, respectively, for non-working wives.

(d) Actual wages for working wives in the sample stand at 69 kopecks per hour; wages non-working wives could expect are estimated on the basis of their level of education and residence at 42–50 kopecks per hour.

(e) Regarding the variables that determine the wife's value of time, it is found that working wives have somewhat fewer children aged 0–3 but that more of those they do have attend nursery schools and fewer stay home compared to those of non-working wives. Working wives do not have fewer children, however — altogether, they have more. This may imply that many women take leave when they have babies but go back to work as soon as possible. A higher number of children may affect the offered wage (negatively) and income needs (positively), but these effects, of course, can only be found with multivariate analysis.

There is only a small absolute difference when there are additional non-working adults in the two kinds of families: 21 percent of families with a working wife have non-working females in the family (14 with older women, i.e., *babushkas*) compared to 17 percent (12 percent *babushkas*) in those with non-working wives. It is difficult to attach any importance to this difference.

c. The equations

Most of the variables in Table 8.5 were included in at least some of the logistic, maximum-likelihood, functional estimation of the participation rate and the ordinary least squares estimation of the supply of hours. Let us take these two equations in sequence.

Labor-force participation (LFP)

The dichotomous variable of participation in the labor force is transformed into a probability function that a certain woman will join the labor force via a logistic function of the general form:

$$P = \frac{e^{\beta x}}{1 + e^{\beta x}},$$

where P is the probability, X the vector of explanatory variables, and β the vector of coefficients (see Gronau, 1978, p. 14; Nakamura *et al.*, 1979). The marginal effects of X on P are $\delta P/\delta X = \delta P(1 - P)$ and are dependent on P and are thus non-linear in P.[7]

Table 8.6 presents results of three alternative specifications of the logit equations. Interesting results from other estimates, not shown, will be mentioned in the discussion. The population for the equations in Table 8.6 consists of all 1,016 married women, some of whom (26) are above the retirement age. Other estimates were made only for women between the ages of 25 and 44. The three equations differ in two respects: first, equation (1) has family income per capita (excluding the wife's earnings) as the only variable for "non-wife" income, while equations (2) and (3) have a breakdown of the family income into the husband's earnings, other non-wife earnings, and non-wage income. The second difference is that equations (1) and (2) include, as an explanatory variable, the natural log of the expected hourly wage, while equation (3) includes instead a dummy variable for residence in a large city (Moscow, Leningrad, or Kiev). It turns out that these two variables offset one another when both appear in one equation. The expected hourly wage for all women was estimated from an earning function of working women, based on their level of education, work experience, and place of residence (see Schultz, 1977, p. 16).

The equation estimated is presented in Table 8.7 and here, too, produces results similar to equivalent estimates elsewhere. As can be seen, there is a positive return to education: the lower the educational level, the lower the offered hourly wage. The difference between an advanced degree and 8 or less years of schooling is about 80 percent of the wage of a university graduate. There is also a positive and declining return to experience, and wages in big cities tend to be higher than in small ones. Being mostly an instrument in this study, no further discussion of this earning function is

Table 8.6. Labor-force participation rates of women: logit estimates

		Eq. (1)		Eq. (2)		Eq. (3)	
		Coefficients	t value	Coefficients	t value	Coefficients	t value
1.	Per capita income[a] (nonwife)	−0.0077	−3.6453	..	..	..	..
2.	Husband's earnings	..	..	−0.0029	−3.1166	−0.0025	−2.7680
3.	Other members' earnings[a]	..	..	−0.0012	−1.1672	−0.0016	−1.4708
4.	Nonwage income	..	..	−0.0037	−3.1724	−0.0037	−3.1474
5.	Years of schooling	0.1985	4.0527	0.2034	4.1085	0.2741	7.4547
6.	Expected hourly wage (ln)[b]	1.9492	2.1962	2.0274	2.2373	..	..
7.	Living in a large city[c]	..	..	..	..	0.7718	1.8897
8.	Being a student	−1.7671	−4.1678	−1.7682	−4.0868	−1.7151	−3.8623
9.	Age 45–54	−0.6194	−1.9287	−0.5977	−1.8450	−0.4343	−1.3697
10.	Age 55+	−1.9106	−4.0400	−1.9603	−4.1578	−1.9595	−4.1321
Number of children							
11.	Aged 0–3	−0.8185	−3.0658	−0.6309	−2.3784	−0.7889	−2.9861
12.	Aged 4–6	0.6371	1.3020	0.8687	1.7341	0.8104	1.5740
13.	Aged 7–11	0.1080	0.3113	0.3085	0.8856	0.3496	0.9981
14.	Aged 12–16	−0.0098	−0.0397	0.1682	0.6863	0.2936	1.1866
15.	Nonworking females	0.0987	0.3544	0.3231	1.1707	0.4472	1.5857
16.	Constant	1.9849	1.8327	1.8031	1.7287	−0.1420	−0.2820
17.	Likelihood ratio/*df*	174.9	11.0	180.2	13.0	177.4	13.0
18.	Pseudo R^2 for model	0.30	..	0.31	..	0.30	..

Note: Participation is established if the respondent declared herself worker or employee during the last *normal* year of life in the Soviet Union *and* reported on monthly wages.
[a] Net, monthly, in rubles.
[b] Calculated from a regression equation including level of education, work experience, and city size (see text).
[c] Large cities are Moscow, Leningrad, and Kiev.

Table 8.7. Wage equation of married women (no. of observations = 978)

	Coefficient	t-value
Educational level (dummy variables)[a]		
Advanced university degree	0.224	2.912
Incomplete university education	−0.326	−6.593
Completed technical school	−0.362	−12.678
Completed general high school (9–11 yrs)	−0.410	−11.540
8 years or less of schooling	−0.529	−8.395
Residence in Moscow, Leningrad, Kiev[b]	0.080	2.409
Residence in cities above 500,000[b]	0.086	2.580
Residence in cities 250,000–500,000	0.056	1.854
Years since end of schooling (Ex)	0.024	5.452
$(Ex)^2$	-0.453×10^{-3}	−3.675
Constant	−0.426	−10.495
$\bar{R}^2$/standard error of equation	0.315	0.333

Note: The dependent variable is the naturallog of hourly wage of wife in the public sector.
[a] The omitted schooling variable is complete university education.
[b] The omitted residence variable is cities below 250,000.

warranted (see also alternative estimates of earning functions for women in Chapter 7 above).

Most of the results are consistent with the usual hypotheses and with behavior in other countries. The coefficients for family income are all negative and, with the exception of other members' earnings, are also highly significant. The coefficients of expected wages and of years in school are all positive and significant, and so is the coefficient of residence in a large city in equation (3) in Table 8.6. As expected, we find that students and older women tend to have lower LFP rates. Finally, the existence of children under 4 also discourages participation. The existence of other non-working females in the family has the right sign but is statistically non-significant in the equations presented. Different formulations, like the product of other non-working females with children aged 0–3, did not produce better results, but in some of the probit estimates near-significant t scores were obtained. Other variables for which non-significant coefficients were estimated in early trial runs are residence in medium-sized cities (as compared with small ones), the existence of a private plot, the presence of non-working males in the family, the work status of the husband (blue-collar or white-collar), and, most important, the total number of children from 0 to 16 years of age.

A number of more refined observations on the equations should be made. Older children do not seem to significantly affect the decision to participate except through their negative impact on per capita income. This may be one explanation for the higher positive values of their coefficients in equations (2) and (3) in Table 8.6, where income per capita is not included. Nonetheless, the high positive coefficients and near significance of the number of children aged 4–6 is quite surprising. Could it be a backlash effect of women who had just had younger children and are rushing back to work? If so, it points to the temporary nature of the effect of young children on the lifetime labor participation of their mothers.

It is interesting to note the higher effect of the family's non-wage income compared with that of the husband's earnings. Theoretical considerations may have it both ways, but if the additions to the husband's earnings are secured by his working longer hours, then the opposite of what we found should occur: to an equal negative income effect one should add the negative effect of heavier overall time pressure on the household (Gronau, 1983b). The higher negative coefficient for non-wage income in our case may reflect women's input of household time in securing those incomes.

In principle the coefficients for the schooling variable should indicate whether participation is specifically affected by the level of education, beyond its effect through wages. According to Gronau (1978, pp. 11–12), the expected sign for such a coefficient is theoretically non-determined since it depends on whether a higher level of education gives more support to

household work or to labor-market activity. In the Soviet case, we hypothesized that the difficulties of using advanced schooling in the home, which
is poorly equipped and serviced, and the clear non-pecuniary benefits of
having a "mental" rather than a "physical" job should generate positive coefficients for education. The difficulty is that of multicollinearity between
education and wages. Let us report that when the series of the educational
variables (as in equation 1) is added to the participation equation, it
generates positive coefficients, although not always significant ones, and that
at least part of this positive effect comes at the expense of the wage
coefficient.

The substitution between the expected wage and city size makes it difficult to determine the true sources of the effect on the offered wage. It
results at least in part from the lower labor-force qualifications of women
residing in small cities. However, note the higher value of the coefficient for
years in school in equation (3), where the expected wage variable is excluded.

The marginal effects of the various variables on PAR at the point of
average participation can be calculated by dividing the latter by 10
$[P(1 - P) = 0.105]$. Instead of presenting all the marginal effects for
elasticities, we present in Table 8.8 selected estimates of the LFP of women
under different sets of assumptions related to their economic and demographic status, and the sensitivity of the rates to changes in the variables.
Most of the simulations are based on equation (1) in Table 8.6, unless otherwise indicated. The benchmark estimate (line 2) is based on average levels
of variables for the population of Soviet urban European married women
between the ages of 17 and 44, and with no account taken of the existence
of children 4 to 16.[8] The sample average is higher than the Soviet average
because the wage rate and the level of education of women in the sample are
higher, a positive effect that is partly offset by higher family income. The
Soviet benchmark estimate of PAR is close enough to the mark (remember
that students and older women, all with lower LFP rates, are not represented
in the base estimate).

The effects on PAR of alternative demographic patterns are presented
in lines 4–7. In an average family with one small child the wife's PAR will
drop 9.2 points, 11.6 points compared to a situation with no children at all.

Table 8.8. Participation rates of women under different conditions

	Expected participation rate (%)	Difference from line 2
1. Sample average (age 17–44) (a)[a]	94.0	+8.4
2. Soviet average (age 17–44) (a)[a]	85.6	..
3. Soviet average (age 17–44) (b)[a]	86.9	+1.3
A. As in line 2, but family has		
4. No child 0–3	88.0	+2.4
5. One child 0–3	76.4	−9.2
6. Two children 0–3	58.7	−26.9
7. One child 0–3, one child 4–6	86.0	+0.4
8. One additional year of schooling	87.9	+2.3
9. 50% increase in family income	80.5	−5.1
10. 50% increase in women's wage	92.8	+7.2
11. 50% reduction in women's wage	60.3	−25.3
12. R50 increase in nonwage income[b]	81.2	−2.7
13. R50 increase in husband's income[b]	81.8	−2.1
14. Residence in large city[c]	91.6	+8.2
15. Age 45–54[d]	79.8	−8.2
16. Age 55+ (retirement age)	52.0	−35.9

		Difference from line 5
B. As in line 5, but family is		
17. Poor, with 2 children 0–3[e]	25.2	−51.2
18. Poor, with 1 child 0–3[e]	43.3	−33.1
19. Poor, age 45–54, no children 0–3[e]	47.8	−28.6
20. Poor, age 55+, no children 0–3[e]	20.1	−56.3
21. Rich, 1 child 0–3 (a)[f]	87.8	+11.4
22. Rich, 1 child 0–3 (b)[f]	93.8	+17.4
23. Rich, no children 0–3 (a)[f]	94.3	+17.9
24. Rich, no children 0–3 (b)[f]	97.2	+20.8

(Notes on following page.)

Notes to Table 8.8

a Assuming 0.26 children aged 0–3, 0.14 children aged 4–6, 0.21 children aged 7–11, and 0.28 children aged 12–16 (as in sample).

Net monthly income (R per month)	Sample	Soviet
Nonwife income per capita	87	70
Husband's earnings	214	171
Other earnings	37	30
Private income	38	30

   Women's hourly wage: The Soviet wage is estimated at roughly 80 percent of the Sample wage.

   Women's schooling: Sample = 12.7 years; Soviet = 9.3 years.

   Income and education figures for the Soviet average based on data in Chapter 4 and the Appendix.

   Average estimates based on equation (1) in Table 2. Soviet estimate (a) excludes and (b) includes the effect of children 4–16.

b The increments are calculated from a Soviet average, estimated from equation (2), which is 83.9 percent.

c The increment is calculated from a Soviet average, estimated from equation (3), which is 83.4 percent.

d The increment is from a participation rate of the Soviet average, but with no children 0–3, which is 88.0 percent.

e A poor family has R50 per capita monthly of nonwife family income; the wife has four years of schooling and is paid the minimum wage.

f A rich family has R140 per capita monthly of nonwife family income; the wife's hourly wage is R1.08 (both double the average). In variant (a) the level of education is kept at 9.3 years, but in variant (b) it is raised to 13 years.

With two small children, 0–3 years of age, PAR will go down 29.3 points. If we include the effect of older children, despite their non-significant coefficients, it is found that by the time one child becomes older than 3 at least the average level of PAR is reestablished. In the sample every fourth wife on the average has a small child. An exogenous increase in the fertility rate that will make, say, every third wife have a small child at any given time (a significant change) will reduce the overall PAR by about one point, provided that all other variables remain constant.

Among the other "marginal" rates presented in lines 8–16 we would like to emphasize the high sensitivity of PAR to the women's wage rate. A 50 percent decline in the wage means bringing it down to the pre-1973 minimum wage of R50 per month. This sensitivity is much higher than those, in opposite signs, of non-wife income sources. This lends support to claims by Mincer and others that the rise in women's wages is the dominant force in increasing women's participation over time. It should also underscore the presumed effect of raising the minimum wage in the Soviet Union between 1959 and 1973 from between R27–35 to R70 per month (McAuley, 1979, pp. 200–1). Of course, other relevant changes were also taking place during that period. Note that the effect of one additional year of schooling raises PAR 2.3 points beyond its effect through the women's wage rate.

In part B of Table 8.3, PAR rates are estimated for women belonging to families with a number of variables removed from the average at the same time. It is first observed that upon moving from a minimum-wage minimum-subsistence status family with two small children to a family with all incomes twice the average and no small children, PAR goes from 25.9 to 97.2 percent. The corresponding range of change of PAR in response to changes in income, wages, and education alone (with one small child) is between 43.3 and 93.8 percent. A second implication is that an equi-proportional rise in wages of both husband and wife has a positive net effect on the woman's PAR. This could be learned indirectly by comparing lines 21 and 22 with line 5. If there was, indeed, a rise in the relative pay of women state employees during the 1950s and 1960s (see McAuley, 1981, pp. 24–25), it can be counted as another factor that helped to raise women's participation rates.

Hours worked

The equation of weekly hours of work was run with a similar array of variables as the participation equation, excluding only city size and years of schooling. Instead of expected or estimated hourly wages, actual wages are included. Two new variables have been introduced: one a dummy variable of being a teacher, to account for the institutionally determined shorter hours, and another for the selectivity bias, a bias caused by the exclusion of non-working women. The selectivity-bias variable is computed from the probit maximum-likelihood estimates of the participation equation (Nakamura *et al.*, 1979, pp. 791–92). It "absorbs" the additional number of hours offered by those who made the decision to work.

As mentioned above, the variability of hours under Soviet conditions is very limited. Three-quarters of all women reported working the regular 41-hour week, and another 100 women reported working between 35 and 47 hours. This leaves the regression results at the mercy of outlier observations, some of which include measurement errors. In a cleanup operation we had to exclude 49 observations, but even then the results should be considered questionable. Nevertheless, part of the limited variability of weekly hours has to do with a long-term choice of occupation rather than with short-term adjustments. This was the reason for introducing the dummy variable of "being a teacher."

The results (Table 8.9) reflect both the Soviet situation and the resulting data problems. With the one exception — husband's earnings — all family-income variables have the right, negative sign, but none of them is statistically significant. None of the age variables is statistically significant, but the positive coefficient signs for more hours and for older women are quite surprising; they probably have to do with the occupational structure of these women. Most of the coefficients for having children are positive, while we expect them to be negative, and the coefficients for non-working females are negative where they should have been positive. The only consolation is that none of these coefficients is statistically significant. The coefficient for selectivity bias is positive, as it should be, and significant. It should be mentioned that in alternative equations with all 891 observations we did get statistically significant negative family-income and small-children coefficients.

Table 8.9. Weekly hours worked: regression analysis

	Equation (1)		Equation (2)	
	Coef-ficient	t-value	Coef-ficient	t-value
1. Per capita family income[a]	..	..	−0.0018	−0.4086
2. Husband's earnings[a]	0.0021	1.1441	..	..
3. Other members' earnings[a]	−0.0039	−1.6376	..	..
4. Nonwage income[a]	−0.0010	−0.4091	..	..
5. Hourly wage (ln)	−3.8725	−6.7463	−3.8266	−6.7553
6. Age 26 or less	−1.0087	−1.6196	−1.0650	−1.7922
7. Age 45–54	0.8407	1.6270	0.7645	1.4754
8. Age 55+	2.2704	1.5841	2.2668	1.5935
9. Being a teacher	−9.7990	−17.3294	−9.8542	−17.4641
10. Number of children 0–3	0.3185	0.7413	0.3912	0.8747
11. Number of children 4–6	0.5608	1.1368	0.5176	1.0459
12. Number of children 7–11	−0.1240	−0.3045	−0.0820	−0.1999
13. Number of children 12–16	0.2954	0.8153	0.3295	0.9313
14. Number of non-working females	−0.2325	−0.5938	−0.2654	−0.6747
15. Selectivity bias[b]	0.9267	2.1068	1.0797	2.4776
16. Constant	42.3093	39.9630	42.4052	38.4960
17. R^2 corrected/SD	0.38	4.81	0.38	4.81

[a] Net, monthly, in rubles.
[b] See text.

Finally, even after allowing the teacher's dummy to "explain away" 10 weekly hours, we get a robust negative hourly-wage effect on hours. The negative elasticity of hours to changes in hourly wage, at the point of averages, is just about 0.1. In other words, around that point women will reduce their work load by one hour when their hourly wage grows by about

25 percent. This is a *backward-bending supply function for hours* but with a rather moderate slope. It is interesting to note that when "being a teacher" is not included in the regression, the negative elasticity of hours with respect to wages is almost twice as large. This may be another indication of the fact that the negative correlation between hours and pay has more to do with a long-run choice of occupation, assuming a permanent pressure on time, than with short-run adjustments to temporary time pressures, adjustments that are almost impossible to make (other than quitting the labor force). On a per-hour basis, at least, wages for teachers, nurses, and medical doctors are relatively high among women's jobs. But even with all the above reservations, a backward-bending supply curve of hours worked under Soviet conditions of pressure to work should not be considered unreasonable. Indeed, it may underscore the reality of time pressure and emphasize the need for additional income as the main stimulus to work. The main conclusion from the hours equation is, however, that here the room to respond to changes in economic and demographic conditions is limited, even more than for the decision to participate.

4. Life cycle participation, fertility, and education

In this section, equations (1) and (2) are estimated on the sample of complete families with working wives. Non-working wives had to be excluded because of lack of data on life-participation of women who did not work during the survey period. This exclusion creates a selectivity bias, which is corrected by including in the equation a selectivity bias variable estimated from a probit equation of participation. Equations (1) and (2) are estimated both separately and simultaneously in a number of formulations, as seen below. Theory calls for simultaneous estimation since, in the long run, decisions on participation and fertility are mutually dependent.

a. Life-participation and fertility (equation 1)

The proportion of years available for work that women actually work — their lifetime commitment to the labor force — should reflect both the long-term, durable determinants of participation as well as the temporary ones resulting from the presence of small children. In such long-term decisions the wife's schooling should play a more important role than schooling at one particular point in time. This is also the natural variable to combine with fertility, which we discuss below. Likewise, permanent income rather than current income variables should be used to capture the long-term income effects. Let us point out, however, that although it is long term, the variable we observe is *ex post*; it is not clear to what extent it also reflects the decision about long-term participation taken early in life, together with decisions on fertility and so forth, and to what extent it is the outcome of external events that occurred in the course of one's life. It should be mentioned that since the sample for life-participation includes only working women, the estimation cannot pick up the permanent non-participants, and this clearly weakens the results.[9]

The estimated equation presented in Table 8.10 reflects what we consider to be the best picture of long-term participation. It is a two-stage least-squares (2SLS) estimation for the fertility variable, and it underscores

Table 8.10. Life participation of working married women: complete families (590) (2SLS)

Variables	Mean	Coefficient	t-value
Relative participation (dependent variable)	0.906		
Educational level (dummy variable)			
University (reference)	0.471		
Technical school	0.269	−0.0726	−2.787
General high school (9–11 years)	0.176	−0.2031	−5.142
8 years or less	0.081	−0.2467	−3.312
Age 45–54	0.315	−0.1469	−5.8431
Number of births	1.315	−0.0717	−1.757
Selectivity bias	0.137	−0.0543	−0.444
Constant		1.1310	19.956

the importance of education and fertility in long-term decisions about work. The findings of these and other estimations are discussed below.

(a)   The level of education is a dominant determinant of life-participation. Indeed, in equations that include wages as well, the wage coefficients are not statistically significant and the educational levels hold their own. According to Table 8.10, the life-participation of technical school graduates is 7 points lower than that of university graduates, that of high-school graduates is 20 points lower, and that of those with less education — almost 25 points lower. For the average working career of 17.9 years, these effects translate into 15 months, 3.5 years, and 4.3 years of work, respectively.[10] Since the education level of non-working women is significantly lower than that for working women, the results must be more robust for the entire sample of completed families. What is found is not so much the effect of education on prospective wages as a decision to participate that is either the outcome of education or part of one and the same decision, early in life, to obtain an education and to pursue a career in the labor force. This interpretation is consistent with the findings presented by Goldin (1982) on the historical patterns of the growing LFP of American married women.

(b)   When the mutual dependency of fertility and participation is recognized, fertility gets a negative and almost significant coefficient. Every additional birth reduces the life-participation of working women by 7 points. Translated into absolute figures, every child born causes a work recess of some 15 months for an average working career of almost 18 years. Here, too, the inclusion of non-working women (at the time of the survey) might increase this effect.

(c)   A reduced-form equation for life-participation (which, instead of fertility, includes the structural variables that determine fertility, not shown), shows that it is the variable of age at marriage that is "responsible" for the negative effect of the number of births on life-participation. This adds another element to a joint decision or sequence of events at an early stage of life that affect the rest of life.

(d)   The algebra of life-participation is such that if interruption of the work career in order to bear and care for children occurs early, or if the woman does not start working directly after finishing school — participation should grow with age. In lieu of this, the introduction of a variable for older age is mainly for control purposes. The negative coefficient was somewhat surprising, until we discovered that there is a sizable group of women between the ages of 45 and 54 (and some younger) who started working outside the home (in the sample) very late in life.[11] On average, they are less educated and most do physical work. This may be one manifestation of the campaigns staged by the Soviet authorities to enlist non-working women into the labor force during the late 1950s and 1960s.

(e) So far the analysis has not succeeded in finding a good variable for long-term non-wife family income that behaves in the expected way. We tried the level of education of the husband, and although it generates positive coefficients, they are not significant.

(f) Finally, the selectivity bias has the "wrong" negative sign (see Nakamura et al. 1979, pp. 791–92), but is never significant. We resist the notion that this result may imply that non-working women (at the time of the survey) are not distinct from working women. Indeed, we have shown this to be untrue.

e. Fertility (equation 2)

Fertility competes with a mother's time in all aspects of LFP — short- and long-run participation, hours worked, and qualitative aspects of women in the labor force. No wonder that both decisions, when taken together, depend on the same vector of variables — wages, income, and level of education — in a way that makes it almost impossible to separate, as claimed by Mincer (1963). No wonder that in most cases one expects coefficients of opposite signs, with the notorious exception of the income variable, and negative mutual effects of one on the other (Mincer, 1963; Ben-Porath, 1973a, 1973b, 1982). On the income side one may also find a degree of complementarity when the need to provide for an extra (unanticipated) child forces women into the labor force at a late stage in life (Schultz, 1977, p. 26).

The story of the Soviet Union is one of pressures on fertility from all directions. Continuous revolution up to the mid-1930s, the second world war, voluntary and involuntary movement of population, and perennial shortages of housing in the cities all created insecure and unstable conditions and economic hardships far from conducive to having children. The numerical surplus of women, created mostly by the war, had similar effects. In addition, one should add strong economic and other pressures on women to join the labor force and, at least indirectly, to acquire the needed schooling beforehand or concurrently. All the above must make reduced fertility the ultimate response, the ultimate endogenous variable. However, if it is considered that labor-force participation is only one of the list of variables above, and that life-participation is measured *ex post*, mostly after decisions or factors affecting fertility are established, it is perfectly possible that the assumed (mutual) relationship between decisions about fertility and participation are reversed; it is the former that affects the latter.

Indeed, the estimated results show this. The first fertility equations estimated, a 2SLS equation with participation as an independent variable, and a reduced-form equation including all the determinants of participation, showed no effect of participation on fertility.

In view of these findings, the equation underlying the results presented in Table 8.11 is formed as a partly reduced form (Schultz, 1977) and excludes participation related variables. For the sake of consistency with the life-participation equations, the equation is based on completed families with working wives. The inclusion of a selectivity bias variable (which is negative and significant, as it should be) makes it very similar to the equation based on the entire sample of completed families.

The relevant fertility variable is the number of children ever born. The life-participation and especially the fertility equations require families with long life spans, so these two equations are estimated on a subsample of "complete" families, defined as families whose youngest child is 4 years old or older, or childless families with wives older than 30 (see Lehrer and Nerlove, 1981).[12] The choice of independent variables is discussed below along with the findings.

(a) A number of variables were found to identify the fertility equation and to distinguish it from the life-participation equation: the age at marriage, the number of rooms in the apartment, and the existence of a private plot. All have clear and robust positive coefficients, as should be the case, and

Table 8.11. Fertility of married working women: complete families (653)
(2SLS)

Variables	Mean	Coefficient	t-value
Number of births (dependent variable)	1.315	..	..
Educational level (dummy variables):			
University (reference)	0.471	..	..
Technical school	0.269	0.1548	2.256
General high school (9 years or more)	0.176	0.3348	3.277
8 years or less	0.083	0.8839	4.728
Age 45–54	0.315	−0.0167	−0.234
Number of rooms	2.408	0.2357	6.481
Owning a private house (= 1)	0.263	−0.1664	−2.563
Having a private plot (= 1)	0.063	0.4612	3.891
Age at marriage	24.0	−0.0199	−3.170
Selectivity bias	1.367	−1.3821	−4.417
Constant	..	1.2593	1.853
$\bar{R}^2$/standard error of regression	..	0.14	0.672

indirectly affects life-participation. The age at marriage is introduced either
as a test variable, indicating a tendency toward higher fertility, or as an
exogenous event, not completely planned, that creates a situation conducive
to having more children if married early or less if married later. While in
each case both fertility and participation are affected, if the marriage age is
partially exogenous, participation is affected indirectly through fertility.

Having a private plot provides an opportunity for the wife to be productive and to rear children under more agreeable conditions than if she
entered the labor market. The choice to have a private plot may also indicate
the rural origin of the family, where there is a tradition of higher fertility.

Housing shortages are continuously cited as a major factor affecting low fertility. We are not aware of a statistical analysis that has demonstrated this obvious fact. It would be nice if more could be said on the strong housing coefficient, but since it registers an *ex post* situation, it cannot be considered the description of the *ex ante* supply of housing to the family, the variable that is being sought.

(b) Since fertility has declined over time, one might expect to find more children to older wives — definitely a positive coefficient in an equation where the wives' level of schooling is already accounted for. The negative (though non-significant) sign comes as a bit of a surprise and may be explained by the fact that the representative women in the group were already 30 years old in 1953, when the Soviet baby boom got underway. Or it may be explained by a degree of under-reporting of children who had already left home.[13] In any case, the inclusion of the age variable takes care of a reporting bias, if one exists.

(c) The sign of the income effect on fertility, the debate that over-shadowed many other issues for such a long time, has been considered of less than primary importance (Ben-Porath, 1982, p. 59). Our investigation did not identify a clear variable to represent income or a clear sign for such an income effect. The schooling level of the husband — a surrogate for permanent income — produced a weak and utterly insignificant coefficient.

A second possible candidate is the ownership of a private house or apartment. Most Soviet urban residents live in apartments rented from the government and pay low, heavily subsidized rent. Only a small minority (much smaller than the 20 percent in our sample) can afford to buy their own apartments, which are of much higher quality. This variable has a negative and highly significant coefficient that may point to a negative income effect. It may, however, represent an alternative form of investment to having children. The competition between the two can manifest itself directly, or indirectly through the need of wives to help finance the purchase of an apartment by working.

(d) Since fertility is a life-cycle phenomenon, it was decided to include the educational level of married women rather than their wages in the equation presented. This also conforms with the participation equation. As such, it clearly captures the impact of the wage and of the level of education. It demonstrates a clear and negative relation with fertility. Technical-school graduates have 0.15 more children than university graduates, and high-school graduates and those with less schooling have 0.33 and 0.88 more children, respectively. This is the opposite of the relationship found between schooling variables and is responsible for part of the response.[14] In alternative estimations it is found that when the women's expected wage replaces the schooling variables it generates a negative and significant coefficient, and when both schooling and wage variables are included, the wage coefficient acquires a positive sign, which is never significant while the negative schooling coefficients are somewhat larger. This last result is most likely the outcome of multicollinearity between schooling and wages. If not, it may give some support to the notion proposed by Berliner (1983) on the basis of a model developed by Ben-Porath (1973b), that in the special conditions of the Soviet Union the own wage effect on fertility may not be as negative as in a market economy or may even turn positive. We are very skeptical that our findings support such a view; in our judgment, wage and schooling have a positive effect on participation and a negative effect on fertility.

5. Conclusion

The analysis in the two preceding sections demonstrated that Soviet women do react and respond to changes in the economic environment along similar lines to women elsewhere.[15] It was further shown that, while the short-run decision about participation is heavily determined by the expected wage, other family income, and the presence of small children, the longer-term decisions about participation are influenced by the level of education and by fertility — fundamental decisions normally made early in life. The decision on weekly hours is much less responsive to economic variables and we hypothesize that the decision results from the unavailability of part-time work in the Soviet Union, an option of which many women might have availed themselves. This conclusion is supported by the backward-bending supply function of hours that was estimated.

The findings in this chapter disagree on one point with results presented by Gregory (1982, pp. 26–27) and Kuniansky (1983), and implied by Berliner (1983, p. 151 and Table 1, p. 142). In these studies there is a negative effect of education on participation (and a positive one on fertility). Gregory considers the finding "surprising"; Berliner implies it only for the upper end of the educational range (only for women with secondary specialized education or more); Kuniansky finds it to hold on average. These studies are based on quite different populations and data bodies and on variables differently defined than ours, so that there is ample room for obtaining different statistical results. We doubt very much whether an overall negative relation between education and participation rates of women can be established. A non-linear relationship with change of sign at very high levels of education is less unlikely and deserves further study.

The general conclusion mentioned above has not, however, addressed itself to the two more difficult questions. (a) To what extent can the economic and demographic variables considered alone explain the high level of participation observed, or are non-economic factors also at work? (b) Are the responses of Soviet women to changes in the economic and demographic variables more muted or restricted than in other countries? (This is, in some sense, a different aspect of the first question.)

Very little can be learned on both questions by comparing coefficients of determination of respective equations or individual coefficients with underlying elasticities. It is very difficult to find two studies that will be similar enough for such comparisons to be revealing. We would, however, like to mention the rather high pseudo-coefficient of determination in the participation equations — around 0.30 — to make the point that the response to the economic variables as a group is important (see also, for comparison, Nakamura *et al.*, 1979, p. 793).

A more direct, though somewhat speculative approach to the first question is by asking: what changes in the economic and demographic variables should be made to bring down the participation rate to the level considered "normal" in market economies, say 50 percent, for married women aged 25–44? Using equation (1) in Table 8.6 above, one could affect such a change by, for example, increasing the number of small children from 0.26 to 0.33 *and* reducing women's hourly wage by approximately 45 percent and their level of education by two years, offsetting the loss of income with an increase in "non-wife income" to keep family income per capita constant. The effect of all four changes together would bring the participation rate down to about 51 percent. This simulation experiment demonstrates that it would take unrealistic changes in the parameters of the equations to bring the rates of participation down to "normal" levels. Although we do not have the necessary comparative data on hand, such changes seem to us to go far beyond what is needed to bring conditions that surround Soviet women to a level on par with those of women in the market economies they are compared with. If that is true, there is room left for factors not included in the equation, such as "persuasion" or higher social and ideological norms.

In response to the second question we can report here on results of labor participation (and hours) functions for a group of Soviet married women (a sub-group of the larger sample), once in the Soviet Union in the early 1970s and a second time in Israel approximately 3–4 years following migration at the end of 1978. The sub-group is not a representative sample of the larger group, and every woman was five years older in 1978 and had gone through various family and other changes. But they did make decisions on work in a society where the rate of participation of married women is about 30 percent (Gronau, 1978, p. 16). There are two main findings: first, their LFP in Israel is 74 percent, much higher than that of Israeli married women but lower than their previous rate of 87 percent in the Soviet Union. Second, all the regression coefficients in the participation and hours equations are larger, more responsive, in Israel than in the Soviet Union. In many cases non-significant Soviet coefficients turn significant in Israel, including the hours equations. Full analysis of the comparison must wait for further study, but the early results seem to point to the fact that the response in the Soviet Union to economic and demographic conditions is somewhat muted by the social demand that women should work. The participation rate of Soviet women in Israel, higher than that of Israeli women, could be a manifestation of investment in human capital that is more directed toward outside work, or of the taste for such work developed in the Soviet Union, or of both and many other factors (Ofer, Vinokur, Eliav, 1982).

An alternative approach to the second question is to examine to what degree the coefficients derived from the cross-section analysis can "project" the historical, long-term participation developments. Such a projection can be attempted with the help of the life-cycle participation and fertility equations. This is easier said than done: in addition to the usual differences between cross-sectional findings and historical developments, there is also the problem of non-correspondence of the available historical data to the immigrant sample. Although the equations are estimated on a sample of European urban families, the available data on participation are for the entire population; there is limited information on participation rates for the urban or non-agricultural population, and that only for the 1959–70 period. In addition, there are no data on wages by sex. Crude estimates under sets of alternative assumptions, however, produce two main results that seem to hold within a wide range of assumptions on participation and on the explanatory variables. The first result is that the participation equation overestimates the change of participation over time. Even with modest assumptions about changes in the wages of women, which is by far the dominant variable, and assuming, for example, that there was no increase in the relative pay of women (see McAuley, 1981, p. 26), estimated participation rates for 1940 and 1950 amount to 20–30 percent as compared with actual rates of at least 50 percent and most probably 60 percent for the urban segment of the population for the same period. The second result is that the equation for life-participation consistently underestimates the changes in *absolute* participation over time.

The underprediction of historical trends of *absolute* participation by the *life*-participation equation is first explained on technical grounds. The relationship between the rates of growth of participation and of life-participation is like that between a marginal and an average change and thus depends on the respective initial levels and on the rate of change of participation. If the initial levels are similar, and participation grows very rapidly, life-participation will lag behind participation; it will catch up when the rates of growth of participation start to slow down.

An added complication in our case is that the life-participation equations cover only working women. If those not working are different — that is, if they have lower, or zero levels of *life* participation — the life-

participation rate may even decline when women who have not worked
previously for a considerable period join the labor force.

According to projections based on the equations, life-participation in
1940 would have been about 67 percent and in 1950 about 77 percent, far
above the *actual* participation figures, as compared with estimated Soviet life-
participation figures of 83 percent for 1973 and 85 percent for 1980. The
entire change of 18 points is brought about by reduced fertility and a rise in
the level of education in almost equal shares. The probable effect of wages
is left to be expressed through education. The first result is highly consistent
with claims by Becker (1981) and Mincer (1963) that the rise of women's
wages is the main driving force behind the historical trend of increased participation (see also Goldin, 1982, pp. 14–15).

What makes us somewhat uneasy about this result is mainly that the
countervailing force of non-wife family income is so weak, unlike the results
of American studies. This weakness is the main reason why the equation
over-predicts the historical increase in participation. What is more important,
however, is that it is at odds with the accepted wisdom that, certainly in the
past and even today, women are virtually forced to work in order to make
ends meet, given the deliberately low wages of men.

Our feeling is that even if the small income effect reflects the present
cross-section situation, it definitely does not reflect the true income effect of
past years. It is also possible, however, that the weak income effect in the
cross section is an outcome of data problems that we cannot identify.

An alternative explanation for over-predicting historical changes is that
the earlier decades saw much stronger application of exogenous pressure on
women to work, and that over the years some of these pressures were
replaced by direct and indirect economic incentives. The latter refer to the
increased level of schooling for women, resulting partly from their understanding that if they have to take jobs it is better to secure white-collar ones.
Clearly much of the impact of increased schooling is reflected in the wage
effect.

Whether by economic incentives, ideological education, or sheer
pressure — if a norm is established early in the game that women want to or
expect to work, or even expect to be pressured into work, investments in

human capital are directed toward this option and family plans are made. In the following generation there is the added effect of daughters growing up in homes of working mothers. These norms are self-perpetuating in the sense that they make the decision to work outside the home closer to optimal and may help explain the very high participation rates of the 1970s. This is so even when other conditions are not fully met, when there is still a heavy household burden and inadequate cooperation by the husband, or when the number of suitable white-collar jobs is inadequate and part-time work is not allowed. The extra pressure is directed to high divorce rates, even lower fertility, and lower investment in human capital and in effort on the job. This must be a major explanation why, although women's schooling is rapidly catching up with men's, their relative wages have hardly increased.

Can the present analysis help to predict what is in store for the Soviet Union with respect to women's LFP? At present levels of fertility and exogenous conditions one should not expect the participation rates to go down. Assuming that male and female wages will continue to grow at least at the same rate, that no new non-wage sources of income are provided, and that household conditions will not get worse, the analysis in this chapter indicates that women will continue to have a high inclination to join the labor force. Indeed, the continued replacement of older, low-educated, first-generation-urban women with young, educated, urban-born women of the new generation may even raise the participation rate. If, however, policies designed to raise fertility levels are introduced — including better facilities for children and better conditions for mothers to take a longer temporary break for work and rear young children at home — then participation rates may east somewhat (see McAuley, 1981, and Chapter 7 above). They may also go down if the social pressure on women to participate fails to be fully internalized as part of women's personalities and values. With labor parti-cipation rates very close to the attainable maximum (for non-Moslem urban married women), even continued increase in women's wages can hardly push them much further. Nonetheless, unless policies to encourage fertility are implemented or there are adjustments in the household sector and the labor market to help mothers there will be a decline in women's participation in the labor force.

Notes

1. Summaries and surveys of the relevant Soviet and Western literature on all these topics are included in Gregory (1982, 1983). Other important studies also containing extended reference lists are Lapidus-Warshofsky (1978, 1982) and McAuley (1981).

2. A few examples are Mincer (1963), Schultz (1974), Liebenstein (1975), Schultz (1977), Gronau (1978), Easterlin (1980), Becker (1981), Lehrer and Nerlove (1981), Goldin (1982); see also Ben-Porath (1982).

3. Detailed summaries of the relevant Soviet (and Western) literature on many of these topics are included in Dodge (1966), Sacks (1976), Lapidus-Warshofsky (1978, 1982), McAuley, (1979, 1981), Gregory (1982, 1983), Berliner (1983). See also Chapter 7.

4. The proportion of women of working age rose from about 50 percent in 1926 to 56.6 percent in 1950 and then declined to 50.9 percent in 1970 (USSR Census Bureau, 1959, p. 12; Eason, 1963, p. 54; Rapaway, 1976, p. 4).

5. Other data underlying this discussion were obtained from the returns of the 1959 and 1970 Soviet population census and from *Vestnik Statistiki*, No. 11 (chapter on women in the USSR), various years since 1975.

6. Data on fertility, marriage, and divorce are from the returns of the Soviet population census (*Vestnik Statistiki* and *Naselenie SSSR*, various years).

7. A second method used is a maximum-likelihood (probit) estimation of PAR = bX, where PAR is the dichotomous participation rate and b the vector of maximum-likelihood coefficients. From the maximum-likelihood functions we estimate the selectivity-bias variable to be included in the conditional hours (and wage) equation of the working women (Nakamura *et al.*, 1979, pp. 791–93). Since results of the logit and probit methods are highly consistent, we only show the logit estimates, which are more easily translatable into marginal effects and elasticities.

8. When they are included the rate goes up 1.3 points; see notes to Table 8.8 for more details.

9. The following are figures for relative participation, potential labor-force experience, and actual LF experience for working married women in complete families by age group and schooling level:

	Mean	Age 45–54	University	Technical	General	Less than 9 years
Relative participation	0.85	0.76	0.95	0.88	0.73	0.61
Potential experience (years)	21.2	30.8	17.7	20.8	25.0	34.1
Actual experience (years)	17.9	22.9	17.2	18.4	17.8	20.5

At present the potential experience of women with 8 years of schooling or less is measured from age 13 (the average age at which the group finished school), which is a mistake that will be corrected in future analyses.

10. The inclusion of the selectivity bias variable in Table 8.10 is designed to correct for this selection bias. The fact that the selectivity bias is insignificant may indicate that the bias is not very important; that is, women who did not work during the year of the survey are no different from those who did work in their long-term attachment to the labor force.

11. This is an assumption. The data do not include information on the timing of work, only on the number of years spent in the labor force.

12. The choice of age 4 as the cut-off point is based on the fact that only children below this age negatively affect the LFP of their mothers. It is recognized that some children may still be born even to complete families, but given low fertility in the Soviet Union and that two children are the goal of most urban European families, the bias created should not be very serious. The cost of further limiting the definition of complete families is to reduce the size of the sample.

13. The number of children even born to women with children of Great Russian nationality is estimated at 2.33. If their level of education had been similar to that of the sample, the figure would have gone down to about 1.6, as compared with 1.46 children per woman with children in the sample. The calculations are based on *Vestnik Statistiki* (1982, No. 1, pp. 64–66).

14. This is evident from the equation that includes the participation rate, in the form of smaller coefficients for the schooling variables.

15. There are similar results for the United States (Heckman and Willis, 1977) and other countries: Canada (Nakamura *et al.*, 1979, p. 793) and Israel (Gronau, 1978, p. 15).

Appendix
Demographic and economic characteristics
of the sample and of the Soviet urban population

1. Introduction

This appendix is devoted to a survey of the main demographic and economic attributes of the ISIP sample and its main patterns of economic behavior, and to a comparison of the above with corresponding characteristics of the Jewish population and of the entire European-urban Soviet population (JP and UP respectively). This survey provides an opportunity to observe the distinct characteristics and patterns of behavior of the UP and of the JP in the Soviet Union. Some of these characteristics are the basis for the reweighting of the sample discussed in Chapters 1 and 4. The survey also provides data on variables, or aspects that are not analyzed further in one of the books and in this way helps to complete the economic picture of all groups (JP, UP, and SP — the sample population).

2. The demographic, social, and economic composition of the sample

Tables A.1 through A.13 present basic data on the various social characteristics of the sample population and, wherever possible, provide comparable data on the distribution of these properties in various "parent" or "target" populations, whose behavior we are trying to study.

a. Geographic distribution

The geographic distribution of SP differs from that of both UP and JP in that it is heavily concentrated in the most western areas of European USSR, mainly in areas annexed during or after 1939. As shown in Table A.1, more than three-fifths of SP came from the post-1939 areas in which only 13.8 percent of JP and 8.4 percent of UP live. Such a high concentration

Table A.1. Distribution of the soviet urban population by republic

	Sample population (SP) (1)	Jewish population 1970[a] (JP) (2)	Urban population 1970[b] (UP) (3)
	(millions)		
Total number	3,443	2.1	149.6
Population in 7 Soviet western republics	3,359[c]	1.9	126.6
	(percentages)		
Total	100.0	100.0	100.0
RSFSR	19.3	42.6	69.6
Ukraine	37.5	41.0	22.3
Byelorussia	5.2	7.8	3.6
Moldavia	28.6	5.2	1.0
Lithuania	5.0	1.2	1.4
Latvia	4.1	1.9	1.3
Estonia	0.4	0.3	0.8
Pre-1939 areas	38.4	86.2	91.6
Post-1939 areas[d]	61.6	13.8	8.4

[a] Source: *Census 1970*, Vol. IV, Table 2, pp. 12–15.
[b] Source: *Narkhoz 1973*, p. 10.
[c] The remaining 84 persons are distributed as follows: Armenia — 7; Azerbaijan — 46; Georgia — 10; Kazakstan — 7; Kirghizia — 4; Uzbekistan — 10.
[d] Includes the three Baltic republics, Moldavia, and the following Oblasts: Kaliningrad (RSFSR), Grodno and Brest (Byelorussia), and Volyn, Rovno, Lvov, Zakarpatskaya, Ivano-Frankovsk, Chernovtsy, and Ternopol (Ukraine).

reflects quite closely the structure of Soviet immigration to Israel, which contains a disproportionately high number of emigrants from the Baltic states. A similar picture is drawn from the breakdown of SP by republic: the sample significantly underrepresents the Jewish and urban populations of the USSR[1] and overrepresents them in Moldavia, Lithuania, and Latvia. The proportion of SP coming from the Ukraine is very close to that of JP but, owing to the high proportion coming from the western annexed areas, it is still much higher than that of UP. Byelorussia, on the other hand, is over-represented for UP but underrepresented for JP.

Of all the SP–UP and SP–JP differences, the most important is certainly the one that cuts across the pre-1939 borders. There is good reason to believe that the social and economic environment, as well as the behavioral habits of the population in the post-1939 areas differ significantly from those in Russia proper. Yet because most of SP from the pre-1939 areas come from Moscow, Leningrad, and Kiev (unbalancing this group as well), we have so far been unable to make the necessary adjustments for both populations when "average" or aggregate magnitudes or patterns of behavior are estimated.

Another geographical factor that may have a significant effect on the results is the distribution of the population by city size (Table A.2). Such differences exist in the Soviet Union on both the supply side (goods and services, housing, wages, work opportunities in general or in particular occupations), and on the demand side (social background of the population, duration of stay in urban locations).

Table A.2 shows the distribution of SP, UP, and some data for JP by city size and for three major cities. Again, there are fairly wide SP–UP differences. Two cases of high one-city concentration strongly affect the SP distribution: there are 645 persons from Kishinev and 467 persons from Chernovtsy in the sample population, very possibly resulting in abnormally high percentages for the 250,000–499,000 and the 100,000–249,000 size groups, respectively. For this reason, column (2) shows the distribution *without* the inhabitants of these cities (although this may, in turn, yield an underestimate of the relevant percentages). We observe that 14–21 percent of SP lived in small cities (of up to 100,000 inhabitants), 20–46 percent lived

Table A.2. Distribution of Soviet population by city size and for three major cities

	SP (1)	SPᵃ (2)	JP 1970ᵇ (3)	UP 1974ᶜ (4)
Total number (millions)	3,443	2,331	1.9	149.6ᵈ
Percentages				
Total	100.0	100.0	100.0	100.0
Cities under 50,000 inhabitants	9.1	13.4		33.1
50,000–99,000	5.4	7.9		9.8
100,000–249,000	20.5	10.2		
250,000–499,000	25.7	10.3		
500,000–1 million	11.1	16.4		12.3
1–1.8 million	7.8	11.5		6.8
Cities				
Kiev	6.5	9.6	7.8	1.3
Leningrad	5.7	8.4	8.4	2.5ᵉ
Moscow8.3	12.2	12.9	4.9ᵉ	

[a] Excluding 192 families (645 persons) from Kishinev and 142 families (467 persons) from Chernovtsy; see text.
[b] Source: Katz (1973, Table A.2, p. 4).
[c] Source: *Narkhoz 1973*, pp. 22–32.
[d] Entire urban population (as of January 1).
[e] 2.8 and 5.0, respectively, if small peripheral towns are included. The difference should be subtracted from the percentages of cities up to 250,000 inhabitants.

in medium-sized cities (100,000–500,000 inhabitants), and 39–58 percent lived in large cities of over half a million inhabitants; 20–30 percent lived in the three major cities of the Soviet Union.

This distribution of SP reveals a much higher concentration in large cities as compared with UP, of whom over 40 percent live in small towns, and 30 percent in medium-sized cities, less than 30 in large cities, and only 9 percent in the three largest Soviet cities. The SP distribution is apparently closer to that of JP, as indicated by comparable data on the three largest cities in the Soviet Union (and other cities, not shown here) and supported by other sources that emphasize the tendency of Jews to congregate in large cities.[2]

Thus, whenever inferences on UP are sought, the different spread of SP and UP among cities of various sizes must be taken into account. In addition to the special treatment accorded to the high proportion of SP from Kishinev and Chernovtsy, special attention must be paid to the relatively high concentration of SP in Moscow and Leningrad, which in many respects differ from all other places in the Soviet Union, and to the underrepresentation of Jews in small towns.

b. Demographic characteristics

The restrictions on the selection of SP families affected their size and composition and created comparison problems with both UP and JP. Specifically, the exclusion of one-parent and non-working families (students or retired persons) tends to increase SP family size (since many of the excluded persons were one-person families) and to increase the number of children and the number of working persons per family. These built-in biases must be kept in mind when the comparative data on family size and composition (Tables A.3 and A.4) are considered.

The average SP family size (3.39) is similar to that of UP for the 7 western republics, but about 2 decimal points larger on average than that of JP in the republics for which information is available (Table A.3, column 8). Some measures of the bias created by the problems mentioned above can be gained from column 9 in Table A.3, where data on the family size of two-parent families of UP are presented. Such families are 0.18–0.20 larger, on

Table A.3. Family size in the Soviet Union: urban population (1970) and sample

	Total	% families with n persons						Average family size	Two-parent family
		2	3	4	5	6	7+		
	(1)	(2)	(3)	(4)	(5)	(6)	(7)	(8)	(9)
Sample	100.0	15.5	44.1	29.2	9.3	1.3	0.7	3.39	3.39
USSR	100.0	25.2	30.3	26.6	11.1	4.0	2.8	3.49	3.67
7 western republics									
Total								3.39	3.57
Jewish								3.14^a	..
RSFSR									
Total	100.0	26.0	31.5	26.8	10.7	3.4	1.6	3.40	3.58
Jewish	100.0	38.0	28.5	22.9	8.2	1.9	0.5	3.1^a	..
Ukraine									
Total	100.0	26.7	31.7	27.6	9.9	2.9	1.2	3.35	3.57
Jewish	100.0	37.3	31.3	21.6	7.6	1.8	0.4	3.1^a	..
Byelorussia									
Total	100.0	22.0	29.4	31.6	12.2	3.5	1.3	3.54	3.56
Jewish	100.0	30.6	28.0	27.7	10.3	2.7	0.6	3.3^a	..
Moldavia									
Total	100.0	26.2	31.2	25.7	10.2	3.9	2.8	3.44	3.57
Jewish	100.0	33.5	30.9	24.4	8.8	2.0	0.5	3.2^a	..
Total population[b]									
Lithuania	100.0	24.9	31.8	27.6	10.8	3.3	1.6	3.42	3.56
Latvia	100.0	30.9	34.6	23.6	7.9	2.2	0.8	3.19	3.36
Estonia	100.0	31.9	33.7	24.9	7.3	1.6	0.6	3.75	3.32

[a] Source: *Census 1970*, Vol. VII, Table 30, pp. 272–303.
[b] Source: *Census 1970*, Vol. VII, Table 26, pp. 234–37.

average, than average UP families, and the average UP family size for the 7 western republics (3.57) is 0.15 larger than that of SP. Because UP includes families headed by students and retired persons, this difference still somewhat underestimates the SP–UP difference. It may thus be inferred that the SP family size is about 0.2 people smaller than that of UP. If the difference in UP family size between columns 8 and 9 can be assumed to be the same for JP, then it can also be concluded that the family size of SP is very similar to that of JP.

The biased geographical spread of SP seems to have only a minor effect on the above conclusions for both comparisons.

The restrictive family definition of SP also shows up in the comparisons of size-distribution of families (columns 2–7). The percentage of two-person families in SP is much lower than either in UP or in JP, and the proportions of three-person (and to a lesser degree four-person) families are higher. No "compensating" higher proportions are observed for larger families. The size distributions also demonstrate the much higher proportion of two-person families in JP than in UP, and the lower proportions of larger-sized families, thus underlining the fact that JP (and SP) families are smaller than UP families.

The average number of children per SP family is 1.14 (see Table A.4), somewhat smaller than that for UP (1.25). If correction for the excluded types of families could be made, the difference would definitely increase, because most of the excluded families have no children and many others have only one child. Moreover, it seems that the true adjusted deficiency of children in SP is even larger than in average family size. This we conclude from the fact that while the unadjusted UP average family size (3.39) is the same as that found for SP, the unadjusted average number of children is higher for UP. If this is true, it follows that SP families contain more adults, i.e., more members that do not belong to the nucleus family (e.g., grand-parents, etc.).

There is no comparative data on JP family composition, but the similarity to SP found in other respects makes it reasonable to assume that JP families have fewer children and somewhat more other family members (for families of the same size) than do UP families. These differences from

Table A.4. Family composition: Soviet urban population, 1970, and sample

	Total	Percentage of families with n children				Average number of children per family
		0	1	2	3+[a]	
Sample	100.0	19.2	50.4	28.2	2.2	1.14
USSR[b]	100.0	19.6	41.5	30.0	8.9	1.30[c]
RSFSR	100.0	19.7	43.6	28.8	7.9	1.27
Ukraine	100.0	22.5	42.5	29.4	5.6	1.19
Byelorussia	100.0	17.4	38.0	35.5	9.1	1.38
Moldavia	100.0	22.8	39.7	27.1	10.4	1.27
Lithuania	100.0	20.0	40.4	30.6	9.0	1.30
Latvia	100.0	23.9	47.8	24.6	3.7	1.09
Estonia	100.0	22.9	45.4	27.2	4.5	1.10

[a] 3+ assumed to equal 3.2, and 4+ assumed to equal 4.
[b] Soviet data calculated from *Census 1970*, Vol. VII, Table 32, pp. 380–95.
[c] The figure for the 7 western republics is 1.25.

the target population, in size and composition, must also be taken into account when family income and expenditures per capita or per consuming unit are considered.

The special characteristics of the sample are also apparent in the age distribution of SP. Because we chose families in which at least the husband was employed, the able-bodied population (men aged 15–60, women aged 15–55) constitutes as much as 70.9 percent of SP compared with 62.8 percent for the RSFSR urban population (Table A.5). Thus the proportion of persons over the age of 60 in SP is only 5.2, as against 10.7 for the comparison group. There is also a bulge in the 20–29 year age group, which may reflect the emigrant character of SP.

Table A.5. Age distribution of SP and the urban population of RSFSR, 1970

	Sample population			Urban population of RSFSR		
	Total	Men	Women	Total	Men	Women
Number of persons (millions)	3,443[a]	1,662	1,781	81.0	37.1	43.8
Percentage breakdown						
Total	100.0	100.0	100.0	100.0	100.0	100.0
0–9	14.7	15.0	14.2	14.5	16.2	13.2
10–19	14.8	14.3	15.4	19.0	20.9	17.3
20–29	21.6	20.5	22.7	15.3	16.8	14.0
30–39	15.2	15.6	14.8	17.3	18.5	16.3
40–49	17.2	17.0	17.5	14.0	13.2	14.7
50–59	11.3	14.2	8.6	9.2	7.5	10.6
60–69	2.7	2.1	3.3	6.9	4.8	8.7
70–79	1.9	0.9	2.7	2.9	1.7	3.9
80+	0.6	0.2	0.8	0.9	0.4	1.3
Able-bodied population as percent of total population	70.9	73.3	68.6	62.8	67.3	59.0

[a] Sex was not identified in all cases for youngest and oldest categories.
[b] Men aged 15–59, women aged 15–60.

Source: *Census 1970*, Vol. Soviet, p. 18.

c. Labor-force characteristics

Concerning the age distribution of the working population, fully comparable data by sex was not available (Table A.6), so that we had to use general data for the RSFSR. A bulge is again evident in the 20–29 age group, whereas the immediately younger and older age categories are underrepresented. The dip in labor-force participation (LFP) among the young is no doubt related to the high education level of SP, but we have no ready explanation for the underrepresentation of the 30–39 age group.

The sample of 1,016 families includes 2,146 working people,[3] or 2.11 workers per family. This figure is significantly higher than the 1.80 per family found for "worker and employee" families as estimated from Soviet sources for 1973.[4] The gross LFP rate for SP is 62.3 percent, compared with an overall figure for Soviet UP of 52.4 percent, and about 55 percent for the 7 western republics.[5]

Table A.6. Distribution of working population by age, SP and RSFSR

	All employed	Men	Women	Working population of RSFSR
Number of persons (millions)	2,146	1,127	1,109	56.2
Percentage breakdown				
Total	100.0	100.0	100.0	100.0
Under 20	2.7	2.0	3.5	7.7
20–29	39.6	27.6	34.0	23.1
30–39	23.8	23.1	24.6	31.0
40–49	26.0	24.8	27.4	25.3
50–54	9.8	12.2	7.3	6.6
55–59	5.4	8.5	1.9	4.4
60+	1.6	1.9	1.4	1.9

Source: *Census 1970*, Vol. VI, p. 459.

The real differences in both the number of workers per family and LFP rates are much smaller when the proper adjustments are made so as to make the populations more compatible. First, the official figure of 1.80 workers per family is taken from the returns of the 1970 Census,[6] and the true figure may be higher for 1973. This is assumed from its constantly increasing trend over 1959–70. According to the Census returns, the number of workers per urban family was 1.56 in 1959, but increased to 1.80 in 1970.[7] Extrapolating from this trend to 1973 produces a figure of 1.86–1.87. Secondly, when we narrow the population base to 7 western republics only, we pick up another 0.01; when we further narrow it down to only families with at least one worker (as are, by definition, all SP families), the figure goes up to 1.94 for 1970.[8] The figure thus may be 2.00 per UP family, still without taking into account the fact that UP includes (while SP excludes) one-person families with a lower-than-average number of workers per family.

There may, however, still be a small difference between SP and UP that could be explained by the larger number of adults per family and other, as yet unidentified, factors.[9] We are also unable to determine whether this high work activity is a specific SP feature or whether it also characterizes JP.

To complete the picture of the amount of work performed, Table A.7 also presents data on the number of hours devoted by various groups of SP to work in different types of jobs. As seen in the table, the average SP worker spends 42.1 hours at work each week, 39.1 of which are regular working hours in the main place of employment and another 1.2 hours are spent on overtime work at the same place. Furthermore, an average of 1 hour per week is devoted to additional jobs in the public sector and 0.8 hour is devoted to various forms of private work. For those who work overtime or outside their main place of employment, the additional working hours comprise a much higher proportion of their work week than indicated by the above figures. Just over 10 percent of all workers do some overtime work for an average of 12.3 hours a week. About 8 percent of them spend 11.9 hours on additional public jobs, and nearly the same proportion spend an average of 10.1 hours weekly supplying privately produced goods and services.

The last two work categories mentioned are not included in official Soviet statistics on hours worked, so for comparison purposes we use the figure of 40.3 hours. The regular working week for most Soviet workers and employees (W&Es) is 41 hours, although for some groups (some industrial workers, medical workers, teachers) it is shorter. The figure given for actual average number of weekly hours of Soviet sources for all W&Es is 39.4 (*Narkhoz 1973*, p. 590), 0.9 hour less than the comparable SP figure (see section e. below for elaboration). Since SP includes a much higher proportion of teachers and doctors than UP, the adjusted gap may be even wider. As in the case of the number of workers, all working hours must be taken into account when income and wage comparisons are made.

Table A.7 also shows that on the average men work longer hours than women, and that the average difference of 4.4 hours is made up of 2.7 hours in the main place of employment plus 1.7 hours of extra work — which is performed mostly by men. At least part of this gap in the main place of employment is due to the high proportion of women in the teaching and medical professions.

d. Sex and level of education

The SP labor force (Table A.7) is made up of 1,127 men (1,011 are heads of families), comprising 52.5 percent of the labor force, and 1,019 women (47.5 percent). As can be seen in Table A.10 below (line a), the male proportion of UP is about 50 percent. This 2.5 percent difference may reflect, in part, the exclusion of one-parent families (most of them headed by women) from SP, and from the inclusion of singles in the population to which the UP figure relates. The difference, while small, may cause differences in average wage or family income if the male-female wage gap is sizable, as it indeed is (see below).

The major labor-quality element dealt with here is the level of education (ED) (Table A.8). With respect to this key factor, SP reflects very well the level of education of JP, both standing considerably higher than that of UP. The proportion of those with at least some higher education is 43.5 percent for SP and 39.8 percent for JP, compared with 10.4 percent for UP. About two-thirds of all SP, and almost 60 percent of JP workers had specific education beyond general secondary school, as against less than 25 percent for UP labor. At the other end of the scale, those with incomplete elementary

Table A.7. Number of workers and hours worked, by sex and type of job

	Total	Main place of work		Additional jobs	
		Regular	Overtime	Public	Private
All employed					
1. Number of persons	2,146	2,142	218	176[a]	168[b]
2. Average hours worked per week for those employed in each category	42.1	39.2	12.3	11.9	10.1
3. Average hours worked per week for entire group	42.1	39.1	1.2	1.0	0.8
Family heads (men)					
1. Number of persons	1,011	1,011	137	128[a]	109
2. Average hours worked per week for those employed in each category	44.4	40.0	12.5	11.9	10.8
3. Average hours worked per week for entire group	44.4	40.0	1.7	1.5	1.2
All men					
1. Number of persons	1,127	1,127	145	139[a]	117[b]
2. Average hours worked per week for those employed in each category	44.2	40.0	12.5	11.9	10.5
3. Average hours worked per week for entire group	44.2	40.0	1.6	1.5	1.1
Women					
1. Number of persons	1,019	1,015	73	37	51
2. Average hours worked per week for those employed in each category	39.8	38.2	11.9	12.1	9.2
3. Average hours worked per week for entire group	39.8	38.1	0.9	0.4	0.5

[a] Seven other persons reported earnings from an additional public job, but did not report the number of hours worked.

[b] Six additional men reported earnings from a private job, but did not report the number of hours worked. Five of the men were heads of families.

[c] Five heads of families were not employed.

Table A.8. Level of education: urban labor, Jewish labor and sample working population

	Sample			Urban working population[a]			Jewish working population[b]		
	Total	Men	Women	Total	Men	Women	Total	Men	Women
All levels	100.0	100.0	100.0	100.0	100.0	100.0	100.0	100.0	100.0
Completed higher education	39.1	40.0	38.1	8.8	9.2	8.4	35.7	36.8	34.5
Incomplete higher education	4.4	4.4	4.4	1.6	1.7	1.4	4.1	4.4	3.7
Completed technical school	22.4	17.7	27.7	13.2	11.4	14.9	19.3	17.8	20.7
10+ years of schooling	18.2	19.3	17.0	18.8	17.6	20.0	19.2	17.1	21.2
7–9 years of general schooling	10.3	11.4	9.0	32.5	34.1	31.0	13.7	13.9	13.5
4–6 years of general schooling	4.8	6.2	3.2	19.5	21.9	17.1	6.2	7.7	4.7
Less than 4 years of general schooling	0.7	0.9	0.6	5.6	4.1	7.1	2.0	2.2	1.7
Average number of years[c]	13.0	13.0	13.0	9.3	9.3	9.3	12.4	12.3	12.5

[a] Seven western republics

[b] Five western republics (Estonia and Lithuania not included). The specific weights are based on the distribution of the population rather than of the labor force.

[c] Assumed number of years for education categories, from top of table down: 16, 14, 13.5, 10.5, 8.5, 5.5, 1.5.

Sources: Jewish population calculated from *Census 1970*, Vol. IV, Tables 58–60, 66–67, pp. 614, 618, 621, 633, 635; other figures calculated from *Census 1970*, Vol. III, Table 6, pp. 408–558.

education account for 5.5 percent of SP and 8.2 percent of JP — but over 25 percent of UP labor. More than half the workers in UP had only 9 years of schooling or less, compared with 15.8 and 21.9 percent respectively for SP and JP. Rough transformation of the level of education categories into number of years of schooling produces similar results: the average number of schooling years for an SP workers is 13, compared with 12.5 for JP and 8.2 for UP. Similar gaps are found when only men or only women are compared; the somewhat different sex composition between populations does not affect the comparisons to any significant extent.

Data on ED in the individual republics are not shown; however, when differences in the geographical distribution are controlled for, the SP–UP gap

Table A.9. Years of schooling of the working population: sample[a]

	All employed		All men		Women	
	Number	Percent	Number	Percent	Number	Percent
Total	2,146	100.0	1,127	100.0	1,019	100.0
Years of schooling						
18+	210	9.8	152	13.5	58	5.7
15–17	695	32.4	341	30.3	354	34.7
12–14	530	24.7	223	19.8	307	30.1
10–11	381	17.8	207	18.4	174	17.1
7–9	211	9.8	124	11.0	87	8.5
4–6	103	4.8	70	6.2	33	3.2
0–3	16	0.7	10	0.9	6	0.6
Average number of years of schooling	13.0		13.0		13.0	

[a] The data presented here differ slightly from those shown in Table A.6, particularly in the lower educational grouping, because slightly differeent definitions were used in these two tables.

Table A.10. Employment status: Soviet urban population, 1970 and sample
I. All employed

	Total	Workers	Employees	*Kolkhoz*
Sample (absolute number)	2,146	615	1,531	..
Percent				
(a)	100.0	28.7	71.3	..
(b)	100.0	28.7	71.3	..
UP: USSR percent				
(a)	100.0	64.7	34.4	0.7
(b)	100.0	64.7	34.4	0.7
RSFSR				
(a)	100.0	65.4	34.2	0.3
(b)	100.0	65.4	34.2	0.3
Ukraine				
(a)	100.0	64.9	33.1	1.8
(b)	100.0	64.9	33.1	1.8
Byelorussia				
(a)	100.0	64.2	35.2	0.4
(b)	100.0	64.2	35.2	0.4
Moldavia				
(a)	100.0	61.2	35.2	3.4
(b)	100.0	61.2	35.2	3.4
Lithuania				
(a)	100.0	64.3	35.1	0.3
(b)	100.0	64.3	35.1	0.3
Latvia				
(a)	100.0	63.3	36.0	0.5
(b)	100.0	63.3	36.0	0.5
Estonia				
(a)	100.0	63.6	35.8	0.5
(b)	100.0	63.6	35.8	0.5

Source: Soviet data, *Census 1970*, Vol. V, Table 4, pp. 25–33.

II. By sex

Men				Women			
Total	Workers	Emp-loyees	*Kolkhoz*	Total	Workers	Emp-loyees	*Kolkhoz*
1,127	419	708	..	1,019	196	823	..
100.0	37.2	62.8	..	100.0	19.2	80.8	..
52.5	19.5	33.0	..	47.5	9.1	38.4	..
100.0	71.4	27.8	0.8	100.0	58.1	41.0	0.6
50.1	35.8	13.9	0.4	49.9	29.0	20.5	0.3
100.0	72.4	27.2	0.4	100.0	58.7	41.0	0.2
49.2	..	..	..	50.8	..	..	..
100.0	70.4	27.8	1.7	100.0	59.2	38.5	1.9
50.4	..	..	..	49.6	..	..	..
100.0	68.3	31.1	0.6	100.0	60.2	39.2	0.3
49.0	..	..	..	51.0	..	..	..
100.0	66.9	29.9	3.1	100.0	55.6	40.4	3.6
49.4	..	..	..	50.6	..	..	..
100.0	70.0	29.5	0.4	100.0	58.6	40.7	0.2
50.5	..	..	..	49.5	..	..	..
100.0	60.0	29.1	0.9	100.0	56.9	42.5	0.2
48.8	..	..	..	51.2	..	..	..
100.0	70.2	29.0	0.8	100.0	57.4	42.4	0.1
48.7	..	..	..	51.3	..	..	..

becomes even wider.[10] Although other minor factors may bias the figures somewhat, none can change the order of magnitude of the ED gap, which is a major source of concern for any meaningful SP–UP comparison. In Table A.9, which presents the distribution of SP labor by years of schooling as reported by the respondents, and in Table A.8, a similar pattern of male-female differences in schooling emerges for all population groups. Women tend to concentrate rather more in secondary-technical schools (probably teacher colleges and nursing schools), and rather less than men in universities, especially in the pursuit of higher degrees. On the other hand, a higher proportion of women complete general secondary school, while more men leave school after less than 10 years. At least for SP, these differing patterns ultimately yield the same average ED as measured by years of schooling.

e. Social groups and occupational structure

The wide SP–UP differences in schooling must be expected to show up in corresponding differences in the social and occupational structure. The labor force (and the population) in the Soviet Union is divided into three main social groups: "workers" (*rabochie*) — mainly holders of blue-collar jobs earning wages; "employees" (*sluzhashchie*) — salary earners who are mainly white-collar workers; and *kolkhoz* members. Since this last group is not represented in SP and is virtually excluded from UP, the discussion here centers on the proportions of workers and employees.

As seen in Table A.10, SP includes only 615 workers who make up only 28.7 percent of the SP labor force, compared with 64.7 percent in UP (USSR). The somewhat higher proportion of men in SP and its biased geographical distribution (a higher proportion coming from Moldavia with a low proportion of UP "workers") probably accounts for only a minute part of this sizable gap: only 37.2 percent of working men in SP are "workers," compared with nearly double that figure in UP; and only 19.2 of SP working women are "workers" compared with three times as many in UP. Likewise, even the relatively low percentage figures for UP workers in Moldavia (lowest among the 7 western republics) far exceed the SP figures: 61.2 for both sexes, 66.9 for men and 55.6 for women.

Table A.11. Level of education by work status: sample and urban population (percent)

	Entire labor force			Workers			Employees		
	Total	Men	Women	Total	Men	Women	Total	Men	Women
Level of education									
Higher and professional	65.9	62.1	70.2	12.5	13.8	9.7	87.4	90.7	84.6
Regular school:									
10+ years	18.2	19.3	17.0	40.0	41.3	37.2	9.5	6.4	12.2
7–9	10.3	11.4	9.0	28.8	26.5	33.7	2.9	2.5	3.2
4–6	4.8	6.2	3.2	16.1	16.0	16.3	0.3	0.4	0.1
Less than 4	0.7	0.9	0.6	2.6	2.4	3.0	0	0	0
Urban population[a]									
Higher and professional	23.7	22.5	25.0	4.4	4.8	4.0	60.9	68.1	56.0
Regular school:									
10+ years	19.2	18.1	20.1	18.9	19.3	18.4	19.6	15.3	22.5
7–9	31.9	33.4	30.4	40.9	42.0	39.5	15.6	12.0	18.0
4–6	19.2	21.4	17.0	27.5	28.2	26.6	3.3	3.9	3.0
Less than 4	6.0	4.6	6.5	8.3	5.7	11.5	0.6	0.7	0.5

[a] Entire urban labor force. Calculated from *Census 1970*, Vol. V, Table 4, p. 26; Table 7, p. 66.

This completely different workers-to-employees ratio for SP is strongly correlated with the SP–UP gap in the level of education, as shown in Table A.11, where the ED for workers of different status is shown. As seen in this table, the SP–UP difference for "workers" alone (columns 4–6) and "employees" alone (columns 7–9) are much narrower, both for each sex separately and for both sexes combined, than those for the entire working population (columns 1–3). Nevertheless, the within-group SP–UP differences are still large. Of all the white-collar employees in SP, 87.4 percent acquired some kind of professional training, as against only 61 percent in UP. Especially low by comparison is the corresponding rate for UP women: 56 percent as compared with 84.6 percent for SP women. Likewise, 12.5 percent of blue-collar SP workers have higher or professional education and more than half completed general high school, compared with only 4.4 percent and less than one-third, respectively, of UP workers.

It must be emphasized, however, that the different workers-to-employees ratios between SP (and most probably JP) and UP provide an explanation of the different ED levels only in the technical sense, as both differences are two dimensions of the same phenomenon. Still, SP–UP comparisons performed within the work-status groups, or with this variable being controlled, account for a good part of the differences in ED.

The occupational distribution of the labor force among various non-agricultural working populations is compared in Table A.12. Here, UP refers to the non-agricultural rather than to the urban Soviet labor force (which includes non-agricultural workers in rural areas). In addition to the percentage breakdown for the various populations, the SP/UP ratios of the proportions in each occupational group are also calculated (column 7). The picture presented in the findings are similar, but much more detailed that the one seen above for work-status groups.

Looking first at the comparison between active labor forces, we see again the much lower proportion of workers and the higher proportion of employees in SP (observe the ratios in column 7 — 0.42 for the first group and 2.29 for the second). We may derive some comfort from the fact that for "production workers," a key group in any investigation, the difference is no greater; rather, it is a bit smaller. We find that for white-collar occupations

Table A.12. Occupational distribution of the non-agricultural working
population: Soviet Union (1970) and sample

	Sample			USSR			Ratio sample
	All emp-loyed	Men	Women	Total for compa-rison	Men	Women	(1)/(4)
					(1000s)		
	(1)	(2)	(3)	(4)	(5)	(6)	(7)
Total	2,146	1,127	1,019	91,655	47,165	44,490	
Total reported in detail	2,146	1,127	1,019	88,487	44,942	43,545	
Percentage breakdown (total %)	100.0	100.0	100.0	100.0	100.0	100.0	
Workers	*28.7*	*37.2*	*19.2*	*68.9*	*77.1*	*60.4*	0.42
Production	22.3	33.0	10.4	47.3	72.0	21.8	0.47
Services	6.4	4.2	8.8	17.4	8.8	26.2	0.37
Others	..		..	4.2	−3.7[a]	12.4	..
Employees	*71.3*	*62.8*	*80.8*	*31.1*	*22.9*	*39.6*	2.29
Agricultural employees	0.1	0.1	0.1	..	..	..	..
Production supervisors	6.5	10.5	2.2	1.5	2.5	0.6	4.33
Technicians and engineers	21.0	23.2	18.4	9.5	10.4	8.6	2.21
Engineers	16.2	20.3	11.7	6.9	8.7	5.2	2.35
Technicians	2.8	2.2	3.5	1.1	0.9	1.3	2.55
Others	1.9	0.7	3.2	1.5	0.9	2.1	1.27
Medical staff	10.6	5.4	16.4	3.1	0.7	5.6	3.42
Head doctors and administration	1.0	1.1	0.8	0.07	0.06	0.07	14.29
Doctors and dentists	4.8	3.3	6.6	0.7	0.4	1.1	6.86
Auxiliary staff	4.0	0.7	7.7	2.2	0.2	4.3	1.82
Others	0.8	0.3	1.4	0.1	0.07	0.2	8.00
Educational staff	12.9	9.6	16.6	5.6	3.4	7.8	2.30
Higher education	4.9	5.9	3.7	0.9	1.0	0.7	5.44
School teachers	8.0	3.6	12.9	4.7	2.5	7.1	1.70
Entertainment and culture	4.6	4.4	4.8	1.4	1.2	1.6	3.29

(cont.)

Table A.12. (cont.)

	Sample			USSR			Ratio sample
	All emp- loyed	Men	Women	Total for compa- rison	Men	Women	(1)/(4)
					(1000s)		
	(1)	(2)	(3)	(4)	(5)	(6)	(7)
Journalists and writers	0.8	0.7	0.9	0.2	0.1	0.2	..
Entertainment administration	0.7	0.5	1.0	0.5	0.6	0.5	..
Entertainers and artists	2.2	3.1	1.2	0.3	0.4	0.2	..
Library staff	0.8	0.1	1.7	0.4	0.04	0.7	..
Law	0.6	0.5	0.6	0.1	0.2	0.1	6.00
Communications	0.05	..	0.1	0.7	0.2	1.1	..
Trade	4.0	4.2	3.6	1.8	1.8	1.9	2.22
Management	2.0	2.8	1.0	1.2	1.1	1.3	1.43
Shop assistants	0.8	0.5	1.1	0.3	0.2	0.4	2.67
Others	1.2	0.9	1.6	0.3	0.5	0.1	..
Planning and accounting	9.9	3.6	16.8	5.7	1.7	9.9	1.74
Administrators	1.2	1.5	0.8	0.1	0.2	..	12.00
Economists	2.0	0.5	3.6	0.8	0.3	1.3	2.50
Accountants (bookkeepers)	5.5	1.6	9.7	3.0	1.1	5.0	1.83
Others (incl. secretaries)	1.3	..	2.6	2.8	0.2	5.5	0.46
Communal services	0.9	1.1	0.7	0.2	0.1	0.2	4.50
Administrators	0.6	0.7	0.4	0.1	..	..	..
Others	0.3	0.4	0.3	0.04	..	..	..
Government administration	0.3	0.2	0.5	0.5	0.6	0.3	0.60

[a] The figures for men were obtained by subtracting the figures for women from the total; the inconsistency is in the Soviet source.

Source: Census 1970, Vol. VI, Table 2, pp. 14–23; Table 18, pp. 165–69.

SP employees are concentrated to a higher degree than the average for all employees in high-education occupations, both among and between the various occupation groups. Such a higher than average concentration is found for managers, in both production and planning (compare the average concentration for employees of 2.29 with 4.33 for production supervisors and 12.0 for planning administrators); for medical employees, especially doctors (3.42 and 6.86 respectively); for employees of high educational and scientific institutions (5.44), and for lawyers. Relative proportions that are below the average for employees are found for some medical employees, mainly nurses (1.82), for school teachers (1.70), and for accountants (1.83). It should be emphasized, however, that even in these cases the proportion of the total employed in each occupation is still higher in SP than in UP. The conclusion is that SP workers not only overconcentrate in white-collar occupations, they overconcentrate *within* that group in those occupations that demand high levels of education and responsibility; but "higher responsibility" goes only up to a certain point. This clearly corresponds to our findings about the educational levels of SP and UP. A similar comparative picture is found when men and women are considered separately. In both SP and UP there are more women than men among doctors, nurses, school teachers, and accountants, but for SP women the degree of concentration is much higher.

The high concentration of SP in employee groups that require a high level of education should be expected to affect its industrial structure as well, at least to some degree. In general, highly educated workers are more highly concentrated in various service sectors (especially public service) than in material production sectors. Given these *a priori* expectations, the findings presented in Table A.13 — the industrial distribution of the labor forces — are quite encouraging. As in Table A.12, the UP population consists of all Soviet employed persons except those working in agriculture. As can be seen, 30.2 percent of the SP labor is concentrated in manufacturing (compared with 37.7 percent of UP), 7.1 percent in construction (11.6), and 9.3 percent in trade (9.6). Among the branches of "material production," the SP–UP gap is wide only in transportation — 4.1 percentage points for SP and 10.0 for UP. For material production as a whole (excluding agriculture) we have about 54 and 71 percent, respectively, a fairly large difference, but not as large as that

Appendix: Demographic

Table A.13. Industrial distribution of the labor force by economic sector: Soviet Union (1973) and sample

	Sample			USSR (1973)[a]		
	Total	Men	Women	Total	Men (1,000s)	Women
Total	2,146	1,127	1,019	87,137	41,712	45,425
Percentage breakdown						
Total	100.0	100.0	100.0	100.0	100.0	100.0
Manufacturing	30.2	34.6	25.4	37.7	40.2	35.5
Agriculture, fishing and forestry	2.0	2.5	1.5	..	..	..
Transportation	4.1	6.3	1.6	10.0	15.8	4.6
Communications	1.0	0.7	1.3	1.7	1.1	2.2
Construction	7.1	10.5	3.4	11.6	17.1	6.4
Trade	9.3	8.3	10.4	9.6	4.8	14.0
Other material production				1.3	2.0	0.6
Communal services	10.8	12.3	9.1	4.0	4.0	4.1
Health, social security and sports	12.4	6.8	18.5	6.3	2.0	10.3
Education and culture	13.3	8.5	18.5	10.0	5.6	14.0
Arts	0.7	1.1	0.4	0.5	0.6	0.4
Science and scientific services	6.2	7.0	5.4	4.3	4.6	4.0
Banking	0.8	..	1.7	0.5	0.2	0.8
Administration	2.0	1.3	2.7	2.4	1.9	2.9

[a] Calculated from *Narkhoz 1973*, pp. 578, 583. Data exclude workers in agriculture, fishing and forestry.

between the respective occupational structures. In the non-material branches we find relatively high concentrations of SP labor in communal services (10.8 as against 4.0 in UP) and in health services (12.4 vs. 6.4), and smaller "excesses" in education (13.3 and 10.0) and science (6.2 and 4.3).

As in the case of social groups, the differences here between SP and UP seem to be more marked among women than among men, especially in the division between material and non-material production: just under 44 percent of SP women work in material production, compared with 63 percent of UP women. Even so, the higher percentage of men in SP has only a negligible effect on bringing the industrial distributions of SP and UP closer together.

There is only scant information on the socio-economic structure of the Jewish population and labor force in the Soviet Union. But if we are to judge from the comparisons between the levels of education of SP, UP, and JP, we have to conclude that the socio-economic structure presented by SP is much closer to that of JP than to that of UP.

Two conclusions arise from the above description of the sample. First, SP is not very far in its demographic-social-economic structure from the Jewish population of the Soviet Union, but it is quite distinct in these characteristics from UP. A second conclusion follows directly: although only minor adaptations of the sample are needed in order to examine the economic behavior and environment of JP, major changes must be made when studying UP. Indeed, in studying the Soviet economy and the economics of UP, two approaches are taken: (a) when aggregate macroeconomic or "average" economic variables for UP are sought, a reweighting of the socio-economic cells of SP must be performed so that it will conform to the structure of UP. In this way one can calculate the average wages, incomes, expenditure patterns, and income distribution of UP. (b) A comparative study of specific groups in SP which, although they may be over- or under-represented in SP compared with UP, are still quite similar to their UP counterparts. For example, there are some 615 blue-collar workers in SP, of whom 433 work in production. While under-represented in SP for UP purposes, they can be directly compared with blue-collar workers in UP. It is quite clear that some adjustment will have to be made, but the two groups are certainly more similar to one another than SP and UP as a whole.

3. Income and wages

This section presents our findings on wages, family income, and their size distribution for SP and (bearing in mind the SP–UP structural differences) compares the returns with corresponding official Soviet data or non-Soviet estimates for UP.

The average net money income per family of SP and its sources are presented in Table A.14. Total income per SP family averages R385.2 or (with an average family size of 3.389 persons) R113.7 per capita. Of this income, 91.7 percent (R353.1) is from work; 4.7 percent comes from other private sources (including agricultural plots), and only 3.6 percent originates from the government in the form of various social-security type payments, scholarships and student stipends.

In Table A.15 we compare SP family income with the estimated monthly income of a UP family in the USSR in 1973. The figures are derived from official Soviet data. The exact computations and sources are summarized below.

1. Average per-worker gross wage is computed for all non-agricultural workers and employees in the *7 western republics* of the Soviet Union in 1973.

2. To arrive at net wages, income tax and single-parent and small families taxes are deducted.

3. The number of workers per family is estimated for *urban families* with at least one worker, also in the 7 western republics. These data are contained in the returns of the 1970 Census. As explained earlier, this brings UP closer to the family characteristics of SP. The estimated figure for 1970 (1.94) is raised to 2.00 for 1973 in accordance with the general long-term trends observed over 1959–70.

4. The other family income elements are estimated by combining the wage-income, as estimated above, and the structure of total family income of industrial workers based on Soviet family budget studies.

5. Finally, for the computation of income per family member, the figure for the average full (two-parent) urban family size in the 7 western republics is taken (3.57 from Table A.3). This family group differs from the one

Table A.14. Net family income per month

	Income in rubles[a] (1)	Percent of average total income (2)
Average total income	*385.2*	*100.0*
Net income from work	*353.1*	*91.7*
Main place of work	321.2	83.4
Extra public jobs	13.3	3.5
Extra private jobs	18.6	4.8
Net income from Social Consumption Fund	*13.8*	*3.6*
Old-age pensions	6.7	1.7
Disability pensions	2.9	0.8
Survivors' pensions	0.5	0.1
Child allowances	0.2	0.1
Other allowances	0.5	0.1
Students' stipends	3.0	0.8
Income from subsidiary agricultural plot	*2.4*	*0.6*
All other sources of income	*15.9*	*4.1*
Rentals	0.8	0.2
Assistance from relatives	7.2	1.9
Miscellaneous	8.0	2.1

[a] The ruble figures correspond to the average income from the given source for all families.

Table A.15. Net monthly family income: sample and Soviet urban population (rubles)

	SP (1)	UP (1973)[a] (2)	Difference (rubles) (3)	Percent difference (4)
A. Findings				
1. Total income	385.2	293.0	92.2	31.5
2. Net income from work	353.1	248.2	104.9	42.3
3. Social Consumption Fund	13.8	31.4	−17.6	−56.1
4. Subsidiary plot	2.4	5.0	−2.6	−52.0
5. Other	15.9	8.5	7.4	87.1
B. Explaining the difference			*Cumulative*[b]	
6. Total family income	385.9	293.0	92.2	92.2
7. Deduct items included in SP but not in UP[c]	−39.9		−39.9	52.3
8. Deduct non-wage income[d]	−24.1	−44.9	20.8	73.1
9. Average family income from main place of work	321.2	248.2	73.0	73.0
10. Deduct SP wage income at main place of work resulting from more workers per family	−16.7		−16.7	56.3
11. Family income from main place of work	304.5	248.2	56.3	56.3
12. Wage per worker at main place of work	152.3	124.1	28.2	
13. Total income from work per worker	167.2	124.1	43.1	

[a] Families of non-agricultural workers and employees in the 7 western republics.
[b] Cumulative difference in rubles.
[c] Including R18.56 from private work, R13.34 from additional public sector jobs, and R7.98 from undisclosed sources.
[d] Including payments from Social Consumption Fund, assistance from relatives, subsidiary plot and other non-wage income.

for which the number of workers was estimated in that it includes non-working families and excludes one-parent working families. As both these types of family tend to be smaller than average, the two differences may offset each other as far as the impact of family size is concerned.

Compared in this fashion, SP family income is found to be R91.2 (31.5 percent) higher than the average income of UP family income (estimated at R293.0). On a per capita basis the differences are even greater, as the average size of the UP family for which the calculation was made is larger than that of the SP family: R113.7 for SP as against R82.1 for UP — a 38.5 percent difference.

As can be seen from Table A.15, the R92.2 SP–UP difference is made up of an even wider difference, of R104.9, in net wages, with another R7.4 coming from unspecified private sources in SP. These differences are only moderately offset by smaller SP incomes from the Social Consumption Fund (SCF) payments and from subsidiary agricultural plots.

Some of the SP–UP income differences result from unequal coverage, in definitions and in estimating errors; some — the major ones — result from differences in the demographic-social-economic properties of SP and UP. In order to isolate the latter, which are more interesting, let us first mention the technical sources of difference. Some of them result from the crude nature of our estimates of UP income, as explained in detail in Table A.26 below. Other sources for specific differences are summarized below:

1. Official Soviet wage estimates do not include income derived from private work or from additional work in public jobs outside the main place of employment. For SP families these two sources of income amount to R18.6 and R13.3, respectively; together with income from undisclosed sources they come to R39.9 per family (see Table A.15, part B). All these incomes clearly also exist for UP families, but there is no information on their size.

2. A large portion of the rather wide SP–UP difference in money income derived from SCF payments (line 3) may be explained by the exclusion from UP of one-parent families that receive more from this source.[11] Other parts of the gap may be explained by other differences in the structures of SP and JP compared to UP (family size and composition,

residence in annexed areas, level of education). We have no reason to believe that the SP returns represent lower SCF payments to JP families.

3. Although we have adjusted the UP wage in order to take account of the lower wage of agricultural employees (see Table A.26), we have not been able, as yet, to account for possible lower wages in rural areas, nor for higher income derived from subsidiary agricultural plots by rural residents.[12] This may explain some of the wage differential and a good part of the difference in income derived from private plots.

4. The periods for which incomes are reported are not entirely consistent. Only about 36 percent of SP families reported income for 1973, about one-third reported for 1972 and earlier, and just under a third reported for 1974 and later. The annual change of average income in the Soviet Union amounts to 3–5 percent so that the bias created by this factor cannot be significant.

5. There are good reasons to conclude that the SP data underestimate family income. One such reason is the fact that average monthly *expenditures* as estimated by our study total R399.5, or R14.3 (3.7 percent) higher than the average income. It is possible, however, that at least some of the underreporting is in income categories that are not included in the official Soviet data.

6. After taking out all the non-compatible wage elements there still remains an SP-UP difference of R73.0 in family wage income from the main place of work (line 9). This is partly (R16.5) explained by the 0.11 difference in workers per family between SP and UP (line 10). An additional small difference may be due to the longer (by 0.9 hour) weekly hours worked by SP workers on their main job (see Table A.7).

When all the above factors are considered, the adjusted per-family wage income difference is reduced to R56.3 and the per-worker difference to R82.2 (lines 11 and 12, respectively). These differences, not considering small biases and errors and factors mentioned but unaccounted for, should result from differences in the demographic and socio-economic characteristics of SP and UP.

A first rough estimation of the significance of SP–UP differences in level of education, work status, and sex is performed by computing a synthetic

Table A.16. Net earnings of groups of workers: sample and estimate for UP
            (rubles per month)

A. SP and UP wage rates: various adjustments

		Men (1)	Women (2)	Total (1) (3)	Total (2) (4)
a. Workers	SP	*163.1*	*102.7*	*144.1*	
	UP	163.3	102.2	135.5	135.6
b. Employees	SP	*198.4*	*122.7*	*158.0*	
	UP	181.1	111.4	139.3	153.0
c. Total (3)	SP	*185.2*	*118.9*	*154.0*	
	UP	168.2	106.0	136.8	151.7
d. Total (4)	SP	*185.2*	*118.9*	*154.0*	
	UP	172.9	110.9	148.9	141.6

B. Analysis of SP–UP wage differentials (rubles)

	SP (1)	Estimated UP (2)	SP – UP (3)	(3) Cumulated (4)	UP (5)	Estimated UP – UP (6)
Net wage	154.0					
Adjusted for:						
Sex composition		151.7	−2.3	−2.3		
Work status		148.9	−5.1	−7.4		
Sex and work status (cumulative)		141.6	−5.0	−12.4		
Education + the above		136.8	−4.8	17.2	124.1	12.7

(1) Adjusted for sex composition and level of education.
(2) Adjusted for sex composition.
(3) Adjusted for work status and level of education.
(4) Adjusted for work status.

average wage of wages for eighteen different groups of SP workers and the corresponding proportions of those groups in UP. In addition to sex and work-status (worker or employee), the groups are also distinguished by up to five different levels of education,[13] chosen in accordance with available Soviet data. The UP weights are for the urban W&E labor force for the 7 western republics combined, for 1970. The results of the computations are shown in Table A.16. Starting from the end result, the UP wage is estimated at R136.8 (Part B), R12.7 (or 10.2 percent) above the official Soviet figure of R124.1 (Table A.15). The adjustments made explain nearly 60 percent of the original SP–UP gap of R29.9. Given the still very crude adjustment for differences in the level of education, this should be considered a good result in the sense that it strengthens confidence in the sample's returns.

The rest of Table A.16 consists of an analysis of SP and estimated UP wage differentials by the factors considered. Cells 1a to 2b compare specific sex and work-status wages adjusted for differences in educational levels; cells 3a, 3b, 1c and 2c do the same for all workers, all employees, all men and all women, respectively. Cells 4a–4d and 1d–3d show the estimated UP wage for the relevant group with no adjustment for differences in the level of education. A detailed analysis of the differences in presented in Part B.

The SP–UP difference in sex composition explains only a very small part (R2.3) of the SP–UP wage gap, despite the marked male-female wage differentials found in SP (see below). A more important factor is the difference in the composition by work status between the two populations: it alone explains R5.1 (about 30 percent) of the total explained gap (Part B, line 4). In addition to the "pure" effects of sex and work status, there is also an additional effect, that of the interaction between them, resulting from the fact that the SP–UP work-status difference is much larger for women than for men and that women's wages are lower. Finally, the pure adjustment for differences in the level of education is estimated at R3.7, or about 27 percent of the entire adjustment.[14] In addition, there is clearly a large interdependency between education and work status, shown here under work status. It is interesting to note that when adjusted for differences in education, the sex-work-status specific SP–UP wage gaps become very small for workers (R0.1 for men, R0.5 for women) but remain wide for employees

Table A.17. Net monthly wages by type of work and sex: sample population

	Total income from work	Main place of work					Other jobs	
		Total	Regular	Premiums	Additional work[a]	Other remuneration	Public	Private
A. Entire labor force								
1. Number	2,146	2,142	2,142	1,105	115	692	179	173
2. Earnings (category)	167.14	152.42	129.43	28.75	51.71	16.25	76.38	108.96
3. Earnings (group)	167.14	152.13	129.18	14.80	2.77	5.24	6.30	8.78
4. Percent of group's total earnings	100.0	91.0	77.3	8.9	1.7	3.1	3.8	5.3
B. All men								
1. Number	1,127	1,127	1,127	674	64	457	142	122
2. Earnings (category)	207.56	183.95	152.80	33.15	60.55	19.13	80.69	125.86
3. Earnings (group)	207.56	183.95	152.80	19.83	3.44	7.76	10.17	13.62
4. Percent of group's total earnings	100.0	88.6	73.6	9.6	1.7	3.7	4.9	6.6

(cont.)

Table A.17. (cont.)

	Total income from work	Main place of work					Other jobs	
		Total	Regular	Premiums	Additional work[a]	Other remuneration	Public	Private
C. All women								
1. Number	1,019	1,015	1,015	431	51	235	37	51
2. Earnings (category)	122.43	117.70	103.48	21.86	40.63	10.66	60.46	68.53
3. Earnings (group)	122.43	116.95	103.07	9.24	2.03	2.46	2.20	3.43
4. Percent of group's total earnings	100.0	95.5	84.2	7.6	1.7	2.0	1.8	2.8
D. Female/male ratios								
1. Number in category	0.904	0.901	0.901	0.639	0.797	0.514	0.261	0.418
2. Wage in category	0.590	0.640	0.677	0.659	0.671	0.557	0.749	0.544
3. Average number of hours in category[b]	0.900	0.939	0.955				1.017	0.874
4. Wage per hour in category	0.680	0.701	0.738				0.669	0.656

[a] Including overtime.
[b] Based on data from Table A.7.

(R16.0 for men and R11.2 for women). This is a direct result of our inability to better distinguish between levels of education at the upper end of the educational scale. We therefore hypothesize that when such finer distinction is possible, the remaining SP–UP gap will be significantly narrowed.

Table A.17 presents data on the size and structure of wages of SP working persons by family status and sex. The main findings are first that wages from the main place of work account for 91 percent of the average income from work for all employed, 88.6 percent for men and 95.5 percent for women. Out of total wages, 77.3 percent (about 85 percent of wages in the main place of employment) are received as regular salaries and wages, and nearly 10 percent are in the form of premiums, while all other kinds of payment are very small on the average. For women, payment over and above regular wages are even smaller. Second, only 9.1 percent of total wages are paid for work outside the main place of employment, 5.3 percent of that for private jobs. The corresponding figures are higher for men (10.9 and 6.6) and lower for women (4.6 and 2.8). These, however, are averages across all workers, including those who had no additional jobs. Those who did hold such jobs (see Table A.15 for the figures) earned an average of R76 from additional official jobs (28.4 percent of their total income from work) and about R109 from private jobs (37.6 percent of their total wages). Finally, the most striking result, however, is the wide wage difference between men and women (Table A.17, part D).[15]

4. Level and structure of expenditures and consumption

The total monthly expenditure per SP family, according to the survey returns, amounted to R399.5, some R14.3 (3.7 percent) higher than the average income from all sources (Table A.18). Of the R399.5 spent, R29.6 (7.4 percent) were saved and another R8.0 were paid for mortgages and installment-plan purchases. If these latter items are regarded as savings, total savings rise to R37.6 or about 9.4 percent of total spending (or income). Transfer payments (assistance to relative and repayment of private debts) amount to R5.7, which leaves R356.2 for consumption. Table A.18 presents the expenditure breakdown in a degree of detail never shown in official

Table A.18. Monthly family expenditures: sample

	Rubles[a]	Percent[a]
Average total expenditure	399.5	100.0
Food and beverages	182.4	45.7
Foodstuffs	160.9	40.3
Restaurants	13.0	3.3
Alcoholic beverages	8.5	2.1
Tobacco and tobacco products	5.3	1.3
Clothing and footwear	43.0	10.8
Purchases	37.1	9.3
Cleaning and repair	5.8	1.5
Household goods	31.5	7.9
Purchase of durables	17.3	4.3
Purchase of non-durables	7.1	1.8
Installment-plan payments	4.7	1.2
Personal ornaments	2.4	0.6
Education, entertainment and personal services	54.7	13.7
Vacations	20.8	5.2
Entertainment	11.7	2.9
Books, correspondence, hobbies	10.1	2.5
Personal care and hygiene	4.8	1.2
Medical care	2.4	0.6
Children's formal education	2.5	0.6
Children's extracurricular lessons	2.3	0.6
Housing	25.6	6.4
Rent	7.8	2.0
Credit payments on co-op apartments	3.3	0.8
Electricity	4.0	1.0
All other utilities	4.2	1.0
Maintenance	2.8	0.7
Telephone	2.4	0.6
Domestic help	1.1	0.3
Transportation	9.9	2.5
Public transport	7.6	1.9
Private transport (including maintenance)	2.3	0.6
Additional expenses	17.4	4.4
Assistance to relatives and friends	4.9	1.2
Organizational dues	4.2	1.0
Insurance	2.8	0.7
Payments on private debts	0.8	0.2
Professional services	0.2	0.05
Exceptional expenses	3.3	0.8
Other	1.1	0.3
Savings	29.6	7.4

[a] The ruble figures correspond to the average amount spent by all the families on each expenditure category. Column (2) presents the figures listed in Column (1) as a percentage of average total expenditure.

Soviet sources. In Table A.19 we compare the expenditure structure of SP with that of UP families. In Table A.19 we also use our estimate of total net money income for a family of workers or employees in the Soviet Union as an estimate of total expenditure. Such a procedure yields an SP–UP income gap of 51.2 percent. It should be remembered, however, that at least part of this gap is artificial, as explained in the previous section. For lack of better data, at least at present, the percentage of the breakdown of total expenditures for UP is taken from data on families of industrial workers.[16] This over-estimates the SP–UP differences among comparable groups:

a. With total expenditures considerably higher, SP families spend more money than UP families on almost every expenditure category. The only exception is clothing and footwear, and we suspect some underreporting in this category in our sample.

b. In two expenditure categories — education and housing — we find that SP spending is also relatively much higher than for UP. This reflects a high income elasticity for these categories, and different tastes of a population with a high proportion of white-collar workers and intelligentsia.

c. Higher relative SP spending on housing, culture, and services are compensated for by lower relative spending on clothing and, to a lesser degree, on household goods, but not by lower relative spending on food. In fact, food expenditures in SP are 2 percentage points higher than in UP. From what is known about income elasticities in general, expenditures on food should have sustained the main impact of increased relative spending on housing, culture, and services. It is thus left for further investigation to find out how much of this ambiguity is a result of reporting errors and how much represents a real economic phenomenon peculiar to the Soviet Union. There is some independent evidence pointing to an exceptionally high income elasticity for food in the Soviet Union.[17] It may also represent, as some suspect, specific Jewish tastes. Such a special taste element that operates to reduce food consumption is reflected in the very low consumption of liquor, which increases the burden of explaining the higher food consumption.[18]

Engel's laws are upheld when the consumption patterns of various groups within SP are compared (Table A.20). Thus, the proportion of food in total expenditure declines with the level of education and with city size.

Table A.19. Monthly family expenditures: sample and USSR (1973)

	Sample		USSR (1973)[a]		Differ-ence in rubles	Differ-ence in percent
	Rubles	Per-cent	Rubles	Per-cent		
	(1)	(2)	(3)	(4)	(5)	(6)
Total monthly family expenditure	399.5	100.0	264.3	100.0	135.2	51.2
Food and beverages	182.4	45.7	115.5	43.7	66.9	57.9
Clothing and footwear	43.0	10.8	51.5	19.5	−8.5	−16.5
Household goods	31.5	7.9	22.7	8.6	8.8	38.8
Education, entertainment and personal services	54.7	13.7	22.7	8.6	32.0	141.0
Housing (including heating fuel)	25.6	6.4	9.2	3.5	16.4	178.3
Tobacco and its products	5.3	1.3				
Transportation	9.9	2.5	23.0	8.7	9.6	41.7
Additional expenses	17.4	4.4				
Savings	29.6	7.4	19.6	7.4	10.0	51.0

[a] Total expenditures = total net money income per family of workers and employees (as in Table 15 above). Percentage breakdown: families of industrial workers.

Source: Column (4) — Expenditures breakdown: *Narkhoz 1973*, p. 632; see Vinokur and Ofer, 1979.

Table A.20. Average structure of monthly expenditures by employment status and family size

	Entire sample	Employment status of family head		Family size (no. of persons)			
		Worker	Emp-loyee	2	3	4	5
Number of families	1,016[a]	359	652	157	448	297	114
Average total expenditure (rubles)	399.5	348.9	428.4	326.7	383.3	432.2	478.1
Average percentage breakdown							
Total (percent)	100.0	100.0	100.0	100.0	100.0	100.0	100.0
Food and beverages	48.4	50.6	47.2	48.2	48.2	48.1	50.3
Tobacco and its products	1.4	1.6	1.3	1.4	1.5	1.2	1.4
Clothing and footwear	10.4	11.2	10.0	9.4	10.6	10.6	11.1
Household goods	7.1	7.0	7.2	6.7	7.2	7.2	7.1
Education, enter tainment and personal services	13.5	11.5	14.6	12.6	13.9	13.9	11.9
Housing (including heating fuel)	6.6	5.9	7.0	6.5	6.6	6.8	6.2
Transportation	2.4	2.1	2.6	2.7	2.3	2.4	2.6
Additional expenses	4.0	3.9	4.1	5.0	3.9	3.9	3.5
Savings	6.1	6.4	6.0	7.4	5.8	6.1	6.1
Average expenditure per capita (rubles)	123.4	109.2	131.6	163.4	127.8	108.1	91.6
Average expenditure on food and beverages per capita (rubles)	56.0	51.9	58.3	70.5	58.4	49.3	43.9

[a] Five family heads are not employed.

Differences in the opposite direction are observed in most cases for expenditures on education and entertainment, housing, and transportation.[19]

Comparable data on the consumption levels of various food groups of the Soviet population are presented in Table A.21. SP is compared with four Soviet population groups: (a) the entire Soviet population in 1973; (b) workers and employees, 1973; (c) industrial workers in selected centers, 1971; and (d) *kolkhoz* families, 1971. Group (b) is, of course, closest to SP in composition. The comparisons show two very unlikely results; we can offer an adequate explanation for only one of them. The much lower figure for sugar in SP is accounted for by the fact that while the Soviet data include both direct and indirect consumption of sugar in the category, SP includes only the former. We still lack a good explanation for the unrealistic figure arrived at for the consumption of fruit and melons in SP. Our guess is that for some reason most interviewees reported summer-time consumption levels. The figure may also have to do with the high percentage of Moldavians interviewed.

Otherwise the figures look quite reasonable: SP families, with higher incomes than all the Soviet groups presented, consume much more meat (except for group c, which is highly restricted) and many more eggs; somewhat more dairy and fish products; and less potatoes and bread (which means more proteins and less carbohydrates). The lower figure for vegetables in SP may be related to the fruit-and-melon problem mentioned earlier.

Consumption patterns of entertainment services of SP are presented in Table A.22. The questions included were presented to only one person in each family, so that we have the answers for 389 male family heads, 476 wives, and 147 adult sons or daughters. We consider the average as representing consumption per adult. According to this table, each SP adult goes to the movies once a week, visits the theater and the concert hall once a month, and attends some other cultural event also once a month. According to official Soviet data, the per capita figure for movie-going among the urban Soviet population is 19 visits a year (22 in Moldavia; see *Narkhoz 1973*, p. 742). On a per-adult basis this may amount to close to 30 visits per year. The difference, while correct in its direction, seems to us quite wide. Total spending on entertainment per adult, as calculated from Table A.22, amounts

Table A.21. Annual consumption of food items per capita: sample and Soviet data (kgs.)

	Sample	Data derived from Soviet sources			
		A	B	C	D
1. Meat and animal fats of all kinds	73.7	53.0	56.3	81.4	48.5
2. Milk and milk products	+400.0	307.0	311.5	388.6	368.7
3. Eggs (units)	298.0	195.0	193.0	275.0	291.0
4. Fish and fish products	19.2	16.1	17.2	18.1	14.9
5. Sugar	16.1	40.8	39.9	35.5	42.4
6. Vegetable oil, margarine	9.8	7.3	7.1	..	..
7. Potatoes	76.6	124.0	117.7	115.7	199.6
8. Vegetables	81.8	85.0	89.8	97.9	70.0
9. Fruit and melons	152.5	40.0	..	48.5	33.9
10. Bread and bread products	133.9	143.0	137.7	119.6	177.7

Sources:
A. Total Soviet population, 1973; *Narkhoz 1973* (p. 630).
B. Workers and employees, 1973; Vinokur and Ofer, 1979.
C. Industrial workers in selected industrial centers, 1971; *Narkhoz 1922–72* (p. 384).
D. *Kolkhoz* families in selected locations, 1971; *Narkhoz 1922–72* (p. 384).

to R83.7 per year. If only adults are considered, the implied family spending is about R208, a much higher figure than that reported as total family spending on entertainment (R140). This gap can be explained, on the one hand, by a possible underestimation of the costs when answering one question with no detailed breakdown; on the other hand, it may be caused by a tendency to report on "norms" rather than on actual consumption.

Table A.22. Frequency of cultural activities: sample

	Number of visits per adult per year	Average price per visit	Annual expenditure per adult (rubles)
Movies	51	0.48	24.5
Theater	12	1.83	22.0
Concerts	11	2.09	23.9
Museums and exhibitions	4	0.38	1.5
Lectures	3	0.36	1.0
Sporting events	8	0.95	7.4
Other cultural activities	1	2.63	3.4
Total	90	0.91	83.7

5. Consumer durables and housing conditions

Ownership of durables is part of the wealth and well-being of the family, on the one hand, and contributes directly to its current consumption level on the other. The data presented in Table A.23 demonstrate without a doubt that SP families have a much higher level of ownership of durables than does the entire Soviet population. We do not have comparable data for UP, but we do have some indication that the advantages of SP, while smaller, hold for that comparison too. As seen in the table, almost all the SP families owned a refrigerator, compared with just about half of all Soviet families; 90.2 percent of SP families owned a TV set (67 percent of Soviet families) and 10.6 percent of SP owned a car (compared with 3 percent in the entire population). Only in sewing machines and bicycles do SP families lag behind, and these certainly may be considered "poor relations" among durable goods.

We have seen that SP families spend a higher proportion of their income on items related to their level of housing. The direct data collected

Table A.23. Ownership of consumer durables: Soviet families (1973) and sample (per 100 families)

	Sample (1)	Soviet population (1973) (2)
Refrigerator	93.8	49
Mixer	29.9	
Washing machine	68.6	60
Vacuum cleaner	76.1	14
Sewing machine	52.8	59
Television set	90.2	67
Phonograph	40.5	
Radio	73.1	74
Tape recorder	40.3	..
Camera	49.9	27
Automobile	10.6	3
Motorcycle	3.1	} 8
Motor scooter	1.4	
Bicycle	24.7	54
Boat	2.2	..
Piano	26.5	..
Accordion	10.1	..
Other musical instruments	6.2	..
Bedroom furniture	47.0	..
Diningroom furniture	48.8	..
Study	4.1	..
Garden	3.6	..
Jewelry	8.3	..
Dacha	0.5	..

Source: Column (2) – *Narkhoz 1973* (p. 631).

on the housing conditions of SP support this finding. According to them, the average size of apartment per SP family was (in 1973) 38.6 square meters of "living space," or about 58 square meters of "useful space" (the first excludes and the second includes kitchen, bathrooms, internal hallways, staircases, elevators and other common areas; see Table A.24).[20] In per capita terms, each SP person has 11.2 m^2 of living space or 16.8 m^2 of useful space. These superior housing conditions should be compared with UP apartments with an average size of 42–45 m^2 of useful space, the per capita useful space was 11.6 m^2, and the living space per capita was 7.7 m^2 in 1973.[21] True, the housing conditions in most of the European parts of the USSR seem to be better than average: 13.9 m^2 of useful space in Estonia, 12.7 in Kiev (they are lower in Moldavia [10.1] and in Kishinev [10.5]).[22] In terms of number of rooms, the average SP family had a 2.3 room apartment (47 percent had two rooms, 34 percent had three rooms), or two-thirds of a room per person.

Table A.24. Living area, sample population's housing

	Number	Percent
Total number of families	1,016	100.0
Living space (m^2)		
Up to 20	111	10.9
21–40	514	50.6
41–60	318	31.3
61–80	49	4.8
81–100	12	1.2
101–120	4	0.4
121–140	1	0.1
141–160	3	0.3
No answer	4	0.4
Average	38.6[a]	

[a] Calculated for those families that gave a positive answer.

Of all SP apartments, 15.9 percent were in cooperative houses and some 10 percent (mostly houses) were privately owned; 72.1 percent of all SP families lived in state- and privately rented apartments (Table A.25a). In comparison with UP, SP families are underrepresented among private owners (who concentrate in small cities, mostly owning very old houses, who own about 25 percent of the total stock of housing units in urban USSR; but SP families are overrepresented as owners of cooperative apartments. During the past 20 years, the period in which cooperative construction started, about 8 percent of all the new urban apartments were built as cooperative ventures. They probably represent less than 4 percent of the entire stock. These two offsetting factors may bring the proportion of renting families in SP to about par with UP, or even somewhat higher than that.

Table A.25. Distribution of the sample population by type of housing ownership

	Number	Percent
Total number of families	1,016	100.0
a. *Type of housing ownership*		
State-owned	709	69.8
Cooperative	162	15.9
Private	98	9.6
Rented from private owners	23	2.3
Hostels operated by an enterprise, organization, or private owners	3	0.3
Others	13	1.3
No answer	8	0.8
b. *Type of housing*		
Individual apartment	788	77.6
Rooms in communal apartment	89	8.8
House (cottage, etc.)	87	8.6
Other type of housing	49	4.8
No answer	3	0.3

Another advantage of the SP housing conditions lies in the fact that only 8.8 percent of all families (about 10 percent of those belonging to the socialized state and cooperative sector) still live in the peculiar Soviet mode of communal apartments with shared kitchen, bathroom and hallways (Table A.25b). In 1960, some 60 percent of all UP families living in socialized housing still dwelt in such shared apartments. This proportion sank to around 30 percent by 1973, but it is still three times higher than the corresponding proportion of SP families, and more than twice as high when the entire SP and UP populations are compared. The standard of amenities (hot water, bathtub, running water, flush toilets, etc.) is also higher in SP than in UP apartments.

6. Conclusion

The above data and findings invite several provisional conclusions. (a) The returns of the survey, with all their possible biases, are quite reasonable, as are (at this level of approximation and aggregation) the official Soviet data. The implication is that it is possible to use our detailed data — not given in Soviet sources — to analyze in greater depth many economic aspects of the Soviet Union and of the life of its Jewish and urban communities. (b) The economic position of the European Jewish community in the Soviet Union is above the average for the entire Soviet urban population, with respect to both incomes and housing conditions, and possible also higher than the average level in the specific localities where they used to live. (c) The economic advantage of the Jewish community in the Soviet Union results mainly from larger investment in education and a tendency to concentrate in white-collar jobs, mostly the high-paying ones. (d) Part of the income advantage of SP represents additional sources of income not reported in official Soviet data, which constitute quite a significant part of total income. As shown in Chapter 2, direct reporting on "second economy" activities among the SP was incomplete; further study of the results revealed that non-official sources of income are higher than reported. Unless we assume that non-official income represents a higher proportion of the income SP families, this sheds some light on the extent of such activities in the UP as a whole.

Table A.26. Calculation of net earnings and net family income: Soviet urban
population, 1973

	USSR	7 republics	USSR	7 republics
1. Gross wage per worker			134.9	136.1
2. *Deduct*: Adjustment for exclusion of agricultural workers			−2.0	−2.0
3. Gross wage per non-agricultural worker			136.9	138.1
4. *Deduct*: Income tax			−13.0	−13.2
5. *Deduct*: Bachelor and small family tax			−0.8	−0.8
6. Net wage per non-agricultural worker (4–5)			123.1	124.1
7. Number of workers per family with workers a.	1.98	2.00		
8. Number of workers per family b.	1.86	1.86		
9. Net earnings per family with workers a. (6 × 7)			243.7	248.2
10. Net earnings per family b. (6 × 8)			229.0	230.8
11. Earnings as percent of total net family income		84.7		

(cont.)

Table A.26. (cont.)

	USSR	7 republics	USSR	7 republics
12. Net money income per family with workers a. (9/11 × 100)			287.7	293.0
13. Net money income per family b. (10/11 × 100)			270.4	272.5
14. Non-earnings income as % of net family money income				
(1) Social Consumption Fund (money)	10.7			
(2) Subsidiary plot	1.7			
(3) Other incomes	2.9			
15. Income from Social Consumption Fund a. (14[1] × 12/100)			30.8	31.4
b. (14[2] × 13/100)			28.9	29.2
16. Income from subsidiary plot a. (14[2] × 12/100)			4.9	5.0
b. (14[2] × 13/100)			4.6	4.6
17. Income from other sources a. (14[3] × 12/100)			8.3	8.5
b. (14[3] × 13/100)			7.8	7.9
18. Number of persons per family				
(1)	3.67	3.57		
(2)	3.49	3.39		
19. Per capita income per family with workers (12/18[1])			78.7	82.1
20. Per capita income per family (13/18[2])			77.6	80.4

Notes and sources to Table A.26

Line 1. Average wage per worker and employee (rural and urban), USSR: *Narkhoz 1973*, p. 586; 7 republics: Wages — Statistical yearbooks of the individual republics. The average 7-republic wage is computed as a weighted average of the above weighted by respective individual republic proportions of urban workers and employees of their total number in all 7 republics together. The data are from *Census 1970*, Vol. V, Table 4, pp. 26–33. The individual republic wages and weights are as follows:

	1973 wages	1970 wages
7 republics	**136.1**	**100.0**
RRSFR	140.5	70.79
Ukraine	(125.0)	21.31
Byelorussia	118.9	3.39
Lithuania	133.9	1.37
Latvia	138.8	0.94
Moldavia	149.2	0.94
Estonia	(111.4)	0.82

Figures in parentheses are estimates from previous or later years.

Lines 2, 3. The adjustment to exclude wages of agricultural workers is made by adjusting each republic's (and the USSR) wage using data on wages of agricultural workers and their proportion in each republic force of W & E. The wage data are from the various statistical yearbooks (USSR: *Narkhoz 1973*, p. 586) and the proportion working in agriculture is from *Narkhoz 1973*, pp. 578–9.

Line 4. Income tax is calculated as 8.2 rubles *plus* 13 percent of gross wages in excess of 100 rubles.

Line 5. It is assumed that families pay one third of the total revenue of this tax (the rest is paid by singles). Tax per worker is assumed to be at the proportion of total revenues of this tax to total income tax revenues. The calculations are based on data presented in Bronson and Severin, 1973, Table B–1, p. 393.

Lines 7, 8. The figures are arrived at in two stages. First, data on families by number of workers (*Census 1970*, Vol. VII, Table 3, pp. 396–411) are used to estimate the number of workers per family in the urban population. Second, 0.06 workers per family are added to all figures, to bring it up to 1973. This is done on the basis of an upward trend of this figure from 1959 (1.56 as in *Census 1959*, USSR, Tables 64, 64b, pp. 250–53, to 1.80 as in *Census 1970*, Vol. VII, Table 33, p. 396).

Lines 11, 14. These percentage figures are based on data on breakdown of income of families of industrial workers from family budget surveys as reported in Soviet sources (*Narkhoz 1973*, p. 632). The following adjustments are made: (a) Taxes (8.3 percent of gross income) are deducted from both total income and from wages, to arrive at net income. (b) Income in the form of government services in kind are assumed to constitute 13.4 percent of gross income, equal to the expenditure share on "education, medical and other services from the social consumption fund." They are subtracted from the net income (to arrive at net *money* income) as well as from the total income received from the social consumption fund. (c) The percentages of all remaining items are recalculated with respect to the new total net-money income.

Line 18. Calculations based on *Census 1970*, Vol. VII, Table 27, pp. 238–49, for the urban population. No adjustment was made for changes in family size from 1970 to 1973.

Notes

1. The true SP–UP discrepancy with respect to RSFSR is somewhat smaller than shown in Table A.1 because the UP data also include populations of Asiatic origin.

2. See, for example, Katz (1973, Table A.2; 1976, Tables 15.1 and 15.2, pp. 355–57).

3. Defined as all adults (17+) who reported obtaining any income from work.

4. *Narkhoz 1973* (p. 585); see also discussion below.

5. Based on *Census 1970*, Vol. VII, Table 1, pp. 6–13, and corresponding population figures.

6. The Soviets increased the figure from 1.72 (1972 and earlier) to 1.80 for 1973 and thereafter, presumably on the basis of completed 1970 Census returns.

7. For 1959: *Census 1959 SSSR*, Tables 64, 64b, pp. 250–53; for 1970: *Census 1970*, Vol. VII, Table 33, p. 396 (three or more workers is taken to equal 3.2 workers).

8. *Census 1970*, Vol. VII, Table 33, p. 396.

9. Of the working persons in SP, only four women who reported having no main job could be excluded from the Soviet definition of a working person.

10. This results mainly from the interaction of low ED and the high concentration of SP in Moldavia.

11. The UP figure is estimated from data of Soviet family-budget studies of industrial workers. These studies already exclude students' and pensioners' families. See McAuley, 1977a, pp. 216–17.

12. In addition, income from private plots for UP are based on family budgets of industrial workers who may derive more income from this source than do white-collar employees.

13. University, incomplete university, specialized secondary (*technikum*), general secondary, and less than general secondary. Two educational categories had to be combined when there were insufficient SP observations in individual cells. The source for the UP weights is *Census 1970*, Vol. V, Table 4, p. 26; Table 7, p. 66.

14. Computed as a sum product of the SP–UP weighted wage differentials.

The figure is, of course, also equal to the residual not explained by the other factors.

15. This result is discussed in detail in Chapter 7. The paper which served as the basis for this appendix also included discussion on income distribution, which is covered here in Chapter 4.

16. The breakdown is calculated from official Soviet data that include free services and taxes.

17. Vinokur and Ofer, 1979.

18. SP families spend only 2.1 percent of total expenditure on liquor (Table A.18) as against over 12 percent for UP according to Treml (1975, p. 175).

19. Many of these differences are significant at the 0.05 level or better.

20. For definitions see Smith (1973, p. 406). Living space is about two-thirds of useful space, and the latter is about 80 percent of total space.

21. Smith (1973, pp. 407, 422); Schroeder and Severin (1976, p. 625).

22. Smith (1973, p. 422).

References

Agursky, M. and H. Adomeit. 1977. "The Soviet Military-Industrial Complex and its Internal Mechanism." Mimeo.

Akademiya Nauk SSSR [USSR Academy of Science]. 1979. *Potrebnosti Dokhody Potrebleniye*. Moscow. Referred to as *Potrebnosti*, 1979.

Akinfieva, L. 1979. "Sotsial'no-Demograficheskoe Obsledoranie Naseleniia Odesskoi Oblasti." In: *Demograficheskaia Situatsiia v SSSR*, pp. 90–106.

Aleksandrova, A. and E. Federovskaia. 1984. "Mekhanism Formirovaniia i Vozvysheniia Potrebnostei," *Voprosy Ekonomiki*, 1: 15–25.

Arutunian, Yu. V. *et al.* (eds.). 1973. *Sotsialnoe i Natsional'noe*. Moscow.

Atkinson, Anthony B. 1983. *The Economics of Inequality*. Oxford: Clarendon Press.

Atkinson, D., A. Dallin and Gail Lapidus-Warshofsky (eds.). 1978. *Women in Russia*. Hassocks, England: Harvester Press.

Baldwin, Godfrey. 1975. *Projections of the Population of the USSR and Eight Subdivisions, by Age and Sex: 1973 to 2000*. Washington, D.C.: Bureau of the Census, International Population Reports, Ser. P–91, No. 24. Government Printing Office.

Becker, Gary. 1981. *A Treatise on the Family*. Cambridge, Mass.: Harvard University Press.

Ben-Porath, Yoram. 1973a. "Economic Analysis of Fertility in Israel: Point and Counterpoint," *Journal of Political Economy*, 81 (No. 2, March/April): 5202–33.

   1973b. "Labor-Force Participation Rates and the Supply of Labor," *Journal of Political Economy*, 81 (May/June): 697–704.

   1982. "Economics and the Family – Match or Mismatch? A Review of Becker's 'A Treatise on the Family'," *Journal of Economic Literature*, 20 (No. 1, March): 52–64.

Bergson, Abram. 1944. *The Structure of Soviet Wages*. Cambridge, Mass.: Harvard University Press.

Bergson, Abram.1983. "Soviet Consumption in Western Perspective, 1972–1982" *Economic Notes* (Italy): 194–218.

1984. "Income Inequality under Soviet Socialism," *Journal of Economic Literature*, 22: 1052–99.

Berliner, Joseph. 1959. "Managerial Incentives and Decisionmaking: A Comparison of the United States and the Soviet Union." In: U.S. Congress, Joint Economic Committee, *Comparisons of the United States and Soviet Economics.* Washington, D.C., U.S. Government Printing Office, pp. 349–76.

1977. "Notes on Economy and Family in Soviet Russia." Cambridge, Mass.: Harvard University Russian Research Center Discussion Paper.

1983. "Education, Labor Force Participation and Fertility in the USSR," *Journal of Comparative Economics*, 7 (No. 2, June): 131–57.

Birman, Igor. 1981. *Secret Incomes of the Soviet State Budget.* The Hague: Martinus Nijhoff Publishers.

Bornycheva, B. 1968. *Nash Semeinyi Budzhet.* Knizhnoe Obozrenie, pp. 261–66.

Bronson, D. W. and B. S. Severin. 1973. "Soviet Consumer Welfare: The Brezhnev Era." In: United States Congress, Joint Economic Committee, *Soviet Economic Prospects for the Seventies.* Washington, D.C.: U.S. Government Printing Office.

Bush, K. 1973. "Soviet Inflation." In: Yves Laulan (ed.), *Banking, Money and Credit in Eastern Europe.* Brussels: NATO.

CBS [(Israel) Central Bureau of Statistics]. 1979. *Consumption Elasticities by Income, 1975–76.* Jerusalem.

Chalidze, Valeriy. 1975. *Criminal Russia: Essays on Crimes in the Soviet Union.* New York: Random House.

Chapman, Janet. 1963. "Consumption." In: Abram Bergson and Simon Kuznets (eds.), *Economic Trends in the Soviet Union.* Cambridge, Mass.: Harvard University Press.

1977a. "Soviet Wages under Socialism." In: Alan Abouchar (ed.), *The Socialist Price Mechanism.* Durham, N.C.: Duke University Press.

1977b. "Recent Trends in the Soviet Industrial Wage Structure." Paper presented at the Conference on Problems of Industrial Labor in the

USSR, Kennan Institute for Advanced Russian Studies, Washington, D.C.

1977c. "The Distribution of Earnings in Selected Countries, East and West." Paper presented at Symposium on Technology, Labor Productivity and Labor Supply, Racine, Wisc., November.

1978. "Equal Pay for Equal Work?" In: D. Atkinson *et al.* (eds.), *Women in Russia*. Hassocks, England: Harvester Press, pp. 225–39.

1979a. "Recent Trends in the Soviet Industrial Wage Stucture." In: A. Kahan and B. Ruble (eds.), *Industrial Labor in the USSR*. New York: Pergamon Press.

1979b. "Are Earnings More Equal under Socialism?" In: John R. Moroney (ed.), *Income Inequality*. Lexington, Mass.: Lexington Books.

1983. "Earnings Distribution in the USSR, 1968–1976," *Soviet Studies*, 35(3): 410–13.

CIA. 1975. *USSR: Gross National Product Accounts, 1970*. Washington, D.C.

1988. *USSR: Sharply Higher Budget Deficits Threaten Perestroika.* Washington, D.C. April.

Chizwick, Barry R. 1982. "The Earnings and Human Capital of American Jews." Mimeo.

1983. "The Labor Market Status of American Jews: Patterns and Determinants." Mimeo.

Commission of the European Communities. 1981. *Final Report from the Commission to the Council on the First Programme of Pilot Themes and Studies to Combat Poverty*. Brussels.

Cromwell, J. 1977. "The Size Distribution of Income: An International Comparison," *Review of Income and Wealth*, 23: 291–309.

Desfosses Cohn, Helen. 1973. "Population Policy in the USSR," *Problems of Communism*, 22(July–August): 41–45.

Danilova, E. Z. 1968. *Sotsial'nye Problemy Truda Zhenshchiny-Rabotnitsy*. Moscow.

D'iachenko, V. P. *et al.* (eds.). 1964. *Finansovo Kreditnyi Slovar' i Finan Uy*. Vol. 2, p. 70. Moscow.

Dietz, Barbara. 1986. "Intreviwes with Soviet German Emigrants as a Source of Information for Soviet Studies", Osteuropa-Institut, Munich.

Dietz, Barbara. 1987. "The Quality of Life in Rural Areas of the Soviet Union: Insights from a Survey of Soviet German Emigrants", Osteuropa-Institut, Munich.

Dodge, Norton. 1966. *Women in the Soviet Economy*. Baltimore: Johns Hopkins University Press.

Dogle, N. V. 1977. *Usloviia Zhizni i Zdorovia Tekshl'shchits*. Moscow.

Dostovalov, Iu. and N. Titova. 1984. "Spekuliatsii Po Povodu Raspredeleniia Potrebitel'skikh Blag pri Sotsializme," *Ekonomicheskie Nauki*, 9: 92–97.

Dubovoi, P. 1969. "Uslovia Truda kak Factor Differentsiatsii Zarabotnoi Platy," *Voprosy Ekonomiki*, 9: 57–66.

Dumnov, D. 1984. "Obsledovanie Dokhodov i Zhilishchnykh Uslovii," *Vestnik Statistiki*, 9.

Eason, Warren. 1963. "Labor Force." In: Abram Bergson and Simon Kuznets (eds.), *Economic Trends in the Soviet Union*. Cambridge, Mass.: Harvard University Press.

  1976. "Demographic Problems: Fertility." In: *The Soviet Economy in a New Perspective*. Report to the Joint Economic Committee, 94th Cong., 2nd Sess. Washington, D.C.: Government Printing Office.

Easterlin, Richard. 1980. *Birth and Fortune: The Impact of Numbers on Personal Welfare*. New York: Basic Books.

Ershova, E. H. 1979. "Zhenshchina v Sovremennoi Amerike," *S.Sh.A* (U.S.A.), 3: 32–41.

Evans, Michael K. 1969. *Macroeconomic Activity*. New York: Harper and Row.

Feshbach, Murray, and Stephen Rapaway. 1973. "Labor Constraints in the Five Year Plan." In: *Soviet Economic Prospects for the Seventies*. Joint Economic Committee, 93rd Cong., 1st Sess. Washington D.C.: Government Printing Office.

Fisher, Wesley Andrew. 1980. "The Soviet Marriage Market: Mate-Selection in Russia and the USSR." New York: Praeger, Columbia University, Studies of the Russian Institute.

Frank, Robert H. 1978. "Why Women Earn Less: The Theory and Estimation of Differential Overqualification," *American Economic Review*, 68 (June): 360–73.

Friedman, M. 1957. *A Theory of the Consumption Function*. Princeton: Princeton University Press.

Friend, I. and P. Taubman. 1968. "The Aggregate Propensity to Save: Some Concepts and Their Application to International Data," *Review of Economics and Statistics*, 48 (May): 113–23.

Fuchs, Victor R. 1971. "Differences in Hourly Earnings between Men and Women," *Monthly Labor Review*, 94 (May): 9–15.

Galenson, Marjorie. 1973. *Women and Work: An International Comparison*. Ithaca: Cornell University.

Geiger, H. K. 1968. *The Family in Soviet Russia*. Cambridge, Mass.: Harvard University Press.

Gerasimov, N. V. 1978. *Obshchestvennye Fondy Potreblenia Neobkhodimost', Sushchnost', Napravlenie Razvitiia*, Minsk: Nauka i Tekhnika.

Gilbertson, W.P. and R.C. Amarcher. 1972. "Inflation in the Planned Economies: Some Estimates for Eastern Europe," *Southern Economic Journal*, 45(2): 380–93.

Goilo, V. 1971. "Burzhuasnaia Teoriia 'Chelovecheskogo Kapitala'," *Voprosy Ekonomiki*, 11: 84–92.

1976. "Burzhuaznye teorii vosproizvodstva rabochei sily," *Voprosy ekonomiki*, 2: 78–90.

Goldin, Claudia. 1982. "Long-Term Change in the Economic Role of Women." New York: National Bureau of Economic Research. Mimeo.

Gordon, L. A., E. V. Klopov, and V. Ia. Neigol'dberg. 1974. "Razvitoi Sotsialism: Blagosostoianie Rabochikh," *Rabochii Klass i Sovremennyi Mir*, 2: 53–72.

Gordon, L. A. and E. V. Klopov. 1972. *Chelovek posle raboty... sotsial'nye problemy byta i vnerabochego vremeni*. Moscow.

Green, H. S. and C. I. Higgins. 1977. *Sovmod I*. New York: Crane, Russak Co., Inc.

Greenslade, Rush V. 1976. "The Real Gross National Product of the USSR, 1950–1975." In: United States Congress, Joint Economic Committee, *Soviet Economy in a New Perspective*. Washington D.C.: U.S. Government Printing Office.

Gregory, Paul R. 1982. "Fertility and Labor Force Participation in the Soviet

Union and Eastern Europe," *Review of Economics and Statistics*, 64 (No. 1, February): 18–31.

Gregory, Paul R. 1983. "Soviet Theories of Economic Demography: A Survey," *Journal of Comparative Economics*, 7 (June): 105–13.

Gronau, Reuben. 1973a. "The Effects of Children on the Housewife's Value of Time," *Journal of Political Economy*, 81 (2, Pt. 2, March/April): S168–S199.

1973b. "The Intrafamily Allocation of Time: The Value of Housewives' Time," *American Economic Review*, 63(September): 634–51.

1978. "Wives' Participation in the Labor Force and Their Earning Structure." Jerusalem: The Maurice Falk Institute for Economic Research in Israel (in Hebrew).

1979. "Participation of Women in the Labor Force and Their Wage Structure." Jerusalem: The Maurice Falk Institute for Economic Research in Israel. Hebrew.

1984. "Effect of Women's Earnings on the Inequality of Income Distribution: Israel, 1968–1980." Jerusalem: The Maurice Falk Institute for Economic Research in Israel.

Grossman, Gregory. 1977. "The 'Second Economy' of the USSR," *Problems of Communism*, 26 (5, September–October): 25–40.

1979. "Notes on the Illegal Private Economy and Corruption." In: U.S. Congress, Joint Economic Committee, *Soviet Economy in a Period of Transition*. Washington, D.C.: U.S. Government Printing Office.

1990. "The Second Economy in the USSR and Eastern Europe: A Bibliography" Berkeley-Duke Occasional Papers on the Second Economy in the USSR, Paper No. 21.

Hanson, P. 1968. *The Consumer in the Soviet Economy*. Evanston, Ill.: Northwestern University Press.

Heckman, James, and Robert Willis. 1977. "A Beta Logistic Model for the Analysis of Sequential Labor Force Participation by Married Women," *Journal of Political Economy*, 85 (February): 27–58.

Hedstrom, Peter, and Ringen, Stein. 1987. "Age and Income in Contemporary Society: A Research Note," *Journal of Social Policy*, 16(2): 226–39.

Houthakker, H. S. 1965. "On Some Determinants of Saving in Developed and Underdeveloped Countries." In: E. A. F. Robinson (ed.), *Problems in Economic Development*. London: Macmillan & Co., pp. 212–24.

Howard, D. H. 1976. "A Note on Hidden Inflation in the Soviet Union," *Soviet Studies*, 28(4): 599–608.

Iankova, Z. A. 1979. *Gorodskaia Sem'ia*. Moscow.

ILO. 1977a. *Yearbook of Labor Statistics*. Geneva.

1977b. *Labor Force Estimates and Projections, 1950–2000*. Geneva.

Inoveli, Irina. 1977. "Budzhet Odnoi Sem'i," *Sputnik*, 1: 112–16.

Itogi Vsesoiuznoi Perepisi Naselenia 1970 Goda, 1974, Vol. VII.

Iuk, Z. M. 1972. "Tekhnickeskii Progress i Kvalifikatsiia Zhenshchiny-Rabotnitsy." In: I. N. Lushchitskii *et al.* (eds.), *Proizvodstvennaia Deiatel'nost' Zhenshchin i Sem'ia*. Minsk, pp. 40–44.

Izvestiia. May 21, 1985.

Jancar, Barbara W. 1976. "Women's Lot in Communist Societies," *Problems of Communism*, 25 (November–December): 68–73.

Johnson, D. W. and J. Chiu. 1968. "The Saving-Income Relation in Underdeveloped Countries," *Economic Journal*, 78 (June): 321–33.

Kaiser, Robert G. 1976. *Russia: The People and the Power*. New York: Pocket Books.

Kalinnik, Margarita. 1977. "Dokhody i Rashody Rabochei Sem'i," *Sputnik*, 3: 9–12.

Kapustin, E. I. 1974. "Tarifnaia Sistema i ee Rol' v Organizatsii i Regulirovannii Zarabotnoi Platy." In: A. P. Volkov, *Trud i Zarabotnaia Plata v SSSR*. 2nd edn. Moscow.

Karapetian, A. Kh. and N. M. Rimashevskaia (eds.). 1977. *Differentsirovannyi Balans Dokhodov i Potrebleniya Naseleniia*. Moscow.

Karpukhin, D. N. and N. P. Kuznetsova. 1968. "Dokhody i Potreblenie Trudiashchikhsia." In: *Trud i zarabotnaia plata v SSSR*. Moscow: Publishing House "Ekonomika".

Katsenelinboigen, A. 1977. "Coloured Markets in the Soviet Union," *Soviet Studies*, 29 (No. 1, January): 62–85.

Katz, Zev. 1973. "Insights from Emigres and Sociological Studies on the Soviet Union." In: United States Congress, Joint Economic

Committee, *Soviet Economic Prospects for the Seventies*. Washington, D.C.: U.S. Government Printing Office, pp. 87–94.

Katz, Zev. 1976. "An Introduction to Soviet Jewry." Cambridge, Mass.: MIT Center for International Studies. Mimeo.

Keiser, W. 1971. *The Soviet Quest for Economic Rationality*. Rotterdam: Rotterdam University Press.

Khansberg, E. 1977. "Obiem i Struktura Normativnogo Fonda Zhiznennykh Sredsv pri Rasvitom Sotsializme," *Trudy po Politicheskoi Ekonomii, Uchenye Zapiski Tartuskogo Gosudarstvennogo Universiteta*, 6: 61–84. Tartu.

Kharchev, A. G. and S. I. Golod. 1969. "Proizvodstvennaia Rabota Zhenshchin i Sem'ia." In: G. V. Osipov and Ia. Shchepanskii (eds.), *Sotsial'nye Problemy Truda i Proizvodstva*. Moscow, pp. 439–56.

1971. *Professional'naia Rabota Zhenshchin i Sem'ia*. Leningrad.

Kirsh, Leonard J. 1972. *Soviet Wages: Changes in Structure and Administration Since 1956*. Cambridge, Mass.: MIT Press.

Kolpakov, B. T. and V. D. Patrushev. 1971. *Biudzhet Vremeni Gorodskogo Naseleniia*. Moscow.

Kotliar, A. E. 1973. "Metodologicheskie Voprosy Izucheniia Struktury Zaniatosti Naselenia v Territorial'nom Razreze." In: A. E. Maikov (ed.), *Problemy Ispol'zovaniia Trudovykh Resursov*, pp. 400–34. Moscow.

Kotliar, A. E. *et al.* 1973. "Professional'no-Otraslevaia Struktura Zaniatost Zhenshchin v Promyshlennosti RSFSR." In: A. E. Maikov (ed.), *Problemy Ispol'zovaniia Trudovykh Resursov*, pp. 379–99. Moscow.

Kotliar, A. E. and S. Ia. Turchaninova. 1975. *Zaniatost' Zhenshchin v Proizvodstve*. Moscow.

Kraeger, Constance B. 1974. "A Note on the Size of Subsidies on Soviet Government Purchases of Agricultural Products," *ACES Bulletin*, 16(2): 63–69.

Kriazhev, V. 1985. "Obshchestvennye Fondy Potrebleniia i Sotsialnaia Spravedlivost'," *Ekonomicheskaia Gazeta*, 52, December.

Kunelskii, L. E. 1968. "Sotsial'no-Ekonomicheskoe Znachenie Povyshenia Minimal'nykh Razmerov Zarabotnoi Platy," *Sotsialisticheskii Trud*, 12: 14–22.

Kuniansky, Anna. 1983. "Soviet Fertility, Labor-Force Participation, and Marital Instability," *Journal of Comparative Economics*, 7 (June): 114–130.

Kuznets, S. 1974. *Demographic (and other) Components in Size Distribution of Income* (Preliminary Notes). The Japan Economic Research Center.

1981. "Size of Households and Income Disparities." In: Julian Simon and Peter A. Lindert (eds.), *Research in Population Economics*, 3: 1–40. Greenwich, Conn.: JAI Press.

1982. "Children and Adults in Income Distribution," *Economic Development and Cultural Change*, 30(4): 697–738.

Kýn, Oldrich. 1978. "Education, Sex and Income Inequality in Soviet Type Socialism." In: Griliches, Z. *et al.* (eds.). *Income Distribution and Economic Inequality*. Frankfurt: Campus Verlag, pp. 274–89.

Lapidus-Warshofsky, Gail. 1978. *Women in Soviet Society: Equality, Development and Social Change*. Berkeley: University of California Press.

1982. *Women, Work and Family in the Soviet Union*. Armonk, NY: M. E. Sharpe.

Lebin, B. D. and I. I. Leiman. 1972. "Zhenschchina-Uchenyi, ee Professional'naia i Semeinaia Roli." In: I. N. Lushchitskii *et al.* (eds.), *Proizvodstvennaia Deiatel'nost' Zhenschin i Sem'ia*. Minsk, pp. 136–41.

Lehrer, Evelyn and Marc Nerlove. 1981. "The Labor Supply and Fertility Behavior of Married Women: A Three Period Model." In: Julian L. Simon and Peter H. Lindert (eds.), *Research in Population Economics*. Greenwich, Conn.: JAI.

Lerner, R. I. and Yitzhaki, Sh. 1984. "A Note on the Calculation and Interpretation of the Gini Index," *Economic Letters*, 15: 363–68.

Levin, A. 1988 "O Tekh kto Zhivet Nizhe Srednego," *Trud*, June 26.

Liebenstein, Harvey. 1975. "The Economic Theory of Fertility Decline," *Quarterly Journal of Economics*, 89 (No. 1, February): 1–31.

Liviatan, N. 1964. *Consumption Patterns in Israel*. Jerusalem: The Maurice Falk Institute for Economic Research in Israel.

Lluch, C. *et al.* 1977. *Patterns in Household Demand and Saving*. New York: Oxford University Press.

Lokshin, R. A. 1975. *Spros Proizvodstvo Torgovlia*. Moscow.

Madison, Bernice. 1978a. "Social Services for Women: Problems and Priorities." In: D. Atkinson *et al.* (eds.), *Women in Russia*. Hassock, England: Harvester Press, pp. 307–32.

  1978b. "Soviet Income Maintenance Programs in the Struggle Against Poverty." Paper presented at the Colloquium at the Kennan Institute for Advanced Russian Studies, Woodrow Wilson International Center for Scholars, Washington, D.C.

  1979. "Trade Unions and Social Welfare." In: A. Kahan and B. Ruble (eds.), *Industrial Labor in the USSR*. New York: Pergamon Press, pp. 85–115.

  1981. "The Soviet Social Welfare System as Experienced and Evaluated by Consumers." Report presented to the National Council for Soviet and East European Research, Washington, D.C.

  1988. "The Soviet Pension System and Social Security for the Aged." In Gail W. Lapidus and Guy E. Swenson (eds.), *State and Welfare, USA/USSR: Contemporary Policy and Practice,* Institute of International Studies, University of California, Berkely.

Maier, V. F. 1968. *Dokhody Naselenia i Rost Blagosostoiania Naroda*. Moscow.

  1977. "Aktual'nye Problemy Povyshenia Narodnogo Blagosostoianiia," *Voprosy Ekonomiki*, 11: 47–56.

Malkiel, Burton G. and Judith A. Malkiel. 1973. "Male Female Pay Differentials in Professional Employment," *American Economic Review*, 63 (September): 693–705.

Mamontova, T. I. 1975. "Vliianie Obshchestvennykh Fondof Potrebleniia na Differentsiatsiiu Urovnia Zhizni Rabochikh i Sluzhashchikh," *Sotsialisticheckii Obraz Zhizni i Narodnoe Blagosostoianie*. Sarotovskii Universitet.

Mandel, William M. 1975. *Soviet Women*. New York: Anchor Books.

Marx, Karl. 1966. *Critique of the Gotha Program*. Moscow: Progress Publishers.

Matthews, Mervyn. 1972. "Poverty in Russia," *New Society*, 27 (January):

  1978. *Privilege in the Soviet Union*. London: Allen and Unwin; Madison, Wisc.: University of Wisconsin Press.

  1986. *Poverty in the Soviet Union: The Life-Styles of the Under-Priviledged* in Recent Years, Cambridge, Cambridge University Press.

Matthews, Mervyn. 1987. "Poverty and Patterns of Deprivation in the Soviety Union." Madison, Wisc.: University of Wisconsin Institute for Research on Poverty. Discussion Paper.

Mayer, T. 1972. *Permanent Income, Wealth and Consumption.* Berkeley: University of California Press.

McAuley, Alastair. 1977a. "The Distribution of Earnings and Incomes in the Soviet Union," *Soviet Studies,* 29 (April): 214–57.

1977b. "Soviet Anti-poverty Policy, 1955–1975." Madison, Wisc.: University of Wisconsin, Institute for Research on Poverty. Discussion Paper.

1978. "Women's Work and Wages in the USSR." Department of Economics (Discussion Paper No. 111). University of Essex.

1979. *Economic Welfare in the Soviet Union: Poverty, Living Standards and Inequality.* Madison, Wisc.: University of Wisconsin Press.

1981. *Women's Work and Wages in the Soviet Union.* London: Allen and Unwin.

MEMO — see *Mirovaia.*

Michal, Jan M. 1975. "An Alternative Approach to Measuring Income Inequality in Eastern Europe." In: Z. M. Fallenbucl, *Economic Development in the Soviet Union and Eastern Europe.* New York: Praeger, Vol. I, pp. 256–75.

Migranova, L. A. and N. E. Rabkina. 1976. "Izmenenie Differentsiatsii pri Prevrashchenii Zarabotnoi Platy v Dokhod Sem'i." In: N. M. Rimashevskaia (ed.), *Sotsial'no Economicheskie Problemy Blagosostoianiia.* Moscow: Tsentral'nyi Economico-Mathematicheskii Institut.

1979. "Izmenenie Differentsiatsii pri Prevrashchenii Zarabotnoi Platy v Dokhod Sem'i." *Potrebnosti Dokhody Potreblenie.* Moscow.

Mikesell, R. F. and R. E. Zinser. 1973. "The Nature of the Savings Function in Developing Countries: A Survey of the Theoretical and Empirical Literature," *Journal of Economic Literature,* 2 (March): 1–26.

Mikhailiuk, V. B. 1970. *Ispol'zovanie Zhenskogo Truda v Narodnom Khoziaistve.* Moscow.

Millar, James (ed.) 1987. Politics, Work and Daily Life in the USSR. Cambridge; Cambridge University Press.

Millar, James R. and Joyce Pickersgill. 1977. "Aggregate Economic Problems in Soviet-Type Economies," *ACES Bulletin*, 19 (No. 1, Spring).

Mincer, Jacob. 1963. "Market Prices, Opportunity Costs and Income Effects." In: Carl C. Christ *et al.* (eds.), *Measurement in Economics: Studies in Mathematical Economics and Econometrics in Memory of Yehuda Grunfeld*. Stanford, Calif.: Stanford University Press.

1974. *Schooling Experience and Earnings*. New York: Columbia University Press (National Bureau of Economic Research).

Mincer, Jacob, and Solomon Polachek. 1974. "Family Investments in Human Capital: Earnings of Women," *Journal of Political Economy*, 72 (Pt. 2, March–April): S76–S108.

Minkoff, Jack and Lynn Turgeon. 1977. "Income Maintenance in the Soviet Union in Eastern and Western Perspective." In: J. L. Horowitz (ed.), *Equity, Income and Policy*. New York: Praeger, pp. 176–91.

Mirovaia Ekonomika i Mezhdu Narodnye Otnosheniia (MEMO). 1974. No. 8 (August).

Morrison, Christian. 1984. "Income Distribution in East European and Western Countries," *Journal of Comparative Economics*, 8: 121–38.

Nakamura, Masao, Alice Nakamura and Dallas Cullen. 1979. "Job Opportunities, the Offered Wage, and the Labor Supply of Married Women," *American Economic Review*, 69 (No. 5, December): 787–805.

Narkhoz (Narodnoe Khoziaistvo SSSR) [The National Economy of the USSR]. Various years, Moscow.

Naselenie SSSR [The Population of the USSR]. Various years. Moscow.

Nemchinova, I. I. 1973. "Dokhody i Potreblenie." In: *Dokhody Trudiashchikhsia i Sotsial'nye Problemy Urovnia Zhizni Naseleniia SSSR*. Moscow.

1975. "Differentsiatsiia Dokhodov i Potreblenia Semei Rabochikh i Sluzhashchikh." In: P. E. Slesarev (ed.), *Sotsialisticheskii Obraz Shizni i Narodnoe Blagosostoianie*, pp. 385–91. Saratov.

Nove, Alec. 1982. "Income Distribution in the USSR: A Possible Explanation of Some Recent Data," *Soviet Studies*, 34(2): 286–88.

Novikova, E. E., V. S. Iazykova and Z. A. Iankova. 1978. *Zhenshchina Trud Sem'ia*. Moscow.

Oaxaca, Ronald. 1973. "Male–Female Wage Differentials in Urban Labor Markets," *International Economic Review*, 14 (October): 693–709.

OECD. 1976. *Public Expenditure on Income Maintenance Programmes*. OECD Studies in Resource Allocation, No. 3. Paris.

1979. "Equal Opportunities for Women," *OECD Observer*, 97 (March): 27–32.

Ofer, Gur. 1973. *The Service Sector in Soviet Economic Growth: A Comparative Study*. Cambridge, Mass.: Harvard University Press.

1979. "The 'Second Economy' and National Income Accounting in the Soviet Union: A Conceptual Discussion." Jerusalem. Mimeo.

1990. "Macroeconomic Issues of Soviet Reforms," NBER, *Macroeconomic Annual 1990*, pp. 297–334.

Ofer, Gur, Aaron Vinokur, and Yarom Ariav. 1982. "Absorption in Work of Soviet Immigrants in Israel." Hebrew. Jerusalem: The Maurice Falk Institute for Economic Research in Israel.

Onikienko, V. V. and V. A. Popovkin. 1973. *Kompleksnoe Issledovanie Migratsionnykh Protsessov*. Moscow.

Pankratova, M. G. and Z. A. Iankova. 1978. "Sovetskaia Zhenshchina," *Sotsiologicheskie Issledovania*, 1: 19–28.

Panova, N. W. 1970. "Voprosy Truda i Byta Zhenshchn." In: *Problemy Byta, Braka i Sem'i*. Vil'nius.

Parkhomenko, V. F. 1972. "Nekotorye Problemy Ratsional'nogo Ispol'zovania Zhenskikh Kadrov v Sostave Inzhenerno-Tekhnicheskikh Rabotnikov Sotsialisticheskogo Proizvodstva." In: V. F. Medvedev *et al.* (eds.), *Vosproizvodstvo i Ispol'zovanie Trudovykh Resursov Belorusskoi SSR*. Minsk.

Pavlova, N. M. and N. E. Rabkina. 1976. "Aktual'nye Voprosy Pensionnogo Obespecheniia Starosti." In: *Dokhody i Potreblenie Naseleniia*, Moscow.

Pearce, Dianne. 1978. "The Feminization of Poverty: Women, Work and Welfare," *Urban and Social Change Review* (1–2): 28–35.

Pickersgill, Joyce. 1976. "Soviet Household Saving Behavior," *Review of Economics and Statistics*, 37 (May): 139–47.

Pickersgill, Joyce. 1977. "Soviet Inflation: Causes and Consequences," *Soviet Union*, 4 (No. 2).

1980a. "Recent Evidence on Soviet Household Saving Behavior," *Review of Economics and Statistics*, 62 (No. 4, November): 628–33.

1980b. "Repressed Inflation and Price Controls in the Soviet Household Sector." Mimeo.

Pimenova, A. L. 1966. "Sem'ia i Perspektivy Razvitiia Obshchestvennogo Truda Zhenshchin pri Sotsializme," *Filosofskie Nauki*, 3: 35–44.

Porokhniuk, E. V. and M. S. Shepeleva. 1975. "O Sovmeshchenii Proizvodstvennykh i Semeinykh Funktsii Zhenshchin-Rabotnits," *Sotsiologicheskie issledovaniia*, 4: 102–28.

Portes, Richard. 1981. "Macroeconomic Equilibrium and Disequilibrium in Centrally Planned Economies," *Economic Inquiry*, 19 (No. 4, October): 559–78.

Potrebnosti — See Akademiya Nauk.

Prais, S. J. and H. S. Houthakker. 1971. *The Analysis of Family Budgets*. Cambridge.

Pravda, May 21, 1985; Nov. 21, 1986.

Pryor, Frederic L. 1973. *Property and Industrial Organization in Communist and Capitalist Nations*. Bloomington, Ind.: Indiana University Press.

Rabkina, N. E. and N. M. Rimashevskaia. 1972. *Osnovy Differentsiatsii Zarabotnoi Platy i Dokhodov*. Moscow.

1978. "Raspredelitel'nye otnosheniia i sotsial'noe razvitie," *Ekonomika i organizatsiia promyshlennogo proizvodstva, (EKO)*, 5: 17–32.

1979. "Izmenenie Differentsiatsii Pri Prevrashchenii Zarabotnoi Platy v Dokhod Sem'i." In: *Potrebnosti Dokhody Potrebleniye*. Moscow.

Rapaway, Stephen. 1976. *Estimates and Projections of the Labor Force and Civilian Employment in the USSR, 1950 to 1990*. Washington, D.C.: U.S. Department of Commerce, Bureau of Economic Analysis, Foreign Economics Report No. 10.

Riurikov, Iu. B. 1977. "Deti i obshchestvo," *Voprosy Filosofii*, 4: 111–21.

Sacks, Michael P. 1976. *Women's Work in Soviet Russia: Continuity in Midst of Change*. New York: Praeger.

Sakharova, N. A. 1973. *Optimal'nye Vozmozhnosti Ispol'zovaniia Zhenskogo*

Truda v Sfere Obshchestvennogo Proizvodstva. Kiev.

Sarkisian, G. S. 1972. *Uroven', Tempy Proportsii Rosta Realnykh Dokhodov pri Sotsializme*. Moscow.

1973. *Dokhody Trudiashchikhsia i Sotsial'nye Problemy Urovnia Zhizni Naseleniia SSSR*. Moscow.

1978. "Agrarnaia Politika KPSS i Rost Blagosostoianiia Naroda," *Sotsialisticheskii Trud*, 10: 7–19.

Sarkisian, G. S. and N. P. Kuznetsova. 1967. *Potrebnosti i Dokhod Sem'i*. Moscow: Publishing House "Ekonomika."

Saunders, C. and D. Marsden. 1981. *Pay Inequality in the European Community*. Redmond, Wash.: Butterworths.

Sawyer, Malcolm. 1976. "Income Distribution in OECD Countries," *OECD Economic Outlook* (Occasional Studies). Paris. July: 3–36.

Schroeder, Gertrude E. 1975. "Consumer Goods Availability and Repressed Inflation in the Soviet Union." In: NATO, *Economic Aspects of Life in the USSR*. Brussels.

1977. "On the Measurement of the Second Economy in the USSR." Mimeo.

Schroeder, Gertrude E., and Rush Greenslade. 1979. "On the Measurement of the Second Economy in the USSR," *ACES Bulletin*, 21 (No. 1, Spring): 3–22.

Schroeder, Gertrude E., and Barbara S. Severin. 1976. "Soviet Consumption and Income Policies in Perspective." In: United States Congress, Joint Economic Committee, *Soviet Economy in a New Perspective*. Washington, D.C.: U.S. Government Printing Office, pp. 620–60.

Schultz, T. Paul. 1977. "The Influence of Fertility on the Labor Force Behavior of Married Women." Washington, D.C.: U.S. Department of Labor, Technical Analysis Paper No. 52. June.

Schultz, Theodore (ed.). 1974. *Economics of the Family: Marriage, Children, and Capital*. Chicago: University of Chicago Press.

Severin, Barbara and David Carey. 1970. "Trends in Official Policy Toward Private Activity in the USSR." CIA, Office of Economic Research. Mimeo.

Sharipov, A. Iu. 1968. "Material'nye u Moral'nye Stimuly k Trudu," *Izvestiia*

Sibirskogo Otdeleniia Akademii Nauk SSSR, Seriia Obshchestvennykh Nauk, No. 1, Vypusk, 1: 33–39.

Shishkan, N. M. 1976. *Trud Zhenshchin v Usloviiakh Razvitogo Sotsialisma*. Kishinev.

Simes, D. 1975. "The Soviet Parallel Market." In: NATO, *Economic Aspects of Life in the USSR*. Brussels. Pp. 91–100.

Simis, K. 1982. *USSR — Corrupt Society: The Secret World of Soviet Capitalism*. New York: Simon and Shuster.

Slesarev, G. A. and Z. A. Iankova. 1969. "Zhenshchina na Promyshlennom Predpriiatii i v Sem'ie." In: G. V. Osipov and Shchepanskii (eds.), *Sotsial'nye Problemy Truda i Proizvodstva*. Moscow, pp. 416–38.

Smith, Hedrick. 1976. *The Russians*. New York.

Smith, Willard S. 1973. "Housing in the Soviet Union – Big Plans, Little Action." In: United States Congress, Joint Economic Committee, *Soviet Economic Prospects for the Seventies*. Washington, D.C.: U.S. Government Printing Office, pp. 404–27.

Sonin, M. Ia. 1973. "Aktualnye Sotsial'no-Ekonomicheskie Problemy Zaniatosti Zhenshchin." In: A. E. Maikov (ed.), *Problemy Ispol'zovaniia Trudovykh Resursov*. Moscow, pp. 352–79.

Swafford, Michael. 1977. "Sex Differences in Soviet Earnings." Nashville, Tenn.: Vanderbilt University. Mimeo.

Szalai, Alexander *et al.* (eds.). 1972. *The Use of Time*. The Hague: Mouton

Timashevskaia, M. V. 1978. "Chelovek i Zhilaia Sreda," *Izvestiia Sibirskogo Otdeleniia Akademii Nauk SSSR*, Seriia Obshchestvennykh Nauk, No. 6, Vypusk, 1: 88–93.

Treml, Vladimir G. 1975. "Alcohol in the USSR: A Fiscal Dilemma," *Soviet Studies*, 27 (No. 2, April): 161–77.

  1978. "Agricultural Subsidies in the Soviet Union." U.S. Bureau of the Census, *Foreign Economic Report*, No. 15.

  1982. *Alcohol in the USSR*. Durham, N.C.: Duke University Press.

  1985. "Purchases of Food from Private Sources in Soviet Urban Areas," Berkely-Duke Occasional papers on the Second Economy in the USSR, No. 3.

Trud

Trufanov, I. P. 1973. *Problemy Byta Gorodskogo Naseleniia SSSR*. Leningrad.

Turchaninova, S. I. 1975. "Trends in Women's Employment in the USSR," *International Labor Review*, 112(October): 253-64.

Turchenko, V. N. 1972. "O Nekatorykh Osobennostiakh Truda Zhenshchiny Uchitelia." In: I. N. Lushchitskii *et al.* (eds.), *Proizvodstvennaia Deiatel'nost' Zhenshchin i sem'ia*. Minsk, pp. 141–45.

UNESCO, *Statistical Yearbook 1981*. Paris.

USSR Census Bureau. 1931. *Vsesoiuznoia Perepis' Naselenia 1926 g* [All-union population census, 1926]. Moscow.

⎯⎯. 1959. *Itogi Vsesoyuznoi Perepisi Naselenia 1959 g* [Returns of the all-union population census, 1959]. Moscow.

USSR State Committee on Statistics, Tsentralnoye Statisticheskoye Upravleniye (TsSu). 1972–74. *Itogi Vsesoiuhznoy Perepisi Naseleniia 1970 Goda*. Vols. I–VII. Moscow. Referred to as *Census 1970*.

⎯⎯. 1990. *Sostav Sem'i, Dokhody i Zhilishchye Usloviia Semei Rabochikh, Sluzhashchikh i Kolkhoznikov* (Family composition, income and personal services of families of workers, employees and collective farmers) Moscow.

⎯⎯. 1990. *Sotsial'noe Razvitie SSSR* (Social development in the USSR), Moscow.

⎯⎯. Various years. *Moskva v Tsifrakh*.

Vasil'ev, A. 1974. "A Statistical Comparison of Living Standards in Russia, the USSR and the Capitalist Countries," *Radio Liberty Research*, RL 276/74. September 3.

Velichkene, I. 1970. "Trud i Zdorov'e Zhenshchiny-Rabotnitsy." In: A. Gul'binskene (ed.), *Problemy Byta Braka i Sem'i*. Vilnius, pp. 95–98.

Vestnik Statistiki. Various years. Moscow.

Vinokur, Aaron. 1975. "Surveys of Family Budgets in the USSR: A Review." Jerusalem: The Hebrew University, Russia and East European Research Center. Mimeo.

Vinokur, Aaron, and Gur Ofer. 1979. "Family Income Levels for Soviet Industrial Workers, 1965–1975." In: A. Kahan and B. A. Ruble (eds.), *Industrial Labor in the USSR*. NY: Pergamon Press, pp. 184–208.

Wiles, P. J. D. 1974. *The Distribution of Income: East and West*. Amsterdam:

North Holland.

1975a. "Introduction to Part III: Income Distribution." In Fallenbucl, Z. M. (ed.), *Economic Development in the Soviet Union and Eastern Europe.* Vol. I. New York: Praeger, pp. 253–55.

1975b. "Recent Data on Soviet Income Distribution," *Survey,* 21 (No. 3, Summer): 28–41.

Wiles, P. J. D., and S. Markowski. 1971, 1972. "Income Distribution under Communism and Capitalism" (Parts 1, 2), *Soviet Studies,* 22(4): 344–69 and 22(5): 487–511.

Williamson, J. G. 1968. "Personal Savings in Developing Nations: An Intertemporal Cross-Section from Asia," *Economic Record,* 44 (June): 194–210.

Zdravomyslov, A. G., V. P. Rozhin and V. A. Iadov (eds.). 1967. *Chelovek i Ego Rabota.* Moscow.

Zhenshchiny v SSSR [Women in the USSR]. 1973. Moscow.

Index